Dieter Haller
Tangier/Gibraltar – A Tale of One City

Culture and Social Practice

Dieter Haller, born in 1962, works as a professor of ethnology at the Faculty of Social Science at the Ruhr University Bochum (RUB). The cultural anthropologist did his doctorate at the University of Heidelberg and was a founding member of the Zentrum für Mittelmeerstudien at the RUB. He carried out long term anthropological fieldwork in Seville (1985/86), Gibraltar (1995/96), Texas (2003/05) and Tangier (since 2013), as well as on Brexit (2019/20). His research focuses on ethnology, corruption, cosmopolitism, possession, and borderlands.

Dieter Haller
Tangier/Gibraltar – A Tale of One City
An Ethnography

[transcript]

Bibliographic information published by the Deutsche Nationalbibliothek
The Deutsche Nationalbibliothek lists this publication in the Deutsche Nationalbibliografie; detailed bibliographic data are available in the Internet at http://dnb.d-nb.de

© 2021 transcript Verlag, Bielefeld

All rights reserved. No part of this book may be reprinted or reproduced or utilized in any form or by any electronic, mechanical, or other means, now known or hereafter invented, including photocopying and recording, or in any information storage or retrieval system, without permission in writing from the publisher.

Cover layout: Maria Arndt, Bielefeld
Cover illustration: Dieter Haller
Printed by Majuskel Medienproduktion GmbH, Wetzlar
Print-ISBN 978-3-8376-5649-7
PDF-ISBN 978-3-8394-5649-1
https://doi.org/10.14361/9783839456491

Printed on permanent acid-free text paper.

Contents

Acknowledgements 7

TanGib – Two Places, One City?
Ethnological Views of the Strait 9

1. Myths, rhythms, senses 15
1.1. Geography and power 15
1.2. Rhythm and Senses 16
1.3. On the sea: Boughaz – Straits – Estrecho 22
1.4. Time 31
1.5. Urban planning and architecture 35

2. Theoretical accesses 41
2.1. Structures: Cosmopolitanism, networks, diasporas, cultural areas 43
2.2. Internalizations: Ethnicity, transculturation, trance and obsession,
     penetration, reflection, self 53

3. Access methods 69
3.1. Seville 77
3.2. Gibraltar 78
3.3. Tangier 81
3.4. The regional embedding: Gibraltar, Tangier and their hinterland 83
3.5. TanGib 2019/20 88

4. Common history until 1956 91
4.1 Portugal and England 92
4.2 The 19th century 97
4.3 Treaty of Fez and international statute 110
4.4 The Spanish Civil War and World War II 114
4.5. 1948 Alija and later 122
4.6 The 1950s – Tangier before independence 127

5.	The loosening of Transboughazian bonds	137
5.1.	1956 to 1960 – A special status for Tangier?	138
5.2.	1960ff – Swan song on TanGib. Provisionally?	143
5.3.	1964 to 1973 – Increasing provincialization of Tangier and border problems in Gibraltar	148
5.4.	1973-1999 Tangier struggles through the Years of Lead and Gibraltar integrates into the EU	156

6.	An ethnology of multiple connections	165

7.	Reordering borders, dynamization and a new rapprochement	199
7.1	Dynamization of TanGib	200
7.2	Migration	201
7.3	Infrastructure: Transboughaz routes	204
7.4	Moroccan Gibraltarians	205
7.5	Cultural heritage	209
7.6	Other links between Tangier and Gibraltar	213

8.	Brexit: An ethnography of agony with hopeful glances to the other side of the Strait	215
8.1	Political status	219
8.2	Foreign policy implications	221
8.3	Economy	222
8.4.	Gibraltar and Morocco Business Association (GMBA) and Strait of Gibraltar Association (SGA)	226
8.5.	Social and Cultural links	229
8.6.	Conclusion	233
8.7.	Addendum: Corona	234

9.	Conclusion	237
9.1.	What is the next step with TanGib?	237
9.2.	Conclusions regarding the theoretical approaches	241
9.3	Final remark	245

References		247

Acknowledgements

This text is dedicated to Jon Morgan Searle, former head of the *Garrison Library* in Gibraltar and the editor of *The Gibraltar Chronicle* – the oldest newspaper in the world still in existence today. I owe him too much to mention at this point. He was the first to open doors to TanGib for me. Even more: He was a human being. A second dedication – If one is allowed to do something like that in a scientific publication – goes to my friend Ahmed Halimi (†), who passed away on April 30, 2020. A great soul.

I am also particularly grateful to Philip Saunders, who helped to put the German text into an understandable English version! My thanks also go to Stefanie Hof, Seda Sönmeztürk and Emre Ünal – without their help the final version of the book could not have been completed.

Joshua Marrache, Christian September, Pepe Fuentes Reyes and Abdellatif Bousseta, my main interlocutors in the fields, cannot be thanked enough. Steffen Wippel, Nino Aivashizvili-Gehne, Hafid Zghouli, Lutz Jablonowsky, Ralf Ullrich and Christoph Sandmann gave me helpful feedback on different versions of the work. I also thank my friends and guarantors in Tangier, Gibraltar and Seville from the bottom of my heart: Tamara Dragadze, John Carreras, Corinne Senior Marrache, Mohammed Stitou Zhare and the Ḥamādša of Tangier, Tarik Dervish, Rachid Tafersiti Zarouila, Moumen Smihi, Rica Assayag and her sisters Perla and Fortuna, Hamza Ben Rabah, Benaissa Msiid, Ahmed Mellak, Barbara Ritchie, Annette and Paul Tunbridge, Estrella Abudarham, Lina Searle and her family, Alice Mascarenhas, Dizzy Buckingham, Priscilla and Henry Sacramento, Steve Marin and Brahim Krikaz, the Khemlichi family, Manolo Batista Nieto, Jacques Vignet Zunz, Michel Peraldi, Gil Podesta, Guy Povedano, Kevin Lane, Charles Trico, Joseph Berllaque, Sam Benady, Olga and Ahmed Benchekroun, Trino Cruz Seruya, Jimmy Imossi, Lydia Mifsud, David Weber, Maxine Torrent del Prat, Father Danny Hernandez, Keith Tonna, Tito Benady, Dorothy Victory, Younes Mubarak, Alegria Benaim, Ernest Wiley, Alegria Benarosh, Mustafa Ben Amar, Abdellah Sghir, Ana Gabriela da Silva Araujo Bonnet, Anna Rossi and Paolo Businelli, Abdelghani Aoufi, Mr. Shakkara, Mr. Jamal, Youssef Mribti and Paco Parado. I also thank the members of various online platforms, as well as Johanna Rolshoven. Unusual for an acknowledement is also an ingratitude: At various points in the production and dissemination of knowledge, sometimes people did everything possible to ensure that my research would fail. I was assured of courtesies in the friendliest way but denied access to crucial institutions – especially in Gibraltar. I could write an ethnography on knowledge and power, but I do not want to do so yet, so as not to poison my heart. It is worth mentioning, however, because even in Gibraltar, access to knowledge does not always follow British fair play but denial of access to archives, resources and free research. Names do not need to be mentioned; they are all too familiar to those involved.

TanGib – Two Places, One City?
Ethnological Views of the Strait

Soor el Maâgazine on the *Boulevard* in Tangier – the view pours out over the port and the Bay of Tangier. Similar to the famous *Café Hafa* on the cliffs of *Mershan*, if the weather is good, one can see not only the opposite coast of southern Spain but also the Rock of Gibraltar in the far right background. From there, from the southernmost point again, *Europa Point*, the view extends to the south with a view of Ceuta, Jebel Musa, Parsley Island, the harbor of Ksar es Sghir and, in good weather, of the lighthouse of Malabata and the Corniche of Tangier.

Illustration 1: View of the Straits from Gibraltar, 02.04.2019

Two continents, two countries, two perspectives, two places – but one single city? Up to now, the relationship of the two cities to each other has been narrated and examined primarily from the viewpoint of separation, difference and the drawing of boundaries: Orient vs. Occident, Islam vs. Catholicism, South vs. North, Atlantic vs. Mediterranean. This was influenced to a considerable extent by the integration of Tangier into Morocco (1956) and the creation of the European Union (EU) external border (1991). In this book, I will explain what this traditional focus on divisive elements obscures, namely, the similarities between the two cities, which, at times and in many ways, allow us to speak of a single city. The aim is to salvage these buried relationships both cultural-historically and ethnographically, and to present and relate them to other findings.

I am an ethnologist and my research region is the Strait of Gibraltar. What may sound strange to an English speaking audience is the self description as an ethnologist: in Germany post 1945 it refers to what elsewhere is called social or/and cultural anthropology. But different to Anglosaxon and French traditions focusing predominantly on contemporary cultures, it retains also a cultural historical perspective. Ethnology therefore researches the cultural meaning of social institutions and agency in contemporary and historical perspective.

The present book is based on my field research in Tangier and Gibraltar on transborder, transboughaz (*Boughaz* = Strait) relations in the context not only of Brexit (2019–20) but also on previous field research in Seville (1985/86), Gibraltar (1995/96) and Tangier (2013–14, and since 2014). In this way, I attempt to connect the separation between ethnographic research presently dominating anthropology in the German-speaking world and the cultural-historical approach that has disappeared or been ceded to other disciplines, and, thus, to correspond to truly ethnological research.

In contrast to other disciplines, ethnology is less interested in official discourses or institutional and structural practices but rather on the informal side of life and coping with existence: worlds and wisdom of so-called simple people. Ethnologists want to make the voices of the unheard audible – this was an important concern, especially in colonialism, and it still remains important today. Therefore, it is important to document things, practices and voices meticulously and sustainably in order to contribute to an archive that will provide future generations with testimony about the past.

The North of Morocco and Andalusia have often been studied by ethnologists. Andalusia has even prompted the establishment of a subdiscipline, Mediterranean ethnology, through the research of Julian Pitt-Rivers (1961). At that time, ethnologists were researching mainly in villages, small towns and rural areas. Few colleagues turned their attention to cities at all; Tangier and Gibraltar fell almost completely out of the researchers' field of vision.

At the same time, various ethnologists lived in Tangier, including Edward Westermarck (1909, 1920, 1933, 1968), Karl Emil Schabinger von Schowingen (1967; Guessous 1977), Elisa Chimenti (1935, 1964, 2003), Carleton S. Coon (1933, 1980), Jacques Vignet-Zunz (2016), Tamara Dragadze (1965) and Michel Peraldi (2007b). The city itself, however, was seldom a subject of their work. Hardly any ethnologists lived in Gibraltar, on the other hand, although Gareth Stanton published several texts about the city (1991, 1994, 2009).

Illustration 2a: Antroplogists from Tangier: Edward Westermarck (left) and Karl Schabinger von Schowingen (right)

Illustration 2b: Antroplogists from Tangier: Elisa Chimenti (left), Carleton Coon (middle) and Jacques Vignet-Zunz (right)

Illustration 2c: Antroplogists from Tangier: Tamara Dragadze (left), Michel Peraldi (middle) and Abdelmajid Hannoum (right)

TanGib? What seems strange at first sight turns out to be not quite so absurd on closer inspection, because Tangier and Gibraltar have been connected in many different ways for a long time: Mythical–geographical, rhythmic–sensual, architectural–urbanistic and human–cultural. The list of similarities is not complete, but the message is clear.

Practically until the end of Tangier's internationality, this city maintained special links with Gibraltar for decades, not only socially but also culturally and economically. A considerable part of the smuggled goods leaving Tangier reached Spain via Gibraltar. (Ceballos López 2009: 330; translation by the author)

Their stories have not yet been told. I would like to tackle these in this book under the following guiding questions:

- What findings allow us to speak of a common city of TanGib over the last 200 years?
- Which epochs of consolidation, stabilization and disentanglement of relations can be identified?
- What approaches are there in the context of Brexit to tie in with old bonds and revitalize them or to establish new ones?

Chapter one will offer a first access to the field of myths of commonality in rhythm and sensuality. Different concepts of time and experiences of movement on the water in the face of the other side will play a role and the materiality of urban space, forms of living and relationship of the cities to their topography.

In chapter two, I present theoretical approaches that determine my work in this book. Inevitably, approaches of earlier research are also included. The present work, however, is decisively characterized by a new definition of the concept of the cultural circle, which is capable of thinking both of persistent structures of a longue durée and of process-related and actor-centered procedures. The term definition itself comes from latin *de* and *fines*: From the border. Usually a definition is thought to be separated by other domains by sharp and linear borders. However, this is a limited notion itself, for borders can be thought as lines or as zones. I do prefer the latter. The zonal character of my understanding of a definition is basic to the concept of *Boughazidad* (*boughaz* = Strait in Arabic, *-idad* = -ity/ship in Spanish), i.e. a 'sea community,' which denotes the habitualization and internalization of the spatial relationship between port and sea, can be used to describe a resource that is used by various actors in times of need. Here, I also tie in with the concept of neighborliness of Moroccan thinker Rachid Boutayeb. He understands neighborhood thinking "as an ethic of compassion […], of ambiguity tolerance, whose discourse is not afraid to articulate itself in the language of spontaneity, empathy and cooperation." Boutayeb distinguishes this thinking from thematic thinking, which he regards as an irrational answer understands the coldness of pure reason when it remains trapped in a "logic of exclusion" (2017: 12). It is precisely this kind of neighborliness that I have in mind when I write about *Boughazidad*. It follows seamlessly on the assumption of Franz Boas, who regarded science as meaningless without a heart: "[S]o that one can recognize the humanity of other people" (King 2020: 43). This humanity of other people is usually framed in terms such as "society", which differentiates between a humane "us" from an in/sub/non humane "other". Eric Wolf (1988) has carved out masterfully the european understanding of society linked to polity and history. *Boughazidad* with its focuss on neighborliness, social practice and territoriality could be added to the examples from China and the Muslim World, where other understandings of the social such as loyalty and faith dominate.

The third chapter presents the methodological approaches of my research, both of preliminary work in Seville, Gibraltar and Tangier, and of recent research on Brexit.

Chapters four and five are devoted to the history of the political–economic and demographic interdependence of Tangier and Gibraltar, with chapter five beginning where chapter four ends: In 1956, a crucial year for the relationship between the two cities, since it was then that the International Zone of Tangier not only lost its political status when being incorporated into a newly created Kingdom of Morocco but also marked the demographic break with Gibraltar.

The sixth chapter introduces the reader to networks between Tangier and Gibraltar. As a result of years of research in the region, I have been able to uncover many personal ties between the two cities, family relationships and networks of friendship, neighborhood and working relationships that transcend religious, ethnic and political boundaries. We will jump across the Strait into the other city, so don't forget to hold on to your hat, you might get dizzy when you meet street vendors, multi-billionaires, spies, waiters and smugglers, rabbis and tourists, tailors and dawdlers.

At the beginning of the New Millennium, both cities experienced new dynamizations. Gibraltar developed into an online gambling paradise and Tangier was purposefully promoted by King Mohammed VI, something that had not happened in previous decades since independence. New companies settled and both cities expanded spatially – Tangier in width, Gibraltar in height and out to sea. Chapter seven will look at the dynamism of both cities.

The last chapter, number eight, is largely built on chapters six and seven. Here, I deal with Brexit and its consequences for Gibraltar, as well as Gibraltar's relationship with Morocco in general and Tangier in particular. Informal networks (chapter six) and structural dynamism of previous years (chapter seven) are fundaments on which Gibraltar can build its future after leaving the EU. Chapter eight, however, does not only deal with the hopeful side of a renewed dense cross-border interdependence, for Brexit has unsettled the community deeply and, in some cases, led to agony. In many respects, the high song of a new future is just a whistling in the woods. One does not know yet; the future is open. How the Corona crisis will affect TanGib cannot be foreseen. What is certain, however, is that in Gibraltar, the interest in reestablishing ties with TanGib is much more vital than on the other side: TanGib's margins do not depend on Gibraltar, they are oriented more toward the EU and other regions of Morocco, as well as global world trade.

Finally, chapter nine deals with two questions: What is the next step with TanGib, and what conclusions can be drawn from the material regarding the theoretical approaches. At this point, I will refrain from suggesting answers to these questions. You better read it yourself.

A few remarks on the language used in this book: In Tangier, due to its international character, one often uses different names for one and the same locality. I have tried to reproduce the terms in the local language *Darija*. This sometimes leads to tricky situations. The external market, for example, is called *Soq Barra*. The foreign terms *Zoco*, *Soco*, *Socco*, *Souk* are only used if an informant uses these terms or if they are taken from a text source where the market is called soq barra. It becomes even more complicated with the inner market. Spaniards call it *Zoco Chico*, for the French, it is the *Petit Soco*, but for the Tanjawis of today, it is the *Soq Dahkel*. Again, I generally refer to the native term *Soq Dahkel*, unless vendors (or authors) use one of the other terms, which are of course retained.

Quotations from English have been retained; quotations from other languages have been translated into English.

Street names in Tangier were Arabized or Moroccanized after independence. I have tried to mark this in the text where appropriate, for example, when I speak of *Avenue Hassan II* and notice its former name, *Avenue de Alejandria*.

1. Myths, rhythms, senses

1.1. Geography and power

Talking about myths, the most famous is probably the ancient legend of the Pillars of Hercules, which "border the Strait of Gibraltar (lat. *Gaditanum Fretum*), the most famous being the Rock of Gibraltar (lat. Calpe) in the south of the Iberian Peninsula and the mountain *Jebel Musa* in Morocco,"[1] east of Tangier. "According to the Greek poet Pindar, Heracles placed the inscription 'No further' at the mouth of the Mediterranean Sea to mark the end of the world."[2] This was the Mediterranean world of the Phoenicians, whose graves are located both in Tangier and on the Iberian side. A monument commemorates one of the columns in Gibraltar. The Mayor of Tangier wanted to erect the other column in his city in 2017 but, in doing so, he received a fatwa (Zamane Online 2019).

The myth about the origin of the famous Berber macaques of Gibraltar is also known outside the region: it is said they came from the opposite *Jebel Musa* through an underground tunnel with dry feet to the partner rock.

Myths, symbols and maps are parts of the performative discourse in which agents try to define social worlds and make their view of it appear as a natural perspective, whereby opposing perspectives often experience a denaturalization (Bourdieu 1991). This applies both to the Spanish perspective on Gibraltar and to the perspective of Gibraltarian nationalists. For Spain, Gibraltar is already geographically a 'natural' part of Spanish territory. This argumentation from the time of fascist caudillo Francisco Franco is still relevant today in Spain's political discourse.

The political narrative that dominates in Gibraltar, in turn, also draws on geology. The following argument is made in the video *The Gibraltar Story – Jurassic Rock*, produced by *Knightsfield Ltd.* in 1994, which we will read about later and can be purchased in Gibraltar's souvenir shops and in the *Gibraltar Museum*:

In the Jurassic period of the Earth's age, Europe was separated from Africa by the Thetysocean. The mortal remains of tiny creatures became limestone. 'This

---

1 Wikipedia (n.d.b).
2 Ibid.

Illustration 3 (left): El Boughaz; Illustration 4 (right): Limestone Gibraltar

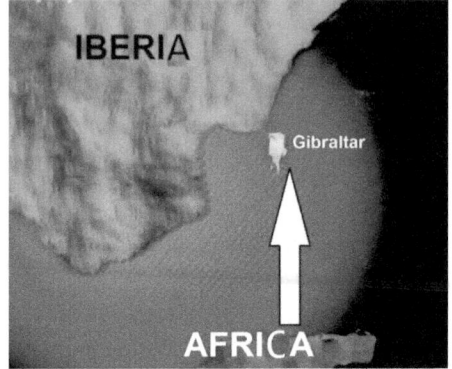

limestone lay about 100 kilometers West of where Gibraltar is today.' The shifting of the Earth's plates 16 or 20 million years ago caused Africa to drift towards Europe, leading to the formation of the Alps, the Sierra Nevada and the Pyrenees. 'Our limestone plate drifted West and attached itself to the other rock.'

The video shows a red African continent moving West, a green Iberian Peninsula that rests within itself, and a white limestone in the outline of Gibraltar that breaks away from North Africa and moves northward toward the Iberian Peninsula, where it eventually docks.

So, different nationalists use geology to substantiate their claims. However, as has already been mentioned, the references to geology, topography and myths around the two places and the 'alleyway' in between – as the Arabs call the Strait – are not the only ones.

1.2. Rhythm and Senses

It is often said that there is a Mediterranean rhythm of life. What is meant by this? Does the Mediterranean have a common rhythm that makes Mediterranean places resemble each other and, at the same time, distinguishes them from places in other regions? Does a typical Mediterranean rhythm exist at all? Instinctively, when we ask this question, most Europeans invoke images and experiences they had as travelers in the countries of the Mediterranean region: Rhythms of movement of people, things, stars, sounds, winds and waves. But how do we approach this question scientifically? How can we say something comprehensible and find out about it? In their rhythm analysis, Lefebvre and Régulier develop a possible approach.

> Rhythm reunites quantitative aspects and elements, which mark time and distinguish moments in it – and qualitative aspects and elements, which link them together, found the unities and result from them. Rhythm appears as regulated time, governed by rational laws, but in contact with what is least rational in human being: the lived, the carnal, the body. Rational, numerical, quantitative and qualitative rhythms superimpose themselves on the multiple natural rhythms of the body (respiration, the heart, hunger and thirst, etc.), though not without changing them. The bundle of natural rhythms wraps itself in rhythms of social or mental function. (Lefebvre/Régulier 2004: 8-9)

Lefebvre and Régulier describe the Mediterranean city as a stage, as a "theatrical city" (Ibid: 96), the concept of the person does not go back to the Mediterranean concept of the mask (lat. *persona*) without reason. But for whom is this city a stage? American ethnologist David Schneider, for example, compared every culture with a theatrical stage on which the individual moves. Norms serve as script instructions for the players (cf. Keesing 1981; Ortner 1984), and the front-stage–backstage analogy comes from Erving Goffman's (1963) stigma analysis, which, in his case, also does not seem to be culture-specific. But what distinguishes the stage of the Mediterranean city from that of other cultures? The theatrical aspect is considered an expression of falsity in German Protestantism, in which inside and outside are supposed to fall into one, which is why the inside has to be carried to the outside in order to be identical. Foucault recognizes it as a central characteristic of modernity in such an emphasis on inner truth through confessional techniques. From this perspective, the theory of Spanish philosopher Ortega y Gasset, who describes the character of Andalusians as narcissistic and inclined towards theatrical self-staging, could be described as premodern[3]. But to whom is the theatricalization directed? For the ethnologists who have worked on Andalusian masculinity, the other men in the context of the bar are the audience for such self-dramatization (Ingham 1964: 97; Aramoni 1972; Giraldo 1972; Gilmore/Gilmore 1978; Brandes 1981: 217; Driessen 1983; Santamaría 1985; Gilmore 1986: 126, 1987: 129f; Corbin/Corbin 1988: 151f). But who judges whether it is a theater, something staged? For whom is the theater a vain game and for whom is it an unreflected matter of course?

Lefebvre and Régulier claim that tourism enhances the stage-like nature of the Mediterranean rhythm of cities: "[T]ourism is added to the traditional and customary use of space and time, of monumentality and rhythms 'of the other' without

---

3   "The Andalusian has a vegetable sense of existence and lives with preference in his skin" (Zambrano/Ortega y Gasset 1984: 243).

making it disappear" (2004: 97f). But if this is so, then the stagecraft must have been there before.

Lefebvre and Régulier do not present findings in this regard, but that is precisely what would be exciting: Wasn't life in premodern Northern Europe just as public and close to the senses as life in the Mediterranean?[4] In any case, the polished cleansing of the ambivalent, the face, the physical contact, the loud conversation, the body odor in modern public space, all point to this. Above all, and this would be of particular interest to the ethnologist, do the inhabitants of the cities even notice these rhythms? And do they perceive them as translocal, i.e. as Mediterranean? If so, what do they mean to them? It is telling that Lefebvre and Régulier have an unspecified "enigmatic individual" roaming the Mediterranean city as rhythm analysts, as if he were Walter Benjamin's flaneur:

> It is thus that we can try and draw the portrait of an enigmatic individual who strolls with his thoughts and his emotions, his impressions and his wonder, through the streets of large Mediterranean towns, and whom we shall call the 'rhythmanalyst'. More sensitive to times than to spaces, to moods than to images, to the atmosphere than to particular events, he is strictly speaking neither psychologist, nor sociologist, nor anthropologist, nor economist; however he borders on each of these fields in turn and is able to draw on the instruments that the specialists use. He therefore adopts a transdisciplinary approach in relation to these different sciences. He is always 'listening out', but he does not only hear words, discourses, noises and sounds; he is capable of listening to a house, a street, a town as one listens to a symphony, an opera. Of course, he seeks to know how this music is composed, who plays it and for whom. (Lefebvre/Régulier 2004: 87)

It can be assumed that the enigmatic individual is neither a local fishwife nor a hotel employee or schoolchild but a stranger from outside, a traveler, a tourist, an artist or a scientist. References to the orientalist discourse on the South are obvious.

As an ethnologist, I can approach this primarily through field research based on participatory observation. Let us look at local experiences in Tangier and Gibraltar.

It is the fact that the other side can be seen that strengthens a longing for the other. Soor el Maâgazine and Café Hafa in Tangier are not the only places in the region where the other is so incredibly close: From here you can see Spain and

---

4   "The entire process of modernisation is aimed at creating a sensual distance and individualising the individual: To muffle noise and minimise shouting in the streets; to whitewash natural odors with artificial ones and thereby standardise them; to regulate looks and gestures; to criminalise touch; to unify the taste inherent in food through industrial mass products." (Cf. Haller 2007: 175ff, translated by the author.)

Illustration 5: View from Dar Baroud (Tangier) across the Strait

Gibraltar, at night and on a clear day, you can even see the headlights of the cars on the other side. Here too, a common ground between *Tanjawis* and Gibraltarians comes to the fore: When the border between Gibraltar and Spain was closed, Gibraltarians were enclosed in an area of 6.8 square kilometers near the Spanish town of La Línea within sight and hearing distance of their friends and relatives.

> 'I was born a few years before the closure of the border between Spain and Gibraltar [1969-1982/85],' says Gibraltarian ethnologist Andrew Canessa. 'My entire childhood and youth was limited to 6.8 km, and I was not allowed to travel in Spain for the first time until I was 16 or 17 years old. I did not cross the border to go to La Línea, but went to Madrid via London. I could practically see Spain from my nursery – and yet it was beyond my reach – it was very strange.' (Bayerischer Rundfunk 2018)

It was similar for the inhabitants of La Línea (Linenses) between 1969 and 1982, perhaps even a little more painful because the inaccessible Rock of Gibraltar sat before their faces like a huge monster. We are dealing with socially closely connected societies on the Strait that cannot escape the gaze of the other.

Access to visible space has also changed for *Tanjawis*: While before 1991, they could cross over to Europe without a visa, today, they can only do so under difficult conditions.

Illustration 6: Closed border between Gibraltar and La Línea

Gibraltarians have been able to travel directly to Spain again since 1982, but even here, the conditions are still unpredictable, as border controls can sometimes take several hours.

Thus, the three cities share the experience of people not being able to move freely in the immediate and visible vicinity but at different times.[5]

Another approach to rhythm research is provided by ethnomusicologist Steven Feld (1984), who measures the world and its cultures acoustically. He has

> dedicated an entire research life to the question of what sound reveals about our world. Or, to put it another way: how human beings and the natural and technical sounds of the world they live in influence each other. [...] He listens to the people [the Kaluli of New Guinea] and realizes that they use the sounds of the rainforest to orient themselves in time and space. Thus, the Kaluli compose songs by singing at and with watercourses. The splashing gives the rhythm and the musical intervals. The lyrics of the songs in turn describe places along streams and forest paths: Water music as a map. The songs of the jungle birds also serve as spatial orientation - and act as an ecological clock. The sounds of birds set the pace for many seasonal and everyday activities. (Feld 1984: 394ff, cit. in Pyritz 2019)

Questions that can be applied to the two cities concern the influence of waves, wind, weather, the cries of seagulls and other soundscapes related to art, performance, habitus and rhythm. Are there commonalities? Were there similarities in the past?

---

5   Beyond the view across the Strait, a visual presence of both cities on the respective other side has been evident at least since 1910. Gibraltarian postcard photographer Benzaquén owned a branch in Tangier and produced images of both cities. Cf. Chipulina (2016).

For "the soundscape of a place can [...] also serve as an indicator of upheavals and disturbances" (Pyritz 2019): In Tangier today – as far as religious expression is concerned – you no longer hear the chimes of the churches or the chants in the synagogues but only the calls to prayer of the muezzin. From time to time, one also hears the music of Sufi groups like Ḥamādša, which, since about 2015, have been able to move increasingly in public space again, after they were previously not able to do so due to Salafi threats. In some places, an acoustic cultural battle is taking place, such as at the *Soq Barra*, where both the *Sidi Bouabid* mosque and the *Cinema Rif* art house are located, the entrance to the medina and tourist venues.

Restaurant *Art y Gourmet* at *Soq Barra*: The muezzin of the mosque calls for prayer and on the roof terrace of the noble restaurant for tourists and local intellectuals sings Judy Garland Somewhere over the Rainbow. Sometimes a boy pushes a cart with prayer CDs across the square, which he loudly fills with the same recordings.[6]

Today you no longer hear the foghorns of the ships in the harbor, which is subject to so many film shots[7]. Nor can the noisy bustle of the port of Tangier, of which Andersen (1863a, 1863b), Lenz (1884) and Savory (1903) gave testimony, be observed in this way any longer. In any case, it is already evident that the ferries between Gibraltar/Tarifa and Tangier are dominated by soundscapes that cannot be assigned to either side but have their own rhythm: The chugging of the engines, the sounds of the wind and sea currents, the strangely muffled sounds that the passengers make. Small, short conversations, no loud roaring like in Tangier, hardly any laughter and only strained silence before crossing over into the other world. When I fly over from Tangier to the other side, to Europe, one of my guarantors says that I am now, like Alice, going behind the other side of the mirror again.

One can transfer Feld's findings to other senses. For it is not only about the sense of hearing and the sense of sight, the other senses are also formative in this corner of the world. You smell the same sea salt in the air, taste the same spices on your tongue and feel the same winds on your skin: The warm *levanter* (the *Chergui* in Tangier) from the east and northeast, the cooler *Poniente* (Moroccan: *Gharbi*) from the Atlantic west. People are exposed to the same atmospheric pressure, common weather conditions, such as the great hailstorm of April 14, 2020, and you feel the same humid cold in your bones.

Annette Tunbridge, pharmacist and political activist from Gibraltar, points to such common realities:

> When the wind comes from one direction, Gibraltarians and *Tanjawis* know exactly which door they have to close to prevent it from slamming shut. Women also know exactly when they should not be styled at the hairdresser's if the weather is such

---

6   Field research diary Tangier, July 17, 2013.
7   The soundscapes of Gibraltar and Tangier still need to be explored in more detail.

that every hairstyle is immediately destroyed. You just know that. If there is a strong wind, the connection with the ferries is interrupted, which then cannot drive. And if the weather permits, they can see each other clearly. It's the same on both sides, we have similarities that show up in practical handling.[8]

And Estrella Abudarham can hardly find words for the *transboughaz* commonality:

Tangier gives her good vibrations. I ask her to be more specific. She does not know how to explain it. I ask if it is the weather, which is similar to Gibraltar, or the air or the light. She says, no, it is not that [...] it is rather an emotional closeness. She would feel at home there, even if she then talked to people and realized that she was British after all. She mentions her mother, who lived in Tangier for a while.[9]

Two other sensual similarities, which will not be discussed in detail here but which underpin the idea of a common cultural area, are music[10] and local cuisine.[11]

1.3. On the sea: Boughaz – Straits – Estrecho

During the research sabbatical in WS 2019/2020, I devoted myself to the relationship between the two places, or rather, the entanglements of TanGib. I could not only rely on my field material collected previously in Gibraltar and Tangier or on the evaluation of chat forums, newspapers and magazines but also on field trips to both localities since the decision for a Brexit in 2016. Several research stays in 2019 and 2020 especially broadened my knowledge.

---

8   Field research diary TanGib, April 1, 2019.
9   Field research diary TanGib, March 5, 2020.
10 Singer Pepe Caserni (Insight Magazine, October 2001), for example, performed at the *Inter Police Ball. The* band "The Terriers were invited to perform their first ever concert in Tangier. Some members of the band and the major part of the instruments, were transported by boat (the *Mons Calpe*), while Sergio Olivera and I had to fly over to Tangier. It was the first time we had ever flown – we had nightmares during the flight from Gibraltar to Tangier!" (Insight Magazine, September 2001). Gibraltarian artists, such as Pepe Palmero (Insight Magazine, November 2003) and Maleni King (Insight Magazine, December 2001), performed not only in Tangier but also in La Línea. The entertainers John Charvetto and Felipe Rodriguez performed not only in Gibraltar but also on Radio Algeciras, Radio La Línea and Radio Tangier (The Gibraltar Chronicle, May 10, 1957). The Gibraltarian Bill Sanguinetti was a comedian and actor and worked for the International Administration of Tangier (Vaidon 1977: 271). These artistic connections no longer exist today.
11 The Gibraltarian national dish *Calentita* is still sold by street vendors in Tangier, also in many other cities of the Mediterranean Sea, for example, in Malta (where it is called *paloma*), in Western Algeria (there they say *karane*) or in Italy (where it is called *farinata*). https://www.wikiwand.com/en/Gibraltarian_cuisine.

Illustration 7: Proyects of fixed railway connections

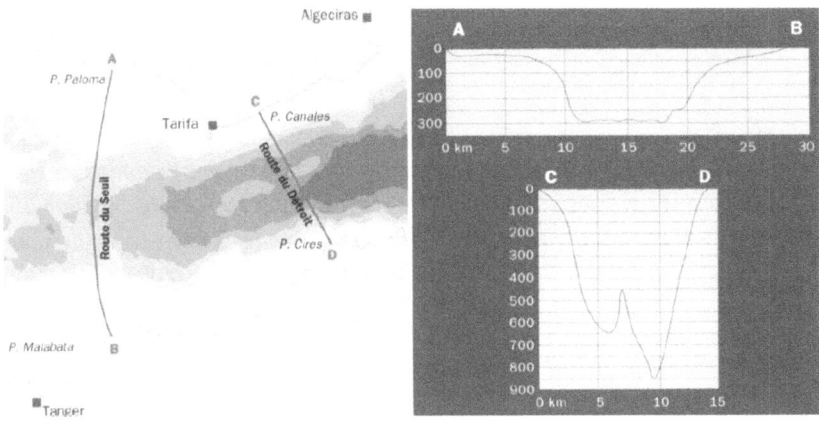

What could be more obvious than to start an approach to the Strait with descriptions of the journey from Gibraltar to Tangier? In theory, there are other possibilities than crossing the Strait by ship: By plane, bridge or tunnel. The former has been used many times in the history of the Strait, the latter has been considered time and again; economist Steffen Wippel (2000) has described the projects in this regard. Time and again, they have inspired fantasies of architects, politicians, economists and artists. None of these approaches to realizing a *lieu fixe*, however, has been able to assert itself so far. Thus, crossings by means of ships or airplanes remain.[12]

If you traveled from Gibraltar to Tangier before 1860, you had to take the feluccas. These had cabins, but these probably did not deserve their name. A traveler wrote in 1857: "There was not in it one single article of furniture of any kind, except a few narrow, thin mattresses, which were spread out in the floor, without sheets, pillows or blankets (Fort 1857: 48ff)." Passengers often preferred to remain on deck during the crossing, which could last between 12 and 30 hours (Vaidon 1977: 71). Let us look at reports of those who took on this crossing. Unfortunately, these are only reports from people who are not from the region itself – neither from Tangier nor from Gibraltar, Ceuta, Tarifa or Algeciras – but rather reports from strangers from the north, whose accounts are perhaps more indicative of the differences, especially when they hope to find in Tangier a promise they think they will not find in Europe. But do they also notice any similarities?

---

12   For flight connections, see chapter 7.

> The English officers returned to Gibraltar in an open boat. Such a journey across this Strait can sometimes be very dangerous. Once two English officers of the evening left Tangier for Cadiz with good winds, where they planned to arrive the following morning. In the night, however, a violent storm broke out, and the boat was considered lost. [...] It was a cloudburst which fell in the Strait between Tarifa and Tangier in the form of a thick and large column on which a thick wave of great circumference seemed to rest [...] That water column seemed to me to be like a pillar on which the vault of heaven rested. The water seemed to fall with such force that it could have crushed a ship, and the sea around it was in violent motion. The weather was beautiful, by the way. A rainbow seemed to surround the column, but after a few minutes it faded and disappeared, write Swedish traveler Olof Agrell and British doctor William Lempriere (1798: 306-307).

Spanish explorer Domingo Badía y Leblich (pseudonym: Ali Bey) describes the arrival in the port of Tangier as a dream and an entry into an absolutely new world, which is as different from Gibraltar as France is from China, as if you were on another planet (Bey 1814: 3).

American author G. Fort (1859: 64) was positively surprised by Tangier when he arrived there from Gibraltar: He thought the city was "cheerful and bright."

Danish writer Hans Christian Andersen arrived in Tangier by ship from Gibraltar on November 2, 1862, where he remained as a guest of Sir John Drummond Hay in *Villa Ravensrock*[13] until his departure on November 9th. He writes about the crossing:

> The crew aboard the steamer was all Moors. The ship was one of the very small ones and leaned heavily on the moving sea; we sailed across the bay to Algeciras and then along the Spanish coast, which was naked and rocky, to Tarifa.
>
> Black, dark stone - sea surf breaks over us. Europe's entire southern tip is a wild mountainous region, burnt and deserted; the city of Tarifa hid behind naked black boulders; only an old, grey-black lighthouse stood out, amidst screaming birds. Africa, which we headed for from Tarifa, towards Tangier, lay smiling and fertile before us.
>
> Behind Ceuta, the country rose enormously, with three mountain ranges in a row, one higher than the other, and one of them as jagged as Montserrat near Barcelona; but now, as the coast stretches towards Tangier, from the Strait to the

---

13 "The room you had given me had the most beautiful view; to the right, over the garden and the green coast, behind the mandarins, one could see the high, blazing mountains of Ceuta and beyond the open Strait towards the Mediterranean Sea, where sailing ships and steamers came and went. Shortly before, from the cliffs of Gibraltar, the Spanish coastal country laid the entire wild coast with Tarifa, Trafalgar Bay and the mountains towards Cadiz. The Atlantic Ocean stretched Westward in its infinity." (Andersen 1863b)

Atlantic, it becomes flatter and greener, like the hills on Själland's North coast. Now, with white walls, flat-roofed houses and above them a lime-white fortress, Tangier.

Behind the town there seemed to be a small glimpse of the desert, vast yellow sand, over which a chain of loaded camels moves. There is no harbour, no protection against the rolling of the sea, even the long, strong breakwater was destroyed by the Europeans when they left their possessions in Tangier.

The steamer stopped quite far out and dropped anchor. A few boats with half-naked, sunburned Moors [...] came towards us, screaming and waving they entered the stairs of the ship. (Andersen 1863b)

In 1879, Gibraltar was connected daily (except Fridays) with Tangier by three small ships, *Hercules*, *Lion Belge* and *Jakal*, writes Austrian Africa researcher Oskar Lenz (1884: 7ff). He focuses decidedly on the passage itself. The ships sometimes leave later because the captains make a "little business" of serving sailing ships as barges. When the weather is bad, the boats are "thrown around," so that one thinks "it must burst apart at any moment." The waves burst in through the "damaged" cabin windows, where they evenly drench the "effects of the passengers." Jewish travelers "moan loudly," Arabs "shout resignedly Allah Kebir" and the Europeans are in an "indescribable state of paralysis." The view of Tangier from the ship seems "quite friendly," Lenz describes landscape and city benevolently. Some hotels are quite bearable and the city has a functioning street-cleaning system. Nowhere, however, does he explicitly compare the two cities.

Spanish Arabist Antonio Almagro Cárdenas imagines himself still in Spain during his visit in 1881, Tangier appears to him like the Albaicín quarter of Granada (López García 2012: 4).

Charles Augustus Stoddard (1892: 210), editor of the *New York Observer*, said that one got into "another sphere" when one crossed the Strait of Gibraltar.

Italian writer De Amicis writes about the passage, but not so much about the thoughts and feelings that overwhelm him during the passage as about his observation of the passengers:

The more noticeable on the outward trip from Gibraltar. Here still ferments the noisy, feverish, brilliant life of a European city, and the traveller, from whatever quarter of Europe he may hail, yet feels himself at home in numberless familiar customs and aspects of life. Three hours later, and the very name of our Continent sounds strange; Christian signifies enemy, and our civilization is unknown, or feared, or scoffed at. Everything, from the very foundations of society to the most trifling details of private life, is metamorphosed, and all indication of the close proximity of Europe has completely disappeared. We suddenly find ourselves in an unknown land, without ties of any kind, and with everything to learn. To be sure the European coast is still visible from the shore, but in our hearts there is a consciousness of immeasurable distance, as though that narrow strip of water were an ocean, those blue, distant hills a delusion. (De Amicis 1897: 3–4).

Illustration 8: Travels of Oscar Lenz

"Like many newcomers, [Frech diplomat Maximilien de la] Martinière must have been unable to distinguish this Jewish and Moorish archetype from Andalusians who made the journey for work or trade. They would have a slight difference in appearance - even dress - and would tend to communicate in the lingua franca, a mixture of Spanish, Arabic and Riffian that they spoke effortlessly. In any case, the chaos of his arrival would quickly upset the Frenchman's arrogant gaze. The ferry dropped anchor very close to the main pier, from where a flotilla of boats full of Moroccans "descendants of ancient pirates" approached, grabbing the ladders to "climb, agile as monkeys, and invade the deck." (Pack 2015: 54)

An English woman, Isabel Savory, reports at the turn of the century:

About six weeks before 1902 was due, Rose A. Bainbridge and myself left behind us the last outpost of England – Gibraltar – with its cluster of civilization round the bottom of the great Rock. Four hours brought us across the Straits; and seen from the deck of the dirty little Gibel Musa, on to which we had changed from a S. & O. at Gibraltar, Morocco shaped itself into a rugged country, ridge behind ridge of low hills and jagged mountains cutting the sky-line. A long white sand-bank lying back in a bay on the African shore, broken at one end by irregular vegetation, gradually developed upon its slopes a yellowish-white, fantastic city, which resolved itself into Tangier. Landing at Tangier among vociferating Moors has been described often enough, and needs no further enlargement. (Savory 1903)

French traveler Du Taillis (1905) describes Gibraltar and Tangier as antitheses. "All here laid out, prepared in the barrenness of the rock for the futile work of battle. And there, on this virgin and already fertile soil, the golden sheaves and green meadows inviting to peaceful labour the energies of our century and our race." But one commonality: Gibraltar is not Europa and Tangier is not Africa. "Gibraltar and Tangier is the Strait, the road of the worlds. Only a few miles away, they are the two points on the globe that are equally well placed to dominate the universe" (Du Taillis 1905: 122).

Finally, Mark Twain writes "[W]e have had enough of Spain and Gibraltar for the present. Tangier is the spot we have been looking for all the time. [...] We wanted something thoroughly and uncompromisingly foreign [...] And lo! In Tangier we have found it. [...] Tangier is a foreign land if ever there was one" (Twain 1920: 64).

In addition to the crossing itself, the question of the first impression of Tangier (Cit. Jebrouni 2019) is less important than the comparison that the travelers make with Gibraltar.

Ali Bey, Fort, Andersen, Stoddard, Du Taillis and Twain focus on Tangier and Gibraltar (Europe), only Lenz and de Amicis write about the passage itself. It seems as if the passage itself recedes behind the need to describe the other as different.

In comparing here and there, orientalist fantasies of Europeans who do not come from the region become manifest: Ali Bey, Fort, Andersen, Lenz, Stoddard, de Amicis, Du Taillis, Twain ... one could add the names of painters and writers, the beat generation, the hippies and also one or the other researcher. For most travelers quoted here, both cities represent antitheses (Stoddard), foreign (Ali Bey, Twain) or unknown (de Amicis) countries.[14]

Mainly in the 19th century, Moroccan visitors to Europe were overwhelmed again and again by the technological development of the Europeans. If you be-

---

14 We find similar things for Spanish travelers. While Ramón Martínez García compares the abysmal differences between Tangier and his country: "At a distance of twenty kilometres there is a difference of twenty centuries" (Martínez García 1989: 25), other travelers speak of a Spanish Tangier. Until the beginning of the 20th century, in 1903, Vicente Vera tells the story of his journey under the title of the Spanish Tangier and describes the work that Spaniards did in the city. What prevails is the value of what is written. The ambitious desire to legitimize the Spanish presence in Tangier is based on mere number games. Pío Baroja, the writer of the '98 generation who traveled to Tangier in 1903 as a journalist for El Globo, sees that the majority of the population speaks Spanish after Arabic, "the Spanish are the most influential, although they are the ones with less authority over French and other European powers" (Baroja, 1989) cit. in. Jebrouni 2019, pg. 50. Translation by the author.

Illustration 9: Ferry between Tarifa and Tangier 2013

lieve Ghouirgate, then Tangier was a transition area for Moroccans, because "the technical and technological progress of Europe can already be felt in Tangier on Moroccan soil. Tangier is already a different world, a strange and wonderful 'elsewhere'" (Ghouirgate 1994: 157). Lenz and Almagro Cárdenas describe Tangier as not so different, and de Taillis is the only one who points out that Tangier is neither African nor Gibraltar European. Since he does not explain what that "neither – nor" would consist of, it is open whether he sees two different transition zones or even a common transition zone.

My own first crossing[15] in February 2013 was not via Gibraltar (there was no direct ferry connection at that time) but via Tarifa. However, my diary notes something connecting between Tangier and Gibraltar:

> On the ferry [...] just a handful of guests, maybe 20 Moroccans and 5 Europeans, thus, almost deserted across the Strait of Gibraltar, a truly lonely journey on this mythical route. We had to queue up at the counter, behind which an official sat in a thickly lined coat, stamped the passports and took entry forms. The ferry had probably been bought from a Greek company or at least it chugged in the Aegean earlier: Behind the official no map of the Strait but of the Aegean Sea. Everywhere also inscriptions in Greek. Especially apart: A complaint box with inscriptions in

---

15   Previously, I had entered Morocco by ferry from Algeciras via Ceuta or by plane.

this language, English, French and German. In the queue behind me, a loudly telephoning young woman with an adventurous language: She jumped back and forth in her sentence between deepest Andalusian and Arabic, so perfect and normal that I could not guess where she probably came from. She swerved between English and Spanish, much like the Yanitos do, but without their accent.[16]

Three weeks later came the second crossing, also via Tarifa. Gibraltar is not in my head, but the passage itself is in my bowels:

> On the ferry of the FRS line. Rarely have I sat in such uncomfortable seats. The ship looks more modern than the Greek island hopper of the other company that brought me to Tangier 3 weeks ago. We are still lying in the harbor – I drove my car onto the ferry and they told me to stop on a sloping ramp, although there was still space in front of me. Strange. Then I immediately stood at the entry queue, they stamped my passport without any problems and put down my entry form, on which I indicated as destination *Tangier, Hotel El Minzah* and as the reason for my journey "tourism," without paying attention to it. Now I am sitting on the bobbing barge in the harbor, outside it is raining harder again and already now it is swaying heavily. I will probably not be able to write much longer, nausea is already announcing itself. At the neighboring table, an older Moroccan sets his watch back one hour. So now it's off to the other world, and when I get out of the car belly of the ferry and into the passenger deck, I have this feeling: Now it's getting serious. Oh dear! Horizons blur. I'm not relaxed at all: Hopefully, the crossing goes well and the entry; hopefully, there is internet in the apartment; hopefully, it's not too cold [...]. Hopefully, I can find something to eat; hopefully, I dare to go by car; hopefully, hopefully, hopefully [...] My goodness, how can one be so worried. Everything's going to be fine. It's chugging out of the belly of the ship and it's 5:05. Are we leaving slowly? Still in port, and I feel faint. Nice words are hard to find there. The announcements are hard to understand or not at all. Only the word "pleasant journey" gets through to me. The ship is turning in the harbor basin and I have to change my position. Otherwise I'll go backwards! Now once again I have to change my position. I hear Spanish and French all around me. The Moroccans are quiet. Still in the harbor, how long does the damn thing keep on turning (5:15 pm)? Now 5:17 pm, we drive out of the basin into the restless Strait of Gibraltar. It is swaying quite a bit. I feel sick."[17]

Further remarks about the Strait, Gibraltar, Tangier and the crossing fall victim to seasickness.

---

16   Field research diary Tangier, February 14, 2013.
17   Field research diary Tangier, March 5, 2013.

Let us change the view from the boat to the view from the land. The land promises security. Thoughts are rooted in what we see, not in our stomachs. In Gibraltar, I make a note:

> I walk up to the top floor of the university building where a café is located. From there you should have a wonderful view over the Strait. And indeed: It is breathtaking. Opposite *Jebel Musa*, then Algeciras, then the bay and *The Rock*. It almost makes me howl. It's so beautiful here. The weather is great too.[18]

On the other side of the Strait, *Café Makina* is the place where my mind opened up during my research. The two oceans, the coast, Spain and Gibraltar opposite ... Yes, *El Boughaz* opens the senses. That is peace.

Illustration 10: Cafe Makina, 2018

Before *Café Makina*, in the course of the urbanistic redesign of Tangier, fell to the modernist sandblasting, so to speak, in order to commodify the cultural *heritage of the city*, I could let my thoughts fly there. But what is this, *cultural heritage*? We had organized a conference on the subject (*"Patrimoine, tourisme et changements politiques dans la région MENA"*)[19] at the Hotel *El Minzah* on February 15 and 16, 2015. There, we no longer understood *Heritage* as a set of objects, artifacts or customs that can be easily collected and classified in a purely empirical sense. Rather, we understood

---

18   Field research diary TanGib, April 2, 2019.
19   https://www.ruhr-uni-bochum.de/archaelogie/mam/content/programm_-_tagung_-_marokko.pdf.

Heritage – with Hall (2005: 25, cit. in Nic Craith 2007: 6) – as a discursive practice by which a community creates its own kind of collective social memory.[20] In contrast to *Heritage*, Tradition refers to lived collective practices. Or as Ullrich Kockel (2007) puts it: *Heritage* begins when a cultural tradition has ended.

Café Makina was then for me a living cultural tradition in a niche that – In my view – had been forgotten and overlooked by neoliberal modernization. I must admit that a good ethnologist would have asked what the visitors thought about the changes of the *Makina* … I did not do that. For me, I needed the *Makina*, an enclave beyond the reach of the market, where one could play tabla in peace and with a little money, watch football and escape the demands of research. Faded photographs of the old Tangier and wooden boats on consoles hang in the main room. The tea costs 5 Dirham. The name of the café comes from the small tables with round milled holes in which the hot glasses could be perfectly placed. Small tables on which Singer sewing machines used to stand. So it was: Heritage?

Old and young men among themselves – and now? *Café Makina* had become a magical and meditative place for me, so I often came here to take walks and excursions into the city. This was promised to me by the experiences that many found in the much better known *Café Hafa* in *Mershan*. This was founded in 1921, made famous by the writer Paul Bowles, by Mick Jagger and the inevitable German hippie icon Uschi Obermaier – *Hafa* can be found in every travel guide. Today, young middle-class people sit on its beautiful terraces with breathtaking views over the Strait of Gibraltar. Much has been written about *Café Hafa*, expat writers have immortalized the café and the rock upon which it is built, as mythical places of nostalgia where you can let your mind go with a glass of mint tea and a Kif pipe. Moroccans themselves especially, who are only 14 kilometers from the promised land, experience their burning desire here: One is within reach of the longed-for other side (but only nearby), which remains inaccessible.

In the years around 2016, *Café Makina* was renovated in the course of exposing the city walls and its temporary terraces were removed. However, the audience has not changed. So: Tradition and *Heritage*?

Now let us look at a difference in the rhythms.

1.4. Time

Tangier and Gibraltar are now subject to different time regimes that structure the daily rhythm. In Gibraltar, the European linear time regime prevails, whereas in Morocco, different time concepts coexist side by side (Abu-Shams/Gonzales

---

20   One example is the distancing of Jews from Tangier in Israel from the other Jews of Morocco (Moreno 2012).

Vasquez 2014: 36). The most obvious difference is that European time is more oriented towards the visibility of the clock. Moroccan time, on the other hand, is mainly structured by the audible fivefold call to prayer, which structures daily routine and physical practices, such as pausing. But of course, Tangier is also partly subject to the time regime of the clock and has been for a long time. Thus, the first clock in Morocco was installed in the Catholic Church *Puríssima Concepción* in *Calle Siaghin* on January 6, 1894 (Marco 1913: 18).[21]

Anselmo Ravella was the only Christian who had been allowed to enter the *Great Mosque*. In 1938, the mosque officials were looking for a trustworthy Muslim watchmaker who could coordinate the clocks in the mosque. But they found none. Opposite the mosque watchmaker Ravella worked in his shop, having had been based in Tangier for already 40 years. Since the watches were too big to bring into his shop and he, as a Christian, was not allowed to enter the floor of the mosque, four strong Muslims carried him on a chair into the mosque. From this chair he repaired the clocks. Because this was too impractical in the long run, he was later granted the right to enter the mosque barefoot. (Martínez Antonio 2010–2011: 290)

Despite the orientation towards linear time, the practice of dealing with time is highly problematic in both cities in some contexts. In Tangier, for example, many people are excited about the question of when, where and in what way one could cross the border into Europe. It is a subcutaneous nervousness that rests dormant in many – and sometimes bursts out. In Gibraltar, too, there is a subliminal nervousness that is connected with the border. But in Gibraltar, it is the crossing of the border into Spain. As this is an old problem and in Gibraltar you can live well – you do not necessarily have to cross to the other side. Spain is not a hope for Gibraltarians, at best a possibility, but mostly a threat: One has to deal with the other side in some pragmatic way. It is impossible, for example, to estimate when the land border with Spain would be open or how long it would take to cross it.

Psychologically stressful is especially the fact that the measures are not always in force and it cannot be estimated by the individual when they will be applied. However, there are various indications that the measures are being reinforced at weekends, during political negotiations between the UK and Spain and in the month leading up to elections in Gibraltar, as well as on the day after the celebration of *Gibraltar National Day*. In the weeks leading up to the *Feria de La Línea* (Autumn Festival of La Línea), border harassment is unlikely.

This is the case every year, explains Mary-Clare Russo (*1955), "so that we can go back over there and spend our money. And every year, after the Feria ends, the harassment is reinstated" (Haller 2000a: 75).

In Tangier, however, the other side is not just a place of pragmatic and problematic everyday planning but a land of hope for the future.

---

21   C. Marco: Historia de la comisión de higiene, pg. 18.

Space also organizes the daily rhythm. Gibraltar is a small, hardly growing community, which at the time of my field research in the 1990s, extended significantly along a single artery – *Main Street* down to the southern tip, to *Europa Point*.

> Here, Gibraltarians often meet several times a day. For one specific strategy, a native term has even been coined: "the Hi-Bye Syndrome." On *Main Street*, distance is created by missing the street with a quick foot and heading purposefully towards the destination, without exchanging with acquaintances except for the ritual avoidance greeting. If you greet an acquaintance with "Hi," you will receive a "Bye" from him. Sometimes you greet with a simple "Bye." (Ibid.: 122)

Gibraltar also has a few side streets like Irish Town or Line Wall Road, which stretch from north to south. If one wanted to escape the narrow space, one had to go to Spain. But today, due to the land reclamation in the former harbor area, new quarters have been added.

Tangier, on the other hand, is a city that is constantly expanding toward the south and east. There is a symbolic boulevard in the city center but no artery that dominates the traffic, instead there is a high volume of traffic throughout the city. Larger distances than in Gibraltar have to be overcome.

Social structure is another factor that influences the rhythm of people's lives. Gibraltar has long been a military colony, a military or militaroid, at least a British habitus was necessary for civilians to rise socially (ibid.: 157). Today, Gibraltar is a service society with a high density of banks, law firms and offices of the gaming industry. Clothing and habitus are more British, not only because of these trades, but also because most young people have received higher education in Britain since the 1970s.

Tangier, on the other hand, experienced an exchange of the majority of its population after Morocco's independence in 1956. Christians, Jews and many old resident Muslims left the city, which experienced a large influx from the rural hinterlands. I have heard the complaints of the old-established many times about *these peasants* who did not know how to live in a city; I have also heard the complaints of the newcomers many times about *these arrogant lazy people* who did not work all day and cheated people. These complaints conceal a central reference to rhythm: An urban Mediterranean art of living (or, turned to the negative: A windy mendacity) is juxtaposed with a rural inland rudeness (turned to the positive: Honest down-to-earthness).

> *Mustafa says:* "We *Tanjawis* are like this: We work to have something and then again not because we like to sleep and enjoy the day. These people from the South have changed everything: They come here to earn money and they work a lot, but

cheaply. They spoil wages and mentality.²² "We have to go slowly, bit by bit. *Tanjawis* don't like to work. Once we have money, we spend it in the café. People from the South, on the other hand, only want money, money, money, not quality of life. *Tanjawis* say: 'Work? No men do, only the donkeys do. Country donkeys who come here.'"²³

Khaled from Essaouira and Abdelladim from Casablanca say: "*Tanjawis* are lazy and sleep until they fall asleep, while we from the south (= Arobia) work hard." The²⁴ other day, Zak from Casablanca said, "*Tanjawis* are racist. They don't like us from the South because we come here to work, and *Tanjawis* are all lazy or crooks."²⁵

Typical for the rhythm of the city, which is perceived by outsiders, especially by Europeans, is the fact that male *Tanjawis* stay in the café for hours without any obvious reason: They sit and comment, drink tea or coffee and look, observe. Or stare and gaze.

But this is what the foreigners experience above all in the Medina and on *Boulevard Pasteur*, i.e. in certain areas that they rarely leave. At the beginning of my research, I did not know that it was part of the *Tanjawis'* self-image to take speed out of the process, to wait and comment and look.²⁶

"What is the first thing that all these men do in the sidewalk cafes, Mohammed asks? They look. And comment. There is a whole science of the gaze, he quotes a French friend who once called it *shufology* (*shuf* = look): the culture of the eyes and the gaze; but I also think that this is a good part of my research methods so far: *Shufology* – the art of looking. In fact, people always looked into your eyes, they looked closely, as if they wanted to see what was inside. Many look closely at who bought what and brought it home in their plastic bags."²⁷

"At Café Cristina, I tell [an informant] that he and his brother would have no problem getting the Shufology diploma because they are trained gawpers and look up every woman's behind. They laugh."²⁸ Only a few years later, in 2019, the shuffeurs' gaze is still directed at women, but less at the people passing by than at their mo-

---

22 Field research diary Tangier, December 10, 2013.
23 Field research diary Tangier, December 27, 2013.
24 Field research diary Tangier, August 7, 2013; December 10, 2013.
25 Field research diary Tangier, December 4, 2013.
26 At this point, it is worth remembering Streck (2010), who refers to Theodor Danzel's distinction between *homo faber* and *homo divinans*. While the former seeks to gain his happiness through work, the latter waits for divine input, experience and *passio*.
27 Field research diary Tangier, July 20, 2013.
28 Field research diary Tangier, July 22, 2013.

bile phone displays. Indeed, the world is no longer a sphere but a flat disc on which you wipe back and forth!

In Gibraltar, people also sit in cafés, and to the visitor from the North, this may seem to be a typical Mediterranean way of life: Staying in pubs, bars and cafés until well into the night and letting the Lord God be a good man. But I made this observation for the first time in 2017, while in my field research records from the 1990s, I find my complaints about the fact that public life in the city dies out at 6 pm, thinned-out street lighting prevails, hardly any pedestrians are visible and pubs – if they were open at all – breathed the flair of the crown glassy gloom of English military pubs. There were hardly any restaurants and cafés in streets and alleys, life was predominantly domestic. This was always explained to me with reference to military tradition: For over 200 years it had not been customary for civilians to be outside after dark (Haller 2000a: 111). That has changed in the meantime – in t times before Corona.

Gender is a key factor in distinguishing the rhythms of Tangier and Gibraltar. Tangier is anything but an Arab city where women would be restricted to the domestic sphere – the women of Tangier are well represented in public and have been considered strong and self-confident since ancient times. Men and women are co-present but they are not co-communicative, as is the case in Gibraltar. They do not sit – except in a family environment – in mixed-gender groups at tables in cafés nor do they speak loudly, as is customary in Gibraltar. Men are also less audible in the cafés than their male counterparts in Gibraltar.

All this indicates that there are hardly any rhythmic similarities between Gibraltar and Tangier on many sensual levels, which have become habitualized in the bodies. I am tempted to say that this is not merely a different time management but a fundamentally ontological difference. Contemplation and idleness are not wasted in Tangier or Gibraltar but are the meaning and purpose of existence, while work is a mere necessity.

1.5. Urban planning and architecture

A sensual commonality, which is rooted in the urban planning of Tangier and Gibraltar, is the ascent and descent from the hills to the sea. There is an upper and a lower town in Gibraltar and in Tangier.[29] Steep alleys, narrow passages, stairs

---

29 "[A]round the Mediterranean and irrespective of the country, many towns have been constructed on escarpments that dominate the sea. In these towns, a distinction is drawn between the lower town and the upper town: steps play a very important role. Generally, there is right around the Mediterranean a remarkable architecture of the stairway. A link between spaces, the stairway also ensures a link between times: between the time of architecture (the

and staircases connect up and down; one may assume that this has a similar effect on the handling of narrow space, the posture when carrying bags and containers, the line of sight when walking and on the musculature of the locomotor system. However, there are no reliable findings on this yet. My assumption that the diagnosis "lumbago" would be just as common in Gibraltar as in Tangier was contradicted by the pharmacist Annette Tunbridge, who said that in cold winds there are no more lumbago or back strain in Gibraltar than in warm weather or when there is no wind. But this is exactly what I think I notice in Tangier through the many complaints of my informants.

The three Mediterranean cities of my research – Seville, Gibraltar and Tangier – share an urbanistic particularity, the so-called *Patios de Vecinos*. These patios are residential buildings arranged around a courtyard. They are usually two-storey buildings where poorer sections of society lived, sharing the courtyard and a water pump that supplied the neighborhood. Such patios are, of course, not only urbanistic formations but also special forms of living together.[30]

Illustration 11 (left): Patio Schott, 1996; Illustration 12 (right): Patio Laredo, 2019

In Gibraltar, many civilians of all religions lived in such patios, because the land that did not belong to the military was scarce and housing conditions limited. The aim of many Gibraltarians was to escape the narrowness of the patios and

house, the enclosure) and urban time (the street, the open space, the square and the monuments)" (Lefebvre/Régulier 2004: 97).

30 Press (1979) has masterfully documented one of these *Patios de Vecinos* in his monograph. For La Línea, see Díaz (2018) and del Manzano Pratts (2019).

control by the neighbors as fast as possible. With the exodus of the locals from the patios to their new apartment blocks, which had been built mainly since the 1970s on land that had been wrested from the sea, the patios remained as housing for Moroccan workers. In the 1990s, they were nostalgically elevated to the birthplaces of a Gibraltarian national identity, where Spaniards and British, Maltese and Jews, Sindhis and Portuguese lived together in harmony (Haller 2000b).

In Tangier, on the other hand, we find patios mainly in the former poorer Spanish and Jewish neighborhoods, in *Brâmil, Jossafat, Hasnona* and neighboring areas. Here, too, the patios were places where people of different religions and nationalities – who, however, belonged to the same poorer or lower middle-class – lived peacefully together.

Until recently, Moroccan workers lived in the patios of Gibraltar (today, these forms of housing have been gentrified), in Tangier, poorer Muslims still live there today.

Illustration 13: Cafe Gibraltar, Tangier

The spread of patios as a form of living on both sides of the Strait can be explained as a heritage of the Andalusian-influenced inhabitants. However, the doubling of the names of streets and hotels is worthwhile considering. In Gibraltar, there is a Lovers Lane, in Tangier a *Calle de los Enamorados*. Both cities have (or had) a *Hotel Bristol*, a Bar called *Hole in the Wall*, a *Café Roxy* and a large natural dune. In Gibraltar one speaks of *The Mount*, in Tangier as well (or of *Jebel Kebir* or *La Vieille Montagne*). In Tangier we find a *Café Gibraltar* and a British *York Castle* and in Gibraltar a *Tangier's Take Away* and a *Moorish Castle*. In both cities there is a Royal Yacht Club, in both places horse races were held on the beach and similar hunting parties existed (the pig hunt in the *Forêt Diplomatique* near Tangier and the *Royal Calpe Hunt* in the hinterland of Gibraltar).[31] *Gorhams Cave* is as important in Gibraltar as the *Gruta de Hercules* in Tangier. An old town quarter in Tangier's medina is called *Bni Ider*; in Gibraltar lived a Jewish family *Benider* (Benady 1989: 151; Babas/Benargane 2018).[32] In Tangier, there was not only the election of a Miss Tangier (Andrè 2003) but also a rosary of female beauty contests, just like in Gibraltar (Haller 2000c).

In both Gibraltar and Tangier, architecture is an important marker within the identity discourse. And this changes in both cities. In Gibraltar, for several years now, more and more land has been reclaimed from the sea and built up with high-rises, which have a disturbing effect on older inhabitants.

On my way to the *Yacht Club*, which is no longer where it used to be because it has been moved, I meet Connie Rossi, 84-year-old sprightly widow. I say to her that the area looks very different from the 1990s. Connie Rossi says that from the Rock you cannot see the sea for all the high-rises. Later, her best friend Heidi Viñas Coreggio adds that even from below, you cannot see the Rock for all the high-rises.[33]

In addition, from most houses of the old town one can hardly see the sea and the view to Morocco is, meanwhile, to a large extent, blocked.[34]

Illustration 14: View from Reclaimed Land onto the Rock of Gibraltar

Rock and sea have been the dominant reference points in the Gibraltarian landscape until now when they are being disempowered by the new architecture.

31　Sir John Drummond Hay justified the *pig-sticking* in the *Forêt Diplomatique*. Sometimes simple soldiers from Gibraltar were sent to Tangier to make the number of participants in the hunt appear more impressive (Finlayson 1992: 44).
32　The family came from Tetuán (Chipulina 2017).
33　Field research diary TanGib, March 31, 2019
34　Field research diary TanGib, February 29, 2020.

In Tangier, the influx from *Arobia*, especially from its rural areas, led to a ruralization of the once cosmopolitan city in the perception of the *Tanjawis*. This is also reflected in the way the city's architectural heritage is treated. "These people," says the local historian Rashid Tafersiti Zarouila, "moved into the old quarters of the medina, but before that they had lived in huts and barracks in the countryside. They have no relationship to the city."[35] Tafersiti Zarouila, who describes himself as a nostalgic and dominates the current book market with nostalgic publications about old Tangier, thus, explains the fact that the old buildings are slowly decaying in many parts. Large parts of the old town, for example, are dominated by European and, even more so, Mediterranean architecture that may seem unusual in other cities in the country: Balconies and windows with grilles or shutters facing the street, stucco and classicist set pieces. However, all this is now threatened not only by the mafia of speculators but also by the careless exploitation of the hicks who have moved in.

***

Back to my place of dreams, not to *Café Hafa* but to the less hypertrophic *Café Makina*, which attracted rather undemanding visitors, dock workers and fishermen. I free myself from my tensions and look out over "the alley." This is what *Tanjawis* call the Strait of Gibraltar. During my year in Tangier – 2013–14 – my thoughts made my inner hoopoe fly off. Because "within us […] there is a hoopoe" that reminds us "that the search, whether metaphysical or specific, for a home is our destiny, that we are not at home at all, that we are perhaps only trapped in what we love, and that there is something within us that drives us out – be it into the big, wide and strange world or into higher spheres: But inside us is a hoopoe." (Weidner 2018: 33)

The importance of the hoopoe is deeply rooted in the popular beliefs, traditional medicine and magic of Morocco (Chimenti 1950). A whole drawer with fascinating contents was opened for me in a herbal pharmacy. The employee Bachir Lahsini explained to me that they do not use parts of the bird as medicine, but as magical substances: The bellows themselves are worth almost nothing. In a way, it is given as a bonus for the really important component, the eye. The eye costs 80 Dirham (about 8 Euro) and is often bought by women who put it into a leather amulet and wear it on their heart: This attracts the attention of the beloved. Dried chameleons and scorpions are sold for the same purpose. The bellows are burned to make the love spell work better. But in reality, only the eye works. The hoopoe "is considered a special bird endowed with magical powers. Its extraordinary qualities can be harnessed because they cling unaltered not only to the living animal, but to the dead as well" (Ventzlaff 2018: 75).

---

35   Field research diary Tangier, April 19, 2013.

Illustration 15: Hoopoe as medicine

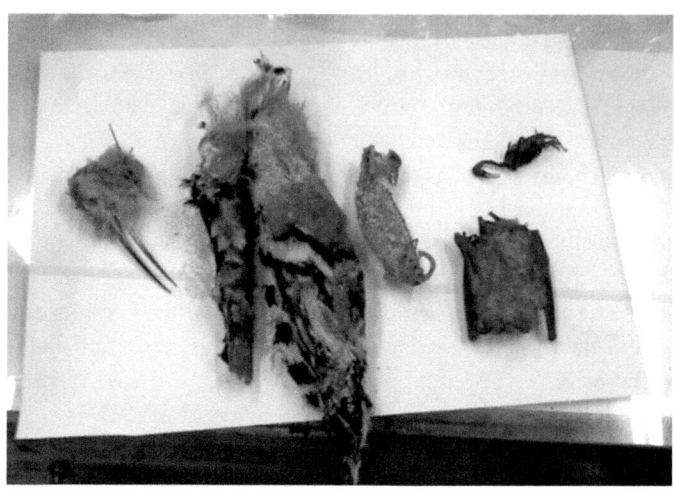

Illustration 16: Hoopoe, Alameda Gardens

At home? Perhaps in the flight of the hoopoe. In any case, home is not necessarily a place, a house. It is more of an existential place: In Islam, man is considered a stranger on earth in this world. Weidner speaks of "the world as a foreign place or exile, gurba" and "strangeness as a human condition" (Weidner 2018). I have lived in Germany, Spain, Gibraltar, the US and in Tangier. My hoopoe flies across the Strait, in spring it nests in Gibraltar's *Alameda Gardens*.

2. Theoretical accesses

> Gibraltar would love you more
> than its neighbor, its sister
> *(Martinez 1953)*

In this line of poetry, Tangier and Gibraltar are not referred to as mere neighbors, but as kin. I go one step further because the focus of this book is on the one city that I strategically call TanGib.[1] However, if one concentrates only on the ties between the two cities, two aspects are lost from view:

- Firstly, one must remind oneself not to neglect those cultural aspects that do not have anything in common.
- Secondly, the regional and transregional embeddings of TanGib must not be disregarded because these are also connected to the two cities and to each other in many ways: Cadiz, Seville, La Línea de la Concepción, San Roque and the *Campo de Gibraltar*, Malaga, Oran, Nador, Ksar el Kebir, Tetuán, Arcila and Laraich.

The *Anthropology of the City* has always dealt with the question of the specifically urban. Cities are "large settlements with an artificially constructed living environment, in which many and various inhabitants interact with each other, but for the most part remain permanently alien to each other" (Antweiler 2004: 286). "Nowhere is the heterogeneity of cultural milieus and social fragmentation greater than in cities. Many city dwellers hardly know large parts of their city themselves, many use urban infrastructure only very selectively and communicate to a limited extent. The city is polyphonic, but many of the voices are barely heard by most residents (ibid.: 289) "[O]nly the principle of inconspicuousness allows for close coexistence in a divided public space. One leaves oneself alone; whoever wants to may remain a stranger; distance is a matter of course" (ibid.: 295).. A problem arises for the two cities and their relationships to each other: Gibraltar and Tangier are undoubtedly cities, but Gibraltar is neither large nor are its inhabitants strangers to each other – on the contrary: The fact that the individual is recognizable at all times is a social

---

1   The object was once called *Tan-Gib* (but with a hyphen) (Loftus 2013).

problem. Tangier is also a city, but until the 1960s, the majority of *Tanjawis* were also either personally known or easily identifiable. This was due to the dense network of civil organizations – schools, hospitals, shops, amusement parks, markets – which the groups shared. Since the 1960s, the population of around 150.000 has grown considerably, and today, a good two million people are said to live in and around the city. "Old" *Tanjawis* complain about this new confusion.

As late as 2018, Antweiler noted that *urban anthropology* in general is very under-theorized.

> At the turn of the millennium, only a few urban anthropologists are still interested in the lively controversies of the 1970s and 1980s about *focus vs. locus* and *anthropology in vs. anthropology of cities*. [...] In recent years the number of application-oriented urban anthropologists has risen sharply, especially in the USA (Cohen/Fukui 1993). But there are also clear continuities. Urban anthropology is still predominantly an ethnology of large cities, and in most cases even very large cities. Special groups or categories, such as minorities, migrants or the poor, continue to be the focus of attention, less frequently also elites. (Antweiler 2018: 2)

The phenomena I am dealing with are also very much under-theorized: We are dealing with two cities that are clearly distinguishable geographically and administratively but which would not have existed for many decades and centuries without each other: Demographic, cultural, social, economic, political, military and symbolic interdependencies between the two are so close that they would not be covered by the conventional approaches of *urban anthropology*.

When social or political scientists today talk and write about global networks, the local background in which people live often fades into the background. Ethnologists have always known that great political and sociological narratives about globalization and the networking of the world are embedded in local contexts and that it is not everywhere as it is imagined in Western science: People still live in their worlds and not in those we imagine based on sociological macro data (Sahlins 2013).

When we talk about relationships between Tangier and Gibraltar and treat them as if they were primarily those of commodity flows, political networks and ideological interdependence, we are wrong. Because specific living environments, local, regional and topographical, are still decisive for how people locate themselves, where they organize their existence and what they orient themselves by.

Perhaps it is precisely this globalization-discursive hubris that assumes that individuals express themselves primarily in virtual, non-face-to-face contacts. Yet, the two cities particularly not only have a past of close interdependence but also a present. In this respect, it is appropriate to treat both cities as if they were a single city in certain eras, two closely connected sub-cities at other times and two units turned away from each other at still other times. Thus, for example, social, family, economic and other networks and orientations of a cultural nature continue to exist in the age of globalization; they have loosened, but not suddenly dissolved. They continue to exist, albeit in a different form than before, sometimes not quite as significant; but they have not disappeared. It is simply that we, as social scientists, no longer turn our attention to these interdependencies and look at the cities precisely in terms of globalization. In this respect, the informal local interdependencies often escape our field of vision. But we look at them in this book. It is important to bring them back into the field of scientific interest.

Certainly, the approach I am advocating here – namely to focus less on the two cities individually than on the relationships between them – is not so easily transferable to the relationships of other cities. I could imagine that there are not many such cases, and in individual cases, it would have to be examined whether the model can be transferred to, for example, Algiers and Marseilles, Berlin and Potsdam, Frankfurt/Oder and Słubice, Buda and Pest, Alexandria and Ismailiya, Bremen and Bremerhaven, Dover and Calais, El Paso and Ciudad Juárez, Malmö and Copenhagen or Athens and Piraeus.

2.1. Structures: Cosmopolitanism, networks, diasporas, cultural areas

TanGib has never been administratively a single city, so that the interrelationships and separations are different from those between West and East Berlin after 1945, between North and South Nicosia or between the individual parts of Beirut during the Lebanese Civil War.

Approaches from cosmopolitanism and network and diaspora studies can be used instead, whereby the networks between the individual diasporic localities of a community play a central role. Beyond these approaches, I fall back on the theories of cultural circles and on various internalization theories.

My research on *cosmopolitanism* (Haller 2015, 2016) is a critique of the current, often inflationary use of the term cosmopolitan in the political and philosophical sciences, which are based on either a social set of rules or an ethical stance. There, cosmopolitanism is often treated as specifically deprived of cultural and historical causes (e.g. Kleingeld/Brown 2002), as an ethical attitude (cf. Römhild/Westrich 2013), for example, in the sense of moral philosophy.[2] Thus, once again, an idea rooted in the West is discussed as a universal model for social forms of society. From an ethnological perspective, I would like to argue that it would be misleading to view TanGib (and other cosmopolitan places) from such a deculturalized perspective as that of a Kantian world citizenship (Harvey 2000). Rather, TanGib's

---

2 Fuhrmann argues similarly (2007: 13).

cosmopolitanism is the result of diverse social practices: Political context, multilingualism, mixed residency, everyday social relations across ethnic and religious categories and common institutions (such as associations or courts, police and administration).³

Illustration 17: Cosmopolis

The high praise for being *Tanjawi* and the values associated with is exemplarily expressed in the following poem by Ouahhab Merzoughi Benshimon. ⁴

Mensaje di corazón a mis paisanos y hijos di mi alta tierra mi perla tanger.
La madre Alta Tánger

Soy *Tanjawi* por eso Soy generoso
Soy *Tanjawi* por eso Me encanta la gente
Soy *Tanjawi* por eso Me encanta la licitación
Soy *Tanjawi* por eso Amo a todas las personas sin excepción
Soy *Tanjawi* por eso Soy paciente con la gente
Soy *Tanjawi* por eso mi gusta aprender
Soy *Tanjawi* por eso respeto a la gente
Soy *Tanjawi* por eso mi gusta hacer el bien
Soy *Tanjawi* por eso soy alto di El rencor
Soy *Tanjawi* por eso soy alto di El Rivalidad
Soy *Tanjawi* por eso soy alto di El Odio
Soy *Tanjawi* por eso soy alto di El Asco.......

---

3   This also applies to other cities, such as Shanghai and Hong Kong (Abbas 2000), Istanbul (Örs 2002) and Alexandria (Ilbert 1997). It is not without irony that the wife of the English writer Lawrence Durrell, Claude-Marie Vincendon, is buried in the cemetery of the Anglican church of Saint Andrews (https://de.wikipedia.org/wiki/Sankt-Andreas-Kirche_(Tanger)). Durrell is best known for his series of novels *Alexandria Quartet*, in which he describes the cosmopolitan life in this Egyptian city, which was not unlike that of Tangier during the period of the International Zone.
4   Online platform A, September 5, 2014.

> Y por ti mi tierra mi quedo siempre alto como tu....ALTA TÁNGER
> A mis paisanos y hijos di mi tierra cantan con migo ANA *TANJAWI* con un comentario.
> Con respeto y amor

Patience, tolerance, equilibrium, respect and love between people are these central values, and they can be acquired. "One can become *Tanjawi*," I was told several times. It is not an exclusive but an inclusive, soft category. Lineage and purity are not part of being *Tanjawi*. Rather, it is a category that focuses on society and location. Sociality is especially important in being a *Tanjawi*: Everyday practical participation in the exchange with other *Tanjawis*. In this respect, being *Tanjawi* is not a question of identity, but rather the practice of mutual identification and, thus, corresponds roughly to the ethnicity approach of Fredrik Barth (1969) and the *Imagined Communities* of Benedict Anderson (1983). But with one crucial difference. In Barth's case, ethnic groups refer to a believed common ancestry or ancestor, just as the nations in Anderson refer to a believed common, long-lasting essentiality. Not time but space plays the decisive role in being *Tanjawi*. Not only those who were born or grew up locally are part of it, but also those who identify with the place and whose identification is recognized by others.

Location-relatedness can mean different things, which Driss Fikri points out to me:

> For some, the fact that you were born in Tangier and have a *Tanjawi* accent is already a *Tanjawi*. Others, even if you were born in Tangier but your parents were born in the Rif and speak *Riffi* at home, you will be considered *Rif* or *Susi* or *Fasi* or *Aroubi* if you are from Beni Mellal, for example. For some Muslim *Tanjawi*, descendants of old city families who lived in the medina, *Dradeb* or Merchán, the residents of the popular neighborhoods who grew up with the wave of the rural exodus of the 60s, 70s and 80s are not considered *Tanjawis*. For some, *Tanjawi* is the Muslim Moroccan who was born or adopted in Tangier, whereas the Indian or Spaniard is a *Hindawi* or *Nesrani*.
>
> Still others have a very broad idea: Not only those who were born or grew up locally are part of it but also those who identify with the place and whose identification is recognized by others. This probably goes back to a diplomatic practice: "As an indicator of this ambiguity, European consuls registered as "residents" anyone who stayed in the city for at least two months; a group that included some 2,000 British tourists who came each year to enjoy the mild winter." (Pack 2015: 50)

What all approaches have in common, however, is the location-relatedness.

Being recognized by Muslims who had remained in Tangier is one of the emotional moments in which *Tanjawis*' common reference to place comes to light. I've heard many stories like that of Maurice Elbaz, who has lived in the United States for 40 years. He tells the story of a visit (around 2012) to Tangier with his second wife and son. He rented a car with a driver to show them around the city. When they passed a certain site, Mr. Elbaz said that his father was the owner. Thereupon the driver stepped on the brakes and asked äre you the son of Albertito?"Mr. Elbaz affirmed and the man burst into tears: he himself had got his first job as a young man with Albertito. [5]

The researched online forums are excellent arenas in which people profess to be *Tanjawi*s and mutually assure each other their *Tanjawi*ness.

> "Me siento orgulloso de ser de una ciudad tan especial y peculiar como Tanger, y la llevo en mi corazón y en mi sangre, siempre la echo de menos, y este es mi barrio donde he nacido plaza de toros. *Tanjawi*/tangerino."[6]

I met Daniel Benaross (* 1940) on one of the online platforms and we exchanged our Whattsapp numbers. So it came to a phone call with Daniel in Carácas/Venezuela. In order to convey the typical convivencia between the groups in Tangier, he told me that in his youth the religious background of the families was known, but that this was not important: "You didn't say *'el judío'* or *'el moro'*. It didn't matter. We were just friends. At school, of course, you spoke depending on which school you attended - for example the French *Lycée Regnault*. At home we spoke Spanish. Amongts each other, we might have started in Spanish and then switched to French, and then back and forth during our conversation. When I started going out with friends at the age of 15 - back then, 007 and Whiskey a Gogo were 'in'. At *Whiskey a Go Go* there were once four English guys at the bar and they turned out to be the famous Rolling Stones. For us it was just four famous English musicians, they visited Tangier like others, because here famous people could move around quite normally apart from the great attention. It was a 'golden youth'. This is the only way to understand why the old participants at the online platforms are so euphoric about that time and the city. The only differences that were actually made were that no one from Tangier was a domestic worker or a gardener: one had hired about maids from the Rif Mountains."[7]

Direct self / external designations (*Ana Tanjawi* = I am *Tanjawi*, *ntina / eres Tanjawia* = you are a *Tanjawja*, *verdadera tangerine* = true Tangerina, *Tanjawi de adopción* = adoptierter *Tanjawi*) or the friendly attribution of characteristics that *Tanjawi*s ascribe to themselves (*Comme un vrai Tanjawi, tu veilles tard*).[8]

Here, however, some further restrictions are necessary, because I am referring here to the current and contextless use of the term. Like all categories, *Tanjawi*

---

5 Field research diary TanGib, 02.10.2020
6 Wael Bghiel, Online platform A, August 4, 2015.
7 Field research diary TanGib, Sommer 2020
8 Karim Almansuri, Online platform A, November 15, 2013.

has changed over time. *Tanjawi* comes from Arabic and has displaced the variety of earlier terms from other languages. Of course, Spanish words in Tangier's Arabic language are losing ground, especially among the young *Tanjawi*s born after 1990. "The most shocking thing for me is," says Driss Fikri, "when young *Tanjawi*s communicate in English with the waiters and hoteliers during their holidays on the Costa del Sol. *Tanjawi*s are increasingly similar to the Filipinos, who have lost the use of Spanish, although they have Spanish surnames." Thus, Spanish has largely fallen out of use in Tangier, as has French, and the previously widespread terms *Tangerino* and *Tangerois* are hardly ever used by the inhabitants. However, they are often used in conversations with Europeans, as most of them do not speak Arabic. When a Muslim informant (*1955), for example, socialized in an Italian school speaks to me, he uses the Italian term *Tangieri*.

The contextualization of the speech situation can also narrow down the generally open concept of *Tanjawi*. "Everything falls apart, nothing is protected," is the opinion of Paul Allemand (*1962 in Tangier), who sees his own childhood environment – he experiences himself as a stranger in his own city – dissolving. He speaks Arabic as a foreign language, his mother tongue is Spanish. I often experience conversations with locals in his presence. The interlocutors always perceive him first as a European and often stage themselves as true *Tanjawi*s. Most of the time, Paul Allemand lets them believe that they are dealing with a European, before presenting himself as a local. As a rule, he then asks the interlocutors about their family and neighborhood.

If Paul Allemand recognizes the other as *Tanjawi*, they indulge in mutual courtesy and look for mutual acquaintances in the further conversation. If the interlocutor finds no mercy, then he breaks off the conversation and whispers to me regularly (analogously), "That's no *Tanjawi*, just someone who moved here from some dump." I use this example because – regardless of Paul Allemand's individual efforts to position himself – the counterparts are actually newcomers, mostly from *Arobia* (the former French protectorate, which began about 70 km south of Tangier). In the perception of *Tanjawi*s, the influx from these regions, especially the influx from its rural areas, led to a ruralization and orientalization of the once cosmopolitan city.

Gibraltarians were one of the pillars of the cosmopolitanism of International Tangier (Ceballos López 2019: 546). However, even in Tangier and Gibraltar there are discrepancies between the ideology of cosmopolitanism and its practice. In the ideology, differences and conflicts which naturally exist in social and cultural reality are faded out. An example of this is the handling of homosexuality, which is presented as accepted on the discursive level but has not proved unproblematic in practice:

> She [Bibi Andersen] was crucified in Tangier and now in Spain we praise her. How hypocritical. In Tangier they also crucified the artist Rogelio del Monte, whom they called 'La Rogelia' with a very bad undertone.[9]

Little tangerino Manuel Fernández Chica (*1954), the son of a taxi driver and a seamstress of the cleaning shop *Amaya* in *Rue de Fez*, became a woman named Bibi Andersen after emigrating to Málaga.

Bibi is described as a great phenomenon in Online platforms. She was tall, wore curls and had a natural presence. She was a little fat and had a beautiful face. After school, she worked in the Quintero supermarket in *M'Sallah*. Later, she worked in a company that made fuse plugs for electrical installations.[10] She rose to become one of the biggest stars of Pedro Almodóvar's films and became – especially in the times of the Spanish *Movída* (1980s) – the symbolic epitome of multiple transgressions. While today old *Tanjawis* use her as an example of Tangiers tolerance, the commentator reminds us of the violence inflicted on little Manolo.

Elsewhere (Haller 2000b, 2001b), I have pointed out that the ethos of cosmopolitanism minimizes conflicts between groups: It undermines the very fabric of these divisions. Rarely, therefore, do differences and conflicts appear as openly as in the following example on online platforms, which are characterized by a discourse of mutual acceptance:

> I always hear that the three religions existed side by side in an exemplary manner, but it was not so. I remember when I was a child, seeing groups of Jewish children walking down the street and being persecuted and harassed by groups of Catholic or Moroccan children, especially Catholics, who teased and annoyed them in order to take away their headgear. I am ashamed to have behaved in this way, I was not aggressive and secretly felt it was inappropriate behaviour, today two of my dearest friends are Jews.[11]

Here, too, the contradiction between a *cosmopolitanism of confession* (the hegemonic ethos of peaceful coexistence) and a *cosmopolitanism of practice* (social interaction) is addressed quite openly. The speaker in this quote refers to the fact that as a Catholic child he tore the *kippoth* from the heads of Jewish boys – a behavior of which he is ashamed today. It is interesting to note that at that time he did not feel aggressive but rather as someone for whom it was quite normal.

Within the religious groups, too, cultural fault lines and hierarchies are becoming apparent, beyond cosmopolitan discourse. Thus, "[t]he hegemonic discourse of Ashkenazi intellectuals, like the paternalistic modernization efforts by Ashkenazi

---

9   Online platform A, Pepe Montero Robles (d.n.n). Translation by the author.
10   Field research diary TanGib, February 25, 2020.
11   Online platform A, Pedro Perales Cuesta, September 30, 2019. Translation by the author.

political bodies [...] orientalized the Sephardim, many of whom – especially the descendants of Jews expelled from Spain – once[12] were part of an aristocratic [...] world order."

The orientalization continues within the Sephardim. In Gibraltar, for example, the actual or claimed origin of ancestors plays an important role in the prestige of a family. The highest prestige is given to the (possibly even aristocratic) origin from Spain. This is followed by the 'Islamic-oriental' Jews from the cities of Northern Morocco. At the bottom of the hierarchy are those descended from 'Islamic-oriental' Jews from rural areas of Morocco. Characteristics which in Ashkenazi discourse characterize the Sephardim as a whole (especially the abundance of children, patriarchal family structure and submission of the woman, parallel cousin marriage, political conservatism, 'irrational' religiosity (Bahloul 1994) and which have their parallel in the discourse of early Mediterranean ethnology [e.g. Banfield 1958; see also Peristiany 1976; Gilmore 1987; Herzfeld 1987]) are applied by the real or supposed descendants of the *megorashim* (refugees from Spain) to describe the *toshabim* ('indigenous' Jews of North Africa) (Haller 2000a: 290).

Conclusion: We have to distinguish between the ideology of cosmopolitanism and cosmopolitan practices. And: strong local roots do not exclude cosmopolitan attitudes, practices and social forms of society at all, but often virtually condition them. After all, the cosmopolitans of Tangier in particular[13] may have seen themselves as citizens of the world, but first and foremost, they were citizens of a city that carried the world and the cosmopolitan within itself. Therefore, the cosmopolitanism of Tangier, and probably every cosmopolitanism, cannot be understood in isolation from its specific local worlds of experience (Haller 2016: 51). This is exactly what would also decenter the Eurocentric view of cosmopolitanism as an ethical attitude. And here it is important to recall Johannes Fabian's (2007) consideration that individuals select elements of the past according to a procedure in which both the remembered and the forgotten are significant. So, it is important to ask which elements are remembered (here: the harmony of living together) (Moreno 2012) and which are not remembered (here, for example, the discrimination of Manolo Chico and the inner-Jewish hierarchies).[14]

Network research classically focuses on primary and secondary social networks of an ego, whose bonds are differentiated and classified according to various param-

---

12   On the activities of French Jews in North Africa, see Schroeter (1994: 189).
13   I am not referring to the expatriate artists, seekers of meaning and writers who stayed in the city for only a short time, as if prayed down in a rosary, but who had a decisive influence on its image and myth, but to *Tanjawis* of all three religions.
14   Trevisan Semi and Sekkat Hatimi (2011) also take this approach in their study of the memories of Jewish-Arab Convivencia in Meknès.

Illustration 18: Malabata

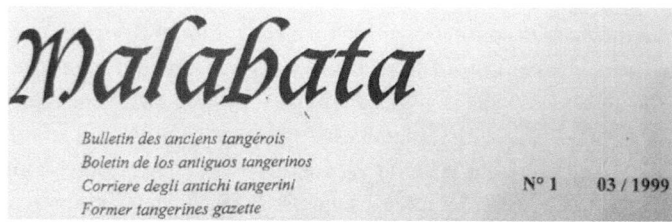

eters.[15] Ethnology has explored this particularly in the relationship constellations of *patron-client research, brokerage*, ritual kinship and friendship, especially in the Mediterranean region. Bourdieu added to these more functional approaches that of social capital, which was largely contoured by his experiences in Algeria. "The Kabyles," he writes, "taught me that the social world is to a large extent what you want it to be" (Bourdieu 2010: 359). Informers and companions, like Mouloud Mammeri or Abdelmalek Sayad, were crucial in this. From Mammeri, Bourdieu learns *tamusni*, the Kabyle wisdom. This is something like social learning. Mammeri says,

> My father's visit to the market lasted half an hour, and the rest of the time he spent meeting people and talking to them; they did the same thing. In a way, this was training on the job, both conscious and diffuse. [...] Learning came through practice. It was not abstract learning. At the same time, it was a matter of orienting one's actions to a certain number of rules and values without which *tamusni* cannot exist. A *tamusni* that is not fully accepted, that is not lived, is only a code. The *tamusni* is an art and a lifeworld, i.e. a practice that is acquired through practice and has practical functions. (Bourdieu 2010: 369-370)

This changes Bourdieu's understanding of the social role of speech and the conditions of its utterance, mediation and perpetuation (Bourdieu 2010: 365), and can be applied to social networks, which we will encounter in this work, especially in Chapter 6. For in Tangier, the evening paseo, sitting in the cafes, *shufology* and the seemingly idle wandering (which is often a search for opportunities) are the techniques that practice social skills and bonds.

The concept of *diaspora* is often applied to all kinds of groups that are spatially characterized by the separation of locality and old homeland. Not only the Jews

---

15 *Expansion* (number of contact persons within Ego's network), *concentration* (type and manner of function(s) that the contact persons perform), *intensity* (frequency and quality of contacts), *permanence* (duration of the relationship), *recruitment* (basis on which membership of a network is based) and *effectiveness* (influence of networks on individual dyads).

Illustration 19: Bharat Ratna

and the Sindhis of TanGib are part of worldwide diasporas. In Gibraltar, for example, these are the expats once stationed in the colony who have a relationship with different locations. In Tangier, this concerns the former Christian and Jewish inhabitants and probably also the majority of the old Muslim *Tanjawis*. Many of them live in Spain, Israel, France, Canada, Latin America, Belgium and the Netherlands. Around the turn of the millennium, they participated in the publication *Malabata* and today in online forums dealing with Tangier. Elsewhere (Haller 2001a, 2003), I have argued that the analytical value of the concept of diaspora could be strengthened by focusing on third spatial relationships that are characteristic of the diaspora but often neglected: The lateral relationships. It, therefore, makes sense to examine, for example, the Hindu communities of TanGib not only regarding their relationship to TanGib and Sindh but to the most diverse communities of their network, to Hyderabad and Aden, to Alexandria, Bombay and Lagos, to Hong Kong and Tenerife (Haller 2003).

Many Jews from Tangier (including the ancestors of a lot of my informants) and other Moroccan cities moved to Latin America in the 19th and 20th centuries and often became particularly wealthy there, especially during the rubber boom.

They went with the intention to send money back to their impoverished families, which they faithfully did, and to return when they could, which they also did – part of the 'back and forth' migratory tradition.

At first they come on long 3 month voyages aboard slow sailing ships. With the advent of steamships to Brazil, the trip only took 3 weeks and the emigration volume increased dramatically and frequent return trips to Morocco with the accumulated wealth became practical. The wealth of the returning sons contrasted sharply with the abject poverty at home and spurred even more sons to seek the Amazonian *eldorado* and incidentally leaving largely female Jewish populations behind. Records of the *Alliance Israelite Universelle* show that many families survived largely on the money sent home by their sons in the Amazon. (Malka, no year)

Illustration 20: Jewish Tangerinos in Iquitos/Perú

If you like, the TanGib region represents an area of multiple and condensed relationships and commonalities – ethnologists have introduced the concept of a *cultural area* for just such a condensed network. Even the diffusionist cultural studies were rarely so narrow-minded that geographical spaces were understood as containers, and the focus of research was not exclusively placed on the 'inside' of the space, but always also on the external connections. Graebner already wrote that the characteristic of a cultural area is *"not absolute* unity of cultural relations [...] *nor absolute continuity* in the distribution of all individual elements, but rather the simple fact that a certain complex of cultural elements is characteristic of a certain area and is *mainly* limited to it" (1911: 132f).[16] Cultural spheres were merely auxiliary constructions to grasp geographical regions where a condensed exchange took place. However, they must be intertwined with a temporal depth. This did not mean that space had to be 'grasped' in the sense of a geographical or even national container (Trimborn 1958: 12ff; Bornemann 1967: 104; Petermann 2004: 583ff; Haller 2018: 75). In its original sense, such circles are not closed, but the connections to the outside are no longer as close as those to the inside. The people of Tangier and Gibraltar also make this clear to us, because their stories sometimes take us far away and we suddenly find ourselves in Smyrna and London, in Alexandria and Corfou, in Boudnib and Marseilles, in Amsterdam and Iquitos, in Oran and in Georgia.

2.2. Internalizations: Ethnicity, transculturation, trance and obsession, penetration, reflection, self

The term "Single-Border-Society" used by Driessen (1992) is closely connected with this understanding of cultural circles. However, as far as TanGib is concerned, it cannot be clearly described as a either a community or a society: Interactions often take place face-to-face, with the actors often having the same interests as those on the other side of the border. In this respect, one can speak about a *community*. On the other hand, the unit is large and impersonal enough to reflect the characteristics of a *society*. But it is not an autonomous unit, even less autonomous in the organization of its social relationships. Approaches of formal and informal community institutions exist today between Gibraltar and its hinterland as well as between Tangier and Gibraltar. However, the three territories are parts of different nation-states. Joint initiatives such as that of Gibraltarian journalist Jon Searle, who has set up a journalists' association of Spaniards, Moroccans and Gibraltarians, are important but rare. Brexit and Corona make it seem necessary again for the present (2020) to take up local/regional cross-border forms of cooperation (see Chapter 8). Common interaction and identification are still there for the resources.

There is a tradition in ethnology, which was represented, for example, by Adolf Bastian or, in sociology, by Georg Simmel, and to which, today, mere lip service is

---

16   Translation by the author.

Illustration 21: Jon M. Searle

often paid, but which is largely buried or, at best, implicitly concealed in the actual production of the text – namely, that by looking at the other, a new view of one's own can also be gained, or better: That the knowledge of the other is inseparably connected with the knowledge of one's self. And it is the gaze of being recognized by the other that is banished by a variety of symbols, gestures and rituals, from amulets against the evil eye to figures of terror and integration rituals, which Kramer (1987) has so brilliantly worked out.

Simmel (1908) has often been understood to focus on the gaze that constructs the other and the self – but what if the gaze creates a similarity between the other and the self and, thus, blurs the boundaries between them? I will work this out using the example of ethnicity:

Excursus: Ethnicity

The fact that the external perception of Jewish and Muslim *Tanjawis* often has a homogenizing tendency that helps to formulate the ethnic is broken by a closer look at the details. The Jews who had fled Spain, for example, could not do much with the old-established Berber Jews; culturally, the groups were alienated. Nor did the Muslims represent a homogeneous group. For centuries, the local Muslims, originally from the Rif, dominated the fortunes of the city. In the late 19th century, however, Tangier also became a center of attraction for craftsmen, traders and intellectual Muslims who came to the city from other Moroccan regions in the course of modernization. "They inserted themselves in the economic sphere, building alliances across communal boundaries, deploying their capital and linking up with non-Muslim investors to launch new building projects, putting aside ancient religious and tribal loyalties in search of new forms of wealth" (Gilson Miller 2010: 147). Not ethnicity, but jointly internalized culture – so my argument goes – is more significant in the case of Tangier.

The international Tangier has often been depicted in literature as a space of either-or: The cosmopolitan lightness of the sense-seeking bohemian, on the one hand, and the closed space of Muslim families, on the other. In my opinion, this image is wrong; it hides the multiple forms of transitions and encapsulation, as well as the individual possibilities of moving around in this space (cf. Nasri 2006: 9). In order to capture these experiences in the social fabric of the international Tangier and to cast them in pictures, I resort to a culinary metaphor: The cheese fondue. Different types of cheese (ethnicities, religions, nationalities) merge together in a pot (Tangier) of hot oil (the use and sharing of the same space). It is true that all cheeses are somehow merged with all others (common ethos of being *Tanjawi*). This can be seen from the threads that are extended when the chunks are fished out. All the original ingredients of the fondue have changed. But not all of them melt completely or at the same speed, nor do they melt with all varieties in the same way. Some of them can be clearly tasted in their texture, shape, color and flavor when enjoyed, while others are hardly recognizable.

In everyday discourse, *Tanjawis* and southern Spaniards often focus on a common descent – in a friendly way. Genetic research from 2000 actually shows that Moroccans and Spaniards are very closely related. From a genetic point of view, both Arabic- and Berber-speaking Moroccans are Berber. The genetic influence of Arabs (from the Arabian Peninsula or the Middle East) is minimal in both Morocco and Spain (Bosch et al. 2000). These findings open up three possibilities: Either Berbers and Iberians already belonged to the same or a similar pre-Islamic group; or the Spaniards were significantly influenced genetically by Muslim conquerors after 711; or today's Moroccans were strongly influenced by *Moors* (Muslims who were forced to convert to Christianity) and Jews[17] who were expelled from Spain after 1492. These findings are at odds with the dominant national historical narratives of Spain and Morocco: Spain, which for a long time formulated its past in distinction to Muslims and North Africans; Morocco, which sees itself as an Arab rather than a Berber nation.

---

17 Adams et al. (2008, pp. 725ff) show that "10.6 per cent of the Y chromosome gene sections examined" of male Spaniards and Portuguese "from North Africa, and a full 19.8 per cent largely correspond to the type of Sephardim living today." The current higher distribution of North African genes in the Northwest of the Iberian Peninsula is probably due to the more consistent expulsion of the Moors and *Moors* from the south.

Genetic findings per se are not particularly relevant for ethnologists, because "scientific methods are not able to distinguish genetic ancestry from identities that guide actions" (Meier 2019: 939). What is important for us is what people make of these findings. What meaning they deny or assign to them, in which contexts and for whom they become effective.

Gibraltar played no role during my field research in Spain in 1985/86, nor did Tangier, but Morocco and the Muslim as well as the Jewish past of Al-Andalus did. It was also still in the period of reorientation of the country after the collapse of the regime of Francisco Franco. At that time, the national narrative of a homogeneous Spanish nation was broken up, and this was also evident at the political level: The regionalization of Spain after 1975 led politically to the discovery of characteristics of what was (regionally and locally) one's own, to the recovery of these as a heritage and to making them the basis of legitimacy for political demands. In Andalusia, it was inevitable that Jewish and Muslim pasts would also be involved. These findings were popularized through festivals, rituals and publication series such as the *Biblioteca de la Cultura Andaluza*. Many young Spaniards searched for their family roots beyond the fading national Francoist narrative: Muslim centers were founded in Seville, young Spaniards converted to Islam in Granada, and many of my informants claimed – real or fictitious – Muslim or Jewish ancestors for themselves (Duran 1992; Bahrami 1998). At that time, all this took place on a hedonistic, colorful, light and liberating level: Al-Andalus and its tolerance offered an ideal counter-projection to Franco's fascism and a possible blueprint for a democratic Spain.

In Gibraltar, the genetic link only played a role in so far as the aim was to prove at all levels that Gibraltarians were not Spanish. This was important because the Spanish claim to the territory was based, among other things, on the genetic argumentation that Gibraltarians were not a "real" population (Spain 1965; Cordero Torres 1966; Barcía Trelles 1968) but merely rabble from the Spanish lower classes or all corners of the Mediterranean, artificially rounded up by Britain. Sociologist Rico (1967) provided an example of the scientific support for this argument.[18] Gibraltarians tried to take up this argument and turn it around: It was precisely their diverse origins that led to the formation of their own emerging national identity which I researched in 1996/97. Multi-religious and multiethnic references played a major role, but it is striking that both Sephardic Jews and Muslims were excluded at the time and the importance of the Spanish inhabitants of the hinterland was kept

---

18   According to Rico (1967), Great Britain imported all kinds of rootless individuals without any national pride and without any form of political organization. The heterogeneous origin of Gibraltarians is especially a thorn in his side. Rico describes them as delinquents, deserted soldiers, pimps, prostitutes and political refugees. In summary, Gibraltarians do not represent a population for the Franco government that could benefit from paragraph 2.

small, i.e. all three groups that could have reinforced a demographic localization in the region.

During my field research in Tangier (2013 ongoing), genetic references to the other side of the Strait of Gibraltar hardly played a role for my informants. While older *Tanjawis*, who had experienced the time of the International Zone themselves or were shaped by it as children, lamented the segregation of the city due to the departure of the Spaniards and Jews and the influx of Moroccans from "the South and the younger *Tanjawis* saw themselves primarily as Moroccans. And indeed, as Arabic Moroccans. Berber references were only addressed, for example, if their own parents or grandparents had moved into the city from the Rif mountains – otherwise my informants saw themselves primarily as either *Tanjawi*, Arab or Moroccan, without a precise ethnic reference.[19]

When my informants, most of whom did not come from academically educated classes, spoke of "the Spanish" and emphasized the proximity between Spaniards and Moroccans, they argued by invoking language, geographical proximity, the Spanish character of Tangier and cultural set pieces (music, soccer, food) – but ancestry, origin or even genetics played no role. For people in the region are connected in many ways: Historically, economically, but also through family relationships, bi- or multilocal ownership, as well as culturally and socially (cf. Canessa 2019). Italian writer Edmondo de Amicis (1897) had already described the region as a space of mixture and ambiguity:

The guide aroused me at last from my reverie and escorted me back to the hotel, where my usual dislike to being among entire strangers was for the first time in my life mitigated by the circumstance of their being all Europeans, Christians, and clad like myself. There were about twenty persons seated at table, of both sexes and various nationalities, offering in themselves a pretty fair example of that strange mingling of families and interests which prevails in those parts. A Frenchman born in Algiers married to an Englishwoman of Gibraltar; a Spaniard from Gibraltar married to the sister of a Portuguese consul from the Atlantic coast; an elderly Englishman accompanied by a daughter born in Tangier and a niece from Algeria; families who wandered back and forth from one continent to the other, or scattered up and down the two coasts, talking five languages, and living half like Arabs, half like Europeans. Hardly had dinner begun when a lively conversation sprang up,

---

19   It seemed striking to me that the struggle for the cultural autonomy of the Berbers, which was fought in other parts of the country and also in the sciences (see Qadery 2016), in part very emphatically, and which was also legally secured in the recognition of the Berber by the 2011 constitution, did not seem to play a role in Tangier itself. Perhaps it is because this question did not particularly shape my work and I, therefore, did not pay attention to it. But the presence of Berber letters in public seemed to be limited to public building projects in which all national languages provided information – as in Berber.

now in French, now in Spanish, interspersed with Arabic words and upon topics which were certainly far enough removed from the ordinary subjects discussed by Europeans. (De Amicis 1897: 11f)

It is true that España (1954: 58) emphasizes that the life of the natives in Tangier has a decidedly Spanish undercurrent, which was joined above all by "los hijos de Gibraltar y la israelita." However, it has become increasingly difficult since the end of the 20th century from an ethnological point of view to make a distinction between Gibraltarians and Tangerinos. Certainly, there are birth registers in the archives, but what do these numbers tell us?[20] There are no figures as to whether someone was a Gibraltarian in Tangier who later settled back in Gibraltar but whose children remained in Tangier. Or whether it was a British officer who served in both Gibraltar and Tangier, married a Gibraltar Catholic and retired in old age in a villa on *The Mount* in Tangier. Or whether it was a subject of His/Her Majesty registered in Gibraltar, but who was engaged in smuggling in both cities. A quotation from (historically) recent times sheds light on this – Manuel Jurado, an informant, tells us:

> Many Gibraltarians moved to Tangier [in the early 1940s] for fear of a German invasion. My godparents were both from Gibraltar. In 1960 I left for Gibraltar because I had met my present wife there. My parents lived in Tangier until 1964. Today they live in Spain. (Haller 2000a: 47)

The mixture is particularly evident in the example of the names of Jewesses of Tangier: These were strongly influenced by Gibraltar. A Sephardic Gimol was now called Molly, a Raquel became Kelly, Rebecca became Rica, Myriam became Mery, Simhat became Simy (Sebat 2016). Inhabitants of the *Campo de Gibraltar*, Tangier and Gibraltar, themselves spoke largely the same lingua franca, which was characterized by the mixture of Spanish with English and a dash of Arabic and Jewish words.[21]

> At the end of the 19th century, in their notes on Morocco, Eduardo Cañizares y Moyano (1895) refer to the Europeans who came to live in the city. 'The number of people living in the city of Tangier is calculated at 5,000' (Cañizares y Moyano 1998: 41). They attribute this large number to economic prosperity and also to the cosmopolitan aspect:' [...] reason why there are countless painters who came to Tangier. In its streets and markets, Arabs of different races mingled with blacks, Jews and Europeans, each wearing the costume of their country and speaking their own language. Sometimes it happens that in the same group two or three different languages are heard, spoken by the same person, depending on the interlocutor

---

20 http://www.nationalarchives.gi/gna/CensusAbstracts.aspx#here.
21 Online platform A, Julián Nunes Rocha, August 8, 2019.

to whom it is addressed. This leads to a confusion that is surprising and pleasing (Cañizares y Moyano, 1998, p. 41). (Jebrouni 2019: 49)

Sabir is another characteristic of the weak meaning of ethnicity in the sense of a believed common descent. This lingua franca, which is based on Romansh, is now considered to be extinct. It was spoken in the cities of North Africa. It was Spanish to the west of Algiers, Italian to the east, and has been French since the conquest of Algeria by France in 1830 and the publication of the *Dictionnaire de la langue franque ou Petit Mauresque*. However, there are also words in it that go back to Occitan, Catalan, Hebrew and Arabic. The existence of numerous common languages that are partly still spoken today counter the disappearance of *Sabir* at the end of the 19th century. Since the *Sabir* was never a uniform, codified language but a pragmatic lingua franca, it survived in the *Pataouete* Algiers (Borutta 2014: 219). In Tangier, the Europeans spoke a French-Spanish mixed language (*Frangpanol*) and Jews had a colloquial language that was speckled with Hispanic-Arabic, the *Haketija*. Even today, Tangerian dialect, *Darija*, is strongly influenced by Spanish words, the *Yanito* of Gibraltarians is a mixed language anyway and words from the *Darija* and *Haketija* are often used and understood among the descendants of *Tanjawis* in Gibraltar. I call this diverse, nonuniform mix of languages based on historical forerunners *Sabir*, with which one can still communicate excellently in TanGib.

Another decisive factor in the development of *Tanjawi* identification among the residents of Tangier is the diplomatic regime that has governed the fortunes of the city since the late 19th century.

Realistically, people in Morocco (Gilson Miller 1991) were even more cautious about representatives of foreign powers than in the Ottoman Empire, where similar developments had taken place, for example, in Smyrna – albeit earlier than in Tangier. Since Sultan Mohammed Ben Abdallah in the late 18th century, foreign diplomats had not been allowed to settle in the capital Fez but had to live far away in Tangier, the diplomatic capital of the country until the 20th century.[22]

The foreign nations placed mostly Moroccan Jews, who served them as dragomen, under their protection. Some families worked for one nation (e.g. the Attias for Brazil, the Toledano for the German Empire, the Castiel for the Netherlands), others worked for several countries (e.g. the Abensur [Laredo 1936: 95ff] for Denmark, Great Britain, Austria-Hungary and the USA, and the Nahon for Belgium [Laredo 1936: 435], Denmark, Germany and France). For the Moroccan court, the Makhzen, Tangier was supposed to take on the function of a cultural 'quarantine station,' which was supposed to keep the threat from the powerful foreign countries to a minimum. The dragomen acted as a protective filter between Makhzen and the foreigners.

---

22   More information in chapter 4.1.

Such an understanding of the nation falls back on pre-nation-state ideas. Here, I join Tagliaferri: "[N]ational identity is used with the meaning of identifying themselves according to the place of origin and of being born subjects of the same sovereign" (Tagliaferri 2016: 87, FN 3).

In this climate, it was also possible to marry between nations, but mostly only within the same social class.

This not uncommon practice was not confined to the urban area of Tangier but rather linked the city very closely with Gibraltar on the other side of the Strait. The question of whether someone is Gibraltarian or Tangerino is based on the false assumption often made these days that there must be a cultural identity that is ethnically determined.

The to and fro between Gibraltarians and Tangerinos shows that the decisive category is that of culture – not that of a confession but as a practice. This approach is also taken by the Swedish ethnologist Löfgren (1999), who demonstrates that the idea of national identity has historically been created by various practices of differentiation that were practically carried out at borders through border controls. However, confession and practice do not usually fall into one.

The impossibility of an ethnic separation of the two cities[23] proves itself in family histories such as the following:

Roque de Soto Lyons was associated with several important families of Gibraltar and Tangier: the Molinari, the Artesani, the Sanz de Soto and the Garassino. In the mid-nineteenth century, his Scottish father, Mr. Lyons, married a young widow, Rita de Soto, in Gibraltar.[24] She gave her children the surnames of her two husbands. These included Rock or Roque, as he was called in Tangier. Roque married Elisa in Tangier, a daughter of Antonio Molinari, a Briton of Genoese descent (Ceballos López 2009: 155f). Like other Genoese, he fled to Gibraltar and became a British subject there. He was sent by the British to Morocco to claim the debts that Moroccan sultans had with the British. He was paid in gold bars, which he transported to Tangier in sacks and piled up in the cellar of his house.[25] From there they were picked up by British soldiers and taken by a small warship to Gibraltar. The marriage of Roque and Elisa produced three daughters, Lydia, Celia and Angeles. The first daughter, Lydia, married Emilio Sanz Barriopedro, one of the leading figures of Tangier. Both are the parents of the art and film critic Emilio Sanz de Soto (1924-2007). (Manzi 2005)

---

23 Ceballos López (2019: 546) mentions the following families who came to Tangier from Gibraltar: Abrines, Garassino, Carrara, Baglietto, Molinaro, Cavilla, Lyons, Licudi, Artesani and Sanguinetti.
24 Mr. Lyons was the trustee of the estate of Lord Sackville-West. One of Sackville-West's illegitimate daughters, Vicky, became the mistress of Virginia Woolf (Manzi 2005).
25 The maids had rings made from the gold dust that remained in the cellar (Manzi 2005).

The second daughter, Celia, married John Joseph Artesani, also of Genoese descent, who had come to Tangier from Gibraltar in 1927. Angeles finally married the Casablanca-born Italian Guglielmo Garassino, the brother of Gian Batista (Baccio), who in the 1920s had the now-decayed *Garrasino Castle* built as a restaurant near Malabata. Sanz de Soto said about his family:

> "But there was a complete uprooting, because these people were not English, nor Italian or Spanish, but, without realizing it, cosmopolitan, because they had a little bit of everything." (Manzi 2005; translation by the author)

Similarly, another family, that of Brian Riley, shows the same difficulty to deal with a concept such as ethnicity in the *Boughaz* area:

> Well as far as I know, my great-grandfather went over to Morocco in the 1910s looking for work and they ended up in Casablanca. The family story is that my great-grandad lost all his money [...], such that he was bankrupt and went to Morocco to seek his fortune (he did not find it). He had seven children, of those, my grandad and a sister came back to Gibraltar in the 1930s. The rest stayed in Morocco settling in Casablanca and Agadir owning restaurants and car workshops. In the 60s, they all started coming back to Europe. Most went to France as they had been born in French Morocco but some of the older ones who had been born in Gibraltar came back here. [They] left because of Moroccan independence, Islamophobia, the usual. My grand-aunt who was the last to leave [in 1975], hated Moroccans. Yes, to Larache and Tangier, I believe. They tried to expropriate her restaurant when her husband passed away; she was given the option of co-owning it with a Moroccan owner or leaving. She sold it on the sly and fled to Gib. My mum's [family] is ex-mercantile middle class come down the scales to basically working class.
>
> As for Tetuan. My dad was born there [...] My grandfather went to Ceuta-Tetuan after his family, parents and sister, died of tuberculosis in the early 1920s. My dad's family is very much working class. Originally my paternal ancestor was an Irish soldier in the Peninsula War who settled with his Sevilla wife after 1814 in Gibraltar. [...] my Lane grandfather spent seven years fighting in the Civil War in Morocco, so one of the first to be captured. He was first imprisoned in Ceuta [...]. My grandmother and the British embassy argued for his case, but I think that much more significant was Stalingrad [...] When the Nazis lost that one, Franco decided to release all prisoners from allied countries he still held (basically UK and US).[26]

Such diversity of origin is not unusual in Gibraltar and Tangier. The concept of ethnicity, so vainly defended today, also fails in other personalities. Let me give a few examples:

---

26 Communication on Messenger, Easter Monday, 2020.

Illustration 22: A gibraltarian-tangerino family tree

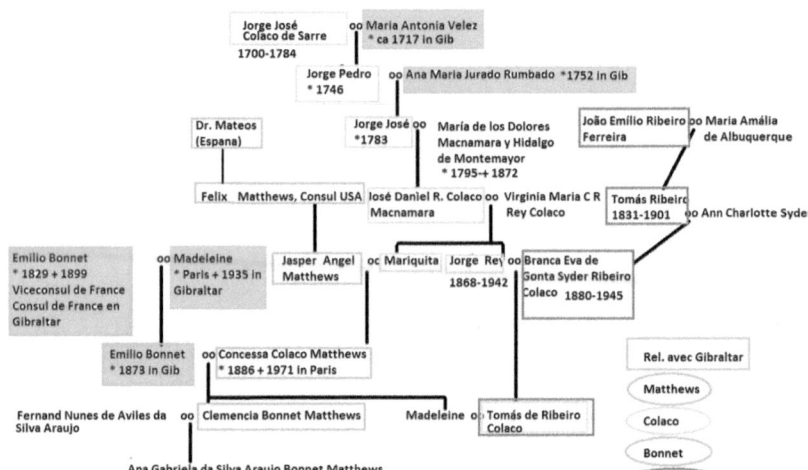

- The oldest Christian family in Tangier, the Portuguese family Colaço, is also partly from Gibraltar.[27] The French vice-consul in Gibraltar, Emile Raymond Bonnet (1829-1899), who lived in Tangier from 1876, also belongs to this family (Laredo 1936: 124). The Matthews family branch was originally Spanish and bore the name Mateos – this was then anglicized. The last descendant of Colaço, Ana Gabriela da Silva Araujo Bonnet, whom I met in 2020 at the age of 92, she passed away December 3rd 2020, but maintained good relations with Gibraltar until her old age.[28]
- The Katzaros family, who owned an impressive villa with a park in *Rue de Fez*, were originally from Greece and became British and Catholics. But the

---

27 Tomás Ribero Colaço (*1899 Lisboa) married Madeleine Matthews Bonnet (*1908 in Tangier +2001) in 1928. She was the daughter of Emilio Bonnet (*September 15, 1876 in Gibraltar), French Consul in Gibraltar. Tomás is the son of Jorge Rey Colaço (*1868 in Tanger +1942) and Branca Eva Colaço (born de Gonta Syder Ribero Colaço), and brother of Clemencia Bonnet Matthews. Jorge Rey is the son of Jorge Daniel Colaço y MacNamara (*1831 in Tangier), he married Virginia Marie Claire Victoria Raimunda Rey Colaço. The Colaços married several times into Gibraltar. Jorge Rey is brother of Mariquita Colaco. Their daughter Concessa married Gibraltarian Emilio Bonnet in 1906. Both are parents of the aforementioned Madeleine and her sister Clemencia. Clemencia is the mother of the now very old Ana Gabriela da Silva Araujo Bonnet. https://www.myheritage.de/names/jorge_cola%C3%A7o.

28 Field research diary TanGib, February 17, 2020.

Katzsaros were both Gibraltarian and *Tanjawi*. John Thomas Katzaros, Secretary of the *Assemblee Legislative*, married Miss Emily Lucy Mosso (*1895) from Gibraltar, but of Italian descent.[29]

- One informant states: "My grandparents on my fathers side were Portuguese, my mother's father was of irish and her mother of Italian descent. My father grew up in La Línea, mi mum in Larache […] I am a mixture of so many countries, but my origin, my roots and basically all my emotions ate Tangerino. I will always be attached with my soul to Tangier, where I was born and where I wish to end my days, smelling its aroma of jasmin and damas de noche."[30]
- Austro-Hungarian Vice Consul Dr. Maximilian Schmidl was originally sent to Tetuán by Baron James de Rothschild in 1861. He founded the school of the *Alliance Israélite Universelle in* 1862 and married Elizabeth (Betsy) Bathsheba De Moraville from Gibraltar, originally from the Hachuel family (Mitchell Serels 1996: 363). He lived in Tangier until his death in 1910 and worked there as a doctor who operated on many women free of charge.[31]

"My mother was born in 1908 in Tangier and lived herself in Gibraltar with her husband […]. My grandfather on my mother's side married a very young woman in Tangier in 1896. She died in Gib but was buried in Tangier in 1921.[32]

Other inhabitants of TanGib were themselves not of mixed origin but were connected to both parts by marriage or profession. Here are a few examples of many:

- Sason Azancot (+1889), translator for the US Consulate in Tangier, was married to Luna Seruya from Gibraltar (Laredo 1936: 105).
- Mr Benaroch owned a haberdashery shop at 54 Rue Siaghines. In 1953, he married, Madame Mattana, and moved to her in Gibraltar.[33]
- David Herbert recalls in his memoirs many trips he took to Gibraltar (Herbert 1990).

As a special trouvaille, a small fashion in the early 1870s among the British to give their children Arab names should be noted: Sir William Kirby Green had his daughter Farida baptized; Mr. Taylor's son was given the name Alfred Hassan.[34]

---

29 Gibraltar Magazine, September 2009; Field research diary TanGib November 1, 2019.
30 Mimi Carvalho Smith, Online platform F, August 13, 2017. Original in Spanisch, translated into English by the author.
31 The Brentan family, descended from this couple, owned the *Compagnie Nord-Africaine Intercontinentale d'Assurances* on Boulevard Pasteur. Online platform A, FO8ES, October 22, 2013.
32 Online platform B, Ruthie García Mifsud, October 7, 2012.
33 Field research diary TanGib, March 6, 2020.
34 Reference from M 27 SF, June 26, 2020.

But there is no question that, above all, the successful interethnic and religious relationships were documented. How many lovers could not officially unite because the person in love belonged to another religion or lineage, although they were of the same social status? Data here are more than meagre, because apart from literary texts in which such things are discussed, only family archives or *oral history* passed down through the family could be used. But the people concerned have either passed away, their descendants know nothing about it or do not want to talk about it. One will have to rely on gossip.

As on those about Nena Madison, the Spanish spouse of a rich British industrialist, and Elisa Baeza, daughter of the Spanish police chief of Tangier. Nena and Elisa had fallen in love with each other. After the relationship became known, Elisa was smuggled to Gibraltar in a wickerwork suitcase.[35]

In this context, material on failed or suppressed relationships would be particularly helpful to support my thesis on "class before ethnicity/religion" in Tangier.

Illustration 23: Simita Benatar

The relationships of families of both cities with each other become the basis not only of local novels (Benady/Chiappe 2011; Ceballos López 2015; Martínez 2016; Sacramento 2016; Sancho Bisquerra 2019) but also of works of world literature. Spanish author Vincente Blasco-Ibañez in his novel *Luna Benamor* (del Castillo Navarro

---

35   España (1954: 189) reports this story; he gave the participants pseudonyms.

2003), for example, created the model for *Lunita Laredo*. This, in turn, was modeled on Simita Benatar, a lady from the Cohen family in Tangier.[36] *Lunita Laredo*, a young Jewish woman from Gibraltar,[37] had been promised to marry Isaac Nuñez, a Jew from Tangier; she became the model for the mother of the heroine *Molly Bloom* (Corrales Castilla 2003) in James Joyces' *Ulysses*. Likewise, the title heroine in Ángel Vásquez' novel *La vida perra de Juanita Narboni* (1976) is also the daughter of a Gibraltarian.

All these are proof that what we differentiate today in ethnic, cultural and religious terms was interwoven in *transboughaz* TanGib in many ways.

Ultimately, the cultural identity of TanGib must be redefined, beyond ethnicity. For the dominant version of ethnicity today assumes that it is a shared belief in actual or fictitious descent. The root metaphor, the search for a common origin, is subject to such notions.

> If ethnology is by definition a discipline that seeks to understand across borders, what could be more legitimate for the ethnologist than navigating between the territorial waters of these two great disciplines of history and geography to overcome the sinuous flow of the diversity of registration possibilities to appreciate the world. (Simenel 2014: 21)

The Berbers of the Atlas Mountains, with whom Simenel spent two years, are thought of as origin and boundary:

> "The origin is a first epoch as well as a starting point in the historical and geographical trace to which the ideal past of an individual or a group can be traced back. The border is just as much a border as a foundation work, since the drawing of a border represents a historical perspective for an area and thus for the memory of a group." (Simenel 2014: 22)

Origin is, therefore, in the Berber sense, the reference point for a beginning, but with which this reference point is filled depends on the respective present:

> "With this permanent registration of the origins, some facets of the past are forgotten while others are brought to the light of memory." (Simenel 2014: 27)

It can be argued not only on the basis of ethnological but also historical (Meier 2019: 99-116) findings that the notions of ethnic groups as rooted family trees are also the results of nation-state thinking in the 19th and 20th centuries. In Tangier and

---

36 Radiosefarad (above).
37 "James Joyce, in his seminal modernist novel Ulysses, has his character Molly Bloom, reminisce about her home town, Gibraltar: I was a bit wild after when I blew out the old bag the biscuits were in from Benady Bros [...] That was my grandfather's grocery shop in Engineer Lane!" (Benady 2020).

Gibraltar, "hybridization of groups was regarded as valuable and where individuals were not obsessed by any limpieza de sangre" (Tagliaferri 2016: 111).

In Tangier this is of course also due to the fact that *Tanjawis* - at least Spanish, Muslims and Jews from lower classes - share a common *Boughazi* culture, as well as common occupations such as Fishermen, goatherds, craftsmen, construction workers, roustabouts, cooks, prostitutes, small shopkeepers. Many informants told me that Tangier was actually an Andalusian town. Of course, this is not true if one is committed to the family tree metaphors. But it is true culturally: Tangier was a Spanish city without being dominated by Spain. The inhabitants españiolized themselves culturally: Italians, French, Portuguese, British, Swedes... Even in the French *Lycée Regnault*, for example, the children spoke Spanish among themselves during recess. Paul Allemand spoke Spanish with his relatives (and parents) from France, Spain, Italy and Germany. This not only concerns the generation of *Tanjawis* born around independence, but also the older generation from the 1920s and 30s. "The French customs chief, Serrault, also spoke perfect Spanish."[38]

That root and stem metaphors do not dominate as much as in clearly national regimes is evident in many *Tanjawis*: The origins and ancestry of individuals are diverse and are only partially shared with other *Tanjawis* identified as 'equal.'

The same is true in Gibraltar, despite all attempts by Knightsfield Ltd. and its narrative petrified in the *Gibraltar Museum*. The idea of the cultural sphere in the original sense of the word reflects this better: Culture as a manifold condensed socio-spatial experience and identification.

A second component is added: Since there is no common root, the common ground lies in the internalization of cultural otherness of the ones co-present. Rachik (2012) and Burke (2014) point out that until the 1980s, the Moroccan intellectual landscape carried French as an internalized other within itself. The scientific policy of King Hassan II, who deceased in 1999, aimed precisely at driving this interwovenness (e.g. Kant, Montesquieu, Heidegger and Durkheim) out of the minds of Moroccan elites (Lakhmari 2016; Mousjid 2018b). As an aside, it should be noted here that Eurocentric sciences generally also purge the internalized other and interwoven.[39]

---

38   The informant Paul Allemand quoted here (telephone conversation on May 22, 2020) is mentioned here as a representative of many of the guarantors.

39   Using the example of Durkheim and Bourdieu's handling of Maghreb material or Arab thinkers from North Africa, I have elaborated on this elsewhere (Haller 2020). Durkheim, for example, conditioned the Maghreb material he received from Hanoteau and Letourneux by eliminating those aspects of Kabyle's social structure that ran counter to his theory of organic and mechanical solidarity. Bourdieu, on the other hand, paid tribute to his Algerian colleagues Mammeri and Sayad as independent scholars and thinkers, but French sociology long regarded them merely as suppliers to Bourdieu's works.

We find such internalizations not only in science but also in everyday life. For the traditional *Tanjawis* – at least for the older generation – Andalusians and Jews are the internalized others. They 'know' the Andalusians and Jews of North Africa, have lived with them for a long time and shared streets, work world and leisure time, played football together and visited cinemas together.

One can fall back on various theoretical approaches to such internalizations:

- In accordance with the concept of *transculturalization* developed by the Cuban ethnologist Fernando Ortíz (1940), cultural contact alters both cultures that are thought of as purely cultural but does not necessarily – as in the case of hybridization – become a new third entity.
- The incorporation of the foreigner, as I learned in Moroccan Sufi popular Islam with their *cults of trance and possession*: Everyone believed in the existence of spirit beings, the djinns, who are selfish and can do both good and bad to man. There are Muslim, Christian, Jewish and Pagan djinni. From the perspective of the canonical Islamic school of law, any contact with the djinns should be avoided and, if it happens that they do infect people, they must then be exorcised from the bodies of the infested (*Roqya*). Regarding Moroccan Sufis, the Ḥamādša, which I have been researching since 2013, the aim is to bring the djinns into permanent harmony with the infested in their bodies through rituals, trances, exstases and breathing techniques in order to banish their dangerous side. Especially the integrative handling of the infestation by a foreign religious spirit can be seen as an attempt to incorporate the foreign and to deal with it as part of oneself (cf. Haller 2016).
- The principle of *mutual interpenetration* or, as Italian philosopher Emanuele Coccia proclaims in his philosophy of plants – Die Wurzeln der Welt, "the comprehensive within the comprehensive and vice versa." "The paradigm of this interpenetration was already called the breath (*pneuma*) in antiquity; breathing, breathing means in fact exactly this experience: what contains us, the air, becomes what is contained in us, and vice versa, what is contained in us becomes what contains us" (Coccia 2018: 23).

In addition to this internalization of the Other, we find – especially historically – an identification with a common culture of the region. One can fall back on different approaches here:

- Hermans' concept of the *dialogic self* as a dynamic variety of voiced positions in an expanded dialogic mental landscape includes others in the social world and imagines others with whom it is intimately intertwined. This self is both multivocal and dialogic (Hermans 2001).

- Similar to Coccia, according to the *Sufi reflections* of Ibn Arabi, the comprehensive is contained within the comprehensive and vice versa, and breathing techniques play a central role in Sufi rituals (cf. Neumann 1981).

Illustration 24: Trance and Possession, Zaouia Hamdouchia

Both habitualized phenomena (the internalization of the other and the negation of otherness through the reference to a common space) I would call – as has already been mentioned – *Boughazidad*. It is still brought to life today in specific contexts by actors, sensual and discursive, sometimes even political. And they often have a connecting effect and always relate to each other (Daoud 2017: 14). Condensed references as in a cultural area.

3. Access methods

The present book is based on several intensive ethnological field studies since the mid-1980s, with participatory observation as its central method. In addition, work with historical material was significant, especially the evaluation of local print media.

The evaluation of literature and of forms of media communication (newspapers, magazines, online forums, etc.) is as much a part of this as the continued exchange with informants from the entire region. I have researched various online platforms, whose names I cannot disclose here for reasons of anonymity, over several years and have used material from various of these forums in this book. I call them online platform A, B, C, D, E, F, etc. I pseudonymized most informants but kept the origin of the name (e.g. the bearer of a Spanish first name and an Arabic surname was given a different Spanish first name and a different Arabic surname). This was essential in order to reflect the cosmopolitan background of the speakers. To further anonymize the speakers, I mostly erased the year and added " (d.n.n)" – which means: date available but not necessary to be mentioned.

A large part of the online material I have used is based on older *Tanjawis* (those born before 1960) of all religions. These are people who have at least acquired their formative years (childhood and youth) in Tangier. However, in the period under study from 2013 onwards, children and grandchildren are increasingly active in these forums (I would estimate them at around 10 per cent). It can be seen that these are Christian and Jewish *Tanjawis* who live mainly abroad (especially in Canada, Spain, France, Brazil, Venezuela and Israel), but the vast majority of Muslims still remain in the city. In terms of content, a distinction can be made between forums that focus primarily on the history of the city and those that focus primarily on the preservation or reestablishment of social ties. A separate term was even created for the specific context of Tangier: *Nostangie* – nostalgic longing for the international Tangier.

"Nostalgia, in the sense of a 'longing for what is lacking in a changed present [...] a yearning for what is now unattainable, simply because of the irreversibility of time' (Pickering/Keightley 2006), is a central notion that permeates present-day discourses and practices. Theorists see in it a distinctive attitude towards the past inherent to contemporary culture, "a reaction against the irreversible" (Jankélévitch 1983) to be found everywhere and now often commodified. It is, the result of "a new phase of accelerated, nostalgia-producing globalization." (Robertson 1992; Ange/Berliner 2015: 2).

Therefore, nostalgia is not only due to intentions for understanding a past but also critically engage with the present.

Whereas, according to William Cunningham Bissel, nostalgia is understood as a result of late-modern insecurity which "may likewise contribute to both ethnographers and their interlocutors' intensified interest in nostalgia," (Rubin 2016: 661) I would rather point to the fact that longing for an idealized past is inherent to all – and even pre-late-modern – national myths and to many literary texts based on a lost childhood. Perhaps it is even justified to call it an anthropological constant.

In the case of Tangiers, nostalgia for most participants in the online forums I researched is not only a sweet or bitter celebration of a past lost, but also of contemporary commonality and bonds between those scattered around the globe and the intentions to pass one's experience over to their offspring.

Participants assure each other of their common belonging to the city of Tangier. By omitting political and religious topics (according to the netiquettes), common memories are cultivated, the deceased are remembered and the image of mixed religious tolerance is invoked. Memories of childhood friendships, of the old residential quarters, of neighbors play a central role. Only rarely do breaks in the image of the tolerant Tangier come to light – the previous chapter of this book referred in this respect to interreligious prejudices and the discrimination of little Manolo, who later became the famous transsexual actress Bibi Andersen.

In addition to these personal, mostly benevolent confrontations, the history of the city plays a role in all forums: Famous people are discussed, certain buildings ... However, a few single historical incidents in the context of independence (such as the 'rampages' of 'activists' or 'lunatics' in 1952 and 1955) are also repeatedly addressed.

Memories and the 'myth of Tangier' take up a large part of the contributions. As far as the present is concerned, it plays an increasingly important role in the contributions in the forums during the years of my research. Former *Tanjawis* report on visits to their old hometown; *Tanjawis* who live in places with many others – Toronto, Malaga, Brussels, Tel Aviv – report on 'homeland meetings'; *Tanjawis* who remain in Tangier post photos or reports on new developments, especially architectural and urbanistic ones. It also seems that more and more (even younger) Moroccans are joining the forums. This assumption is based on the observation that there are increasingly contributions in Arabic script. The basic tone of these contributions is also to praise Tangier as tolerant and diverse, and as different from the rest of Morocco. Pride in the city's special character is detectable. Perhaps this is also a light form of resistance to the nation state and is due to the fact that the city has been undergoing a transformation for the past ten, fifteen years, which threatens and causes the architectural witnesses of the past – and of an old identity – to disappear.[1]

These new contributions are not only in Arabic script, but also in the 'transcription' of the local Arabic dialect, *Darija*, with Latin letters and Arabic numerals. Here we are with the language of the contributions in general. Most of them are in Spanish, in French or in Frangpagnol. *Haketija*, the local Sephardic-Spanish language, is also used in the contributions but only in the form of specific expressions understandable to everyone (such as '*ya hasra!*,' a written sigh that says 'so it is', or 'z'L', which is Hebrew *Zichrono livracha* and means 'of blessed memory'). Very rarely do participants express themselves in other languages, such as English, Portuguese or Italian.

All in all, it can be said that in all forums, tolerance and the good life in Tangier are praised, and the maintenance of the ties with this city finds an expression. This memory is very different from the myth created by the foreign writers (such as Burroughs, Capote, Orton, etc.) who worked in Tangier for mostly only a short time: A city of sexual freedoms, drug use, orientalist desires and libertinage. The images of the city expressed in the forums, on the other hand, are nourished by the experience of one's own socialization on the ground, the neighborhoods and the relationships lived. Nevertheless, they are memories of mostly elderly participants and, thus, also present nostalgic versions of a past time.

In this respect, we are dealing not only with spatially but also temporally disparate sources. I would like to use the term 'memory bag' for this, because it reminds us to shrink-wrap memories and freeze them in the context of follow-up research in the hope of thawing them again at some point. This is what Fabian described as *memory work*: "What people tell us or how we 'in the field' would be of little use unless we can remember it when we are back from the field"(2009: 195). I would add: And when we are back in the field. In this way, we often remind our interlocutors of things they have forgotten or which are no longer important to them today. I like to work with culinary metaphors and I was thinking, for example, of the image of freezer bags in which food is preserved in a freezer. You know that they are there but you do not need them for the time being. Sometimes, they lie at the bottom of the deep freeze, you do not throw them away even though you know that they might no longer be enjoyable. And if you do, then only in a very distorted state of taste. Working with such memory bags is central as an ethnologist who works on material from previous research again and again, revisiting

---

1 Cf. Moreno (2012) for the dissociation of Jews from Tangier from those of other regions of Morocco, which is cultivated in Israel.

fragments of conversations he vaguely remembers, but who is put back on track by reading the old field research records. Suddenly, connections come to light that seemed ephemeral and meaningless during the research itself and which one has only noted down because one has learned in methodological training to document even seemingly unimportant experiences since one never knows where one would be driven to by research.

The endeavor to salvage and work on commonalities that have been neglected up to now is naturally subject to the risk that, for its part, temporally divisive aspects may be belittled or even denied and, thus, generate an ahistorical permanent presence of the temporal. It is, therefore, particularly important not to project findings from one period into other periods without reflection but to locate them in their respective historical context.

The diverse information and findings about TanGib which I have come across during all the years of research have never before been systematically collected and analyzed.[2] In none of the books about Gibraltar that I have read since the 1990s – and believe me, there have been countless – have I come across more than anecdotal and ephemeral stories and references about TanGib (e.g. Serfaty 1958; Mesod Benady 1974-1978, 1996; Jackson 1987; Howes 1991; Finlayson 1991, 1996; Sam M. Benady 1993; Sam Benady 1994; García 1994; Jackson/Cantos 1995). In the books about Tangier, e.g. De Tejada (1906), Laredo (1936), Landau (1952), Malo (1953), España (1954), Aleko (1956), Hart (1957), Vaidon (1977), Mitchell Serels (1996), Assayag (2000) and Ceballos López (2009), on the other hand, the references to Gibraltar are somewhat more evident, especially in publications about the history. But even there, the relationships are nowhere systematically addressed.

It is important to note that publications about TanGib were not published in national but in local and sometimes only in personal contexts. This is especially the case with the publications of local historians such as Tito Benady, Sam G. Benady and Rachid Tafersiti Zarouila: The publications on TanGib appear in *Khbar Bladna*, a local publication series, Gibraltarian books are hardly ever published in supra-local but mostly in local series. Similarly, publications on La Línea are also published without any recognizable publication reference or are self-published. Why is this? It can be assumed that the authors

1   either want to keep the upper hand over historiography in the local context, or that
2   they do not seek a national publisher because they are seeking a local readership anyway, or

---

2   This was already complained about in 1955 – not much has changed since then (L'Eurafricain 1955: 43).

3 cannot find one because the findings were not collected professionally but are unsystematic, eclectic or the result of hobby research.

Embedding these local publications in a national or international academic or literary discourse hardly ever takes place. This is unfortunate, as they seldom provide unsubstantiated nonsense but often valuable and significant data and insights that deserve to be fed into an iternational discourse.

Most publications of this grey literature are certainly committed to a – mostly unconscious and unreflected – political agenda. As Borutta and Lemmes (2013) have pointed out, the historiography of the Mediterranean (or its subregions) usually fails because of its writers national thinking: One focuses on the national and, thus, cuts the connections to the outside world. This is particularly evident in Gibraltar, which has experienced a veritable boom in publications (e.g. Serfaty 1958; Benady 1974-1978, 1979-1980, 1989, 1992, 1993, 1996; Finlayson 1991, 1996, 2018; Lamelas 1992; Benady 1993; Benady 1994; Chipulina 2013, 2014a, 2014b, 2016, 2017; Galliano 2003; Garcia 2014; Searle 2019) in the last 30 years that stand in the context of the search for national identity. The same can be observed in Tangier, although this is not so much a political project as a way of preserving memories for the generations that have followed the Christian, Jewish and – to a lesser extent – Muslim inhabitants of the International Zone (Landau 1952; Aleko 1956; Vaidon 1977; Woolman 1998; Assayag 2000; Toledano 2010; Tafersiti Zarouila 2012; Guignet-Boulogne 2015; Vignet-Zunz 2016). It remains to be seen whether this literature will one day be used for political purposes – such as the regionalization of Morocco – in the future. In any case, they are available as resources for this. Texts are also memory bags. Some, however, are hardly ever defrosted, others never.

The finding of mutual neglect in the local publications is strange, since both cities have always been strongly dependent on each other over the centuries and – so I maintain – have always shared a common cultural area with their respective hinterlands. I will argue that, despite the weakening of the diverse relationships between Tangier and Gibraltar after 1956, commonalities still exist today and allow us to speak of a *Boughazidad*: The habitualized internalization of the other and the negation of otherness.

The books on Gibraltar which deal with aspects other than military history were written in light of the political background of the self-positioning of civilians towards Spain and the motherland. Moreover, this only happened after the opening of the border in 1982 (for pedestrians)/1985 (for vehicles), i.e. at a time when Tangier no longer played a decisive role in the everyday life of Gibraltarians.

This is also evident in the publication landscape itself:

> When I post the photo of the Gibraltarian *Take-Away Tangier's* in June 2019 in one of the online forums and ask who could tell me something about the connection of

the take-away to Tangier, one of the administrators informs me that the page, "It's only for photos, videos and paintings of Gibraltar, if you want other information about Tangier's it's better you join other groups as posts not to do with Gibraltar will be deleted, thanks."

Illustration 25: A Take Away in Gibraltar

I have to think of Marshall Sahlins (2013: XIII) and his statement that the worlds of our informants do not revolve around our worlds. Had I interpreted the *Boughazidad* too much into my material when I misinterpreted the photo of Take Away *Tangier's* as an indication of a TanGib community?

I had a similar experience with the publication series *Khbar Bladna* in Tangier. The editor informed me that the manuscript I submitted on the relationships between Tangier and Gibraltar contained "too much Gibraltar" for a book series on Tangier. Both reactions were incomprehensible to me but pointed out that I had assumed that the ties between the two cities, which I thought I could see everywhere, must also be of interest for an online forum or a publication series. This was obviously not the case. Now one could speculate a lot about possible motives, but what is interesting is the finding that Tangier and Gibraltar are not seen as an internalized other in the respective forums.

Here is a little digression about my dreams. My dreams often take place in landscapes or cities where I have lived. The topology of my dream landscapes is relatively stable, but sometimes they flow into each other at different points. The following dream is typical:

> On the (as always in these dreams) futile search for the shop of my friend Estrella in Gibraltar, I come across a synagogue which I had never seen in real life and which from the outside looks more like a baroque church. It is Shabbat and the Jews leave the synagogue in black suits and hats. I know that I am out of place. I don't want to disturb anyone and I go outside the city walls, and suddenly I am in Tangier and looking for the *zaouia* of the Hamdouchi Brotherhood. Today, everyone is in the big square, someone tells me, they are all celebrating. It's the *Soq Barra* in Tangier, but it looks like the university square in Heidelberg. By 'all,' the informant referred to various cultural groups of different religions, including the Hamdouchi, a *fantasia* (equestrian games), but also bookstores, a flamenco group, circus artists and stalls like at a German street festival.[3]

My dreams often become fields of encounter and contact with phenomena that are actually unheard-of and separated from each other: They make it possible to bring things together that are not usually brought together. Can anything methodological or otherwise unattainable knowledge about the object of research be deduced from the dreams? Certainly this one: Since I started working on a *transboughaz* research project, I have internalized the subject matter so much that it is updated in my night sleep. So when I place the internalization of the Other at the center of my central concept *Boughazidad*, my dreams warn me against seeing *Boughazidad* unquestioningly everywhere. Just because I myself have internalized the concept does not mean that my informants do the same. But just as authors in their scientific work must critically examine their own internalizations, so must they do with the statements of their informants. It is important to perceive findings, but not to become blind to what is happening outside the focus.

The lack of awareness of the ties between the two cities in publications about Tangier is mainly due to demographic and political reasons. Most of the books focus on the *myth of* Tangier. They are either designed to document the Tangier of the Zone Period, i.e. the processing of a loss; or they focus on the myths of foreign artists and writers who were enthusiastic about the Orient – and Gibraltar does not belong in this picture (Jebrouni 2019). In addition, many *Tanjawis* who were closely associated with Gibraltar had left the city after 1956; at the same time, many Moroccans with no connection to Gibraltar moved to Tangier from other regions

---

3   Frequently recurring dream sequence since 2014.

of Morocco. This reduced the regional ties even further. Moreover, the fixation of Morocco on Spain and the EU since the mid-1990s led to the fact that interest in the tiny territory of Gibraltar took a back seat.

The other city plays no role today in the school curriculum of both cities. In Morocco, even the school subject 'local affairs' has been abolished, so that not even something about the history of their own city or region is taught.[4] In Gibraltar, on the other hand, history lessons are very important, especially since the time of national identification. Tangier, however, is hardly present there.[5]

I cultivated different approaches in my research in the region. These were due not only to the context of my academic environment (in Heidelberg rather social anthropology and cultural history, in Frankfurt/Oder and Bochum rather cultural anthropology and ethnology) but also to the circumstances under which I conducted the respective research. With my research in Seville I wanted to prove myself as a doctoral candidate, with the research in Gibraltar as a postdoctoral candidate. In Tangier, on the other hand, I had no qualification work in mind, but was able to develop and carry out my own ways of researching and writing.

All three cities in my fieldwork had one thing in common at the time of the research: They were all facing major urban restructuring that transformed the cities profoundly.

In Seville, this took place within the framework of Expo 1992 on the occasion of the 500th anniversary of the discovery of America by Columbus. This was already discussed in the city during the 1985/86 and 1988 research and there were first signs of the upcoming urbanistic reconstruction.

In Gibraltar, land had long been wrested from the sea to increase the surface area of the community. But the fundamental rearrangement of the harbor, military bastions and newly reclaimed pieces of land only became apparent on a big scale in the new millennium.

In Tangier, too, the central transformations of the city as a whole by the royal development plans, such as Tangier-Métropole, were still to come, although the first tentative steps had already been taken at the time of the start of research in 2013.

The urban planning and lifeworlds of my research, thus, took place in contexts that have now been moved out of the center of urban life. These are living worlds that have not disappeared but have been subjected to lasting transformations. I am even tempted to say: Worlds that have not yet been so thoroughly commodified and subjected to neoliberal access to such a decisive degree, as is the case today.

---

4   Personal communication, Noreddine Chraibi, December 2, 2019.
5   Personal communication, Heidi Viñas Coreggio, December 2, 2019.

3.1. Seville

I had cultivated a primarily cultural and historical approach in writing my Sevillian material. Out of fear and caution. I myself did not have the courage to write more ethnographically when I published the results of my research on *Machismo and Homosexuality in Andalusia* in my dissertation (Haller 1992; Haller/Romer 1992). I tried too hard to hide the stigma of my own homosexuality in the text.

My most obvious intention was to write an ethnography of gay and transvestite life in Seville (1985-1988) – at a time when Spanish society as a whole was undergoing a profound democratization and hedonization: The *Transición* – the transition from Francisco Franco's fascist regime to a constitutional monarchy was complete, but the processes of social opening, best illustrated by the movies of Pedro Almodóvar (in which an already mentioned woman from Tangier, Bibi Andersen,[6] played an important role), were still virulent and far from complete. The questioning of gender roles and sexual norms was obvious.

What was to become an academic life topic, however, was not clear to me at that time – although it was already laid out in the dissertation: The concern with border-drawing processes, with exclusion mechanisms and the establishment of normality. By placing transvestites at the center of my research, I focused on border crossers and tried to focus on the border-drawing processes between actors with hetero- resp. homosexual identities. I was not only interested in focusing on the perspective of the transvestites themselves but, above all, in the function transvestites played within Andalusia's sociocultural classification system.

Seville itself was a wonderful initiation into field research life – not only in terms of my research topic but also in terms of the culture of this city (and especially at that time) in general. Spain had become a member of the then European Community just a few months before I came to Seville. The country was still very different from other EU countries; it was still uncommon, for example, to be able to buy German products at reasonable prices and local products dominated the market. The 1992 World Fair was still many years away. Local mentality was marked by Francoism and the detachment and liberation from it. In Seville, people voted left and worshipped the elderly civil war heroine Dolores Ibarruri. In the gay venues one could hear the songs of Isabel Pantoja and Rocío Jurado. The tranny bar *Tibu's*, where you could buy the house's *chapero* (hustler) at bingo after the establishment closed early in the morning, was a place to get drunk. Or in the tranny cabaret *Prisma* and in the pompous bar *Garlocchi* with its statues of Virgin Mary and fragrant candles. People danced to Sevillanas and to kitschy hits from the Franco era but also to the Spanish equivalent of the *Neue Deutsche Welle*, with performers like Alaska

---

6   Bibi was a companion of Angie Van Pritt, who performed in the *Prisma Cabaret* of Sevilla.

Illustration 26: Cabaret Prisma, Sevilla (1985)

y Dinarama, Mecano, Martirio de Pasión and Golpes Bajos. Everybody was smoking marijuana like hell and the very modern sniffed cocaine. As a young person, I enjoyed life in this fascinating city to the fullest with everything that came along. I could say it was a time of upheaval – but what time isn't? In any case, Francoism had not yet disappeared and democracy had not yet been fully established (after all, only four years earlier, Lieutenant Colonel Tejero had attempted a coup d'état). It was a transitional period of excess and, therefore, ideal for investigating border-drawing processes.

3.2. Gibraltar

After my doctorate, I did not always want to be seen as just the ethnologist who is perceived as a competent contact person for questions of gender and sexuality but as an ethnologist without hyphen or addition. In order to qualify for a habilitation, I was, therefore, looking for a completely different subject, but one that should be in the same region. My linguistic competence, with a command of Andalusian Spanish and English, drew my attention to the British crown colony of Gibraltar: It was sufficiently different from the Andalusian background of my dissertation and far enough away from it to allow me to discover a new subject. Nevertheless, I did not have to learn a new language and would possibly even be able to draw on

Andalusian findings of the preliminary research. I researched what was currently a political issue in Gibraltar and came across the so-called smuggler crisis: While smuggling had been the basis for local subsistence in the decades and centuries before, it had been democratized to a great extent in the 1990s. It was no longer only the classic smuggling families Victory,[7] Olivero[8] and Vinet (Cartwright 2009) who organized the smuggling, but the smuggling had been individualized by cheap loans to young people for the purchase of speedboats.

Illustration 27: Mediterranean Contraband Triangle

In Gibraltar, therefore, the transformation of a social order based on social ties into an individual-dominated society could be studied in detail. Peraldi (2007a: 6) rightly points out that smuggling is often folklorized, especially that of small and poor people who either try to skim off a small profit from the great inequality between the ex-colonists and the ex-colonizers, or from their own friendship networks to benefit.

> But this folkloristic vision only points to a part of a nebula which brings together multiple forms of articulation between local trade and transnational peddling [...] specialized trade rather reserved for specific categories, such as these young people, sons of apparatchiks of the regime in Algeria, sons of wealthy migrants in France, who take advantage of their easy access to visas, when visas are introduced, to 'make their pocket money' by selling luxury products bought in Europe in their circles of relatives. (Peraldi 2007a: 6)

---

7   Personal Communication. Informant, name and date available but not necessary to be mentioned.
8   Field research diary Gibraltar, December 24, 1996.

So it would be misleading to restrict the research on smuggling exclusively to local and regional relationships; it has long been part of larger networks. Spanish entrepreneur, smuggler and sixth richest man in the world at the time, Juan March (Umbría Quiñones 2019: 24ff), for example, already dominated the entire Western Mediterranean between Tangier, Genoa and Palermo in the first half of the 20th century. He fled from the Spanish Republic to Gibraltar in 1933.[9] March played a central role in the Second World War: by donating 12 million dollars to the family Franco, he helped to prevent Spain from going to war on the German side, for example, and attacking Gibraltar.[10] The existence of the British military base guaranteed the Allies access to the Mediterranean and, ultimately, made an American invasion of Sicily possible.

My publications on Gibraltar go back to the research project *From a place of deployment to a tax haven: The influence of political-economic transformation processes on the formation of national and ethnic identities using the example of Gibraltar*. The project, supervised by Werner Schiffauer and his Chair of Comparative Cultural and Social Anthropology at the European University Viadrina (Frankfurt/Oder),[11] was funded by the *German Research Foundation (DFG)* during the two-year period. I collected material during a one-year stationary field research in Gibraltar.[12] Gibraltar was then still a British Crown Colony with a Governor appointed by the Crown. It is not without pride that I would like to say that I am one of the few contemporary colleagues who has actually carried out research in a real colony and who is, therefore, able to analyze colonialism not only historically and retrospectively but also through own observation on the ground.

My research in Gibraltar was socioanthropological: I wanted to explore how a society deals with the transformation from a military to a financial economy. But on the ground, another topic proved to be more relevant to understanding Gibraltar society: The relationship with neighboring Spain, which claimed the territory for herself. This claim was made in different ways; paradigmatic for this was what happened on the land border. Although both Spain and Gibraltar belonged to the European Community, Spanish authorities harassed cross-border workers. On the other hand, both Gibraltar and its immediate Spanish hinterland, the *Campo de Gibraltar*, continued to live largely from large and small-scale smuggling: Food, alcohol, perfume, petrol, hashish and other drugs. Furthermore, both territories were located in the south in close proximity to Morocco. The situation at the Strait was complicated by the existence of the Spanish exclaves on African territory, Ceuta and

---

9	Time Magazine 1933.
10	BBC 2018
11	1996-1997.
12	February 1996 - February 1997.

Melilla, and some tiny islands off Morocco's coast. This highly complex geopolitical situation, in which Spain, Great Britain, Morocco, the EU and the USA played the dominant roles, affected the existence of the civilian population of the small colony in many ways: In the social fabric, religions, sport, national discourses and elsewhere.

In Gibraltar, I felt like a data collection machine – at least that is how I described myself in my field notes at the time – which ticked off appointment after appointment and in the evening, exhausted with a bottle of wine and hastily cobbled together food in front of the TV, collapsed unhealthily. All relationships in the field, when I look back, were in the service of a goal-oriented question to be answered on a logocentric basis. My research habitus in Gibraltar closed many doors for me, denied me many miracles: I had learned a lot about history, social structure, even about unofficial discourse, but I had hardly participated in the private life of my informants. With my monograph (Haller 2000a), I wanted to pay my respects to Gibraltarians whom I had the privilege of meeting in their blessed place.

3.3. Tangier

My research in Gibraltar had been going on for some time when I decided to go to Tangier. In the years between Gibraltar and Tangier, the phase of the free researcher's bullock tour fell.[13] I could hardly allow myself a new field of research during these years of professional establishment.

The search for new subjects in Seville or Gibraltar did not appeal to me. Instead, I thought of the Moroccan city of Tangier, firstly, since it was unknown to me but was located in 'my' research region, secondly, it would provide me with a completely new facet – the experience of a non-European culture, and thirdly, it would be an exciting field because major infrastructural projects promised to plough the city.

These projects concerned the ports of Tangier in particular, so I would make them the focus of my research. I was particularly interested in the effects that this transformation would have on the simple *Tanjawis* and their coping with existence. It took me several years before I could do research there for a year – the minimum time for a new field of research.

I wanted to approach things in Tangier differently than in my previous research: Firstly, because I actually found the research method in Gibraltar unhealthy, but also because I had learned that my research habitus in Gibraltar closed many

---

13   Teaching at various institutes, guest professorships in Granada and Hamburg, an assistant at New School University/New York and a DAAD professorship in Austin/Texas lay in between, and in 2005, the appointment to a newly established professorship for social anthropology in Bochum.

Illustration 28: Tanger Ville

doors for me. I was able to proceed differently in Tangier – not only because of my previous Gibraltarian experience but also because I did not carry out any qualification work in Tangier as I did on the other side of the Strait. In Tangier, I was also not committed to any foundation that would have financed me. I was, therefore, free from outside institutional or financial pressure and could explore what was happening. That is a great freedom and should actually be the normal state of affairs for explorative scientific research: Not to be restricted by question-blinders from the start but to search broadly in the field for the relevant questions that come from the culture we are addressing. This approach is becoming increasingly impossible today due to the synchronized, goal-oriented and economized working conditions at universities, therefore, I felt it a great mercy to be able to cultivate this old and meaningful approach in Tangier.

This meant that I could try to let things and questions come to me – and not search for them in advance. The fact that I was not – as in the previous research – moving within a Euro-American context, in which time regulations, forms of communication, secularization and the constellation of values ultimately privilege the individual as a central actor, was, of course, a confounding factor. In Tangier, I was confronted with world conceptions in which individuals are regarded as less free from a Western point of view, because they and their optimization, improvement and capacity to act are not the sole points of reference, but because man is placed in a cosmos of external forces that sometimes make him their plaything: Allah, *ba-*

raka, the worlds of the spirit beings (Haller 2016, 2018).[14] I also experienced this as a relief: Here, it is not exclusively up to the individual to be the forger of his own happiness, but there are also external forces that determine the individual's prosperity and ruin decisively.

It should be added that this research also focused on other boundaries than those of gender or nation states: The ontological boundaries between humans and spiritual beings (*ǧnūn*), which I researched in the Sufist brotherhood of the Ḥamādša (Haller 2016, 2018).

3.4. The regional embedding: Gibraltar, Tangier and their hinterland

Neither of the two parts of the city nor TanGib as a whole can be understood without embedding it in the regional hinterlands. This applies in several respects: Historically, demographically and politically.

As has already been mentioned, at present, the Strait is characterized by the existence of various territorial peculiarities: Gibraltar is British, but Spain claims the former colony as its own territory. Ceuta and Melilla are Spanish cities on North African soil, they are claimed by Morocco as are the islands of Perejil, Chafarinas and Alborán, the Peñon de Velez de la Gomera and the Peñon de Alhucemas.

From the Gibraltarian point of view, their home town is not only intertwined with North Africa but especially with the immediate Iberian hinterland, the *Campo de Gibraltar* in the province of Cádiz. A few historical facts:

When Gibraltar was awarded to Britain in 1712, its pre-population left the Rock and founded the city of San Roque in the immediate vicinity. The border remained largely open in the 19th century, only interrupted when epidemics raged (Jackson 1987: 249).

Between the first half of the 19th century and the 1950s, Gibraltar and the Campo de Gibraltar in many ways developed as an interwoven borderland society, in some respect even institutionally anchored.

The inhabitants of neighboring La Línea were especially considered to be close to Gibraltarians. In Spanish, línea simply means 'line.' The name refers to the military line between the British and the Spanish. Originally, between 1730 and 1735, a defensive line with several fortifications was built. This line was located on the isthmus, half a mile from the defensive positions of the Rock.[15] From the 1810s on-

---

14 Finally, in Tangier, in addition to modernization, I explored another border relationship – that between people and spiritual beings in the context of Moroccan Sufism.
15 England fought on the Spanish side in the Napoleonic Wars. When the French reached San Roque, the Spanish general Francisco Ballesteros sought help in Gibraltar in the form of money and weapons. The Spanish general Castaños and the British commander Sir Colin Camp-

Illustration 29: Borders at the Strait of Gibraltar

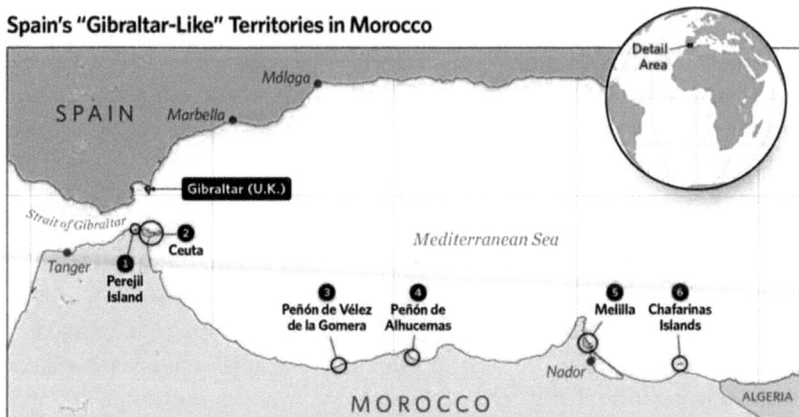

wards, a settlement of poor huts was established behind the line of fortifications, mainly inhabited by residents of San Roque, such as bar owners, workers, traders and craftsmen, who worked for the British garrison. Later, Andalusians from other places in the *Campo* and even from Cádiz moved to La Línea, then Portuguese and Genoese from Gibraltar. Several British subjects also settled in the *Campo* (Stockey 2019). In 1869, the inhabitants of La Línea applied for independence from San Roque – but in vain. The San Roque city council argued that the inhabitants of La Línea were only a temporary population, thanks to the Spanish military, and that

bell agreed to destroy the fortifications on the Isthmus so that they would not fall into the hands of the French.

they were economically dependent on the British colony. Nevertheless, in 1870, La Línea became a separate unit, independent from San Roque, and in 1931 it was granted municipal rights.

Gibraltar often served as a refuge site for Spanish liberals during the Spanish civil wars of the 19th century. Spaniards also found political asylum in Gibraltar during the Spanish Civil War 1936-39. In the first three days of the Civil War, around 5000 fled[16] to Gibraltar, including many Britons who lived in the Campo.[17]

Gibraltar politician Isaac Abecasis was born in 1929. At the beginning of the Spanish Civil War the Abecasis family fled from La Línea – at that time, La Línea and Gibraltar was un pueblo unido (a united town). In 1939, Abecasis was evacuated to Morocco. All relatives who lived in Morocco have moved to Israel.[18]

Illustration 30: Culture Area

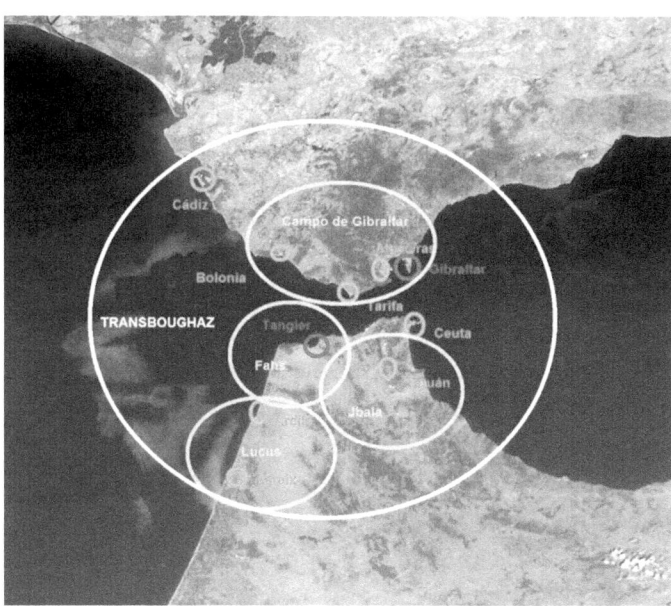

---

16 There is no clarity about the number of refugees. Jackson (1987: 270) speaks of 4000 in the first weeks.
17 The Gibraltar Chronicle, Special Edition, July 22, 1936; cit. in Finlayson (1996).
18 Abecasis describes himself as a "very militant British Gibraltarian"; Israel, however, does not offer him a perspective for life. "Quiero el mejor para Israel – pero desde lejos" (I want the best for Israel – but from afar). "Gibraltar 100 per cent." Field research diary Gibraltar, August 13, 1996.

Most of the Spanish Civil War refugees were taken by British destroyers into National Spanish or Republican territory, others returned to Spain only after the end of the Civil War. About 500 Spaniards remained permanently in Gibraltar (Jackson 1987: 272).

After World War II, Gibraltarians again moved to La Línea due to the lack of housing, where the cost of housing and food was much lower than on the Rock. Many built or bought their own houses in the *Campo* but kept their British nationality. As an example of this, we will get to know the Marrache family in chapter 6.

Gibraltar and the *Campo*, thus, formed a cross-border society in the first half of the 20th century. This can be seen not only in the cultural Hispanization of Gibraltarians but also in the Anglicization of Linenses (even today, the local vocabulary of the inhabitants of La Línea is full of Anglicisms). The two towns were also connected in other aspects: In the 1920s, for example, Gibraltarian brothels, then located in *Serruya's Lane*, were[19] closed down by order of the governor. The prostitutes moved to La Línea and settled in a street popularly known as *Calle de Gibraltar*.[20] They mainly served military and civil clientele from Gibraltar.

These close ties diminished after World War II and particularly since 1965: Spain, which still claimed Gibraltar as her own, tried to wear down its population by means of all kinds of harassment.[21] When I conducted research in Gibraltar in 1996/97, the primary experiences of harassment by Spanish authorities at the border were placed in the long context of these hostilities. This was still partly the case in 2019. Implicit in this is the conviction of Spanish moral superiority: 'The Spanish' are still mentally influenced by fascism. An example of this is the verdict of Major Richard Vasallo (*1950):

> I'll tell you something: The Spanish have a fascist mentality, they're tyrannical [...] This lousy nation probably thinks it can take on Britain! [...]. (Haller 2000a: 89)

Causally responsible for the persistence of that mentality branded fascist is school education in times of Franco. The liberalization of Spanish society since the *Transición* is denied or reinterpreted into the negative in Gibraltarian hegemonic discourse. For the hatred of Spain was accentuated by the harassment that culminated in the closure of the border in 1969.

After the opening of the border in 1982 (for pedestrians)/1985 (for vehicles), Spain was considered by religious Gibraltarians as a source of a loose way of life. The representative of one of the religious groups in Gibraltar, for example, assures me

---

19	Also known as *Callejón del Peligro* (Benady 1996: 35).
20	The connection between borders and prostitution is highlighted in Donnan and Wilson (1999: 91ff, 143ff).
21	The last paragraphs of this chapter have been taken, in part literally, from Haller (2000a) and translated into English by the author.

that Francoism had its good points, because of the high moral standards: "Twenty-five years ago, I was on holiday in Spain and a boy was arrested by a policeman for wearing shorts!"[22]

After the death of Franco, the "morality was much lighter and it affected the ethical standard even in Gibraltar."[23]

Children took drugs, had sex and used obscene language. The notion of loose living and the libertinage in Spain can be understood through the background of a small society in which total social control developed due to its tiny and closed territory. In fact, visits to Spain are often the only way to satisfy forbidden desires.

In addition to loose lifestyles and crime, diseases are also localized in neighboring countries. It is widely believed that the ugly oil refinery in Campamento[24] on the Bay of Algeciras was built to 'poison Gibraltarians.' The lung cancer rate in Europe is higher than in any other region.

The land border with a fence (*verja*) and border controls function as a

> "protective barrier against the influences of evil (illness, crime, police arbitrariness, unemployment, poverty) that can constantly threaten it from the environmental exosphere [here: Spain] and violate its sacredness" (Müller 1987: 29).

The alignment of economic and social living conditions between Gibraltar and Spain after 1985 reinforced the demarcation of the social sector, which, in habitus, descendance and language, was most similar to the inhabitants of the *Campo*. I could notice this, for example, during the 1996 election campaign: The supporters of the *Gibraltar Socialist Labour Party* (GSLP) with a working class background and a habitus similar to Andalusians are characterized by the most anti-Spanish discourse. By contrast, the voters of the conservative *Gibraltar Social Democrats* (GSD), with its more Anglo habitus, are the most open to talks and negotiations with Spain.[25]

On the other side of the Strait, in Tangier, since my field research in 2013/2014 until today, I have only sporadically encountered myths of togetherness as far as Gibraltar is concerned. If you take a closer look at the history of the city, a different picture emerges. However, these are knowledge assets of only a few local historians. Gibraltar no longer has any specific meaning for large parts of the population. Today, the population of Tangier consists mainly of immigrants from other parts of Morocco; they only got to know the period of close connections with Gibraltar from stories. As a rule, they know nothing about the history of their own city or even that of the city on the other side. And the border 'to the North' is more impenetrable

---

22 Interview with Rabbi Ronnie Hassid, April 23, 1996.
23 Interview with Rabbi Ronnie Hassid, April 23, 1996.
24 We will learn more about the background of the oil refinery in chapter 6.
25 The last paragraphs of this chapter have been taken, in part literally, from Haller (2000a) and translated into English by the author.

than before anyway – so why should the mental horizon of the new *Tanjawis* only extend to Gibraltar and not immediately to Spain or Europe?

But Andalusia as a whole or even 'Spain' are, in a certain way, considered as a part of their own, due to the proximity. The conquest of the Iberian Peninsula by Tariq Ibn Ziyad is generally considered. Moreover, 'Spanish' mentality, cuisine, social ways of binding and culture are *Tanjawis'* internalized Other, an inseparable reference point for the commonality with the people of the Northern coast. People have lived together in Tangier for too long for Spanish to be something foreign. Anyone who settles in Tangier always has the other side in mind, and in sight. *Zurqaqq* – the alleyway – is what the Strait is called in the local dialect.

Historically, *Tanjawis* have had a similar experience to Gibraltarians: Both were expulsed –Gibraltarians to the hill of San Roque, *Tanjawis* to the hill Tanja Balia.[26]

Tangier has three immediate hinterlands: Fahs, Lucus and Jbala. Fahs is a small region, extending about 35 kilometers to the present mega-port of Tangier-Med in Ksar es Seghir in the east and about 15 kilometers to the south. Lucus includes the cities in the south: Asilah, Laraich and Ksar el Kebir. Jbala is the mountainous area between Taza, Ouazzan, Chefchaouen and Tetuán. Many of the people who moved to Tangier during the Zone Period came from here. The Jblis are Arabic-speaking Berbers, often with Hispanic roots, who are different from the Berbers of the Rif area. They were the classic backwoodsmen at that time, but nowadays the old Jbli families are considered to belong to the old-established *Tanjawis* or, at least, are considered 'similar to *Tanjawis*.' The 'real' strangers come from somewhere else today. Demographic changes in the city may have started in 1956, but they could only become noticeable with the massive influx of people from the south, from Arobia: This is the name given to the former French protectorate, which began about 70 km south of Tangier.[27] Since the 1980s, but intensified by the designation of Tangier as a development area by King Mohamed VI in the new millennium, Arobia symbolizes 'the foreign' for many and, thus, plays a central role in the discourse of self-determination.

3.5. TanGib 2019/20

A decisive rupture in the close relations between Gibraltar and Tangier took place in the years around the incorporation of Tangier into the new Moroccan nation-state. I could evaluate various newspapers from this period in this regard. Special

---

26 *Tanja Balia* actually means 'old Tangier,' a name that can only be explained thus: After Britain withdrew, the inhabitants of *Tanja Balia* returned to Tangier; for these returnees, *Tanja Balia* was their old Tangier, while the historically old Tangier became the new Tangier to them.
27 For other sources, *Arobia* already begins between Asilah and Laraich (Hillali 1988).

attention was paid to the publications between 1955 and 1959. However, only the reporting in *The Gibraltar Chronicle* could be fully taken into consideration; most newspapers from Tangier were hardly available from the period in question and only ephemerally from the years close by: Only isolated copies of the newspaper *Tangier Gazette* from 1950-1955, complete from 1955-1961, *Cosmopolis* isolated issues from 1946-53, *España* only from 1953, *La Dépeche* Moroccaine *de Tangier* (first half of 1956).[28] This material was incorporated particularly in chapters 4 and 5.

Ethnographically, in 2019/20, I was able to draw on several connections with friends, acquaintances and other informants established during previous field research in Gibraltar (1990s) and Tangier (2010s). Since my time in Tangier, I had visited this city constantly and frequently for research purposes. Relations with Gibraltar, however, had been interrupted for some time, so I was surprised at the careers that some of my informants from the 1990s had pursued since then: Little Fabian, who was then considered a young hope of the *Labour Party*, is now *Chief Minister*; young politician and historian Joe Garcia is now Deputy Chief Minister; Dominique Searle, whom I had met as a young journalist, is now spokesman for the Gibraltarian government in London (The Diplomat 2016); Roy Clinton, who at the time left me his BA in Economics at the University of Birmingham, is now interim chairman of the opposition party GSD; Deepak Ramchandani, who worked as a salesman in a perfume shop, became the beautician of a *Miss India* and then a *Miss World*. Several informants and friends have passed away. However, new contacts could be won over in 2019 and through various online platforms.

I am probably one of the few Germans who wished, indeed longed, for the United Kingdom to leave the EU (Brexit). Not at the time when it was decided in a referendum in 2016 but in 2019, when Brexit was imminent on several occasions. It was to take place in April 2019, and I traveled down to be there when Gibraltar, as part of Britain, would have to leave the EU. But nothing happened. Would it take place on October 31, 2019, as announced later? There have long been voices denying this. Of course they were right. Damn it! Teresa May and Boris Johnson boycotted my research project: There would be no way to study what happens in Gibraltar after Brexit if there is no Brexit. Or, if it were to be postponed indefinitely…

In the summer of 2019, I could motivate three students to go on a research trip to Gibraltar to take a closer look at the – in the broadest sense – preparations made for a Brexit in October 2019.[29] Afterwards, I traveled to Tangier to continue my research on the relations between Tangier and Gibraltar – as I had already done for

---

28　The journals were not a complete source. All editions of the *Tangier Gazette, España* and *Cosmopolis* available in the *Spanish Biblioteca Española Juan Goytisolo* could be consulted there, *La Dépeche Marocaine de Tangier* in the *Elisa Chimenti* Foundation and *Tangier Gazette* in the Légation Américaine.

29　The Promos Program of the Ruhr-University Bochum supported this project.

years. It was possible to twist the original research question pragmatically: What is happening in Gibraltar in preparation for Brexit? Is the pressing Brexit an occasion for research into relations across the *Boughaz*? What initiatives are emerging from Brexit for TanGib? What resources can these initiatives draw on? Does *Boughazidad* play any role in this?

Similar to April 2019, the October deadline passed silently.

Considering these conditions, the idea to research TanGib, therefore, had to have two sides to it: One cultural-historical and one contemporary ethnological. The cultural-historical side was ensured by the evaluation of the publications listed in the bibliography, the ethnological one by the partly retrospective revision of the field materials from Gibraltar (1995/96), Tangier (2013-19) and the current material on TanGib (2019 ff).

Gibraltar, as an appendage of the United Kingdom, finally left the EU on January 31, 2020, as announced by the government of British Prime Minister Boris Johnson.

Chapter eight, then, will deal with the field research on TanGib in times of Brexit. I will address both the structural preconditions and the informal and institutional ties that link the two cities in the present.

Finally, the last chapter deals, inter alia, with the implications of the material for the future of relations between Tangier and Gibraltar (9.1.).

4. Common history until 1956

Because of its location at the entrance to the Mediterranean Sea, Tangier, Gibraltar and the Strait are in a central geopolitical position whose control major global players have struggled for over the centuries – to name but the most important: Phoenicians, Carthaginians, Romans, Visigoths and Vandals, the Caliphates, Spain, Great Britain, the USA, the EU, the Gulf States, China and most recently Iran[1]. This is not the place to go into all the details of these historical connections. Therefore, I will provide only a few central data for the time until 1956.

Illustration 31: Gibraltarian Currency

In 711, Gibraltar was the first place on the European mainland to be conquered by the Moors under the leadership of army commander Tariq Ibn Zayid. The Arabic name *Jebel al Tarik* (Mount of Tarik) became the present day 'Gibraltar.'

Moving forward in history, one will involuntarily come across the Caliphate of Cordoba, the Almohad Empire[2] (which at times stretched from Senegal to France)

---

1   In the summer of 2019, Gibraltarian authorities detained the Iranian tanker *Grace 1* in the port of Gibraltar for several weeks. The EU accused Iran of smuggling oil to Syria in violation of EU sanctions.
2   Gibraltar was then called *Madīnat al-Fatḥ* (City of Victory) (Lane 2016: 209).

and the Almoravid Empire. During these periods, both Tangier and the Rock of Gibraltar were under the same dominion.³

In 1333, the Moroccan Merinid dynasty conquered Gibraltar, in 1355, Isa Ibn al-Hassam appointed himself King of Gibraltar and in 1374, the rock was given to the Nazarites of Granada. In 1471, Portugal conquered Tangier. In 1580, Portugal was united with Spain, so that Tangier and Ceuta also came under Spanish sovereignty.

Castile conquered Gibraltar in 1462, and the Duke of Medina Sidonia sold Gibraltar in 1474 to a group of Jewish converts, which he expelled two years later (Lamelas 1992). With the conquest of the last part of Al-Andalus (1492), Jews and Muslims living there, as well as their converted descendants or those who had only converted for appearances' sake but had been discovered, were expelled in several waves. Apart from the Ottoman Empire, Morocco in particular, especially the city of Fès and then the cities of Tetuán and Tangier became points of contact for the displaced people. Many Moriscos (descendants of Iberian Muslims who fled to North Africa) joined the corsairs of the Barbarian states, and refugees from Extremadura founded the pirate republic of Salé on the Moroccan Atlantic coast.

4.1 Portugal and England

Great Britain particularly had long had an interest in the entrance to the Mediterranean Sea, as it allowed it to control the trade routes from the Middle East to North-Western Europe – and after the construction of the Suez Canal in 1867, the lifeline of the British Empire. Tangier came into British possession in 1661 as a dowry of Portuguese Princess Catalina de Braganza. The North African city was then considered the "brightest jewel" in the crown of her husband, King Charles II (Landau 1952: 24), who, however, was dependent on the approval of the English parliament for the financing of the renewal of the fortifications in Tangier. In the end, Tangier was administered by Catholics who were partisans of their faith and whom the Protestant king did not want to support from his private purse. This led to the withdrawal of the British in 1683 and the writer and *Secretary for the Navy* Samuel Pepys was entrusted with the organization of the withdrawal. He noted in his diaries the idea that Gibraltar should be taken in order to compensate for the loss of Tangier. However, due to the costly adventure in Tangier, this did not happen for the time being.

After the loss of Tangier, the conquest of Gibraltar in 1704 and its protection by the *Treaty of Utrecht* (1713) between Great Britain and Spain was particularly si-

---

3   Daoud (2017) provides a broad and well-founded panorama of the connections between the two coasts before the time we are mainly interested in here.

Illustration 32: Portuguese Tangier

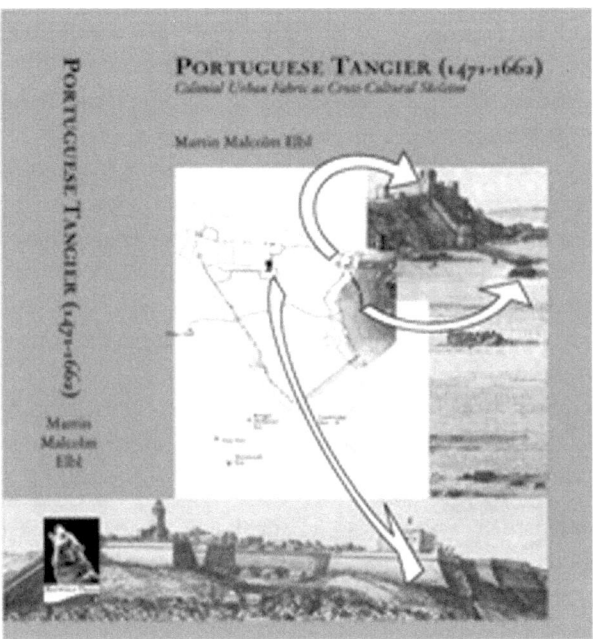

gnificant.[4] Some 120 years later, Admiral Nelson believed that the loss of Tangier was one of his country's greatest mistakes and that a reconquest was essential to secure Gibraltar and British interests (Vaidon 1977: 42). One of the first governors of Gibraltar, Roger Elliott (1665-1714), was actually born in Tangier (Ceballos López 2009: 328).

The civilian population in the British garrison of Gibraltar arose from the need to supply the military with food and raw materials. Crucial to this in the first century of British rule were the Sephardic Jews of Morocco and their networks and Muslim subjects of the sultan. The *Treaty of Utrecht* prohibited Jews and Moors from establishing themselves in Gibraltar.

That all Moors or Jews subject to the Emperor of Morocco shall be allowed a free traffic to buy and sell for thirty days in the City of Gibraltar, or Island of Minorca, but not to reside in either place, but to depart with their effects, without let or molestation, to any part of the said Emperor's dominion.

---

4   However, there had been English attempts to conquer Gibraltar earlier, around 1625 and 1656 (Martínez Ruiz 2005: 1053).

However, this restriction was unilaterally lifted by Great Britain after Spain, in breach of the treaty, laid siege to the Rock, which was, thus, cut off from the supply of goods from its Spanish hinterland. It can be assumed that the acceptance of Muslims and Jews is also due to the distrust of the British administration towards the Catholic residents (Heeter Smith 2016).

After the second (1720) and third sieges (1727/28), official agreements were concluded with the Moroccan sultan to guarantee the duty-free export of goods from Morocco. Again, it was mainly the Sephardis of Morocco who organized the trade. Although the first paragraph of the treaty of 1729 again stipulated, during several Spanish sieges of the 18th century, relations with Morocco guaranteed the supply and survival of the colony, providing drinking water (Jackson 1987: 191, 199), food[5] and raw materials of all kinds.[6] Muslims lived partly in Gibraltar itself.[7] Tangier, on the other hand, maintained close economic relations not only with Gibraltar but also with the Campo de Gibraltar.[8]

Demographically, the two places were also connected early on. A member of the community was married to a Gibraltarian and a Jewish woman from Tangier at the same time:

> Aboab was married to a Jewish lady in Gibraltar in the 1760s, but as she could not bear children, or so it seems, he adapted the Jewish Law in Morocco so as to marry a young lady, who Lopez de Ayala describes as beautiful and young but that when her husband and she were invited to the governor's residence she would wear a wig because of loss of hair. What he did not understand was that she did it for religious reasons, covering her hair was a sign of purity and modesty. [A]bo[ab] even paid for burial plots for both of them, next to each other, in London. Of course, the plots were never used. The first wife got her money and moved. And the second one went against the wishes of her husband. He wrote that if she wanted to benefit from his inheritance she should not marry [...] ever, a widow for life. Still, she

---

5   Until 1815, Moroccan traders slaughtered their cattle and sheep in a slaughterhouse which was located in Irish Town on the site of the later police station (Benady 1996: 25).

6   In City Mill Lane, for example, there was a candle factory that purchased wax from Morocco (Benady 1996: 29).

7   So, Benzimra's Alley was also called *Callejón del Moro*, after a Moroccan merchant who lived there at the beginning of the 19th century (Benady 1996: 34; also see Jackson 1987: 124 ff).

8   Such relations existed, for example, in the late 18th century between Tangier and Tarifa: "Because of its proximity to the African coasts, Tarifa has followed the vicissitudes that have marked the history of Morocco with great attention over the centuries. [...] At the end of May, on May 28th, Jorge Juan signed the Peace and Trade Treaty on behalf of Carlos III, which was intended to help strengthen the ties that bound the people of Tarragona to their Tangierino neighbors and to place them under international protection from now on. [...] In the first half of 1768, 109 boats left Tangier, many of which followed the course of Tarifa, although in a smaller proportion than in previous months" (Posac Mon 1990: 63; translation by the author).

married an Italian Jew, and got something, but the rest of the estate went to close relatives.⁹

Illustration 33: Commercial City

Towards the end of the 18th Century, Spain besieged the fortress again several times. During the Great Siege (1779), Moroccan-born Jonah de Abram Pariente was the representative of the sultan in Gibraltar (Benady 1992: 50).

In 1780, Alawid Sultan Mohammed III (1757/1759-1790) saw an opportunity to expel the diplomatic corps in Morocco based in Tangier. The sultan had sided with Spain for a short time. All Europeans, except the Spaniards, had to leave the city by January 1, 1781. The sultan wanted to sell Tangier to the Spanish for 100.000 $. At that time, the British already provided the largest diplomatically protected contingent in Tangier with 709 subjects. The British Consul fled pell-mell to Gibraltar, after he had quickly burned the Consulate archives (Vaidon 1977: 34). However, when the British proved to be more powerful during the siege of Gibraltar, Mohammed III allowed them to return to Tangier. In 1786 (Vaidon 1977), Tangier officially became the diplomatic capital of the Alawid Empire.

Diplomacy and trade were closely linked and, as a result, diplomats and traders from Morocco played a central role in supplying Gibraltar. However,

> [W]hereas Barbary Moors came and went and no doubt made their fortunes both legitimately and illegitimately by supplying Gibraltar, the Barbary Jews found it much more convenient to become residents. (Chipulina 2014a)

---

9 Personal communication, Sidney Delmar, July 7, 2019. See also https://en.wikipedia.org/wiki/History_of_the_Jews_in_Gibraltar

Aaron Cardozo (1761-1834), for example, was sent by the Governor of Gibraltar to Tangier in 1793 to get fresh beef – Cardozo was a friend of the sultan's brother[10]. Cardozo's father-in-law was the British Vice-Consul, Isaac Diaz Carvalho. Isaac Diaz Carvalho's son, David Diaz Carvalho (*1726) was born in Gibraltar and leader of the local Jewish community (Benady 1989: 157).

Another important Jewish actor who linked the two cities was Jehuda Benoliel (*1772). He was a friend of Cardozo and acted as Moroccan (and Austrian) (Serfaty 1958: 19) consul in Gibraltar.[11] Benoliel's influence was so strong that he was able to prevent the attack of the Sardinian fleet on the Kingdom of Morocco through diplomatic skill.[12]

> Because of Morocco's role as supplier of the British garrison, there was constant sea traffic with Tangier. Gold coins from Morocco were shipped to Benoliel in exchange for Spanish dollars. The proceeds of customs and taxes levied in Northern Morocco could be transported to the southern capital of Marrakesh, by way of Benoliel in Gibraltar, who would ship the money to Essaouira. The overland route from Essaouira to Marrakesh took only a few days, in contrast to a much more arduous and risky land journey from Tangier. Benoliel was also well positioned to ship other commodities to Morocco requested by the sultan – such as textiles, or grain in time of drought – or to negotiate the purchase of ships. (Schroeter 2002: 125)

Benoliel, Arengo and Cardozo

> got together and they decided to bring over a quarter of a million pounds in gold coins through Portugal and England to Gibraltar. And these guys came up with all this money to pay the officers. And obviously they divided whatever was left between them. Even with what they divided [...] the amount was such that my grandmother [...] used to tell me that her great aunt used to say they used to go into the house with real barrels of gold coins. So her grandfather Solomon, when he was born, was weighed in gold here in Gibraltar and the money was given to the poor and from the moment he was born until the moment he died he was known as El niño de oro, the Golden Boy. These are things that used to happen here very commonly [...].[13]

---

10 https://gibraltar-intro.blogspot.com/2012/01/chapter-2_7266.html
11 https://gibraltar-intro.blogspot.com/2012/01/chapter-2_7266.html
12 https://gibraltar-intro.blogspot.com/2013/08/1772-benoliel-family-yahuda-bulil.html
13 Field research diary Gibraltar May 16, 1996.

4.2 The 19th century

In March 1808, the British conquered Parsley Island (in Moroccan Arabic: Leila, in Spanish: Isla Perejil). Three hundred soldiers from Gibraltar are said to have been stationed on the tiny island at that time (Daoud 2017: 192). The tiny island is still is a subject of dispute between Spain and Morocco, in order to put pressure on the Spanish garrison in Ceuta.

The great powers of the epoch, however, persisted in the Strait even in times of peace, influencing both cities. An example of this is the *Three Brothers* affair:

> In July 1822, a Gibraltar-based ship, Three Brothers, flying a British flag, was captured by one of the Spanish privateering coastguards while on its way to Tangier. This set off a train of legal arguments which would last several years and involve four governments: Britain, France, Spain and Morocco. The Three Brothers was carrying a British register and a Mediterranean pass, and a passport from the Civil Secretary in Gibraltar. This passport included a bill of health certifying that the ship was free of disease. Those were all the papers that were needed. Gibraltar was a free port, and the Moroccans did not require a manifest of cargo, so manifests were not carried. Of course if the Spanish coastguard claimed that the ship was smuggling, there was no way of proving otherwise. And it was very difficult to distinguish smugglers from trading ships licitly, because the currents and winds forced ships to hug the Spanish coast until they had passed through the Straits of Gibraltar into the Atlantic. (Pennell 1994: 176)

López García quotes Juan Bautista Vilar, who testifies that Tangier was a vanishing point for Spanish liberals during the absolutist rule of Fernando VII (1813-1833). He says that

> "the proximity of the North African coast to the Spanish Mediterranean coasts and the existence of the Gibraltar springboard, made Morocco, and more precisely Tangier, the destination and base of operations for some emigrants from Southern Spain." (López García 2012: 2).

Some of the exiles converted to Islam. In 1860 657 Spaniards and 130 Anglogibraltarians lived in Tangier (López García 2012: 3ff).

Locally, however, it was, above all, Jewish communities' networks that remained important for the functioning of relations between the cities and for the destiny of the cities themselves. This, for example, became evident in 1825 when Sultan Moulay Slimane demanded the tribute to be paid by Swedish Consul Graberg in advance. Graberg could not raise more than 5000 piasters and asked the Jewish community of Gibraltar to advance him the rest (Miège 1996a: 99).

Illustration 34: 1869 Execution of a Moroccan Jewess (Sol Hachuel)

In 1830, a dispute arose between two Jews from Tangier within a synagogue. The governor wrote to Sultan Moulay Abderrahman (1822-1859) that the synagogues had become "place(s) of strife and dishonor" and that all synagogues should be closed. The sultan agreed to this but was convinced by Judah Benoliel to drop his decree (Benady 1989: 167).

The case of *Sol la Saddiqa* is to be understood in the context of the anti-Jewish positions of Sultan Moulay Abderrahman. Sol was born in 1817 in the medina of Tangier as the daughter of a Talmud specialist with strong connections to Gibraltar (González Vázquez 2015). The girl suffered a terrible fate as she was captured at the age of 15 by the Governor of Tangier, who wanted to marry her. Sol resisted the request to convert to Islam but was accused by a friendly neighbor of having already converted to Islam. Her insistence on the confession of Judaism was, therefore interpreted as a conversion *from* Islam and punished accordingly by the public decapitation that took place in Fez in 1834. Jews and some Muslims still venerate her today as tzadeket (saint). Jews honor her as *Sol HaTzaddikah* ('the just Sol'), Muslims call her *Lalla Suleika* (Holy Lady Suleika).[14] The story of Sol Hatchuel was first published in 1837, in Gibraltar (Romero 1837). The grandson of Sol's brother Yassachar, Solomón Buzaglo, was one of the three representatives of the Jewish-Moroccan deputies in the *Asemblea Legislativa* in the International Zone of Tangier, representing the interests of the entrepreneur Braunschwig.[15]

Benoliel, in addition to his activities as a diplomat and merchant, also had an impact on both communities. He co-founded the *Theatre Royal*[16] in Gibraltar and financed the *Nefusot Yehudah* Synagogue in Line Wall Road and the renovation of the synagogues in Tangier.

Between 1842 and 1920, Morocco had a consulate at 87-89 *Main Street* in Gibraltar, and the Governor of Tangier at the time of Moulay Abderrahman, Sidi Mohammed el Khetib, was a sugar and coffee trader "who, while he exercised the duties of a minister, continued to trade regularly at Tangier and Gibraltar" (De Amicis 1897: 81).

Some Muslims also settled in Gibraltar at this time, running small shops (Oda Ángel 2003: 18).

It seems, however, that in Gibraltar, Jews from Tetuán far outnumbered those from Tangier in number and influence – at least until the beginning of the 19th century.[17] *Abudarham Synagogue* in Parliament Lane – a foundation of Tetuáníes – was then already in the 1820s considered to be a focal point for new immigrants from Tangier and Tetuán (Lombard 1997: 84; Benady 1989: 169). The Jewish community of Gibraltar has increasingly oriented itself towards the communities of Morocco since the middle of the 19th century.[18]

Later, 4000 North African Jews sought refuge in Gibraltar during the Berber Wars (1859/60) (Chipulina 2013). The British administration – supported by the *Alliance Israélite Universelle* and other organizations from London and Paris – set up a refugee camp in North Front, where the refugees remained until the end of the turmoil in the same year (Benady 1993).

---

14   Descendants of Sol's brother still live in Tangier today. I had the honor of meeting one of his great-great-granddaughters during my field research.
15   Personal communication, Sidney Delmar, January 11, 2020.
16   https://gibraltar-intro.blogspot.com/2015/06/1847-theatre-royal-el-godsafedekin.html.
17   This is especially true for the Jews of 1777 (Howes 1991: 71; see also Benady 1989: 145; Chipulina 2014b).
18   When the Archduke and later Emperor of Mexico, Maximilian, visited Gibraltar (1859), for example, the Chief Rabbi of Tangier held a wedding (Benady 1989: 168). In the 1860s, Gibraltarian customs authorities did not allow the kidneys of slaughtered animals to be examined, as required by the Jewish authorities in Tangier. The junta of Tangier nevertheless allowed (exceptionally) the sacrificial animals to be exported to Gibraltar (Mitchell Serels 1996: 65).

Illustration 35: Jewish Refugees in Gibraltar, 1859

Morocco was still crucial for securing a British Gibraltar with supplies of all kinds, but Gibraltar was also important for Morocco and indeed for foreign trade. In the first half of the 19th century, Gibraltar had the fourth largest volume of trade of any Mediterranean city. Gibraltar, thus, replaced Cádiz as Morocco's most important trading partner (Miège 1996a: 70-71). The trade, which, for example, the Moroccan main port of Mogador conducted directly with London, never became nearly as important as Moroccan foreign trade with Great Britain, which was conducted via Gibraltar (ibid.: 71). Since English goods were particularly sought after in Morocco, goods from France, for example, were re-declared as 'English' in Gibraltar (ibid.).

Indeed, as far as the financial sector is concerned, Gibraltar was the most important center in the Western Mediterranean. Moroccan trade with Manchester and Marseilles, for example, was conducted through an account in Gibraltar. This had the advantage that payments and transfers could be made faster than the 90 days it would have taken via London and Paris. The fees and interest incurred were, thus, lower (ibid.: 100). The fast and linked communication was important in financial trading. The economic and financial news of *The Gibraltar Chronicle*, one of the oldest newspapers still published in the world (founded in 1801), was received throughout large parts of the Mediterranean region. Advantages were the British Navy and the many shipping lines that served Gibraltar:[19] News from Britain took less than a week to arrive via the convenient shipping connections, while the French mail from Marseille to Tangier took almost a month (ibid.: 103).

In order to be able to adapt more quickly to the often sudden changes in commodity prices, networks of traders operated in both cities, Tangier and Gibraltar, or owned property and family on both sides. The merchant Giuseppe Viale, Consul of the Kingdom of the Two Sicilies in Morocco, for example, lived and worked in Gibraltar but had a property in Tangier, where part of his family lived (ibid.: 104).

Tangier and Gibraltar were closely linked at an early stage in terms of infrastructure and technology.[20] Until 1860, it was *faluccas*,[21] small Arabic sailing ships that provided the link, as well as two other types of boat: The *mistick*[22] and the *schebecke*.[23]

Francisco Correa,[24] Atalaya and Olcèse guaranteed the naval connections between Gibraltar and Tangier. Correa rented his boat for 40 piasters per crossing (Bendelac/Miège 1995: 55). In 1860, Gibraltar's Bland Line established a permanent shipping connection to Tangier (Woolman 1998: 51).

---

19 Compagnie Bazin (Marseille-Cadiz), Peninsular and Oriental Steam Navigation Company (Southampton-Alexandria), General Screw Shipping Company (Liverpool-Constantinople), Levant Steam Packet Company (Liverpool-Alexandria) and Ligne Deppe (Antwerpen-Marseille) (Miège 1996a: 245).

20 A stopover in Tangier has several advantages compared to a stopover in Gibraltar: Port charges and ancillary costs are much lower, there are better conditions for forward and return freight, and a more suitable route for boats that only use charcoal to navigate the Strait (Cousin 1902: 13).

21 The smaller vessels that traveled between the two cities had a tonnage of less than 30 and a crew of five to six members (Bendelac/Miège 1995: 50).

22 The *misticks* had a main mast, a foremast in the direction of travel and a mizzen mast. It is 50 tons on average and the crew consists of seven to nine members.

23 The *schebecke*, on the other hand, is a three-master with lateen sails, averages 30 to 80 tons and has a crew of five to ten members.

24 In 1837, Joanna Correa was the widow of a Genoese boatman who traveled back and forth between the two towns (Finlayson 1992: 34).

Illustration 36: First Print of the Gibraltar Chronicle

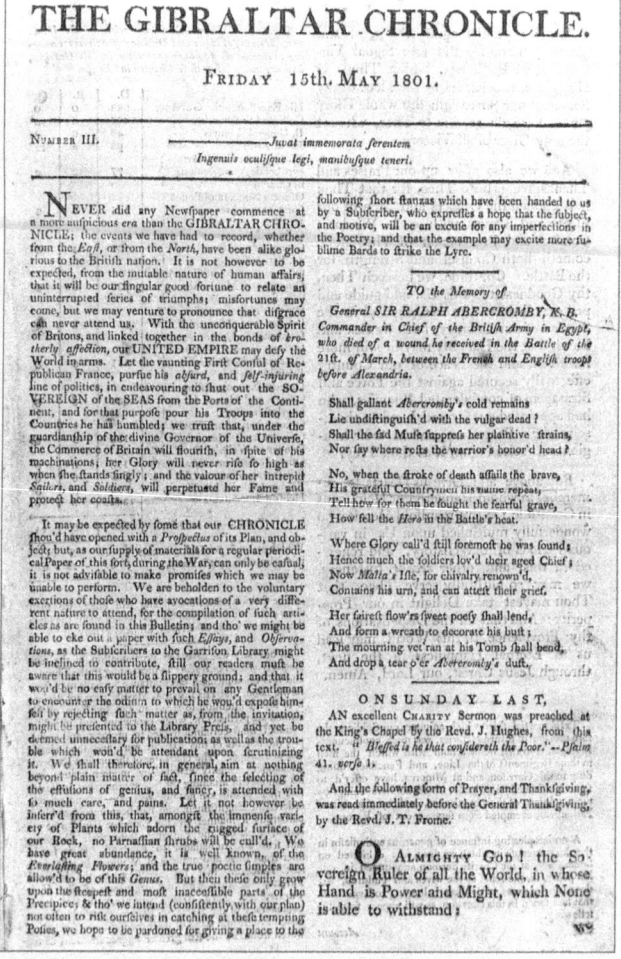

The English postal service was handled via Gibraltar: The first post office opened in 1857[25] and a post office on *Soq Dahkel* only opened in 1892.[26] It was closed down in

---

25 "The British post office had apparently been in operation since 1857, was based at the British Consulate and used stamps from Gibraltar. In 1907, a British post office was inaugurated and its first director was Roque Lyon of Gibraltar" (Ceballos López 2009: 155; translation by the author).

26 "The English postal service had for many years been operated from Gibraltar, where the English correspondence was concentrated and from where it was brought to Tangier by small

1957.[27] Mr. Griffin, representative of the *Telegraph Eastern Society*, opened an English telegraph office in Tangier in 1880. In the same year, the telegraph cables were laid to Gibraltar. But still in 1883, the authorities of Tangier communicated with Gibraltar by heliograph (Vaidon 1977: 107).

Illustration 37 (left): Rue du Télégraphe Anglais; Illustration 38 (right): Steamship Hercules

The ship *Hercules* brought between 50 and 100 cattle – in addition to fruit, vegetables and poultry – from Tangier to Gibraltar twice a week in the 1890s (Stoddard 1892: 207; Chipulina 2014a). The meat came from the farm *El Mediar* of Gibraltarian entrepreneur Abelardo Sastre (Chirop/Martínez 2018; cf. Laredo 1936: 331).[28] As late as 1902, beef, game, poultry and eggs were transported mainly from Tangier to Gibraltar, consequently, were more expensive in Gibraltar (Cousin 1902: 13).

In addition to diplomacy and trade, the relations between Morocco/Tangier and Gibraltar were also intensified in the 19th century. Thus, the sultans of Morocco, for example, Moulay Yazid (1790-92)[29] and Moulay Slimane (1798-1822), requested personal physicians trained by the British. In 1877, Emily Keene, the Sherifa de Ouazzane, brought the first serum for smallpox vaccination from Gibraltar to Tangier (Vaidon 1977: 130). Edward Taylor built the first steam mill in Tangier in 1878 to produce carbonated drinks. He exported part of it via Gibraltar (Miège 1996b: 337). Entrepreneur John M. S. De Moraville was born in Gibraltar but studied in Tangier (Laredo 1936: 228). In 1891, the majority of the British living in Morocco were Jewish, Gibraltarian or both (Miège 1996b: 294).

---

steamers which made the journey several times a week. However, it was not until 1892 that Sultan Moulay El-Hasan granted the English Minister Sir Ewan Smith the right to lease nine premises in the inner *souq* for sixty-five years to build the English postal service. Later, this post office was moved a little further down the road, where it is still located today" (Michaux-Bellaire 1921: 238; translation by the author).

27 The Gibraltar Chronicle, December 28, 1956.
28 Sastre da *Teatro Romea* was founded in Tangier in 1905 (Ceballos López 2009: 255).
29 In 1790, for example, a Dr. William Lempriere from Gibraltar began his work with the sultan, and in 1805, a Dr. Buffa came to Sultan Slimane (Vaidon 1977: 43).

Illustration 39: Moroccan Poultry Vendor in Gibraltar, 1930

The *Forêt Diplomatique* extends in the southwest of Tangier, from Boukhalef and Achakkar down to the river Tahadart. The forest got its name from the hunting parties that the diplomats conducted here. This tradition began in 1866 when the British Ambassador to Morocco, Sir John Hay Drummond Hay, received permission from Sultan Mohamed IV (1859-1873) for *pig sticking* at a distance of two to three hours from the city. In 1892, the hunting parties were officially transformed into an association, the *Tangier Tent Club*, for several years the *institution sociale la plus remarquable* of Tangier. During the First World War, their activities were suspended and the club reached a peak between 1925 and 1935. After the Second World War, the hunts ended (Miège et al. 1992: 34). Later, the citizens of the city adopted this terrain for excursions, picnics and scout overnight stays. Today, the forest is threatened by real estate speculators, as the growing city of Tangier is already pouring down to the nearby hills of the now no longer small hamlet of Mediouna.[30]

The hunts in the *Forêt Diplomatique* resembled those of the upper class on the other side of the Strait. The *Royal Calpe Hunt*, a tradition (Jackson 1987: 222) founded by the British in 1811 and lasting for 129 years, of joint hunting by British and Spanish dignitaries in the cork forests of the *Campo de Gibraltar* is still conjured up

---

30 If you enter *"Forêt Diplomatique Tanger"* into Google, the first seven pages will mainly show ads for apartments or newspaper articles about fires that were probably started by real estate speculators in order to make the actually protected forest accessible for their purposes.

today as a symbol of peaceful coexistence between Spain and Great Britain.³¹ In the late 19th century, Spanish and British economic interests increasingly intertwined throughout Andalusia.³²

In 1868, Drummond Hay proposed exchanging Gibraltar for Ceuta in order to safeguard British interests in the region (Vaidon 1977: 85). This plan was never realized. On the advice of Drummond Hay, Sultan Hassan I (1873-1894) decided to train 200 of his most promising officers in Gibraltar (Woolman 1998: 54).

Illustration 40: Past Times at Forêt Diplomatique 1910

He also recruited British and French officers, one of whom was Harry Aubrey de Vere MacLean of the 69th Foot Regiment in Gibraltar. He became Caid (General) and, thus, the most important man in the Moroccan army. In 1880, six cannons were delivered from Gibraltar to Tangier (Michaux-Bellaire 1921: 136). These and other Armstrong cannons were installed by Caid Edward Silva. Silva, son of Spanish parents, also came from Gibraltar; his military rank was awarded to him by Sultan Hassan I for having produced the first detailed map of Tangier in 1888. In Tangier, he married a Gibraltarian, Margarita Silva (Miège 1991: 85).

In 1880, Gregorio Trinidad Abrines and Antonio Molinari (Ceballos López 2009: 259)³³ from Gibraltar arrived in Tangier and founded the first printing works in the

---

31 King Edward VII and Alfonso XIII were patrons of the hunt before the First World War. The relationship between the two countries was further normalized with the marriage between Alfonso and Princess Elena of Battenberg, a granddaughter of Queen Victoria, in 1906, –except for the irreconcilable positions regarding Gibraltar.

32 In 1892, Great Britain built the railway line between Algeciras and Bobadilla, which connected the Andalusian South to the Spanish railway network; British companies developed the copper mines in Riotinto/Province of Huelva (Jackson 1987: 254).

33 In 1884, Molinari also installed the first telephone in Tangier (Miège 1996b: 324).

Illustration 41: Royal Calpe Hunt

city.[34] Molinari was a photographer and friends with Daguerre, the inventor of photography in France. He worked together with Cavilla, also from Gibraltar, who had run a photography business with his *compagnon*, Bruzón[35]. Cavilla comes from a Genoese family, his father Damian Cavilla (from Gibraltar) was married to Luisa Vantrai, who was born in Tánger in 1844 as the daughter of a French consular officer (Honorio 2015: 2). The first issue of their newspaper *Al Moghreb Al Aksa* appeared on January 28, 1883.

Madame Bruzón also owned a villa in Tangier,[36] which a lover had left to her. She took Antonia Gil y Gil, who had come to Gibraltar from Ronda with her three children, to Tangier as a maid.[37] One of the daughters, Mariquita Molina y Gil, was the mother of Spanish writer Manuel Vásquez. Mariquita worked in the hat shop of Madame Boissonet[38] in Calle Bousselham, which she later took over (Vásquez 2009:

---

34   However, the relations with Gibraltar did not end there: In *Villa Abrines*, for example, lived "Ana Povedano nee Raggio and her son Rodolfo Povedano," whose descendants still live in Gibraltar today. Personal communication, Guy Povedano, November 5, 2019.
35   Personal Communication, Paul Allemand, June 26, 2019.
36   "in the [...] Oxen Souk, today transformed into the Convent of the Adorers" (Vásquez Molina 2012).
37   Afterwards, Señora Gil y Gil entered the service of the Hassan family of bankers. Later, she opened a boarding house for Spanish country girls who were to be prepared for service in the homes of the wealthy in Tangier.
38   Boissonet was a famous Parisian hatter who had to take refuge in Tangier after a scandal that threatened the President of the French Republic.

18f; Pastor de Maria Campos 2019: 80f).³⁹ Manuel Vásquez Molina described in his novel *La vida perra de Juanita Narboni*, the situation of a Spanish woman from Tangier (and daughter of a Gibraltarian), who remains in the city as an elderly spinster after all relatives, friends and acquaintances, as well as other Europeans and Jews, have left the city. The homosexual author gave evidence of how the familiar city became a strange place.

The second printing house in Morocco was opened in 1886 by *Tanjawis* Isaac Toledano and Isaac Laredo, and Gibraltarian Agustin Lugaro (Malo 1953: 127). *El Diario de Tangier* was founded in 1889 by Gibraltarian Adolphe Franceron (Miège 1996b: 326). The fourth newspaper from Tangier, *La Africana*, was also published by a Gibraltarian – Eduard Hauglin (Laredo 1936: 241). The Journal *Cosmopolis* was founded by Anthony Sastre, son of the aforementioned Gibraltarian Abelardo Sastre, and by José de Benito (Ceballos López 2009: 261).

Illustration 42: Pension Gibraltar, Tangier

Gibraltar also played a central role in terms of restoration and the hotel industry. The first bathing pavilion in Tangier was called *Kety la Gibraltareña*. The *Hotel Continental* was opened in 1870 (Tafersiti Zarouila 2012: 213) by John Ansaldo from Gibraltar. *Hotel Bristol* at *Soq Dahkel*, built in the last years of the 19th century, also originally belonged to a Gibraltarian.⁴⁰ *Hotel Calpe* in the *Rue du Statut* (today

---

39 Here, history and stories flow together. In the novel *Entre Costuras* by Maria Dueñas, the young spy Sira buys her outfit in the shop of Madame Boissenet. The model from reality is British spy Rosalind Fox.
40 Padilla from Gibraltar was manager of the Hotel Bristol (De Reparaz 1922).

Pension Gibraltar in *Rue de la Liberté*) goes back to a Gibraltarian entrepreneur, Peter Saccone. The Saccones also owned the *Hotel Marco Polo*. A daughter of Italy's consul of Tangier, Petri, married one of the Gibraltarian Saccones. *Garaje Calpe* car dealership and workshop on *Rue Victor Hugo* also belonged to Gibraltarians.[41]

Eugenio Chappory (+1930) came to Tangier from Spain. He was the representative of Lloyds from London. Eugenio married Inés, the daughter of the Gibraltarian owner of the Hotel Cecil, Anibal Rinaldi. Their daughter Eugenia married Emiliano Rodriguez Marchena, who owned the Huertas de Marchena, a 30,000 square meter property in the city center.[42] The famous Villa Eugenia on the Boulevard in the middle of the property was named after her and is now demolished. In its place is now the residential block Tanger Boulevard.

Diego Jiménez Villalobos, Tangier's leading building contractor and engineer from a wealthy family from Casarabonela (Málaga), was married to a Scottish woman, niece of Bishop Armstrong of Gibraltar. Their son Diego Jiménez Armstrong built, among other things, the *Hotel Gibraltar* (1910).

> The building has an eclectic style that tends towards the modern. The architect decorated the facade with tiles. Wrought iron was used in a very original way to fill the space in the hollow arcades that support the balcony on the second floor. (Mribti 2015; translation by the author)

Father and son Diego Jiménez shaped the cityscape of International Tangier with their buildings in the Medina and the Ville Nouvelle.

Gibraltar also played an important role in the horse races in Boubana. Jockeys came from Gibraltar, as did the horse doctor Benrimoj. Many race horses, for example, those that took part in the horse races on the beach between Malabata and the *Hotel Cecil*[43] were also shipped over from the British colony, belonged to Gibraltarian family Cazés (España 1954: 161). Demographically, Southern Spain, Gibraltar and Tangier grew together closer and closer in the late 19th century. Of the 897 Spaniards who lived in Tangier in 1882, a particularly large number came from the provinces bordering the *Boughaz* (310 Prov. Cádiz, 139 Prov. Málaga, 39 Ceuta, 23 Gibraltar). (López García 2012: 7ff).

Strategically, Tangier remained a desirable place for foreign interests in the late 19th and early 20th century.

---

41 Elias Wahnon, Online platform A, December 7, 2016.
42 In 1937, they traveled to Germany with their sons Luis and Manolo Chappory Marchena. Manolo, in turn, married Concepcion Bisquerra. Manolo "left his five children and went with his young lover to Venezuela." Translation by the author. One of the children was Luis, another Quique (Enrique) and Rodriguito was later known as Dr. Marchena, a distinguished doctor.
43 Online platform A, Germán Obregón, January 14, 2019.

Illustration 43 : 1904 - Kidnapping Ion Perdicaris, Tangier

A significant event brings the USA more strongly into play as an actor in the struggle for influence in Tangier and Morocco. Ion Perdicaris was a Greek-American businessman who had the villa named after him built in 1872. Some of the two hundred trees and plants on the estate, for example, the eucalyptus trees, were imported from Australia. In 1904, the villa became the scene of an international incident, as the Berber rebel Raissouli had kidnapped the (alleged)[44] American in order to demand money and support from the USA in his quest to be recognized as Lord of the North. The American government sent warships to Tangier to persuade the sultan to comply with Raissouli's demands.[45] Although President Theodore Roosevelt had meanwhile been informed that Perdicais had already given up his American citizenship at this point in time, he had the liberation operation carried out to cover up his error. The Moroccan government submitted to American pressure and Roosevelt won the upcoming presidential election in a landslide victory.

---

44   It turned out that Perdicaris was no longer an American citizen at the time of his abduction.
45   In 1975, the incident was filmed as *The Wind and the Lion* and turned into a heterosexual love story: Sean Connery (in the role of Raissouli) kidnapped Perdicaris' wife (Candice Bergen), with whom he fell in love.

As early as 1887, Perdicaris advocated placing Tangier as a neutral free port under the joint control of the great powers (Finlayson 1992: 52). Especially Spain, France, Germany and Great Britain tried to outbid each other. Under the watchful eyes of the United States and Italy, the nations tried to bring Morocco and especially Tangier under their control.

The city and Morocco as a whole were central building blocks of imperial German foreign and colonial policy. Germany (Guillen/Miège 1965) not only tried to guarantee Morocco's independence against the interests of Great Britain, France and Spain as a protecting power but also to shield the many interests of German companies in Morocco – especially Mannesmann. Joseph Lasry, son of Gibraltarian Rabbi Samuel Lasry and an important figure in Tangier, was one of those notables who welcomed Kaiser Wilhelm II on his visit to Tangier in 1905 (Laredo 1936: 150f). The Emperor's visit was intended to underline Germany's commitment in and to Morocco.

Karl-Emil Schabinger von Schowingen worked in the German legation as an interpreter in the years 1902-1914. As a folklorist, he documented Moroccan stories and verses that were recited about markets and cultural and religious customs. Schabinger played a central role in one of the great conflicts of the present day: He implemented the plan of the *Great Jihad*, which Max von Oppenheim sought in World War I, as his successor in the *Department of Information for the Middle East*.

The German Empire attempted with this plan, largely unsuccessfully, to incite Muslim subjects of the British and French to revolt against the colonial powers.

4.3 Treaty of Fez and international statute

When Morocco was divided into a Spanish and a French protectorate in the Treaty of Fez (1912), Tangier received a special status: The resistance of the other nations was too strong to allow the city to be taken over by Spain or France. France, Spain and Great Britain began to work out a status for the city in Madrid in March 1913. During the First World War, the work on it came to a standstill and in the Treaty of Versailles, the three nations could not agree on a solution for Tangier: The Spanish insisted that the inhabitants spoke Spanish, so the city had to be taken over by Spain. The French argued with the dominating influence of the French economy; the British, in turn, distrusted the French and sided with Spain because they considered its administration incompetent, so that Britain, in turn, could extend its influence over Tangier. Finally, on June 29, 1923. the foundation of the International Zone (Zone) was decided, whose existence began on June 1, 1925. The Zone existed, with a short interruption by the Spanish occupation (1940-1945), until the integration into the Kingdom of Morocco in 1956.

Illustration 44 : The International Zone of Tangier

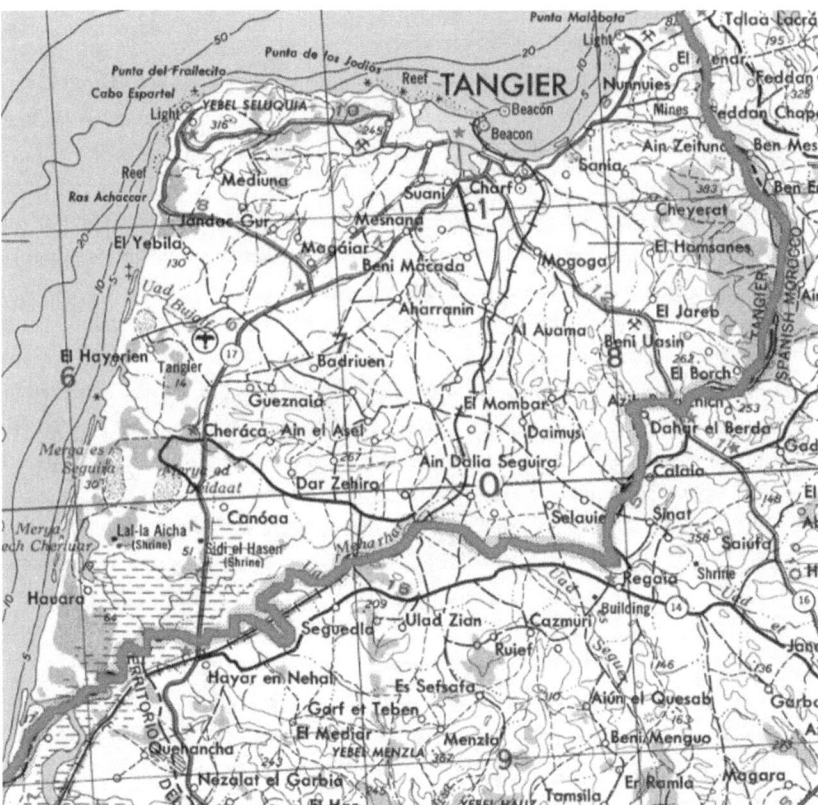

The Zone was a cosmopolitan and multicultural, 355 square kilometers large independent city under international administration. Even during the Zone period, Muslims always made up the majority of the population in Tangier but with strong Christian and Jewish minorities.[46] The Legislative Assembly was chaired by the Mendoub as the representative of the sultan. It had 32 members, including six Muslim and three Jewish subjects of the sultan. In addition, there were four Spanish and four French, three British, three American, three Russian, three Italian, one

---

46 In 1927, Tangier had 60.000 inhabitants, 35.000 of whom were Muslims, 15.000 Jews and 10.000 Europeans. In 1950, 150.000 inhabitants lived in the city, including 75.000 Muslims (mainly from the Rif, as well as 20.000 from Fahs), 43.000 Christians (of whom 20.000 were Spanish, 7000 French, 2500 Italian, 1300 British, 600 Portuguese, 600 Belgian, etc.) and 15.000 Jews (Tafersiti Zarouila 2012: 163, 156).

Belgian, one Portuguese and one Dutch (Ceballos López 2009: 108). The statute of 1923 provided for Spanish, French and British judges, in 1928, it was supplemented by judges from Belgium and Italy, and in 1950, by judges from the USA, Holland and Portugal (ibid.: 112).

> "The humanism of the customs officers pushed them to be interested only in the intentions of the travelers, not in the contents of their suitcases, putting the sign of lchalk on those which, opened, revealed themselves full to the brim with nylon stockings or perfumes. All imports into the zone, except for weapons and narcotics, were authorized and the tariffs so reasonable as to render concealment and fraud unnecessary: 12% at most on ordinary products and 7.5% on goods valuable products, such as silks, jewelry, false stones, gold and silver." (Vernay 1968: 15).
>
> Under the protection of the international administration, Tangier developed into one of the most important financial centres in the Western world. While more or less strict currency controls prevailed in large parts of Europe, the economy of Tangier was characterised by completely free movement of gold and foreign exchange, even after the Second World War [...]. A traditional asylum for endangered money, Switzerland was too close to the Soviet occupation zone in Austria to serve as a sanctuary for those fleeing a possible third world war. The bankers of Zurich and Geneva, sure of the loyalty of their customers, recommended them to turn to the international zone of Tangier, where they had correspondents and even interests." (Vernay 1968: 14)
>
> European – and to a lesser extent overseas – capital fled to Tangier to be stored in the vaults of countless banks before the curious eyes of the local tax authorities. "On the opulent pediments of the Boulevard Pasteur and the Rue Velasquez glittered by the dozen gilded plaques of anonymous companies bearing an abracadabra of letters, followed by the words 'et Cie', 'Ltd', or 'Incorporated'. Some opted for an emphasis: International Consortium of Transactions, Societe Universelle de Commerce et d'Echange, Omni-Trading, Tangier World Company, while others gave only confused indications of origin or intention: Commercial Union of Indochina and Africa, Holland Morocco Trading Company, Societe Zurichoise de Tanger. Very few chose the clarity." (Vernay 1968: 17ff)

At times, in Tangier, a city of some 100 000 inhabitants, there were some 400 companies engaged in banking activities, including 85 banks entered in the local register and therefore generally recognised. In addition, there were 14 branches of major foreign banks, as well as some 50 commercial companies, which were authorised to carry out banking transactions in accordance with their statutes. The rest consisted of "wild" bankers and money changers, most of whom were locals, while the regular banking institutions were mainly in the hands of Europeans and Americans.

The banking secrecy practised by Tangier banks was even more impenetrable than the famous Swiss model. For example, it was not uncommon for the owner of a particular bank account to be unknown even to the head of the bank.

Virtually anyone could start a bank, as there was no official authorisation and virtually no control. Yes, in Tangier, a bank did not need to keep books, to submit annual accounts or in any way to prove its solvency and probity. Periodic efforts to introduce a minimum of official supervision failed every time because of the resistance of leading financial circles. (Milikin 1966)

> "The most effective means of penetrating into the […] mysteries [of the economic realm] was to visit a sufficient number of lawyers and finance men, all of whom tried to demonstrate that the Tangier system could claim, if not originality, at least to superiority. In Switzerland, in Liechtenstein, in Panama too, they said, the government knew how to recognize that 'business is business' […]. But the authorities of Tangier had pushed to an unequaled degree of perfection the art of non-governing by reciprocal annulment of rival sovereignties. They took care, better than elsewhere, of the rigorous application of an almost total non-taxation, allied to an unlimited customs liberalism, the effects of which were multiplied by the fictitious warehouse regime. All goods imported by a Tangier company were in fact considered to be Tangiers, even if the latter resold them without having sent them through the international zone." (Vernay 1986: 18)

Tangier was a class society in which many lived under the poorest conditions. Barbara Hutton, the Woolworth heiress, is described as one of the few outrageously wealthy immigrants who took care of the poor and set up soup kitchens (Green 1992: 16).

Not far from the Zone, the population of the Rif, led by Abdelkrim, rose up against the Spanish protectorate power in the 1920s. The uprising was initially so successful that it led to the world's first republic to prevail against a European colonial power. The Rif Republic existed from 1920 to 1926, but it was battling against the Spanish and French throughout its existence. The British socialist John Arnall, who was sympathetic to the Rifeños, delivered about 400 hand grenades to Abdelkrim in 1922. The group of arms smugglers consisted of *Tanjawis* and Gibraltarians: Eugene Chappory (a member of the *British Chamber of Commerce of Tangier* and owner of the *Hotel Cecil*) and Roque de Soto Lyons (former head of the *British Post Office* in Tangier and founder of *Teatro Tivoli* (1913)) (Ceballos López 2009: 256). Arnall's wife Gertrude, pharmacist Ernest Florentine Bonich and Captain C.S.B. Mundey delivered medicines and relief supplies from the *British Red Crescent Society* to the Rif in 1924 (Sasse 2006: 173). The following dialogue from a completely different context, a crime novel by Edgar Wallace, could have come from smuggling during the Rif War:

"I propose giving Gibraltar a wide berth, and following the coast line to Tangier."
"Tangier wouldn't be a bad place to land if there weren't two of us," he went on.
"It is our being together in this yacht that is likely to cause suspicion. You could easily pretend that you'd come over from Gibraltar, and the port authorities there are pretty slack." "Or if we could land on the coast," he suggested. "There's a good landing, and we could follow the beach down, and turn up in Tangier in the morning – all sorts of oddments turn up in Tangier without exciting suspicion." (Wallace 1922)

Spain finally defeated the Republic of the Rif with the help of French troops and German poison gas.

In the course of the first half of the 20th century, the two cities merged with each other in ever more fields, for example, in terms of infrastructure. In 1931, a seaplane line was opened between Gibraltar and Tangier, as there was no airfield in the colony at that time. It was an amphibious vehicle because it was not always possible to land in the water in Tangier due to the rough sea. But since such planes were expensive and, moreover, technically very vulnerable, the governor of Gibraltar considered another solution: The construction of a runway on the Neutral Territory between Gibraltar and Spain (Finlayson 2018: 90-91).[47]

4.4 The Spanish Civil War and World War II

During the Spanish Civil War (1936-39), Gibraltar and Tangier were safe havens for the defeated Republicans (in Tangier, however, only until the fascist occupation in 1940), for example, for the Ramonet family, whose son Ignacio, as editor of the journal *Le Monde Diplomatique*, founded the globalization-critical movement *Attac* in 1997. The Galliano family of bankers also fled from Gibraltar to Tangier as early as 1936. They obviously feared that the uprising of the Francoist troops could also have Gibraltar as a target. The Gallianos stayed at *Bristol Hotel*, which belonged to Gibraltarian families – first to the Saccones, then to the Romeros. But Tangier was not entirely safe either: A Bland Line freighter, the *Gibel Dris*, was attacked by Spanish bombers, and British warships anchored in the bay were fired upon by Spain (Galliano 2003: 53f).

---

47 But in 1954 there was again a connection with *hidroaviones* (Ceballos López 2009: 155). The newspaper *La Dépeche Marocaine de Tangier* announced the ferry and flight connections daily in its column *Air et Mer*, as well as the ships arriving in the port. Among them are also the connections to Gibraltar.

The civil links between Tangier and Gibraltar did not break off during World War II. So, Señor Podesta,[48] a craftsman and son of a butcher from Tangier, came to Gibraltar in 1940 for professional reasons. There he met his wife, a Jewish-Maltese, with whom he was evacuated to England shortly afterwards. Their son Gil was born there in 1941. After the war, the family moved back to Tangier, lived in *Calle Dante* and then moved over to Gibraltar again in 1949.[49] His mother had converted to Catholicism, and she was now buried in the Catholic family tomb, because her (Jewish) family "had *kicked* her *out*", Gil says.[50] I met him in the 1990s at *Marina Court*, the apartment building where I lived during my fieldwork. Gil and his brother Patrick were the caretakers there.

> When I ask Gil in 2019 what he remembers of Tangier, he says that he attended the French school *École Berchet*. In front of the school there was a large well where camels were led to water. When he returned to Tangier with his father after many years and searched for the grave of his grandfather, who is buried in the Christian cemetery in Bubana, they were referred to the old guard of the cemetery, who sat at the gate and knew all the graves. Before they could say anything, the guard looked at the father and said: "You are the son of *Bachiba*. I recognize you." Gil's grandfather was known in Tangier under that name.[51]

Bachiba not only had a son (the same Señor Podesta) but also a daughter who married into a famous family of Tangier: the Gumperts. This family, originally from Austria-Hungary, provided the guards of the lighthouse of *Cape Spartel* from 1878. Joseph Philipp Gumpert, from Blottendorf in Bohemia, took over the management of this lighthouse at the crossroads between the Atlantic and the Mediterranean until his death in 1899, and his son José Ramón continued the task until 1927.

On December 13, 1911, the Gumperts rescued the passengers of the shipwrecked S.S. Delhi, which was smashed against the cliffs of *Cape Spartel*. Among them was the Duke of Fife, son-in-law of King Edward VII, and his daughters Maud and Alexandra. The goods, which were stored in the belly of the ship, could be salvaged and sent on to Gibraltar.

---

48   Patrick tells us that his father was from Tangier and came to Gibraltar at a young age; his great-grandfather was one of the first "whites" in Tangier, a butcher from Genoa. Field research diary Gibraltar, June 14, 1996.
49   Field research diary TanGib, November 1, 2019.
50   Field research diary Gibraltar, June 14, 1996.
51   Field research diary TanGib, November 1, 2019.

Illustration 45: The Gumpert family, Cap Spartel lighthouse1

The way led in the other direction during World War II: Mainly Gibraltarians and other Europeans[52] sought refuge in Tangier.[53] But Tangier was occupied by Spain on June 14, 1940, the day the Nazis conquered Paris, and it was feared that Spanish republicans, Jews and British living there would be persecuted:

Many Jews fled from Tangier after Germany recovered *Mendubia Palace*,[54] when it became known that a Nazi team had arrived to capture as many Jews as possible and send them to concentration camps. This did not happen, but it did lead several families – especially those who had worked with the Allies – to flee to Gibraltar and settle temporarily in the United Kingdom from there. (Ceballos López 2009: 79; translation by the author)

Gibraltarian entrepreneur Abraham Marrache also moved to Tangier with his wife and children Sam, Joshua and Luna,

---

52 Trudy Gardós, for example, a Hungarian Jewess, arrived in Tangier via Gibraltar, where she opened the bar *Trudy and her Piano* in the *Cine Mauriania* (Woolman 1998: 145).
53 "My mother had her parents in Tangier. So my father decided that we should go to Tangier. [...] I was ten years old in 1936. The war began in '39 [...]. So we moved to Tangier and stayed there for four years. [...] We were about five per cent Gibraltarian," says another source (Cosquieri 2015). Finlayson speaks of 700 (1996: 21) and 719 (ibid.: 147) Gibraltarians.
54 Kurt Rieth, who had organized the assassination of Austrian Chancellor Engelbert Dollfuss, stayed at the Rif Hotel and the German legation in the Mendoubia Palace on *Soq Barra*. Sydney Morning Herald 1944.

"because we could do it privately and because father got on well with the Spaniards (administration in North Africa)." The family lived in *Calle Velasco*, Luna's brother Sam worked as a mail courier. Luna had private tutors and flirted a lot with young men, many parties were celebrated in her magnificent property "but I didn't know in what danger I was: The Germans had all our names to take us to the concentration camp [...] I would have been a second Anne Frank."[55]

Gibraltarian Christians in Tangier were able to send their children to local schools[56] or to the Christian Brothers' school in *Calle Holanda* (Galliano 2003: 70; Ceballos López 2009: 214), which had also been evacuated from Gibraltar. A number of Gibraltarian local celebrities such as Louis Vasquez,[57] Albert Francis[58] and Johnnie Stagnetto,[59] Mariola Russo (Brufal de Melgarejo 2008), James Galliano[60] and Leslie Cardona[61] had previously attended the Christian Brothers' school in Line Wall Lane as children, and then with the same teachers later in Tangier. Once again Francis Cosquieri (2015):

[Four Christian Brothers] went over to Tangiers too [...] in order to be with the Gibraltarians. Brother O'Bryan, Brother Mercy, Brother Healy and Brother O'Toole. They opened up a school – make up school – and one of them came over to Gibraltar – he was allowed to come over back to Gibraltar – and collected [...] Whatever books he could manage, from the Sacred Heart School and he took them over.

Although Tangier was occupied by Spain, the situation during the Spanish occupation was characterized *only* by a deceptive calm. In the end, the Francoists *only* persecuted Spanish Republicans who had found refuge in the city.

Tangier remained a contested trophy – the battle was fought silently, because it was not military but carried out by secret services and intelligence. The British secret service was active against Germany during World War II. The Strait and

---

55 Interview with Luna Benzecry, December 20, 1996. Luna and her husband „married in Tangier [...] He died young around 1954 or 1955. He died of a badly treated fractured leg. My auntie was pregnant with Jackie at the time. It was tragic. He died suddenly on the day of the feast of Purim which is the most joyous of all Hebrew feasts." Personal communication, Joshua Marrache, Field research diary TanGib, November 26, 2018.
56 Tita Stagnetto attended the French school (N.N. 2000: 118).
57 April 30, 2010, http://www.rockjottings.com/docs/1282129904vasquez,%20louis%201.jpg.
58 The Gibraltar Magazine, February 2015 http://www.rockjottings.com/docs/1455830502img44 2.jpg.
59 The Gibraltar Magazine, July 2007 http://www.rockjottings.com/docs/1236448481johnniestag netto1.pdf.
60 The Gibraltar Magazine, September 2010: 24f.
61 The Gibraltar Magazine, March 2008. http://www.rockjottings.com/docs/1236448702lesliecar dona1.pdf.

especially the control over Gibraltar and Tangier had to be guaranteed for the Allies in any case.

Probably the best known representative outside the world of the secret services was Ian Fleming, author of the James Bond novels. Fleming worked at deciphering in Gibraltar within *Operation Goldeneye*. The latter observed the correspondence between Spain and Hitler's Germany, particularly regarding a possible conquest of Gibraltar by Franco's troops. In this context, Fleming also followed Henry Greenleaves, who had opened a contact office of the British secret service in Tangier (Simmons 2018).

Colonel William Eddy was a Briton born in Syria, who later received American citizenship. He organized radio stations in Casablanca, Oran, Algiers, Tunis and also in Tangier that agitated against Germany. He succeeded in hiring the ethnologists, Gordon Browne and Carleton Coon, as agents in Tangier. The group sometimes met at the Buckingham family's *Farhar Hotel* (Fowler 2009: 181; O'Donnell 2014: 34).[62] The Eddy Group knew that there was a German post on the *Mershan Cliffs*, which sent messages to the submarines of the Axis powers in the Strait via infrared links (Vaidon 1977: 238; Galliano 2003: 72).[63] The German base *Luchs* (lynx) at 4 *Rue de la Falaise* was blown up by a bomb in the early morning of January 12. 1943[64]

---

62   The Buckingham family's social activities are regularly reported in the *Tangier Gazette* in the issues I have reviewed between 1955 and 1962.

63   "Spain was not Neutral as everybody has been led to believe. They were Non-Belligerent which meant that although they had not declared war on the Allies they still supported the Axis (Germany and Japan). Proof of this were the three Spanish armed branches of Navy, Air Force and Army (Division Azul) that were fighting alongside Germany in the Baltic and Russian Front. They allowed the Germans to have a tanker the Fulgor in Cadiz harbour where the U-Boats would come in at night to refuel. They had Infra Red Ray stations at Punta Carnero and Tangier (Rue de la Falaise) to monitor the convoys and inform submarines in the Mediterranean and Atlantic they were coming their way. The Tangier one was blown up by the British SOE and they told Franco that the other one would also be blown up if he didn't do something about it, it was removed. The Rescue bomb at Tangier had to do with this episode unfortunately it blew up prematurely. The Italian ship Olterra in Algeciras harbour with its human torpedoes, right under our noses. The spy and sabotage ring of Falangists led by Blas Castro, a fanatic Falangist. The barracks at San Roque had many German instructors teaching many Spanish troops the art of war. Manilva was chosen by Germany to practise the take over of the Rock and on and on. [...]" Tito Vallejo, (Online platform I, April 12, 2013).

64   After rapid intervention by the firefighters who had been driven to the site, they were only able to recover the remains of a woman from the rubble which had been transferred to the French hospital. The hospital, which like many buildings in the area suffered the consequences of the explosion, had numerous windows broken by the explosive wave. Minutes later, an injured man was found near the site and was treated and taken to the nearby Spanish hospital, where his death was confirmed shortly afterwards. At dawn, the two bodies were identified and residents of the villa such as Jonard Quiriacao, a merchant marine Greek who

– shortly before that, the British ship *Rescue* exploded in a first and failed attempt to bring the bomb from Gibraltar to Tangier (Galliano 2003: 72-73).

There was an English spy institution in *Rue Shakespeare*, also in *Mershan* (Pons 1990: 68). From there, young *Tanjawis* were taken down to the coast, from where they were transferred by fishing boats to larger ships. They were then brought to Gibraltar, where they received military training to fight for the national liberation movements against the Third Reich.[65]

In his book *A History of North Africa: The Anthropologist as Agent of the OSS* (1980), Coon reports on "his work in North Africa during the Second World War" and describes his contribution to espionage and arms trafficking under the guise of anthropological research on the ground.[66] Coon developed exploding plastic donkey and camel poo to destroy German tanks.[67]

He did his doctorate on the Berbers of the Rif and then researched tribal structures in Albania, Ethiopia and Yemen. When he died in June 1981 at the age of 76, an obituary in the *New York Times* praised him as "one of the last great anthropologists."[68]

The adventurer Marguerite d'Andurain owned the luxury yacht *Djeilan*, with which she often crossed the Strait between Gibraltar and Tangier. Madame d'Andurain was a dazzling personality who made the Arabic region her home. In 1925, she opened a beauty salon in Cairo; later she traveled to Syria. In Palmyra, she ran the *Hotel Zenobia* and a horse breeding ranch. She converted to Islam and in 1933 planned a trip to Mecca but only got as far as Jeddah. During the war – sources are not quite sure about this – she worked for SS General Reinhard Heydrich. After the war, it was proven that she worked for Austrian Bishop Alois Hudal, who organized the so-called *Rat Line* and was a central figure in the *Odessa Organization*.

It is said that during these passages, Madame d'Andurain smuggled Nazi mandarins: the commander of Treblinka, Franz Stagl; Adolf Eichmann; the head of the Gestapo in Italy, Erich Priebke, and others, to Morocco, from where they were passed on to Argentina, Brazil, Peru, Uruguay or Chile. It is testified that the 'Butcher of Mauthausen', Aribert Heim (Stein 2014), fled to Egypt via Tangier and also that

---

had arrived in Tangier in June 1940 on the ship Florida, and his wife, a Cuban woman named Carmen Ortiz, were identified." (Online platform, Mehdi Zoubairi, December 2, 2016)

65 The uncle of Dominique Pons, who as a Jew was under the protection of the Netherlands, was trained for the Dutch underground army (Pons 1990: 69), and the same happened to the uncle of Rachel Muyal (Rousseau 2019: 22).

66 Wikipedia (n.d.a).

67 https://www.nps.gov/articles/oss-in-action-the-mediterranean-and-european-theaters.htm.

68 Coon (1939) pleaded for a specifically American anthropology, in which archaeology, physical and cultural anthropology were practiced together. This is hardly common practice in the United States today.

Illustration 46 : Notice about d'Andurains possible assessination

MARGA D'ANDURAIN A-T-ELLE ÉTÉ ASSASSINÉE ?

A Tanger, où l'on croit qu'elle est simplement partie son « assassin » est condamné à 20 ans de bagne

Friedrich von Freienfels, concentration camp doctor in Dachau, Mauthausen and Auschwitz, "disappeared" via Tangier (Soto 2014) as *Dr. Pirata* and under the pseudonym *Dr. Luis Gurruchaga*.

Men around Madame d'Andurain often died a strange death. I quote Wikipedia here for a change:

> She came into the focus of the European and US press when she was arrested in Nice at the end of 1946 on the charge of poisoning her godson and nephew [he had written on the back of a metro ticket: "The chocolate Marga gave me tasted strange"], and a second time two years later when she was murdered on her yacht in Tangier Bay. During this time, she was given bold terms to describe her life in the Middle East: "Imitator of the Brinvilliers," "spy and double agent" who "outshines Mata Hari," "Amazon of the desert,"" "ex-queen of Palmyra," "adventurer of 20 crimes" and "poisoner." It was expected in vain that after her arrest she would

be held responsible for a whole series of deaths in her surroundings for which she could not be proved guilty until now."[69]

On the night of November 5, 1948, she was found dead in the bay of Tangier. She had been murdered by Hans Abele and his lover Helena Kuntz, two of their employees and former Gestapo agents (Frattini 2004: 275).

Rosalind Powell Fox was a British spy in World War II and active between Tangier, the Spanish Protectorate, Gibraltar and the *Campo de Gibraltar*. At the Olympic Games in Berlin in 1936 she met and fell in love with Juan Luis Beigbeder, later Franco's Foreign Minister. Franco suspected that Fox was working for the British secret service, but the British refused her entry into Gibraltar (Cecilia 2009). Beigbeder was deposed by Franco and exiled to Ronda. Fox passed away in Guadarranque in 2006, within sight of Tangier and Gibraltar. Her relationship with Beigbeder served as a model for the popular Spanish television series Eltiempoentrecosturas (first broadcast in 2013/14).

British subjects were expelled from the Campo to Gibraltar, as were members of the British Mining Authority of Riotinto (Province of Huelva) during the Spanish Civil War and in World War II. This also concerned sympathizers of the Francoist Regime, such as Montague W. Brown, the director of the *Compañía del Ferrocarril de Zafra a Huelva* (Ramirez Copeiro de Villar 1996: 260ff).

During the Second World War, most Gibraltarian civilians were evacuated from the strategically important military post, especially to London, Northern Ireland, Jamaica or Madeira. There are records of these official evacuations in the *Gibraltar National Archive*, thus, exact figures are available. At the end of the war, the repatriation plan for those Gibraltarians evacuated to Great Britain, Jamaica and Madeira provided for them to be sent back not only to Gibraltar but also, in part, to Tangier.

But those civilians who, like the Marrache family, went to Tangier did this on their own initiative, consequently, there are no official figures available. According to estimates, there were supposed to be approximately 700. These were often Gibraltarians who already had family in Tangier or worked there.[70] Many families of those few Gibraltarians who remained in Gibraltar during the war because they worked for the Ministry of Defence also moved to Tangier, as they could be visited by their menfolk there.[71] Thus, in 1941, the banker's wife Madame Galliano went

---

69 Wikipedia n.d.c.
70 Mary Lou Benson got a job at the British Consulate in Tangier (N.N. 2000: 20). Rousseau (2019: 15ff) also mentions the Gibraltarians in Tangier.
71 "The evacuation did not stop menfolk from visiting their wives overseas. There were also some families like mine that opted to go (at their own expense) to Tangier during the war. In fact that was where I was born. My father stayed in Gib but commuted to Tangier. I know about 10 other Gibraltarians that were born in Tangier during WW2." Online platform C, Donny Cantwell, April 3, 2019. "My family on my mother's side spent five years in Tangier during the war,

to Tangier with her children; her husband joined them when he was no longer considered necessary for the garrison in Gibraltar (Galliano 2003: 70). However, as a precaution, British authorities handed to their representatives in Tangier a list (*Proclaimed List of Certain Blocked Nationals* [Rev IX, July 17, 1941]) of names of shops whose owners supported the Axis powers (ibid.: 71). This list is suitable for questioning and breaking today's narrative of the peaceful coexistence of religions and nationalities. Obviously, the listed German names (e.g. Wissman, Losbichler, Schnitzer, Hafner, Haggenmacher, Bantl, Huber, Jangl and Ballweg) were amalgamated with Hitler's Germany. Some of them have German but others Spanish first names. It can be assumed that they were either embassy staff of the German representation or Hispanic German people who came to Tangier with the Spanish occupation in 1940. The majority of those listed are *Tanjawis*, however, and it not only tells of the fascist amalgamation of local notbales (i.e. Petri, Porte) that are remembered and held in mythical esteem by the elderly participants in the online forums, not only by members of the Italian minority with fascist Italy but also by *Tanjawis* with a Spanish, Portuguese or Flemish background, as well as by some Sephardim from old Jewish families (such as Levy, Bendellac, Chocron, Trojman). A similar list of the collaborators in the Spanish Protectorate (e.g. Tetuán and Larache) also shows Germans (e.g. Renschhausen and Schultz) but only one Sephardic name (Alfonso Benaim Hatchuel). In another document (Meyer 2014: 526ff), three Moroccan nationalist leaders were employed by the Nazis: Abd el Khalaq Torres, leader of the *Nationalist Reform Party*; Brahim Wasani, leader of the *Nationalist Party*; and Ahmed Balafrej.

After the withdrawal of Spain in 1945, the International Statute of Tangier came into force again. The international institutions began to work as before, Tangier once again prospered economically as a financial center and the city expanded spatially into the *Ville Nouvelle* south and east of the *Boulevard*. Undamaged by the war, Tangier was once again a beacon of modernity. The easy life after the catastrophe, which had left the city largely intact, was maintained for a short decade. On the horizon, however, there were already signs of a profound change.

4.5. 1948 Alija and later

Until the 1950s, Gibraltarian Jews were closely linked to Jewish communities in Morocco through family, culture, and social and economic networks and, through

> my father, who worked for the Ministry of Defence, stayed in Gibraltar and would visit when possible, during one of those visits he narrowly missed death when a bomb exploded soon after he disembarked from the ferry." Online platform C, Ruthie García Mifsud, April 3, 2019.

common institutions of religious law, came[72] closest to the type of cross-border society.

> "On holidays, it's good to have a Cohen to give the blessing. When there were Jews in Morocco, we used to bring them from Tangier. We brought someone poor, paid him the fare and gave him a present to bless us. Now it's not like that anymore, there are hardly any Jews left in Morocco," says Momy Levy in 1996, later mayor of Gibraltar.[73]

Tangier, but also Kenitra and Tetuán, became a reservoir for spouses and religious specialists.

> Moroccans who married Gibraltarians Ibgui to Benady, Castiel to Attias, Abergel to Benzaquen, Bensimon to Hassan, Edery to Benamor, Edery to Benaim, Delmar to Massias, Suissa to Benatar [...].[74]

In 1948, 270.000 Jews lived in Morocco and around 15.000 in Tangier. Today, there are fewer than 6000 in the whole country and only a handful in Tangier. After Sultan Mohammed V (1927-1953; 1955-1961) demanded Moroccan independence when he gave a speech in Tangier in 1947, many Jews left the country in an atmosphere of insecurity and impoverishment and emigrated – mostly via Gibraltar – mainly to Israel, Canada and South America.

Of course, the exodus was also spurred on by the founding of the State of Israel, which provided a home for Jews from the Diaspora. During the Israeli War of Independence in 1948, the relatively moderate sultan joined his Arab neighbors and forbade his Jewish subjects to emigrate. In this case, one can speak of the classical *push* and *pull factors* carved out in migration studies.

Between 1949 and 1956, 90.000 Jews left the country. In 1956 (Laskier 1990: 469), the year of the annexation of Tangier to the new nation-state of Morocco, ships transported 150 Moroccan Jews from Tangier to Haifa – via Gibraltar. The *Zion*, for example, docked in Gibraltar on February 24, 1956.[75]

The leader of the independence party *Istiqlal*, Allal El Fassi, announced in March 1956 that Moroccan Jews and Muslims would be treated equally.[76] The attitude of Jews in Morocco, however, was anything but uniform, certainly not regarding their stance toward independence. Laskier (1990: 267f) singles out three main directions that existed within Moroccan Jewry: One group preferred Western education, especially French education. This group preferred to seek their future in the nations of

---

72 Leading authorities of the Talmud and Kabbalah from Morocco became Rabbis in Gibraltar.
73 Field research diary Gibraltar, November 11, 1996.
74 Personal Communication, Joshua Marrache, July 7, 2019.
75 The Gibraltar Chronicle, February 24, 1956.
76 The Gibraltar Chronicle, March 19, 1956.

the West and in South America. A second group saw their future in Israel. Finally, a third group looked for Jewish-Muslim integration or fusion within Morocco. This third group was not homogeneous either, but they put their hopes in the tolerance of and protection by Sultan Mohammed V, and many of their protagonists were active in the Independence Party *Istiqlal*. However, different currents were also in conflict within the party and while most Jews were able to follow the leftist leader Mehdi Ben Barka, they were afraid of the orthodox Muslim wing around Al Fassi. When this wing became established in the party, the leader of the Jewish community in Tangier, David Laredo, no longer saw a secure position for Jews in Morocco because Al Fassi was oriented towards the anti-Israeli policy of Egyptian President Nasser.

More and more Jewish Moroccans left the country. The great wave of emigration from Tangier took place in 1961 and 1962.[77] Jews from all over Morocco gathered on a plot of land behind *Hotel Cecil* (Vaidon 1977: 318-319), which was later called *Campito de los Judíos*. They waited there for an opportunity to leave the country. The Jewish community in Gibraltar, under the leadership of its President Sam M. Benady, QC, and with the active support of the Israeli Consulate and the *Jewish World Agency*, organized a transitional camp in Eastern Beach. The refugees were medically examined there and then flown to Marseille. It was the smuggler family Victory who organized the departure of Moroccan Jews and brought many of them directly to Eastern Beach in Gibraltar. It is said that the family even did this without any payment.[78] One of the nurses, Marcelle Bensimon (Searle 2019: 39ff), came from Tangier and married Sir Joshua Hassan, later Prime Minister of Gibraltar.

> The husband of Marcelle's sister Mery, Nisso Gabai, was a powerful man in the Jewish community of Tangier and beyond (e.g. as Consul Deputy of Italy and President of Casa de Italia), he died on August 16, 2020. Gabai had influence in high circles, he was turned to when there was something to be fixed and arranged. For example, he solved the problem of a young couple. A young Jewess had become pregnant by her Catholic boyfriend and they wanted to get married. In Morocco, however, a marriage was only recognized by the state if it was concluded by a rabbi. But he refused. Gabai sent the two to his brother-in-law in Gibraltar, where they married. As a British married couple, the bond has now also been recognized in Morocco.[79]

Sam M. Benady, QC, whom I interviewed in 1996, writes in his memoirs:

---

77   On October 21, 1957, 250 Moroccan Jews were arrested near Tetuán while trying to leave the country with invalid passports. The Gibraltar Chronicle, October 21, 1957.
78   Personal Communication. Informant, name and date available but not necessary to be mentioned..
79   Fieldnote September 16, 2020.

Most of the refugees had no passports and they were brought in via Spain with the help of the Franco Police. Many embarked on the North African beaches, without any personal belongings, in a small vessel called the Egoz, chartered by the Jewish Agency. I will never forget one terrible night in January 1961 when the Egoz sank in terrible weather with 43 refugees on board. [...] In spite of this tragedy, hundreds of thousands of immigrants went through Gibraltar. (Benady 1993: 84)

Ernest Wiley (*1935) comes from the *Spanish Quarter* in Tangier and has lived in Gibraltar since 1951. His father had been a harbor pilot. At the age of 16, he entered the French diplomatic service. As France's representative in Gibraltar, he issued travel documents to Jews fleeing from Tangier via Gibraltar to Marseille – including the victims on the *Egoz*.[80] The *Egoz* disaster was anti-Semitically instrumentalized, as the action was illegal from a Moroccan point of view: Jews were smuggled out of Morocco in secret.[81]

As a result, there were arbitrary arrests and assaults. Consequently, thousands of tracts were distributed among Zionist activists in Morocco, denying any hope of a prosperous life in the country. This, in turn, fueled anti-Jewish sentiment.

Illustration 47: EGOZ after drowning (Gibraltar)

In addition to this political developement, there is another motive for the emigration of Moroccan Jews: "In the years following Moroccan independence there

---

80   Field research diary TanGib, March 6, 2020.
81   "[T]he Minister of Information, Mawlay Ahmad Alawi, blamed the tragedy on the Zionist organizations which 'incited' Jews to leave Morocco" (Laskier 1990: 485).

were numerous cases of underage Jewish girls being kidnapped and forcibly converted to Islam in order to marry Moroccan Muslims." This happened particularly in 1961/62 and was discussed in the Jewish-Moroccan press as well as in Al-Alam, the newspaper of the dominant Istiqlal party (Elbaz 2015: 48).

The Jewish community of Gibraltar was under the sovereignty of the Sephardic *Beit Din* in London until 1953/54. The resignation of R. Solomon Haham Gaon led to a split within the *Beit Din*, as a result of which, Gibraltar was placed under the sovereignty of Ashkenazi London *Beit Din*. Thus, the Sephardic community fell under the sovereignty of an Ashkenazi court.

In the years leading up to the *Six-Day War* in 1967, most of the remaining Moroccan Jews emigrated in various waves. There was another attack in Tangier in June 1967, this time on the leader of the community.

> His name was Rabbi Yamin Cohen.[82] He became the leader of the Tangiers community. He had a wonderful voice, unfortunately [...] a Moroccan 'crazy' stabbed him in the throat. (Luckily, Rabbi Yamin Cohen's sons were there – they were tall, big guys – and they pulled the aggressor away and got their father to Hospital). He survived and was the person to ask on many religious points. He was a very happy and funny man, well respected by people of all Faith's in Tangiers.[83]

In short: The situation was getting worse and every reaction led to a spiral of counterreactions.

As mentioned before, there are very few Jews left today in Tangier and throughout Morocco. Even though the societies of Morocco and Israel are far apart, there are close and special relations – which cannot be discussed here – between the two countries on many levels (cf. e.g. Kabbaj 2018; Naba 2018; Times of Israel Staff 2018). The port of Tangier plays a special role in this: "In the free port of Tangier, goods from Israel are re-labelled and reloaded for export to Muslim countries, which like to buy Israeli products but value discretion" (Schmid 2018).

There was still a Moroccan consulate in Gibraltar. Ahmed Youssoufi worked there. After his return to Morocco, he settled in Tangier. His son Abderrahman Youssoufi served as Prime Minister from 1998 to 2002 (Mousjid 2018a).

---

82 He originally came from Meknés, worked as a paperboy for the magazine *El Porvenir* and made his Talmud studies on the side. He was married to the daughter of Rabbi Yehuda Benchimol. Online platform A, Maurice Castiel, March 20, 2020.
83 Personal Communication, Joshua Marrache, July 7, 2019.

4.6 The 1950s – Tangier before independence[84]

Morocco had been formally colonized quite late with the Treaty of Fez in 1912. In contrast to Algeria, for example, which had been conquered by France in 1830 (a conquest that was challenged by other powers), Morocco was, especially from a strategic point of view at the entrance to the Mediterranean Sea, the coveted object of France, Spain, the USA, Great Britain and the German Empire. The division into the two protectorates was, to a certain extent, a compromise, in order not to let neither France nor Spain dominate but to still give the other powers a certain influence. In Tangier, this situation, which had already been resolved for the rest of the country in 1912, lasted until 1956, so to speak. In this respect, Tangier can be described as pre-colonial; a refined and sophisticated formulation of the pre-colonial situation dominated, so to speak, until 1956, for it was not dominated by a colonial power in the classical sense.

However, if one does not focus on this unambiguousness but on the dominance of a single foreign power, then Tangier in the Zone period was, at first glance, naturally a colonial city: Natalia Ribas Mateos speaks of a "predominio universal colonialist" (Jebrouni 2019: 13). Nevertheless, there were special features here as well. Firstly, the International Zone (1923) and the period between the Treaty of Fez and the establishment of the Zone (1912-1923) were preceded by a period in which consuls and local authorities took the fate of the city into their own hands: With the creation of the *Comisión Internacional de Higiene y Limpieza* (1888), which not only took care of local health issues but also of customs, public debt control, local taxes and other local matters. This became the *Comisión de Higiene y Policia Urbana* in 1903 (Ceballos López 2009: 59). This commission was made up of Moroccan Muslims and European dignitaries, but mostly local Jewish subjects of the sultan, who were also often the patrons of European nations. This enabled local interests, which were not necessarily always linked to the interests of the sultanate or foreign nations, to be articulated early on.

The International Zone was able to build on these local institutions. There was a Legislative Assembly in the Zone period, but its members were not elected but appointed. As far as the institutions of the Zone were concerned, there were fewer Muslim and Jewish subjects of the sultan on the committees of the city than representatives of the foreign powers. But none of the nations represented were dominant, so that there was never a clear majority in the bodies, which could have been named European-Moroccan along the dichotomy, for example. France, however, had the largest contingent of representatives, for one cannot count only the four representatives of the *Grande Nation* but must add the nine of the Kingdom

---

84   I would like to take this opportunity to thank two colleagues in particular whom I do not want to put at risk.

of Morocco. The sultan was dependent on France (and to a lesser extent on Spain), and his sphere of influence was mainly the protectorates. Many speak of Morocco's political system still being dependent on France.

Regarding Morocco as a whole, Rachik (2012) and Burke (2014) have explored how and what kind of knowledge social sciences have generated about the "simple" natives.

This is true in Tangier in a different way than in the other parts of Morocco, for many locals contributed to knowledge production.[85] The consular system is largely responsible for the fact that it allowed local Muslims and Jews to become protected by the foreign powers. Although these were subordinate to the foreign employers, in the local context, they were anything but powerless as dragomen, translators and negotiators since they guaranteed the maintenance of the system on the spot.

Colonial systems are characterized not only by the fact that the institutional power is in the hands of a foreign power, but the transformation of the mental constitution of the natives as inferior is significant. Even if there were many natives who participated in it: The poorer classes in particular were often not subjects but objects of knowledge production.[86] They were taught that their way of thinking, living and organizing existence was inferior to that of the colonizers. Especially the focus on magical practices, sorcery and the cults of saints became cornerstones for this attitude toward the poor. This also affected poor Jews and Spaniards from the working class, but above all, Muslims of the lower class:

> The representation of the cosmopolitan city literally took shape at the end of the 19th century. Moroccans are part of this world of diversity and are the only inhabitants of Tangier to lose their importance and relinquish dominance to the Europeans. The colonialist character of the texts written by Spanish travelers in past centuries is as undeniable as the undeniable concept of the dream, which is linked to the temporality of Tangier, which feminizes its spaces and its inhabitants and whose sun produces narcotic effects. (Jebrouni 2019: 76-77; translation by the author)

However, as noted elsewhere, the

> "tendency to polarize characterizes much of the literature. Disputes over fundamental values take on a stridently ideological cast, and outcomes are often seen in the absolute, either as total defeat or complete victory for one side or the other. But reality is far more complex,"

---

85 Here, however, a distinction must be made between European/modern educational knowledge and traditional local knowledge, as well as scholars such as Guennoun and others, where Arabic was the language of instruction.
86 However, there were thinkers who tried to change this, for example, Abdelkébir Khatibi.

as Gilson Miller demonstrates in the evolution of Tangier's water system. She shows that "ideas interpenetrated, merged and reemerged in a vigorous dynamic of exchange" (Gilson Miller 2001: 27). That is true for the case of Tangier, as Gilson Miller notes:

> "Not all Europeans in Tangier were enlightened universalists and not all Moroccans were believers in blood brotherhood. A range of attitudes and strategies were part of the cultural baggage of each, and to formulate their encounter in overly simplistic terms would be misleading" (ibid.).

Illustration 48: Scene from El Chergui 1975

In addition to these remarks, locals of all faiths had to adjust in one way or the other to the dominant political and social conditions, which created a structural colonial mentality. This is clearly named – or shown – in artistic works by locals. Vásquez Molina (1962: 20), for example, describes the factotum Hamú, a domestic worker who has established himself in the "classic role of the Muslim who has settled into the sweet slavery of colonialism." The heroine in Moumen Smihi's film *El Chergui*, the wife of a simple imam, observes in one of the most impressive scenes such a vibrant 'Hamú' as he wordlessly shields the arrival of his European master's guests from the simple riffraff with his eyes (e.g. Limbrick 2020: 57). El Ouriaghi (2013: 116) corresponds to this exclusion of Muslims when he writes:

> When talking about multiculturalism or multinationality in Tangier, as if it were an exception that amazes many foreigners, a Frenchwoman says: 'It's very simple, the key is specialization: in Tangier the English are the masters, the French the governors and the Spanish the workers,' and if someone asked, what about the Muslims?, she replied only ironically, as if enacting a great truth that everyone knew: 'The Muslims? Muslims do not exist!'[87]

---

87 cit. in: Jebrouni 2019, pg. 183.

Nevertheless, I can state that religion, ethnicity and origin were not the decisive parameters of Tangier's international society, but nation and class. In the words of Gilson Miller:

> Already at the end of the nineteenth century organisations such as the Commission of Hygiene cut across religious, ethnic and national lines, promoting 'grammars of difference' that did not follow the standard colonial syntax. Residents, both foreign and local, including Muslims and Jews, were absorbed into structures of governance, exercising the rights of citizens in a land in which the concept of 'citizen' in its modern sense did not yet really exist. [...] A crucial element was the membership of the Admission by Moroccan Muslims that the category *'Tanjawi'* included residents of the town who were of Jewish and Christian origin. (Gilson Miller 2001: 43)

Certainly, this does not mean that there were no areas of life in which ethnic and religious groups remained among themselves, or that there were no prejudices of an ethnic or religious nature between the groups. But – even before nationality – class was the dominant structuring feature of the city. So when Aourid (2019) speaks of Morocco at the time of the protectorates as an apartheid society, in which Europeans and *natives* lived spatially and socially separated from one another, this was not the case in Tangier. There was no Jewish quarter here, and members of the most diverse religions often lived in one block, for example, in the buildings *Bendrihen II* and *III* on Boulevard Pasteur.[88] Muslims, Jews and Christians of the middle and lower classes lived together in the medina and in *Dradeb*, as did those of the upper class in *Mershan*. The members of the different religions "shared the same pathways, used the same bread ovens, and patronized the same stores," for example, in the old town quarter *Beni Idder*, which in the 20th century developed into a residential area of the simple classes. A closer look at the microstructure of the quarter shows, however, that the religions lived more densely in individual blocks and alleys than with the other religions (Gilson Miller 2010: 158f).

Many Christians and Jews of the lower classes also lived side by side in the so-called Muslim quarter of *M'sallah*. Moreover, the composition of most school classes, for example, the *École Berchet* and the *Scuola Italiana*, was multi-religious, marriages between Muslims and Christians as well as between Christians and Jews were – although not frequent, at least – not as unusual as Aourid claims for the rest of the country. Muslims, Christians and Jews, who are now over 60 years old, remember playing football together, going to the cinema and sharing other leisure activities. Friends and neighbors of different religions gave each other presents on holidays (Pons 1990: 94; Haller 2000a: 306f).

---

88 Field research diary Tangier, August 11, 2013.

Illustration 49: Christian woman dressed as Jewish bride

"The Jewish friends of Manuel Bautista Nieto's Christian grandmother dressed her as a Jewish bride shortly before she married her husband, who was also a Christian."[89]

However, as I have shown elsewhere (Haller 2001b) about Gibraltar, mixing does not mean equivalence per se. Rather, it is about the *right* mix, which excludes, discriminates against or restricts certain groups in some areas. The only group excluded from the mix in relation to the society of the Zone period was not Muslims per se but the poor Muslims, particularly those who had moved in from Jbala, the Rif and other areas of the North.

What seems unusual to me is that various older Moroccan interlocutors whose families were already living in Tangier during the time of the Zone describe the period of the Zone as 'free' and the time after 1956 as 'colonial.' After the integration into the Moroccan state, Tangier experienced devaluation, impoverishment and desolation. Positions in the administrative apparatus were mainly occupied by Moroccans from the French protectorate. Sadness and annoyance about the relative loss of prosperity is evident in the accounts of many of my interlocutors. The talk of an ethnically and religiously conflict-free period dominates in many of the conversations I have had. It either depicts the illusions and wishes of those born

---

89   Field research diary TanGib, February 20, 2020.

afterwards, because they long for such a time in their present, or it is about personal memories of a happy childhood and youth, because those I can talk to today were, at best, young adults at the time of the Zone. Hardly anyone has experienced the Zone as an adult. In any case, the stories about the Zone period express one thing: The pride of a city and of belonging to it: being-*Tanjawi*.

Like most Moroccan cities, Tangier has its own body of written and oral tradition that makes up the distinctive cultural apparatus of the community, reinforcing a strong sense of local identity. To be '*Tanjawi*', or a person of Tangier, is a mark of pride. This feeling of distinctiveness is bound up with a particular historical consciousness, and is as much a quality of Jewish Tangier as it is of Muslim. Moreover, both groups traditionally shared certain attitudes toward local history, including an obsession with events as signs and symbols, a selective interest in historical 'facts', and an acute awareness of the immanence of God in the affairs of humankind. (Gilson Miller 1991: 587)

I would, therefore, not call the International Zone a colony dependent on a single power in the classical sense, or an exclusive part of the Alaoui monarchy and certainly not a democracy. Rather, it can be described as an international oligarchy and a place of learning for multiple negotiations. As said previously, it resembled more a pre-colonial condition than a colonial one.

The international status of the city and the diverse interests of the powers and their representatives – which sometimes contradicted each other[90] – allowed for a lot of freedom. It is no wonder, therefore, that the Independence Party *Istiqlal* was able to develop during the time of the French and the Spanish Protectorate (Daoud 2017: 483), especially in Tangier (Pons 1990: 80).[91] Like the deposed Sultans Moulay Abdelaziz (1908-1943), Moulay Hafid (1913) and Ben Arafa (1953-1955, 1955-1956), the nationalists of *Istiqlal* were able to retreat. However, the sultans and *Istiqlal* were also under observation in Tangier. Thus, in 1929, the *Oficina Mixta de Información* was founded by the French and Spanish in Tangier in order to observe and fight the activities of the Moroccan independence movement, especially in Tangier itself, as well as in the Spanish Protectorate. Investigations were conducted particularly against Mohamed Sidi Abdellah Guennoun, the *Asociación de Estudiantes Yamiat el Taleb* and the Sufi Brotherhood of the Alawiya (Aixelà-Cabré 2017: 150ff).

---

90 In his life records, German diplomat Schabinger von Schowingen (1967) reports how he sometimes parried the hostile directives from Paris and Berlin together with his French colleague, with whom he got along splendidly.

91 Also see "On April 9, 1951, the *Moroccan National Front* was created in Tangier, bringing together the *Istiqlâl Party* (P.I.), the *Democratic Party of Independence* (P.D.I.), the P.R.N. and the P.U.M." (Benjelloun 1996: 26).

In his speech in Tangier on April 10, 1947, Mohammed V rescinded the unity between the sultanate and France that had been celebrated until then. This date is regarded as a turning point in Moroccan history because it marked the king's alliance with the *Istiqlal* (Joffé 1985: 289).

Geostrategically, after World War II, the Strait remained a central region for world trade and the military and intelligence protection of the areas of interest of the great powers. Espionage was as virulent after the war as it was during the war. British secret agent Guy Burgess, for example, intended to move from Section B of the Foreign Office to Section A, which would have enabled him to advance to the official diplomatic service of Great Britain. In Tangier, however, his public appearances and drunkenness had made it so impossible for him to continue to carry out only secret service activities (Téllez Rubio 2003).

In the early 1950s, anti-European riots (Tafersiti Zarouila 2012: 136f)[92] in the course of efforts to annex Tangier into a possibly emerging Morocco unsettled the European and Jewish local population in particular – Gibraltar was only indirectly affected by this, as a neighborhood observer, so to speak. But, of course, the Moroccanization of Tangier would also affect relations with Gibraltar in a number of ways:

- Many Spaniards living in Tangier were republicans and opponents of the Franco regime. If deportation were to take place – where would they be able to go?
- A good part of the property belonged to the British – what would happen to this property?
- Jews as the link between the two cities would be exposed to a more fundamental reorientation if the community in Northern Morocco and Tangier were to disappear – how would the ties of Gibraltarian Jews to Morocco be compensated?

These overarching questions show that the future of Tangier within a Moroccan nation state would affect its ties with Gibraltar deeply.

March 30th, 1952, was a decisive date for anti-European riots. This event traumatized many *Tanjawis* because it revealed the seriousness of their situation to them (Pons 1990: 201ff).

It was the day of the 40th anniversary of the Franco-Spanish protectorate in Morocco, a Sunday on which a general strike was called to protest against France's refusal to deal with Moroccan independence. The masses took to the streets, plundering and burning shops and buildings, and blood was running, the likes of which had never been seen before in Tangier.

---

92   Tangier Gazette, April 4, 1952.

Police Commissioner Le Grand – a Belgian – said that 85 per cent of the demonstrators were foreigners. On that day, when the morning became cloudy and no rain threatened, all the merchants had closed their doors and only the grocery stores remained open. The demonstrators smashed the shop windows and even set fire to some cars. The situation did not seem to be resolved and the authorities asked the Spanish Zone for help, but, in the end, the local police managed to deal with the situation.[93]

The sources are not sure about the numbers, but there are said to have been about 7 dead and 49 injured; 81 shops and 77 cars were damaged. A list of 22 people to be deported – almost exclusively leaders of Moroccan parties – was drawn up by the international administration, including Abdellah Guennoun (the first Governor of Tangier after independence) (López García 2018).

Further riots followed. On August 3rd, 1955, the knife attack of an 'confused' ('*amok*') Arab took place: Four dead (especially Jews) and five injured.[94] Contemporary witnesses discuss the incident on the online platform A:

Mariceli Medeiros Varga: I was 10 years old in 1955 and I was almost stabbed to death by an alleged madman who killed many people. There was a very big mess and the fear of not being able to go out into the streets because of fear of a big slaughter.
Ignacio Ruíz Antúnez: I think it was the same one who broke into my mother's boarding house with a knife. I remember it well because one of the sons of a police inspector was married to my cousin, who told us, 'Yes, he was very close to your apartments.'
Odilio Batista: It was also said that up at the entrance arch of Soq Barra there was a man with a submachine gun and he started shooting.
Juan Sanz Alonso: Mariceli Medeiros Varga; what you said, [...] that was a madman called Barnisi who started killing at the entrance of the market on *Calle Siaghine*, picking out Christians and Jews who crossed his path. I don't remember if there were 8 or 10 dead and several injured. In *Zoco Chico*, he started to flee and got as far as the train station where he was killed by a policeman called *Llanito* (the Gibraltarian).[95] And yes, the one from Odilio Batista mentioned was the main inspector of the police station in *Calle Sanlucar*.
Mariceli Medeiros Varga: And I also went through the Silversmiths' Street and Tuajin Street and met him in *Siaghin Street*, in the height of *Bodega Chaves*, where there was also a synagogue. I hid there. There were several dead, two of whom I knew, a cousin of my mother's who worked at *Foto Alba* in the *Silversmiths' Street*, he cut

---

93 Online platform A, Mehdi Zoubairi (d.n.n).
94 The Gibraltar Chronicle, August 3, 1955.
95 Green (1992: 158f), on the other hand, writes that Barnissi was taken to Ghandouri prison.

her face and in Calle Tuajin he stabbed a friend of my mother's in the stomach. He only attacked the Europeans.⁹⁶

Illustration 50: Riots in souq Barra, Tangier, September 1955

On March 7th, 1956, 11 people were killed and 22 wounded in Tetuán during anti-Spanish riots.⁹⁷ Six people were killed and 20 wounded in Larache in April.⁹⁸ A little later, knife attacks took place at *Soq Barra* in Tangier with six wounded, and six people were injured.⁹⁹ On August 22, stones were thrown at the police.¹⁰⁰

The fact that Tangier was on the verge of being integrated into Morocco was shown by not only anti-European riots but also the withdrawal of gold: In 1955 it was 50 tonnes, in January 1956 it was 30 tonnes and in March of the same year, it had come down to just 8 tonnes.¹⁰¹ Money was also taken away from Tangier in other ways.¹⁰² Eight hundred companies disappeared and the flight of capital to Uruguay, Great Britain and Switzerland continued (Daoud 2017: 485). At the end of 1959, the old Banco Pariente moved to Genoa and the *American and Foreign Bank* closed before the end of the year (Vaidon 1977: 328). The *Tangier Gazette* complained in March 1960

---

96   Online platform A, various guarantors (d.n.n).
97   The Gibraltar Chronicle, March 7, 1956.
98   The Gibraltar Chronicle, April 11, 1956.
99   The Gibraltar Chronicle, April 27, 1956.
100 The Gibraltar Chronicle, August 22, 1956.
101 The Gibraltar Chronicle, March 22, 1956.
102 On November 9, 1957, a Portuguese woman who tried to bring three million pesetas in 1000 peseta notes to Gibraltar was arrested at the border of La Línea. The money obviously came from Tangier. The Gibraltar Chronicle, November 9, 1957.

that "[M]any banking, business, and industrial enterprises have already shut their doors" (The Tangier Gazette 1960).

During my field research period in autumn 2019, I came across a politically particularly sensitive topic related to the independence movement: Jewish espionage in the service of France during the period of nationalization (1956ff). Unfortunately, I cannot be very specific in this context as it is a threatening matter that probably does not leave those involved untouched even today. The starting point for this topic was the rather harmless but persistent search of an informant – let's call him Reda – for his Jewish roots. Reda's father Hafid was orphaned at the age of four and raised by the sister of her Muslim grandmother, who owned a house in the Kasbah. During his childhood, Hafid had always heard a murmur about the fact that he was actually a Jewish child, but his aunt had destroyed all documents about his father Ahmed. Reda was looking for an answer to the grandfather's rejection by his sister-in law (Reda's grand-aunt). For Hafid, in turn, had passed on the rumors about his Jewish father Ahmed to his son Reda, who has been searching for his roots ever since. One day, as we happened to pass the shop of an elderly informant in the old town – let's call him Adnan – I entered the shop to greet Adnan. Reda followed and I introduced the two to each other. When Adnan heard Reda's family name, he said that he knew his father and grandparents, especially Ahmed, well. He described the physical characteristics of Reda's father exactly, gave names of siblings and then said that Ahmed was a Jew who had married a Muslim woman. Reda was beside himself with joy, for the first time an unknown person confirmed to him what he had always believed. Adnan could describe where the grandmother lived. It also turned out that Adnan was able to confirm what Reda had heard, namely that grandfather Ahmed came from Fez and to Tangier as an officer of the French army, converted to Islam for appearances' sake and, thus, was able to work for France against the Moroccan independence movement *Istiqlal*. Part of the mystery surrounding the behavior of Reda's great-aunt, thus, seemed to have been solved[103] and was confirmed by other informants in the course of further research.[104]

---

103 Field research diary TanGib, October 26, 2019.
104 Field research diary TanGib, February 23, 2020.

5. The loosening of Transboughazian bonds

The long and deep ties established between the two cities began to slowly erode after World War II. This will become clear in the following chronologically arranged line of development. However, this is not a matter of continuous erosion but rather of phases of strengthening or stagnation.

From April 1955 onwards, *Tanjawis* no longer required a visa for Gibraltar for a stay of up to 72 hours.[1] In June 1955, a wireless telephone connection was established between the two cities, making it possible to call the other side without having to wait for hours.[2]

This chapter, thus. begins with renewed encounters between *Tanjawis* and Gibraltarians: "[M]uchos gibraltareños viajaban a Tangier de compras o bien a pasar un fin de semana, especialmente en verano" (Ceballos López 2009: 154).

> Franky was born in Gibraltar, and in 1950 he opened a small dance hall in the *Rue Fernando de Portugal* with his partner Johnny. There the young people met to dance together in the dim light. They did not have a license to serve alcohol, and the inaugurated guests knew that behind the order for a cup of 'Tea of the Innkeeper' was hiding excellent Scotch whiskey. The entertainer and singer Coccinelle, later the most famous transsexual in France, worked at *Franky & Johnny* at times.[3]

Others came over to Tangier because they received an offer of work.

> The parents of Michael Gómez married in Gibraltar in 1947. During the honeymoon, his father received a job offer in Tangier at RCA (Radio Communications of America). John's brothers were born in Tangier in 1949 and 1952, respectively, and he himself in 1962. They lived at 43 *Rue Cujas*, in the *Inmueble Grebler*. John remembers trips with his parents to the *Forêt Diplomatique*. He attended, firstly, the Spanish and then the French kindergarten, later the primary school *École Berchet* and then the *Scuola Italiana*. The grammar school *Lycée Regnault* followed. In 1972, when Morocco started the *Marche Verte* to the former Spanish Western Sahara,

---

1   Tangier Gazette, April 30, 1955: 1.
2   Tangier Gazette, June 11, 1955: 2.
3   Online platform A, Sabeer Noujani (d.n.n).

the Gómez returned to Gibraltar. There Michael attended the Christian Brothers' School of the Irish Brothers. He was teased by his classmates as '*morito*' (little Arab) because English was not his mother tongue. He attended the Bayside Comprehensive School in Gibraltar until 1980. Michael studied Tourism in the UK and received his master's in International Relations. At Warwick University, he wrote his doctorate on *The Moroccan Zone Franche status into its independence*.[4] In the 1990s, he worked for Saccone & Speed, one of the major tobacco, alcohol and food wholesalers.

In a class photo of the *École Berchet* in 2019 I discovered Michael and an informant from Tangier, Patrick Grénard. I did not know they were in the same class and knew each other. Neither of them knew that I knew the other (Gómez since 1996, Grénard since 2013), and I subsequently tried to bring them together. Both reactions were sympathetic but restrained. At school they were not resentful or displeased with each other, but they had nothing to do with each other either, because their interests were too different. They were not friends. There was benevolent indifference. The mothers knew each other superficially when they met in the city, they talked, but they were not friends either, they were just acquaintances. In this respect, both found my request to connect something that never had a previous bond somewhat strange. I suppose both reacted well-disposed because they wanted to show me a friendly courtesy.

This shows that the attempt to work out what Tangier and Gibraltar have in common was also in my own interest to salvage and appreciate what I thought was common. The example of Gómez-Grénard particularly shows that although there may be common ground, it may not be aligned with a deeper interest: *Transboughaz* ties had loosened and people whose lives touched once do not necessarily have to seal these touches in a memory bag. Yet, such relationships have the potential to provide resources for future bonds. I believed myself to have this potential – but the two people concerned were not motivated to thaw memory bags that I thought were just waiting to be brought back to life.

5.1. 1956 to 1960 – A special status for Tangier?

If one takes the cultural circle metaphor and applies it to TanGib and the region around the *Boughaz*, it can be stated that the ties and networks slowly but steadily loosened in the middle of the 20th century. Different time marks were decisive in this process.

---

4   Personal Communication, Michael Gómez, April 27, 2019 and June 25, 2019.

On March 16, 1956, Al-Fassi (the leader of the Independence Party *Istiqlal*) hinted that Tangier would become part of a unified Morocco sooner than planned.[5]

In the Spanish-Moroccan Declaration of April 8, 1956, on the independence of a united Morocco, Ceuta and Melilla were omitted.[6] On May 2nd, 1956, *The Gibraltar Chronicle* informed that there would probably be changes in the status of Tangier and that the sultan's Foreign Minister would discuss the "reintegration" of the Zone into an independent Moroccan state with the signatory states. On May 8, Spain declared itself ready to agree to negotiations.

The Moroccan delegates to the International Legislative Assembly had demanded that until the integration of the Zone into Morocco, the Assembly should only deal with local matters. When this was rejected, the Muslims left the Assembly. In the end, Moroccans had prevailed.[7]

On June 14th, 1956, *The Gibraltar Chronicle* reports that Spain will hand over her protectorate to Morocco within two weeks.

The prospect of a special status for Tangier inspired the international community, the civilians of Tangier and the entrepreneurs in 1956. On July 6th, 1956, the International Control Committee traveled from Tangier to Rabat to announce the approval of the new status of Tangier to Foreign Minister Ahmed Balafrej. It was requested to announce the exact date for this.[8] Balafrej held out the prospect of a special economic, financial and trade-related status. The Court of Justice and some other administrative units remained in international hands, but the police, construction and health services were transferred to Moroccan hands.[9]

Abdellah Guennoun is appointed first governor of the new Moroccan province of Tangier on July 8, 1956.[10] The port workers use the new development to test their strength and on July 13th paralyze the port, especially the ferry port. However, they are, following a request from the new governor, to resume work until the workers' concerns have been settled by an intermediary.[11]

From August 10th, 1956, onwards Moroccan stamps are valid in the North.[12]

On September 4th, 1956, Foreign Minister Balafrej again declared that Tangier would retain a special economic status in order to attract capital to the country.[13] Euphoric hopes flared up briefly.[14] Three days later, the palace confirmed that Tan-

---

5   The Gibraltar Chronicle, March 19, 1956.
6   The Gibraltar Chronicle, April 9, 1956.
7   The Gibraltar Chronicle, May 4, 1956.
8   The Gibraltar Chronicle, July 6, 1956.
9   The Gibraltar Chronicle, July 9, 1956.
10 The Gibraltar Chronicle, July 9, 1956.
11 The Gibraltar Chronicle, July 13, 1956.
12 The Gibraltar Chronicle, August 10, 1956.
13 La Dépeche Marocaine de Tangier, 1956a.
14 La Dépeche Marocaine de Tangier, 1956b.

Illustration 51: 1956 Announcement of a Special Status for Tangier

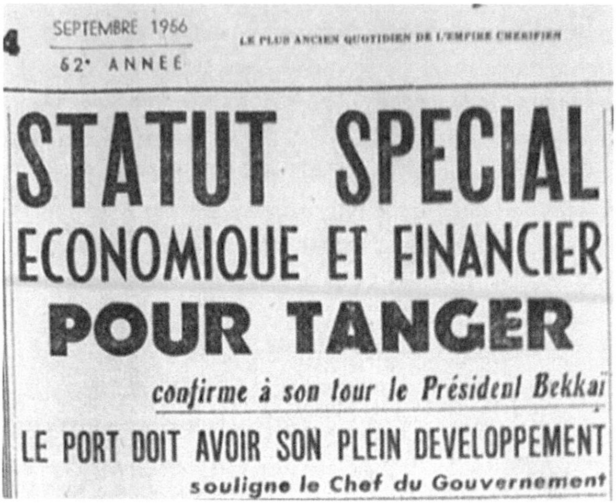

4 SEPTEMBRE 1956

62e ANNEE

LE PLUS ANCIEN QUOTIDIEN DE L'EMPIRE CHERIFIEN

STATUT SPECIAL

ECONOMIQUE ET FINANCIER

POUR TANGER

confirme à son tour le Président Bekkaï

LE PORT DOIT AVOIR SON PLEIN DEVELOPPEMENT

souligne le Chef du Gouvernement

gier would receive a special status.[15] This is reaffirmed on the September 14.[16] On the same day, it was announced that the establishments in the medina serving alcohol would be deprived of this right.[17]

A conference on the new status of Tangier was scheduled for October of 1956.[18] On October 11th, Balafrej announces in a meeting with representatives of the eight protecting powers that the sultan wants to keep the city as an "international meeting place."[19] But riots broke out, which can be classified as minor in comparison to other Moroccan cities:

On October 24th, 1956, a strike took place in Tangier; European and Moroccan companies closed down, so do schools and public services. The ferry *Mons Calpe* and the airline *Gibair* also stopped their connection for a day. Troops were deployed to assist the police. The strike came about as a protest against the appointment of five Algerian independence fighters by France.[20] The toll of blood was particularly high in Meknès: thirty-eight farms were burned to the ground and in addition to the 29 dead, 25 were injured. France announced that it would send 100.000 soldiers if the

15 La Dépeche Marocaine de Tangier, 1956c.

16 La Dépeche Marocaine de Tangier, 1956d.

17 La Dépeche Marocaine de Tangier, 1956e.

18 The Gibraltar Chronicle, July 9, 1956.

19 The Gibraltar Chronicle, 11 October 1956.

20 The Gibraltar Chronicle, October 24, 1956.

Moroccan army could not protect French lives and property.²¹ One day later, the 49.000 French officials in the former protectorate went on strike.²²

On October 29th, the *Final Declaration of the International Conference in Tangier and Annexed Protocol* was drawn up between the Protecting Powers of the International Zone and the Kingdom of Morocco.²³ It came into force on the same day.

Following the integration of the International Zone into the new and independent Kingdom of Morocco, many of its inhabitants settled in Gibraltar and Southern Spain. I have no figures on this. Money-changers, in particular, were leaving the city and settling in Ceuta or Gibraltar. The Sindhis also migrated to Casablanca or Gibraltar (Tafersiti Zarouila 2012: 249):

> In 1996, Mrs. Khalwani who was born in Tangier, had no relatives there now. Her family and that of her husband "moved to Gibraltar and Tangiers at the same time" because, at that time, both places were perfect to do business. Many families lived in both cities at the same time. After the end of the Zone Period, Gibraltar became the main location for family business. Mrs. Khalwani received her British passport in Gibraltar because her father was already a British subject.²⁴

On April 3rd of the following year, it was announced that the second summit meeting of the independent nations of Africa would take place in Tangier in May of that year.²⁵

The *British Post Office* in Tangier existed for 100 years. It would have been closed in 1956, but Morocco wanted to make a gesture of friendship to Britain, so it did not close its doors until April 1957.²⁶

On May 31st, 1957, the International Police was dissolved, one day later the *Sureté Nationale* took over their tasks.

On April 12th, 1957, the Moroccan court again announced that Tangier would be granted some special economic rights, such as exemption from official exchange rates and the possibility of free trade with foreign countries.²⁷

In August 1957th, the sultan announced that Morocco had now become a kingdom and that he would be known from this time onwards as King Mohamed V. At almost the same time, he awarded rights of her import-export merchants to operate without licenses and freedom from income tax until such time as his government decided otherwise. Should any changes be contemplated, he would give

---

21 The Gibraltar Chronicle, October 25, 1956.
22 The Gibraltar Chronicle, October 26, 1956.
23 Strangely enough, we find no mention of the *Final Declaration* in *The Gibraltar Chronicle*.
24 November 17, 1996, from the interview with Geetu and Gope Karnani.
25 The Gibraltar Chronicle, April 3, 1957.
26 The Gibraltar Chronicle, April 26, 1957.
27 The Gibraltar Chronicle, April 12, 1957.

the city five months' notice in which to arrange her affairs. This generous decision, naturally, won genuine respect for the king among Tangerinos (Vaidon 1977: 318).

The special rights provided Tangier a "free money market" according to the royal decree. After months of uncertainty, bankers and businessmen began to regain hope. It was hoped that a large part of Morocco's foreign trade would be conducted through Tangier. The order called for a six-month lead time for any possible changes to these promises. However, Tangier was also losing an important economic advantage to "neigbouring Gibraltar": Luxury goods were now much more expensive in Tangier than in Gibraltar. It was also announced in writing that some restrictions may be imposed on Tangier trade "for reasons appertaining to the general interests of the Kingdom."[28]

The persecution of foreign homosexuals was part of the nationalization efforts in Tangier. The city has always been considered a liberal refuge for gays and lesbians from the repressive countries of the North, as I have pointed out elsewhere (Haller 2016: 275ff). 1957 and 1958 saw spectacular actions against expatriates whose personal lifestyles were considered reprehensible (Sawyer-Lauçanno 1989: 341), especially homosexuals such as Paul and Jane Bowles, David Herbert and others, and Moroccans such as Ahmed Yacoubi.

Illustration 52: Tangier Excentrics and Celebrities

---

28   The Gibraltar Chronicle, September 12, 1957.

In late November 1957, Paul, Jane and Ahmed return to Tangier. The following day Yacoubi is accused of allegedly seducing a German youth and is confined in the jail in Tangier's Kasbah. (It is a period of local governmental persecution of expatriates living in Tangier and Moroccans who associated with them.

> 1958 In advance of leaving Tangier, Paul Bowles transfers ownership of his Jaguar convertible to Mohammed Temsamani, his chauffeur, and Temsamany sells the car and moves to Germany to work. In early February 1958, Paul and Jane Bowles fly from Tangier to Lisbon, Portugal, where they board a boat for Funchal in the Madeira Islands, spending one month there. [...]. Paul Bowles remains in Portugal, staying almost two months in a pension on the beach in Costa da Caparica. Later, he and Maurice Grosser decide to rent a house in Albufeira, Portugal, but don't move in, as Paul is summoned to New York by Libby Holman (n.d.) to work on Yerma. On May 14th, 1958, Yacoubi is acquitted of the charges against him and released from jail in Tangier. [...] Paul and Jane sail to Algeciras, Spain, and arrive back in Tangier near the end of December 1958. Ahmed Yacoubi is now living with an American girl in Tangier. (Lisenbee n.d.)

> Next came a sudden purge – which provoked international headlines – directed at certain Tangerinos during the autumn of 1958. [...] a large number of homosexuals were placed on a black list. A prominent young *Tanjawi* painter had been arrested and put away in the casbah jail for becoming over fond of a 15-year-old German boy visiting. [...] One of the grandees of Tangerino society (David Herbert) got off the hook by inviting the Winston Churchills, who were, luckily, in Tangier Bay aboard Aristotle Onassis' yacht at the time, to dinner. The police were so impressed with the local gentleman's powerful friends that, rightly or wrongly, they left him alone after that. (Vaidon 1977: 324/5)

The ban on young male dancers performing in places such as *1001 Nights*, *El Merhaba Palace* and *El Maghreb* should also be seen in this context.[29]

In 1958, smuggling from Tangier suffered a setback: Boats weighing less than 100 tonnes were banned from exporting tobacco and alcohol (Finlayson 1992: 76).

5.2. 1960ff – Swan song on TanGib. Provisionally?

Tangier and Gibraltar still perceived each other in many areas during this time. In January 1955, for example, an essay about Tangier appeared in *The Gibraltar Chroni-*

---

29   Tangier Gazette, December 14, 1958: 5.

cle, and *The Tangier Gazette* praised this text a few days later as a very appropriate article.[30] The *Tangier Gazette* reported on Gibraltar:

Illustration 53: Tangier-Gibraltar Connection

The *Calpe Institute of Gibraltar* is attended by the Director of the *Tourist Board of Tangier*;[31] a flower show[32] and the *Gibraltar Fair* are held[33] in Gibraltar; the Bishop of Gibraltar visits Tangier[34] and the actress Mary Pickford is a guest in Gibraltar;[35] the Chairman of the *City Council*, Joshua Hassan, has been elected as the first *Mayor of Gibraltar*;[36] the *Governor of Gibraltar* visits Tangier for reasons that are "purely private";[37] *Les Amis de l'Operette* visit Gibraltar, where they perform their farce *Mon Bébé*;[38] the manager of the *Rif Hotel*, Aimé Serfaty, fled to Gibraltar to escape an

---

30 Tangier Gazette, January 19, 1955: 2.
31 Tangier Gazette, May 7, 1955.
32 Tangier Gazette, February 19, 1955.
33 Tangier Gazette, June 25, 1955: 7.
34 Tangier Gazette, May 21, 1955.
35 Tangier Gazette, August 20, 1955: 5.
36 Tangier Gazette, November 25, 1955.
37 Tangier Gazette, April 13, 1956: 4.
38 Tangier Gazette, April 13, 1956: 5.

announced kidnapping;[39] four boys barely escaped an explosion in the *Jungle* of Gibraltar (Searle 2019: 38f);[40] jewel thief Michael Caborn Waterfield, known in both cities as *Dandy Kim*, is on trial in London.

Mutual visits still took place: *The Tangiers Lions Club* met at the *Rock Hotel* in Gibraltar,[41] the *Tangiers Aero Club* made a trip to Gibraltar in September 1957,[42] in the same month, daily day trips were made on the Bland Line[43] and the hospitality industry courted guests from Gibraltar.[44] However, in January 1959, the ferry was also leased to the Moroccan government, which used it to transport troops to the insurgent areas of the Rif.[45]

Some Jewish religious specialists were still living in Tangier, so that Gibraltarian Jews still sought advice and help:

> Isaac Abecasis hands me the circumcision certificate of his son: "Herewith it is confirmed that the so-called Judah Abecasis, son of Isaac Abecasis and Frances Pizarello, who was born in Gibraltar on May 16, 1960, and died on May 7, 1960, is the only one who was circumcised. He was circumcised on September 7, 1960, in Tangier by the authorization of the rabbinical court of Tangier, in the presence of the rabbinical court, which is, therefore, part of the Hebrew confession, given in Tangier on February 12, 1962, was immersed in the ritual bath."[46]

On April 19, 1960, the Royal Charter was finally withdrawn and Tangier fully incorporated into Morocco (Vaidon 1977: 330). The *Tangier Gazette* writes, "[the] guillotine falls" and the "gas chamber is now being prepared."[47] More and more Europeans left the city. Here are some voices of emigrants:

> *Lorenzo Rubio Franco:* I left Tangier in October 1962. My father had worked for the *Moroccan Hispanic Hydroelectric*. He was fired 62 years ago and he didn't want to leave his Tangier, but we had to do it through the Spanish consulate, which deported us to Spain because we had no more money.

---

39 Tangier Gazette, August 31, 1956.
40 Tangier Gazette, January 31, 1958.
41 The Gibraltar Chronicle, July 6, 1957.
42 The Gibraltar Chronicle, September 25, 1957.
43 The Gibraltar Chronicle, August 28, 1957.
44 The Gibraltar Chronicle, October 31, 1957.
45 "During January, 1959, as a change from sailing to Tangier with holiday-seeking passengers, Mons Calpe was chartered by the Moroccan Government to carry troops from Tangier to Alhucemas, on the Mediterranean coast of Morocco, where there was a revolt by the local tribesmen. She landed the troops at dawn without any opposition as had other Bland steamers in the early part of the century, when they too carried out similar functions" (Sanahuja Albiñana 2011).
46 Field research diary Gibraltar, August 13, 1996; translation by the author.
47 *The Tangier Gazette*, March 11, 1960.

> *Rosario Santos Araujo:* I was required to have a work permit (I was born in Tangier). *Luís Guimares Mascarenhas:* [...] I thought the work card was not used. In the beginning, when Tangier was incorporated into the kingdom, there was a royal decree for a few years that declared a free port. There was great uncertainty about the future of non-Moroccans born in the city. This led to a massive exodus of young people looking for other horizons. [...]
> *Rosario Santos Araujo:* [...] I was Dr. Hirt's assistant and I had to apply for the work card. I still have it with me in Malaga. I don't remember if I was 17 years old. It still leaves the pain of being a stranger in your own country.
> *Lorenzo Rubio Franco:* I worked as a trainee in the pharmacy du Boulevard and had to go to the police to get the work card. 14 years, 1960. By the way, the pharmacist's son, Carlos Benaim, is the best perfumer in N.Y.[48]

The *Tangier Gazette* had – in the years 1955 to 1961, which I consulted – one page each on official events in *Tangier* ("Tangier Notes"), as well as an additional local gossip page (*Ruth Maxwell's Tangier Diary* or, since May 1958, *James Joy's Tangier Diary* – James Joy is one of the pseudonyms used by American journalist David Woolman). At the same time, the *Tangier Gazette* had a page *News from Gibraltar*, and since May 1956, another one called *Torremolinos News*. Many Spanish *Tanjawis* moved to Torremolinos, Marbella and Malaga, which at that time started to compete with Tangier as a destination for the international Jet Set. Costa del Sol social climate for the often leftist Spaniards from Tangier was considered the most bearable perspective within the fascist country. Later, another column appeared in the *Tangier Gazette*, the *Casablanca Notes*.

As late as in 1955, Morocco's independence and the possible consequences for the International Zone were not sufficiently addressed in either the *Tangier Gazette* or *The Gibraltar Chronicle*. This did not happen until 1956, and only then did news from the French Protectorate slowly begin to make its way into these newspapers. Until then, Tangier seemed to be largely self-referential. In the following years, the numbers of pages in local papers became smaller and smaller. This was due to two developments: On the one hand, the number of readers decreased rapidly due to the exodus of Christians and Jews and, on the other hand, the local authority lost its decision-making powers – these had been delegated to the national capital, Rabat.[49]

Changes also affected regular trade. This is exemplified by the decline of the company Saccone & Speed in Tangier. Saccone & Speed, originally an importer of beverages, later a food importer, had been operating in Tangier since 1929. The ma-

---

48 Online platform A, various guarantors (d.n.n).
49 Field research diary TanGib, October 24, 2019.

Illustration 54: Announcement Saccone & Speed

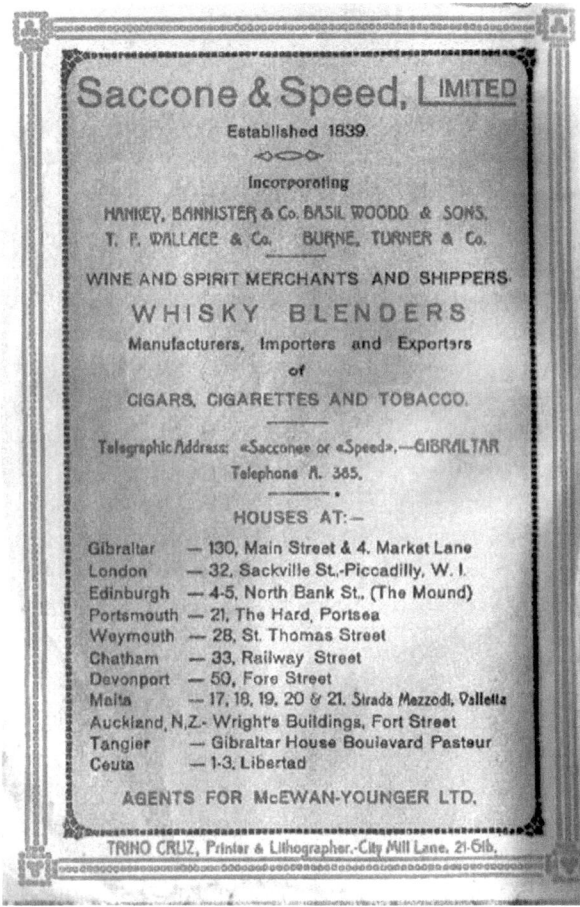

nagers often came from Gibraltar (Garcia 2014: 86). A bottling plant was needed for the export of beer to Morocco, which had to be set up in Gibraltar (ibid.: 108). In 1934, Saccone & Speed received a commission for the sugar trade in Tangier (ibid.: 97). In 1944, the manager of the Tangier department was instructed to buy 2.35 million francs to settle possible obligations in that currency as the exchange rates were fluctuating rapidly (ibid.: 133f). In 1947, a sister company was created for the shops, Lawn & Alder, whose business was conducted through the Bank of British West Africa; this company was dissolved in 1948 and then operated under the name Saccone & Speed (Morocco) S.A. with a capital contribution of 3 million pesetas, as well as through Banco Moses Pariente. If good profits were made, this changed in

1954, as the economic and political situation became uncertain. Saccone & Speed closed its offices on Boulevard Pasteur. In 1955 (ibid.: 175), the company again did good business in both Tangier and Casablanca (ibid.: 176). On April 16, 1960, the special tax and economic rights for Tangier expired. The manager for Morocco was instructed to settle all debts owed to the parent company in Gibraltar immediately, as it was feared that after the end of the special status, it would become difficult to transfer money out of Morocco. At the same time, Moroccan subsidiaries were only to store whiskey, as it was still easy to sell (ibid.: 193). In the course of 1960, the trade of Saccone & Speed in Morocco largely collapsed (ibid.: 196). In that year, the subsidiaries of Casablanca and Tangier also merged with a capital of 50 million francs. It was hoped to establish a free trade Zone in Tangier, a hope that had to be buried in 1961. Saccone & Speed ceased its retail activities and limited its business in Morocco to the wholesale food trade (ibid.: 201f). Saccone & Speed now focused on Spain to compensate for the losses in Morocco (ibid.: 213). In the first half of the 1960s, business in Tangier developed very poorly. An attempt was made in 1966 to revive the retail trade on a small scale (ibid.: 233). To this day, Tangier no longer represents a significant area of activity for Saccone & Speed.

The setback for smuggling, the ban on alcohol, the exodus of Jews, reduced special rights, capital flight, persecution of homosexuals, work permits for European *Tanjawis* that were difficult to obtain, the disappearance of the local press, the decline of classical trade – it was becoming apparent that the overall situation in Tangier was indeed changing. The new Moroccan system gave "the bitch" (*El Kelba*), as Tangier was called in other parts of the country (Green 1992: 17), one kick after another. Very slowly, as Bowles writes in a letter to a friend

> We are still in Tangier, expecting everything to get ‚worse' which it does do, but so slowly that generally we aren't conscious of it, until on certain days everything seems askew and wrong, and one can make [it of all the thing that have altered [...]. (Sawyer-Lauçanno 1989: 354)

5.3. 1964 to 1973 – Increasing provincialization of Tangier and border problems in Gibraltar

There is no doubt that Tangier's reputation was in decline until the end of the 1960s. It was no longer associated with the International Zone or the charm of the rich but with crime, downturn, arbitrariness and decay. An example where all this comes together is in two criminal cases: The Marianne murder case and the Degioanni case.

The *Hotel Charf* was formerly called *Hotel Dante*. It became notorious because the former owner, Michel, had committed a murder of passion in 1967. Michel Zante, who lived in *Calle Verdun*, had an affair with Eduardo Vizcaino, a young man who was engaged at the same time to Marianne Lown, the niece of the local furniture manufacturer Guérin. Marianne lived with her grandmother in *Calle Málaga*. Antonio Carillo Mejias' father discovered the girl's body one morning when he opened Guérin's workshop where he worked. Apparently she had been beaten to death with an iron and strangled with the iron's cable. The police summoned friends of the dead and neighbors, but then suspected Monsieur Guérin, the girl's uncle – who did not like his niece very much – and kept him in prison for two years. But Interpol researched the case further and in 1972, discovered the earrings of the victim in the safe of *Hotel Dante*. There were also photographs of influential high-ranking personalities in compromising positions with young men. Michel Zante had secretly taken pictures of his guests in order to blackmail them. Zante, who was known for clucking back and forth on the *Boulevard* in his red Ford Thunderbird, was also known as a heroin dealer – at least that is what people said. After his conviction, Zante was transferred to Kenitra prison and then deported to France. Others say he escaped from Lazareto/Malabata prison by boat. Later he was shot dead in Marseilles.[50]

The Degioanni case was different. Here feudal arbitrariness obviously played a more important role than in the Zante case.

Italian tailor Giuseppe Degioanni, who lived in *Calle Balmes* and whose shop *Les Ciseaux d'Or* was located in *Rue de la Liberté*, had made 12 suits (*trajes*) for the governor of Tangier, and when he demanded payment of the bill, he was not paid but beaten. He died of this at the age of 59 on September 11, 1969. His wife caused a scandal via the Italian consulate, the embassy in Rabat and the foreign ministry in Rome, so that the costs for the suits was finally paid.[51]

We can only agree with the judgment in Sawyer-Lauçanno: "By the end of the decade, Tangier would largely loose its former international flavor, its perceived decadence and – for many – its charm" (1989: 342f).

What happened to the connections between the two cities? From September 4, 1964, to January 8, 1965, Gibraltar had to do without a ferry connection to Tangier by *Mons Calpe*, because it had to be overhauled in Scotland (Sanahuja Albiñana 2011).

On the other side of the Strait: Spain had never given up its claim to Gibraltar. Elsewhere (Haller 2000a), I have broadly discussed the Spanish arguments put forward in this regard.

It is simply a matter of stressing that Spain renewed this claim in 1964 and 1965, in the context of the pre-UN decolonization movements. Ultimately, Spain sought

---

50   Field research diary Tangier, October 30, 2013; online platform A, Adil Oukach (d.n.n).
51   Field research diary Tangier, November 2, 2018.

before the UN's *Special Committee on Decolonization (C24)* to incorporate Gibraltar into Spanish territory. In order to weaken Spain's position, the British Foreign Office (*Information Research Department*) set up a series of "liberation movements" in 1966 and 1967, which, in turn, aimed to reclaim the Spanish territories in North Africa – Ceuta, Melilla, Ifni, the Rio de Oro and the Canary Islands – demanded the *Front for the Liberation of the Spanish Maghreb*, the *Freedom for Africa Movement* and the *Organization for the Expulsion of Spanish Colonialists from Arab Lands*. Arabic-language leaflets were circulated in Morocco, Algeria and Tunisia and the chairman of the C24, Tanzanian John S. Malecela, was denounced as "unworthy of the name of African brother" and as a Spanish bribe recipient. This was revealed in documents that were only discovered in 2019 in The National Archives in London by Professor Rory Cormac of the University of Nottingham (Norton 2020).

Neither the British undercover organizations nor Spain's requests were crowned with success, so that Spain initiated measures on the border with Gibraltar, which ultimately led to its closure.

> When 1965 saw the beginning of Spain's confrontation of Gibraltar and the banishment of the several thousand Spanish, who along with their forbears, had worked on the Rock for at least a century and a half, Gibraltar simply turned to the ready and willing *Tanjawis* just across the Straits. Having been a small piece of 19th century England with a Spanish accent, the Rock now became an assort of tawdry extension of an increasingly tawdry Tangier with an off-English accent. Meanwhile the Bland Line, which has a monopoly on air and sea travel between Tangier and Gibraltar, made a killing from this built-in gold mine of *Tanjawis* who swarm back and forth in droves. Not only has there been a degree of brain-drain from Tangier which *Tanjawis* cannot afford to lose, but now that so many of them send remittances to their families in the city, Tangier would suffer seriously if a recession or some awful political calamity forced expatriate *Tanjawis* to return to Morocco. (Vaidon 1977: 330)

When Spain closed the land border with Gibraltar (1969), Tangier became the gateway to the world for the imprisoned rock dwellers: Telephone cables between Gibraltar and Spain had been cut as well.

The Bland Line *MV Mons Calpe* served Gibraltar from 1954 to 1986. One of our few links during the border closure. It carried passengers, vehicles and cargo between Gibraltar and Tangier. Many used it to cross to Tangier to catch a Spanish ferry back to Algeciras to visit family in Spain after the border closed.[52]

---

52   Online platform, Rosemary Pillington (d.n.n). Also see Gaggero (2011).

A special mention at this point must go to the skipper of the *Mons Calpe*, Capitan Donald Delf. Captain Delf clocked up 10,000 voyages across the Straits and was highly respected.[53]

"A woman," says Eulogio Barabich, "died in Spain, and the relatives in Gibraltar could not be notified. So the daughter called Tangier in Spain, from there someone called Gibraltar, and before the son from Gibraltar came to Tangier, from there to Algeciras and from there to Spain, the mother was already buried. He arrived at 7:00, and the mother was buried at 4:00."[54]

While mainly Christian and Jewish *Tanjawis* came to Gibraltar until 1969, Muslim *Tanjawis* and inhabitants of other Northern Moroccan regions joined them afterwards. The closing of the border had a variety of effects economically on the relationship between Tangier and Gibraltar. Virtually overnight, the Spanish workforce (about a third of all workers) was replaced by British military personnel, local women (who, thus, entered the wage labor market for the first time), and about 3000 Moroccan workers.[55]

Illustration 55 : Gibraltar Commemorates Moroccan Workers

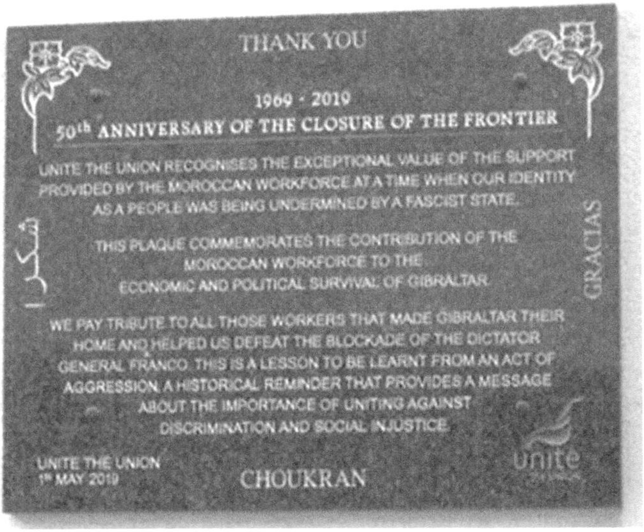

---

53 Insight Magazine, July 2003.
54 Interview with Eulogio Barabich, October 24, 1996.
55 Symbolically, this would be honored on May 3, 2019, with the placing of a plaque thanking Moroccan workers for their help since the time of the closure of the border (GBC 2019a).

In 2013, I met an elderly lady in the Jewish Casino in Tangier who revealed to me that it was she herself who saved Gibraltar from ruin in 1969 after the Spanish closed the land border.

"There was no longer a Spanish workforce in Gibraltar: The trade, the port, the households – Spaniards had worked everywhere. My sister called me and asked me to help her. So I organized everything and sent 3000 Moroccans over there without further ado. If it hadn't been for me, Gibraltar would never have existed today," says the lady proudly.[56]

My interlocutor in the Casino turned out to be Mery Gabay, the sister of Marcelle Bensimon, the wife of former Prime Minister of Gibraltar, Sir Joshua Hassan, who occasionally took me under his friendly wings during my field research in the 1990s.[57]

"Moroccans were recruited by a delegation made up of the Dept. of Public Works, the Ministry of Defence and 'algunos patrones privados'," stressed Mohamed Sarsri, representative of the Moroccan community in Gibraltar.[58]

The son of the Mayor of Gibraltar, Willie Serfaty, led the delegation. He was sent to Tangier to find suitable workers. Above all, carpenters, painters and construction workers were needed. At first, workers were recruited from the areas of Rabat, Casablanca and Kenitra, who spoke a little English (there was a US military base in Kenitra).

Private companies, on the other hand, recruited more in the North, in Tangier, Tetuán and Larache. A few Moroccans were looking for work on their own; they came to Gibraltar alone or as a married couple, but they were not recruited specifically.

Bookseller Mr. Fitoussi says his father worked in Gibraltar and returned to Tangier in 1971 – he himself had not yet been there. His father was always on the ferry *Mons Calpe* and was in Gibraltar for two weeks, then in Tangier at the weekend and again over there for two weeks to work.[59]

Women mainly worked in the household and in the shops, while men tended to do the physically heavy work.[60]

When Moroccans were recruited, there was no other accommodation in Gibraltar other than the *Casemates* where they could have been accommodated. Gibraltarians themselves lived in cramped conditions and the *Casemates*, formerly military

---

56 Field research diary Tangier, December 25, 2013.
57 Field research diary Tangier, December 25, 2013.
58 Interview with Mohamed Sarsri, October 28, 1996.
59 Field research diary TanGib, February 24, 2020.
60 Field research diary TanGib, February 26, 2020.

accommodation, were owned by the government. In 1969, 850 people were accommodated in the *Casemates* and a smaller number lived in the quarries.

In 1996, only about 400 Moroccans were still accommodated in the *Casemates*, in 20 rooms. The government did not allocate the beds in the *Casemates* for Moroccan workers to individuals but to the companies for which they worked. But it was the workers themselves who paid for the beds. It was only after a labor dispute by the *Moroccan Workers Association* in the early 1980s that it was possible to get the beds rented directly to the workers. However, whoever lost his job, the bed was taken away from him.[61]

Before 1984, it was prohibited for them to give birth to children in Gibraltar.

You are not allowed to bring your family here and you have to apply for a visa for visits and pay about 30 GBP in Tangier ("to bring my son to a visit; and he was born here in Gibraltar").[62]

Under the law at the time, children born in Gibraltar would automatically have become British Subjects – something that was to be prevented at all costs. After that, the conditions changed: If both parents worked in Gibraltar, the children could stay and attend school, but as soon as one parent lost his or her job, the child had to leave school.[63]

Food supply in the besieged colony also had to be reorganized. George Desoisa and his *Gibmaroc Group* succeeded in importing fresh products directly from Morocco and providing the population of Gibraltar with a new livelihood.

Other influences from Tangier also affected life in Gibraltar. The conservative Catholic *Cursillo Movement*, for example, spread through Tangier in the 1970s. At that time, only 20 per cent of Catholics considered themselves believers. The popularity of Father Antonio Campos among Gibraltarians was significant. In 1976, he visited the rock

> with a team of Spanish speaking people from Tangier [...] to assist us establish the *Cursillo de Cristianidad Movement* here. He was Spiritual Director of 90 courses at St. Joseph's Pastoral Center and contributed much to establish confidence in the movement.[64]

With success: In the 1990s, 50 per cent of Catholics already described themselves as regular churchgoers.

In the 1960s, Gibraltar and Tangier were also still connected in terms of tourism. The *Target Guide*, for example, promoted the visit of both cities.

---

61 Field research diary Gib, interview with Mohamed Sarsri, October 28, 1996.
62 Field research diary Gib, interview with Mr. Hakim, March 18, 1996.
63 Field research diary Gib, interview with Mohamed Sarsri, October 28, 1996.
64 The Gibraltar Chronicle, November 12, 1996.

Illustration 56: Transboughaz Tourism

In 64/65 the Spanish government started to close the border between Gibraltar and Spain. Up until that time the English came to Gibraltar and rented a car there, very cheap. Gibraltar now owned a huge park with rental cars and no one came to rent them. And here I came up with an idea when I was 18: we took the cars from Gibraltar to Tangier by ferry. We kept them in the *Garaje Universal*, Gibraltar rented the cars to tourists who came to Morocco much cheaper than Hertz and Avis, and I in Tangier handed them over a contract made out in Gibraltar. The customer saved the price of the ferry and got a cheap rental car. I've had over 50 cars floating around in Morocco. After nearly two years, the deal was over when the *Avis Agency of Tangier* finally found out and reported to the local authorities. Papa, who had very good contacts with high authorities, received a phone call one day in which they said: "Tell your son that he has a week to remove ALL Gibraltar-numbered cars that are in circulation in Morocco are."[65]

I remember it well! Got my first proper job [in 1961] aged 18 taking British tourists for a night to Gibraltar and back to Tangier for the tour company called Horizon.[66]

Since the closure of the border also led to a drop in tourism to Gibraltar via Spain, the local government tried to promote Gibraltar as a holiday destination in Morocco.

---

65 Field research diary, 30.09.2020
66 Nino Weissenfeldt, online platform E (d.n.n).

Isaac Abecasis hands me an old *Who's Who* from the 70s, in which he is listed as *Minister of Housing, Postal Services and Tourism*. He had traveled a lot 'to promote Gibraltar.' He thinks he would have loved to convince Moroccans that Gibraltar used to be Arabic in order to attract tourists here, "into their homeland."[67]

Tangier, on the other hand, has always been a refuge for the inhabitants of the rock, especially during the period when the border was closed.[68]

Annette Caruana and Paul Tunbridge were married in 1970 and their honeymoon was to go to Tangier. The flight by helicopter took only 15 minutes. The very young couple had hardly any money and stayed at the *Hotel Bristol*, which belonged to the family of a school friend of Paul's – the Romeros. In Tangier, they made friends with Muslim *Tanjawis* and others, with whom they visited the *Gospel Club* in *Calle Sanlúcar*, for example. 'It was almost like home,' says Annette, 'with the difference that there was a piece of sea between here and there.'[69]

Later, Paul worked for the Gibraltar branch of *Barclays Bank*. To keep their employees from going island feverish, the bank paid for a monthly trip to Tangier.

Not only for young people like Annette and Paul Tunbridge, but also for Gibraltarian libertines of the time, Tangier was a place of freedom where one could live out one's desires. Thus, the cultivation of relations with Gibraltar was especially necessary for the soldiers of the garrison, because there had been no brothels in Gibraltar itself since the 1920s. Thus, excursions of the short-handed soldiers to Tangier were even necessary to prevent attacks on Gibraltarian girls and, thus, to keep the colony calm. There had always been a large selection of brothels in Tangier:

> For the year 1923, for example, and thus the beginning of the International Zone, it is testified that Madame Simone's *École d'Amour* 'was only one of 46 brothels in the city. There are bodies for sale for every taste: Women and young men, dark and fair-skinned, whorehouses for Christians, Muslims and Jews.' (Bayerischer Rundfunk 2012)

If Paris seemed to have sent to Tangier its pornographic magazines banned in France for display, the United States, them, used the resources of eroticism to the rowdy marketing of their products: everywhere posters on which young women always blond, thin and semi-naked, praised the merits of sewing machines, radios and American cigarettes. The shops offered tourists the equivocal junk of Times Square

---

67 Field research diary Gibraltar, August 13, 1996.
68 "In fact in 1953 [...] the Mons Calpe he played a part in the film 'Captain's Paradise', standing in for the British actor the late Alec Guiness, playing the part of a ship's captain plying between Gibraltar and Tangier. The film also included the beautiful actress Yvonne De Carlo. The presence of the film crew caused great interest in Gibraltar at the time." Insight Magazine, July 2003
69 Field research diary TanGib, April 1, 2019.

as well as the luxury goods of the Old and New World (Vernay 1968: 16). Pornographic films could be enjoyed in places like *Le Chat Noir* and *Deux* at *Soq Dahkel* (Woolman 1998: 194). In 1955, the flight between the two cities lasted only fifteen minutes (L'Eurafricain 1955: 119), the boat trip two hours (ibid.: 239). Tangier as a place of temptation even caused a tangible political scandal and a change of government in Gibraltar in 1969.

Bland Travel also offered excursions to the Moroccan Mediterranean coast in 1969 and 1970 to ensure that Gibraltarians did not have Tangier exclusively as an accessible vanishing point. However, this offer was hardly taken up and was, therefore, soon discontinued.[70]

5.4. 1973-1999 Tangier struggles through the Years of Lead and Gibraltar integrates into the EU

The *Years of Lead* in Morocco are the period from the early 1970s until the death of Hassan II in 1999: A time of mildew, oppression, stagnation – but also of economic stability.

> King Hassan II ran a brutally repressive state that liquidated adversaries and was particularly punishing of Berber nationalism. An Arabization policy was put in place, and as Rabat gained control over Tangier, state officials began to erase the Spanish colonial past, knocking down colonial buildings – streets named after Spanish figures like Cervantes and Quevedo would now bear the names of Arab caliphs or Saudi rulers. People would joke that as soon as a street was given an Arab name, it would deteriorate (*uribat, khuribat*). [...] From the 1970s onward Tangier went into decline: tourism dried up, infrastructure deteriorated, water shortages became routine and criminal gangs emerged in the city's *bidonvilles* doing battle with Islamists. Soon clandestine immigration to Europe started, with people boarding boats at night (or the occasional jet ski), trying to cross the Strait to the Spanish coast. (Aidi 2017: 23)

As far as Tangier was concerned, there had been a devaluation of civil institutions, structures and civil ethos. Vaidon speaks of the disappearance of elegant shops, the increasing sloppiness of hotels, the disruption of water supplies, telephone connections, and fires that could hardly be contained because of an unprofessional fire brigade (1977: 389ff).

---

70 "In an effort to offer Gibraltarians some other place of relaxation locally other than Tangier, excursions were run by Mons Calpe to the Moroccan Mediterranean resort of Fnideq during the summers of 1969 and 1970, but this enterprise did not meet with sufficient support and the excursions were withdrawn" (Sanahuja Albiñana 2011).

In short, public order and public services increasingly collapsed in the 1970s and the economy went downhill. Tangier lost its economic privileges and its status as the country's main tourist destination. The promotion of tourism was shifted to Marrakech and Agadir. The 1970s to 1990s are, thus, described as years in which crime, drugs, corruption (Daoud 2017: 487), gang crime and the failure of public services dominated the city.

'Tangier in the 1980s was terrible, especially the dirt,' says *Tanjawia* Luísa Harris. 'Today there is something like street cleaning, back then everyone put their garbage bags in the street and the cats had a nice time at the garbage. The rubbish was spread all over the place and when it rained the streets were dangerous because of the thick smear of rubbish on them. Thank God that had changed.'[71]

King Hassan II,

who had ascended the throne in 1961 shortly after Tangier's annexation to Morocco, is said to have hated the city: its loose morals, its intoxicating vitality, its dubious reputation. Those who had to seek safety from the monarch's henchmen sought refuge within its walls and hid in the labyrinth of its alleys. Tangier and the nearby Rif Mountains were the source of most of the assassins who sought to kill Hassan II. The old king punished Tangier by starving it economically, culturally and socially. (Doering 2007)

In the *Years of Lead*, bells of authoritarianism, persecution of dissident voices and the omnipresent informer services were ringing over the country. The air for breathing became increasingly thin for all those who had different ideas about how to shape the country. The intellectual Nawfal Alaoui specifies the neglect of Tangier by official policy as follows:

In 1971 and 1972, there were coup attempts against King Hassan II. In July 1971, 1400 "apparently misinformed cadets"[72] stormed the king's birthday party but broke off the action when they realized that they had unwittingly taken part in an attempted coup.

In 1972, parts of the air force tried to shoot down the king's plane, which was on its way back from Paris to Rabat, near Tetuán. After the failed coup, three NCOs and two officers fled by helicopter to Gibraltar.

While the NCOs returned home voluntarily, London extradited the officers to Morocco - to the indignation of the British press, because there is no extradition treaty between London and Rabat. The British government's haste is explained

---

71 Field research diary Tangier, July 31, 2013.
72 TIME ONLINE 1972.

by the rock's precarious situation: since the Spanish blockade, Gibraltar has been dependent on labour and supplies from Morocco.[73]

Hassan II had since then given the North the cold shoulder; Tangier was for him "above all the centre of the Rif region known as the rebellious" (Reifeld 2016: 7). We remember the Republic of the Rif. Informants again and again affirmed that after the two coups d'état and after the unrest in the 1980s, the king insulted his people and described the North entirely as a haven for *contrabandistas* (smugglers) and criminals.[74]

King Hassan II did not visit Tangier once during his 37 years of reign. Nationalization policy under Hassan II was partly responsible for the misery of the North, which had led to the unrest: The country was still in the period of decolonization, Moroccanization and nationalization.

On March 2nd, 1973, much changed in Tangier, because on this day the *Moroccanization Law* was passed. This law decreed that non-Moroccans had to accept a Moroccan partner in their company and transfer at least 51 per cent of the shares to him.[75] This affected especially small shops and craftsmen existentially.

The majority of these are 'one-man businesses with family helpers,' shoemakers, greengrocers and similar professions. Although they will not be expropriated without compensation, but the shops may be sold, Prime Minister Osman has announced that the proceeds from these sales may not be transferred. But what do you do with money that you are not allowed to take with you? It won't be much anyway, given the large number of businesses that are becoming vacant [...] France, with its experience in Algeria, is setting up emergency camps. (Caudex 1973)[76]

The situation is simpler for large companies based in Morocco. Here, Moroccanization is said to have stopped at the possibility of bringing Moroccan capital into the business. (Ibid.)

Thus, the remaining foreigners, whether civil servants, such as the parents of French left-wing politician Jean-Luc Mélenchon (*1951 in Tangier), or businessmen with their companies left the country in droves, companies that had offered good jobs in the decades before, especially in Tangier.

---

73   TIME ONLINE 1972.
74   Field research diary Tangier, April 1, 2013, July 20, 2013, July 29, 2013 and January 20, 2014.
75   "In theperiod of Moroccanization of business, it was obligatory to find a Moroccan partner and transfer 51 per cent of the business to him. There were cases of national interest excluded from this decree." Online platform A, Luís Guimares (d.n.n); translation by the author.
76   "Moroccanization was very difficult for some. Perhaps in excess, even if it had its logic. For some, it was very hard because they had to go out of business without food or drink and return home. Fortunately, most of us have changed our lives for the better. So you stay there and all the water returned to its source." Online platform A, Salvador Cruz Herrera (d.n.n); translation by the author.

It is no wonder that in the years that followed, especially in the 1970s and 1980s, many people lived exclusively from the hashish business, because it was the only economical branch in which one could make a living.[77] After all, since the 1970s, Tangier has seen the construction of important properties or luxurious villas, without this being attributable to any explainable real estate fever – writes Peraldi acutely, referring to the visible influence of the drug economy on the city (2007b). I do not want to insinuate that the drug economy was merely a phenomenon of the *Years of Lead*. Far from it. Even today its influence is remarkable. However, the drug economy seems to have influenced the city more significantly and comprehensively in the period in question than it does today (Haller 2016: 176f).

Similarly, the *Yom Kippur* War in August 1973 changed the mood against Jews who remained in the country. They were increasingly exposed to hostility of all kinds. Many left the country secretly, often without informing their families, because they did not have passports. The mood among the remaining Europeans became more precarious, one saw that the Jews were leaving and Jews saw that the Europeans were leaving.

Two conversations about the Moroccanization and the departure of Jews and Europeans I could follow on the online platform A; they both originate from the 2010s. It is about humiliation, loss and mourning:

Conversation I

Juan Luís Pinto Maman: The fatal thing was the Moroccanization of companies and the need to work with a Moroccan who would take advantage of it without bringing anything in. That was true for anyone who had a shop, a kiosk, a dairy, some fields, a shop of any kind. In general, these people left, and the one who did not have this problem, doctor, professor, lawyer, remained in Tangier [...]. Spanish, Italian, French, American, etc. They left in great numbers. Everyone was looking for another place to earn money regularly, usually in the country where one came from, and especially in Spain, where the ships were going. Algeciras, Málaga, Almería and Madrid.

Alegria Kaufman Hassan: [...] Someone should explain why we left the town where we were born. Nobody left because they wanted to [...]. In our souls, it will always be the city we were born in, the city we remember so much, and it will be part of our lives wherever we are.

Lorenzo Rubio Franco: We left on October 12, 1962, and my father, like many others, was fired by the *Moroccan Hispanic Electric Company*, and he wouldn't leave until we ran out of pesetas and francs. The Spanish consulate paid for our repatriation to

---

77   Field research diary Tangier, July 20, 2013.

Spain, because without money you couldn't eat, let alone pay for a trip. My dear father thought of Tangier until he died.

Daniel Abreu: The Spanish also began to emigrate, mainly to Germany, Switzerland and France. So many friends left the Calle de Sevilla that we were alone and sad and wanted to leave. And apart from that, it's better not to devote too much time to it. Then we feel better.

Yacob Cohen: I'm just going to tell you that there was a time when I was 12 years old that we were afraid to leave the house at night. [...] I was very scared in '67. One day I was walking home from school with my brother and they spat in our faces because we were [...] Jews.

Alegria Kaufman Hassan: Rebi Yamin was the one who represented the Jewish community, and the day they stabbed him was the day we saw our lives in danger.

Yacob Cohen: Since that bad day, we no longer went alone to the Rue Siaghine to the synagogues or to the Zoco as we used to do.

Estrella Hachuel: When they stabbed a Jew, they said it was a Hadj, it was allowed and they did not hurt him .... [...] They said he was crazy and that was the end of the story – but for Rabbi Yamin Cohen, King Mulay Hassan II was great, he brought him to Paris and took care of him – we will never forget that.

Juan Luís Pinto Maman: We had Moroccan passports and there was no religion listed in them. When the Nazis arrived in Morocco, they asked the King to give them the Jews. His answer was: "In Morocco there are no Jews, only Moroccan subjects," but at village level we all knew each other, whether we were Jews, Muslims or Christians.

Pedro Perales Cuesta: What Juan Luís Pinto Maman says is true. But from time to time there were some "crazy people" who took the lives of some Jews, as in 55.[78]

Illustration 57: 1965, Rabbi Yamin Cohen

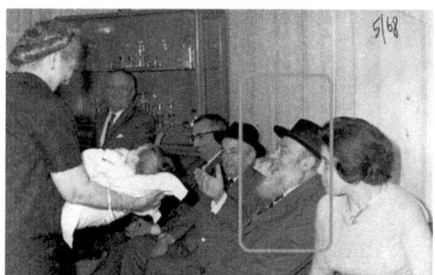

---

78 Online platform A (d.n.n).

5. The loosening of Transboughazian bonds   161

Conversation II

Tomás Fuentes Weidenfeld: We owned my father's gas station until 1974 [...] It was then given a certain person, we were thrown out under the Moroccanization law.
Ahmed M'Barak: They threw you out without giving you anything?
Tomás Fuentes Weidenfeld: Right, [...] exactly, we lost everything we had, the apartment, the cars.
Ahmed M'Barak: Excuse me, I am interested in this topic. Didn't you have any papers confirming that you had bought this, or a title deed? I find it absurd that a country should behave like this,
Luís Guimares Mascarenhas: Moroccanization has not expropriated anyone. They had the opportunity to look for a Moroccan partner, who has a 51 per cent stake in the business, and the other option was to sell the business.
Tomás Fuentes Weidenfeld: [...] Yes, but the partner received 51 per cent. Without bringing in anything, and if you sold, they took advantage of it and didn't give you anything, which means they kicked us out.
Luís Guimares Mascarenhas: [...] I understand, everything was aimed at finding an acceptable partner, but under these circumstances it was difficult to find one.
Tomás Fuentes Weidenfeld: Very well expressed, people used politics.[79]

With the *Green March* in 1975, when Morocco occupied the Spanish colony of Western Sahara, the mood against the Spaniards intensified.

The 1973-1974 decrees on the Moroccanization of land and businesses and the impact of the Green March in November 1975 on the Spanish colony contributed to this and recorded a reduction of 4,150 people in the last two years. (López García 2012; translation by the author.)

An informant tells that hen, at the age of thirteen, his parents urged him to speak French in public instead of Spanish. His sister had only received meat from the butcher because the butcher knew her as a Tangerina. Otherwise she would not have been served. Another informant reports about his own fate:

I left Tangier because I received a letter from the *École Berchet* informing me that I had to take my son out of school at the end of the first semester (December), as from that date it was only open to French and Moroccans [...]. It was also rumored that foreigners born in Tangier would need a work permit to work. I don't know if this was implemented. I had to make an important decision and leave my parents and my brother behind, who are still lying in the Bubana cemetery. [...] Well, I would like to clarify one point. The school problem arose because after Moroccan

---

79   Online platform A, various guarantors (d.n.n).

independence, all French schools were taken over by the French Foreign Ministry and became dependent on it.[80]

Once again, the city experienced an economic downturn and a breakdown of public order. Today in Tangier, they say that the North was starved deliberately because the Makhzen saw the city as a recalcitrant city and the whole North as a rebellious region. Moroccans did not need a visa to travel abroad at that time, only a passport. However, they usually only received this if they had connections. In order to prevent the resulting suffering of the population, which could have been unloaded in the Rif, passports were generously issued there for emigration to Europe.

Nevertheless, some *Tanjawis* also left the country to work in Gibraltar. Abdelghani Aoufi, the owner and operator of *Café Baba*, worked at the *Rock Hotel* in Gibraltar from 1975 to 1996. *Café Baba* plays an important role in Tangier mythology, especially in the echoes of the hippie movement that still is virulent today. It was here that all the artists, writers and actors came to trace the myth in Tangier:

> The cafe has served the kings of both Spain and Sweden; the Grand Duke of Luxembourg; former Secretary-General to the United Nations, Kofi Annan; punk rock legend Patti Smith; numerous actors and filmmakers, such as Daniel Auteuil and Jim Jarmusch; and dozens of mid-20th-century aristocrats. (Shkolnik 2017)

All these strangers were looking for the hidden, the very different, the mysterious character of Tangier. Paul Bowles perfectly embodies the connection between writer and city:

> When I say that Tangier hit me as if it had been a dream city, one must understand the expression in the literal sense. The topography was rich in typically dreamlike scenes: Covered streets resembling corridors, doors on each side leading to rooms, hidden terraces overlooking the sea, streets that were only stairs, dark dead ends, small towns arranged in sloping places so that it looked like the decorations of a ballet drawn against the laws of perspective, with alleys in all directions. There were also tunnels, ramparts, ruins, dungeons and cliffs, all classic places of the 'dream universe.' (Caraës y Fernandez 2002: 24, cit. in Jebrouni 2019: 71; translation by the author.)

But these are European or – more so – American fantasies. Native Muslims (and in former times also Jews and Christians) know the "classic places of the dream universe" as places of their everyday, quite unmystical and unmythical life.

Pictures of John Hurt, Tilda Swinton, Barbara Hutton and Princess Irene of Greece are displayed in *Café Baba*. In Gibraltar, unlike most Moroccans, Aoufi did not live in the mass accommodation in the *Casemates* but in government housing

---

80 Online platform A, Luís Guimares Mascarenhas (d.n.n); translation by the author.

in *Devil's Tower Road*. Aoufi returned to Tangier because he took over *Café Baba* from his father. His grandfather had opened the café in 1942.[81]

American writer, the icon of the literary scene and Tangier lover, Paul Bowles, lived in the city even during the *Years of Lead*. Politics and the decaying structure of the city play hardly any role in his stories. Problems his actors face are not concealed, but they are told laconically. It is important to know that Bowles himself, as a homosexual, was under constant threat from the secret service and in danger of expulsion. He could not afford to politicize the fates of his protagonists or to problematize a social context. Like a veil of timelessness, the *leadenness* also covers the literature and the illusionless style of Bowles.

There are hardly any cultural studies sources from the *Years of Lead* about the disintegration of the city's order because this was hardly a topic that could be addressed, even in the state-controlled media. This is another reason why the book *For bread alone* by Mohammed Choukri (1973) was such a scandal: He spoke of the disorderliness of the city under which his protagonists had to cope with their existence. The explicit sexual passages of his book made it possible to ban the book on moral grounds, behind which the political motivation to ban the book because of its social criticism could hide.

As far as the question of territorial order in the region is concerned, at the time of Hassan II (1961-1999), it was considered whether Tangier should be granted a status similar to that of Monaco to France: As a formally independent principality under the rule of the king's brother, Moulay Abdellah (1935-1983). It was later discussed whether to entrust the possible principality to the brother of King Mohamed VI, Moulay Rachid (*1970). In April 1979, King Juan Carlos I is said to have considered the idea of transferring Melilla to Morocco and awarding Ceuta the status of an International City,[82] as Tangier had previously held it.

During this period, Tangier's gaze tended to be directed inwards and towards the center of Moroccan power, while its links with Gibraltar were of little importance and withered away. At the same time, Tangier was the lifeline for Gibraltar in the face of the cage fever that the Spanish threat of closing the border had triggered. However, the old networks to Tangier were now hardly effective, since the Europeans and Jews had left Tangier. For Gibraltar, Tangier was, thus, a place largely cleansed of the familiar: The facade still stood, *Boughazidad* still existed, but the staff had disappeared or been replaced.

With the accession of the United Kingdom to the European Economic Community on January 1, 1973, Gibraltar also joined the confederation. The territory was given a special status, as Gibraltar was excluded from the rules of the Common

---

81   Field research diary TanGib, February 26, 2020.
82   https://zamane.ma/fr/espagne-les-concessions-de-juan-carlos-inquiet-dune-seconde-marche
    -verte/?fbclid=IwAR1zG_RfuAYLkejoqzjNsPRS9WgcwWpu6pvQttbvLeZtynIAd7d449BQ3fY

Market, the Common Agricultural Policy and the harmonization of taxes – especially VAT.[83] At that time, neighboring Spain was not yet a member of the European Economic Community, so the exemptions were seen as a way of ensuring the economic survival of the colony. However, the people of Gibraltar themselves had for a long time had no say in matters affecting their homeland. It was not until 2004 that Gibraltarians were able to take part in the European Parliament elections. It was not until 1999 that the European Court of Human Rights ruled on this.

Sealed off from hostile Spain, which had closed its land border, ignored by their southern neighbor Morocco, Gibraltarians in the 1970s had only the option of either orienting themselves towards the motherland or to reflect on themselves – with temporary short escapes to Tangier. It is no wonder that the years of the closed border between 1969 and 1982 in Gibraltar are, in retrospect, considered a time of cultural and national self-discovery. I have traced this in detail elsewhere (Haller 2000, pp. 147-241). Morocco, apart from being a place to breathe a sigh of relief from the narrowness of territorial limitations, played a role above all as a supplier of labor. The old networks between Gibraltar and Tangier, however, frayed or disintegrated: In Gibraltar, those groups that were the bearers of *transboughaz* networks –Jews, Spanish Republicans, Britons, Hindu traders – remained, but in Tangier, they disappeared. Europeans and Americans who settled in Tangier during this period – billionaires, eccentrics, writers, hippies – had few ties to Gibraltar. Gibraltar increasingly oriented itself towards Europe in the years following the opening of the border in 1982/1985, trying to tie in with old bonds and create new ones in the local Spanish environment of the *Campo*.

In this respect, it can be observed that Gibraltar's social and institutional commonalities declined steadily between 1969 and 1982 for the *Campo* and 1954 and 1999 for Tangier. The cultural area had developed into two separate regions (*Campo* and North Africa) and an insularized community (Gibraltar). But to what extent did the habitual feeling of connectedness, *Boughazidad*, remain?

In chapters 7 and 8 we will address this question. After the historical preparation (Chapters 4 and 5), the ethnographic sounding out of the networks in the next chapter can now provide a first trace.

---

83   Article 227 (4) of the European Economic Community Treaty and Article 28 of the British Accession Treaty (1972 Act of Accession) stipulates: "The provisions of this Treaty shall apply to the European territories for whose external relations a Member State is responsible." However, Article 28 provides for various derogations for Gibraltar. The Common Agricultural Policy, for example, does not apply, Gibraltar is not part of the Customs Union and is not subject to VAT. Since the first direct elections to the European Parliament, the motherland of the colony has refused to participate in the elections.

6. An ethnology of multiple connections

While I have dealt mainly with historical material in the two previous chapters 4 and 5, the present chapter focuses on the results of ethnological fieldwork. Based on my own experiences and observations, I will trace connections between my sources from 1995/96 and since 2013.

Some people, a few of whom have already been mentioned, will appear at various points in the chapter, therefore, the phrase "already mentioned" will be frequently used.

To this end, in the sense of Baba Farid (+1265) and his proposition "Don't give me scissors, give me a needle! I put together, I don't cut up" (Frembgen 2014: 89), I jump back and forth between the two cities with the intention of tracing a dense interwoven tapestry like a weaving shuttle – and since I am not a weaver, I sometimes go astray in space and time – in other words, beyond the immediate field research. The fact that I sometimes go astray from my original research intention, that I become delirious (*de irare*), is indeed the rule for ethnological research. We go there with a clear idea but then let ourselves go astray and be guided by the people we meet in the field: Our academic questions are not usually the problems that concern the people we are dealing with here. Yes, Marshall Sahlins is right: "Other people's worlds don't revolve around ours" (2013: XIII).

I start in the House of Lilies (*Dar Zambaqía*). This is the name of the property in *Rue Imam Ibn Hanbal* in Tangier's *Mershan* residential area, which I moved into at the beginning of July 2013. Formerly called *Ramon y Cajal*, the street is located between *Avenue Imam Malik* (formerly *Avenue Roosevelt*) and *Avenue Hassan II* (formerly *Avenue d'Alexandrie*). The property and the area are not only an exemplary reflection of the political, economic, cultural and social processes and developments in Tangier since the 19th century but also a perfect example of the way in which the city has developed: The period of the International Zone, the nationalization after the integration of the city into the new Moroccan nation state after 1956, the modernization by King Mohamed VI; the relationship between the upper class and the service personnel; the multicultural history in which Muslims, Jews and Spaniards, French and British, Sindhis and Germans play a role; the diversity of banking houses (Dutch and French institutions), currencies (Pesetas, Pounds, Dirhams

Illustration 58: Dar Zambaquia in Mershan district

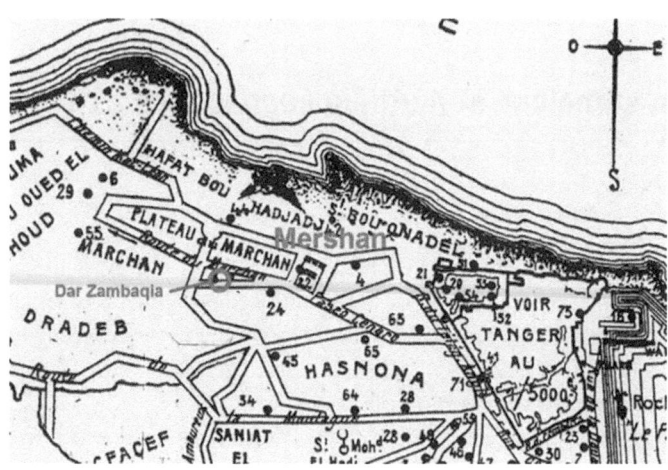

and Dollars) and financial transactions (mortgages, sales and speculation) that appear in the files on the history of the house[1] reflect Tangier as a financial center.[2] It is also an ideal starting point for getting involved in the links between Tangier and Gibraltar.

But let's stay in *Mershan* itself for now. The district is located on a plateau west of the Medina of Tangier, the old town with its *Kasbah*. There, I entered a world of the basal senses, of looking (Simmel 1908), touching and smelling, of the sometimes undisguised physicality and the face; a world of abundance from which those (if one were in postwar Italy) could come who moved to the Borghate, which Pasolini (1955) portrayed so masterfully.

The *Mershan* plateau was not built on until the 19th century. The first building was the Sardinian-Piedmontese Legation, which hosted Italian national hero Giuseppe Garibaldi in 1849/50.[3] The area become urbanized only towards the end of the 19th century urbanized; mainly villas and other two-storey buildings of the upper class were built there. Land was owned mostly by wealthy Muslim and Jewish families. The French Hospital opened in 1893 and the Cherif of Ouezzane settled in the area around 1900. In 1908, after his abdication, Sultan Moulay Abdelaziz (1894-1908) moved to *Mershan*. His vizier Mohamed Mokhri and his Minister of Defense,

---

1   *International Administration of the Tangier Area, Service of the Registry of Territorial Property Jahr.*
2   The private account of Pope Pius XII was also in a bank in Tangier. Online platform A, Tomás Fuentes Weidenfeld, 2018.
3   In 1850, 700 Genoese from Tangier and Gibraltar joined Garibaldi (Daoud 2017: 479).

Mehdi Mnebhi, also moved there and had magnificent villas built. In 1913, the *Institut Pasteur* opened. The palace of the sultan's local representative, the Mendoub, was completed here in the 1920s and in 1970 it was purchased by American publisher Malcolm Forbes. In the 1920s and 1930s, *Mershan* consolidated itself as an upper middle-class residential area (Assayag 2000: 163ff; Mas Garriga 2013).

In 1921, the Café Hafa already mentioned was built on the cliffs facing the sea. Since 2008, the new coastal road has run along the coast below *Hafa*, part of the major redevelopment project with which King Mohamed VI wanted to modernize the city, which has been neglected for a long time since the 1970s and give it a new impetus.

Dar Zambaqía is located in a good neighborhood. *Mershan* offered itself as a residential area if one wanted to explore the Medina: Close enough and far enough apart to practice the right amount of distance and closeness inherent in ethnological work. I was not the first ethnologist who had lived in *Mershan*.

Illustration 59: Edward Westermarck with co-workers and servants in the 1920s

For the great Finnish researcher Edward Westermarck, his *Villa Tusculum* was a place of retreat, collection and reflection. My *Villa Tusculum* was *Dar Zambaqía*. Westermarck had rented his property – at that time on the outskirts of the city, now also located inside of *Mershan* – in 1923 and acquired it a little later, in 1927 (Suolinna 1995). He lived there with his confidant and administrator (Abdessalam) El Baqqali and a servant, El Hadjj. The acquisition of the *Villa Tusculum* allowed Westermarck to realize his dream of a good life (Lagerborg 1951).

Once, when Westermarck had left the city for a longer period of time, he wrote that *Villa Tusculum* was like a sultan's palace without a sultan and that his servants behaved like troops without their general.

Ragnar Nummelin, an old friend and student of Westermarck, visited *Villa Tusculum* in the spring of 1960, and he writes in a letter that El Baqqali lived in the *Villa Tusculum* until his death, which, according to another source, would have been in the autumn of 1942. In 1960, El Baqqali's relatives still lived in the villa, which at that time, belonged to Westermarck's family in Finland.

From *Villa Tusculum* one could look out over the river of Jews, the *Oued Lihoud*, which separates *Mershan* in the West from the Mount, *Jebel Kbir*. The river got its name from Jews who fled in 1492 after the conquest of Granada by the Christian kings and arrived at the mouth of this river (Laredo 1936: 4). Here, the night is especially dangerous, many informants tell me, some speak of female spirits (*ǧinnīyat*), who lured young men to a wet death.

Others refer to smuggler boats that started their journey to Spain from here with people or drugs. The name for one of the sections of the coast, *Bou Qnadel* (Lord of the Lamp), probably comes from those pilots who approached the boats or warned them of enemy ships by showing light signals. Smuggling has always been an important trade in Tangier. Spanish historian Manuel Sanchez Mantero wrote that by the middle of the 20th century, 100.000 smugglers would have been active around the Rock of Gibraltar, including Tangier (Gómez Rubio 1997). These were not always goods that we think of today: Until the 19th century, for example, leeches were also smuggled from Tangier to Gibraltar (Ceballos López 2009: 174, FN 121).

After World War II, Tangier briefly developed into a mafia metropolis: In the early 1950s, famous Italian-American mafioso and smuggler godfather Lucky Luciano resided in the Accordion Building on the *Boulevard* (Ceballos López 2009: 175.),[4] and in 1951, his confidant Jo Renucci (*Petit Jo*) moved to the city. Renucci mainly smuggled tobacco. One of Luciano's most important men in Tangier was Solomon Gozal, a local merchant, the other one, 'Nylon Sid' Paley, who got his name from smuggling nylon stockings, made nearby *Hotel Massilia* his base. Nylon Sid was accused of piracy on the high seas for organizing actions against merchant ships. Exemplarily, he rammed a Dutch ship, *Combatie*, with an 80-ton ship and stole $100.000 worth of cigarettes. In the end, however, Paley was acquitted (Time Magazine 1952).

---

4   Also the jewel thief Michael Caborn Waterfield, known under the nickname *Dandy Kim*, was "*well-known in Tangier and Gibraltar in the* 1950s. The Tangier Gazette 1960

Beyond the big fish, local and regional actors[5] and networks play an important role: As growers, suppliers, transporters, middlemen and coordinators on the ground, etc.[6]

Salomon Gozal was the representative of the Italian 'Cosa Nostra' in Tangier. The entire cigarette and alcohol smuggling from Tangier/Gibraltar/Italy went through his hands. I still remember the day of a wedding in Tangier, when all Italian 'partners' were present.[7]

Someone close to the former most important smuggler family in Gibraltar tells us.

The grandfather was a teacher and used to teach the blind to read braille, later on was a policeman and then moved on to become Chief Sanitary Inspector for Gibraltar.

There was only that family working between Tangiers and Gibraltar. There were a few smugglers in Gibraltar but that family was the best known. The sons were the first. They had a boatyard down behind Victoria Stadium since the 1950s and that's where they used to go every day and do there, work on the launches and an office in *Main Street*. It must have been the early 1950s when they started their business.

They didn't have family connections on the other side. Just people they paid. Most of the clients didn't use their proper names, they used nicknames. Mainly they were clients, not partners. Gib is a small place, as you know, asking around in their own circles and then speaking on the phone and arranging meeting in Gibraltar to discuss business. The sons were also traveling a lot in those days as far as Lebanon and South America. Algeria also they were all over the place.

They were working with ex-RAF launches bought here and they also had Swedish torpedo launches and also had small cargo ships which they used to work with. The bigger ships were used to work as far as Malta and Italy. One of the launches, too, was taken up as far as Malta.

Smuggling in those days consisted of whatever was in demand. Also penicillin was brought back to Gibraltar from Tangiers as it was the neatest source of availability. The family was involved mostly with tobacco smuggling.[8]

---

5   Online platform A, Angel Ortíz (d.n.n): "The owner of the Palace Hotel was an Italian Neapolitan, Mr. Bartuli, who had apparently been in prison in the USA for belonging to the Lucky Luciano gang. He was married to a Jewish woman, Mrs Simmy. And his daughters and sons were our friends [...]." Translation by the author.
6   In 2019, the Tejón family of the *Clan de Los Castañas* will still control drug smuggling in the Campo de Gibraltar (rtve 2018).
7   Online communication, 30.09.2020
8   Personal Communication, Elisabeth Cunningham Olivero, March 7, 2020.

Smuggling and legal trade, of course, are not always clearly separated – one is smuggling and the other is trafficking. Let's stay in Gibraltar for now and look at the Benoliel family, which illustrates the fluidity of the transition between trade and smuggling in the region. During my field research on the rock, I had the honor of making friends with Joshua Marrache, historian of the Jewish community. He tells how:

> Solomon Benoliel was known as the *Golden Boy* because he was weighed in gold when he was born, the gold, the proceeds of the gold was eventually given to the poor of the Town. Solomon's father Isaac and his uncle Judah were sons of Solomon Benoliel who came to Gibraltar from Morocco and was already a merchant by 1760s. They, like all other Jewish merchants, started by dealing as a broker between commercial houses in Amsterdam, London and Leghorn. Their family contacts and understanding of the Spanish, English and, at times, Arabic language gave them great ease in doing commercial transactions, with the permits, that is, of the Governors of Gibraltar and consent of the Emperors of Morocco. They would send brokers to the port of Salé, where they would wait for the sub-Saharan caravans from whom they would buy or exchange goods which were sought after in Europe, such as ivory, ostrich feathers, leather hides, and gold dust from Mali. A very important commodity that was fished for off Moroccan coasts was red coral. This red coral was highly prized in India and China, where it was exchanged for precious stones, Goa being the main port of export of these precious stones, that eventually would make it to the monarchs, aristocrats and courtiers of Europe. The wealthier the family got, the more insular it became, in the sense that, to protect their wealth, they would only marry other families that were at their same level. In more than one will it was expressed that if a Benoliel daughter passed away before her husband, then her husband wouldn't be entitled to her fortune, which go to her children. Judah Benoliel was one of the most powerful of the family. He had contacts with many political and ecclesiastical leaders, including a Pope. During every war between France and Spain against Britain, the Benoliels prospered greatly due mainly to their function as privateers. They owned great ships which would capture Spanish and French ships as prizes. The ships would be sold at the Port of Gibraltar and the cargos of the ships at *Auction Square*, where you find *John Mackintosh Square* today. The Benoliel were not the only Gibraltarian Jewish family as privateers with letters of marque from the British crown.
> Great fortunes were made during the Napoleonic Wars – to this day one can see the amounts of French and Spanish ships bought in as prizes in *The Gibraltar Chronicle* of the time. Napoleon's blockade spurred on ideas in the merchants of Gibraltar, who were 'genetically' economic 'survivors.' Smuggling from Gibraltar had been a curse on the kings of Spain's treasury. Many a time, the Spanish au-

thorities had to correspond with the governors of Gibraltar concerning the matter of the smuggling induced by Jews and Genoese, something that governors didn't take much heed of, seeing they had more important things to care about, such as a convent ball, for example. Smuggling in Gibraltar came under an interesting infrastructure. Smugglers who manned the smuggling ships were usually Spanish residents in Gibraltar. This bought a great deal of conflict between Spain and the British authorities. However, Britain – as long as their home products were being sold together with the smuggled items – turned a blind eye. Many families who benefited from this would eventually settle in England and would start a 'new' life.[9]

Joshua's grandfather Abraham Marrache entered the business of his uncle Joshua Beniso when he was nine years old. He mainly imported tobacco from Havanna, smuggled it on to Spain and, over time, became involved in the trade with other goods, such as chinoiseries and tableware. He bought *Cannon Hotel* in Gibraltar and incorporated it into his growing business.

In the 1920s and 30s, he traded in cork from Spain, which he transported mainly to Germany. During the Spanish Civil War he opened the *Granada Shop* in *Main Street*, where original beads were traded. He had them smuggled to Madrid through an intermediary.

Carmen Polo, the spouse of Franco and known for her greed for jewelry and pearls, had received many of her pearls directly from Marrache's shop. Abraham and his son Sam (*1922) traded in everything that was lucrative and rare, such as Hermeseta (substitute sugar for diabetics). This was scarcely available in Spain at that time, even for the narrow Francoist upper class, so it was ordered in the USA and it was sent from there to Spain via Gibraltar. The trade relations of the family also had a political effect: Abraham became Consul of Venezuela from 1938-1969, and Sam was Consul of Ecuador. The family lived in Tangier during World War II.

> My father used to work for the British delegation in Tangier during the War. Although he was young, he told me once that he was carrying a message to a delegation from one side of Tangier and always had guards following him when he carried something of importance. He got engaged in Tangier to my mother at the age of 16.[10]

Joshua's grandfather Abraham also owned a plot of land in Malabata/Tanger. Samuel Reichmann was present at the funeral of Abraham's wife (and Joshua's grandmother) Rebecca Serfaty. Reichmann had fled from Vienna to Tangier to escape the

---

9   Field research diary Gibraltar, May 16, 1996.
10 Field research diary TanGib, November 26, 2018.

Nazis and was the fourth richest man in the world at the time.[11] Renée Reichmann organized food deliveries for Jews to the Nazi-occupied areas of Europe. With the help of the Francoist High Commissioner of Tangier, General Luis Orgaz, she arranged protection and travel visas for many European Jews.[12] Among the rescued who arrived in Tangier were also about 200 Jews from Rhodes (Ceballos López 2009: 313). The rescued were first accommodated in the harbor in one of the buildings of the entrepreneur Braunschwig. He had founded and financed the schools of the *Alliance Israélite* in Tangier and Casablanca. The Reichmanns also initiated the Talmud School in Gibraltar in the 1970s and financed it for a long time.[13]

Illustration 60: The Reichmann Family

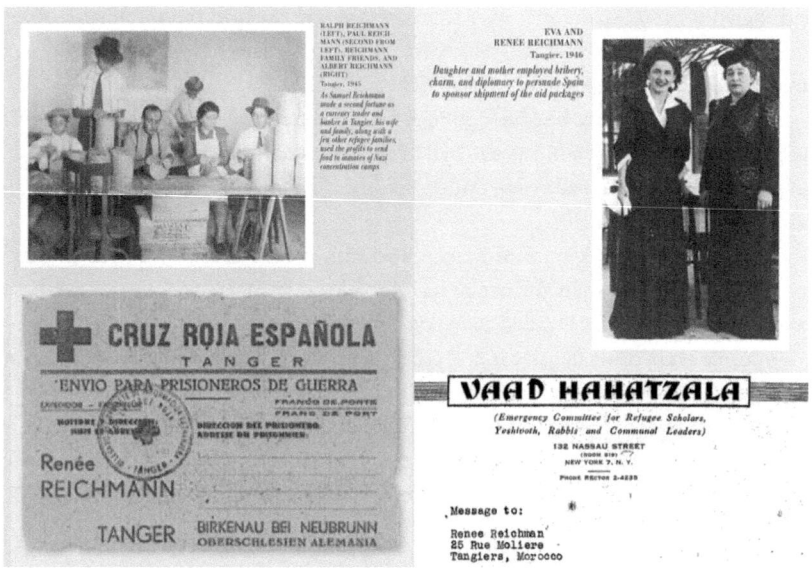

My informant Carlos Betanzos comes from a simple family who physically carried out the smuggling with boats. He describes the smuggling from a different, more practical perspective. Carlos, born in Tangier in 1940 and living in Gibraltar since the 1960s, says

---

11 Personal communication, Sidney Delmar, November 26, 2018.
12 It is said that he was one of the Spanish consular officials who had taken an oath to Franco who were not Francoists but had served Spain before. Personal communication, Paul Allemand, January 11, 2020.
13 Field research diary Gibraltar, May 31, 1996.

6. An ethnology of multiple connections   173

I started smuggling when I was 17, while still living in Tangier. With friends, not relatives. It took me a lot of effort to get in there at all. Once you passed, you were in a better world, you had more prestige, more money, better clothes. The smugglers were normal people, like everyone else in Gibraltar. They weren't Mafia guys. In Tangier and Gibraltar they are not smugglers either, legally speaking, but of course they are for the Spaniards who greeted us with shots. Nor was it drugs, but tobacco, transistor radios and so on. [...] People were also smuggled. Jews were brought from Morocco in small boats.[14] They were smuggled out of Morocco, and the smugglers financed that too. There was once a ship [*Egoz*] with 42 passengers! They all drowned![15]

Mr. Betanzos' entry into the smuggling circles proved to be difficult, because if there were 20 boats, they already had their crew.

Only when something happened on a boat did you have a chance to fill the void. I waited months to be told they needed someone. The voyages were not without problems, the sea, the weather, the coastguard [...] How did they communicate back then? On the radio. There was a cargo agent, the client's delegate in Spain. He came to Tangier and from there to Spain and knew exactly where we were to land. The captain sailed. But the freight officer set the course. The places where we landed were rarely the same. How did the freight officer know that the landing place was not by chance just checked by the police? Lantern signals indicated whether something was going on and where. Sometimes the Civil Guard would take possession of the people with the lanterns on land, but most of the time they didn't tell us which movements meant what, so the smugglers were rarely caught. But many smugglers lost their lives [...] Italy was a particularly difficult place. There was smuggling from Tangier and Gibraltar to Sicily and Genoa.[16] The round trips lasted a month.[17]

I'll break a lance for smugglers! Because smugglers make sure the people get something at a reasonable price that their own state denies them! In the Spanish Civil War, for example, it was penicillin! In Spain, people died and only the rich

---

14 During the Spanish-Moroccan riots in the hinterland of Ceuta (1859), 3800 Jews had already fled to Gibraltar. The British administration – supported by the *Alliance Israélite Universelle* and other organizations, and London and Paris – set up a refugee camp in the North Front, where the refugees remained until the end of the turmoil in the same year (Mesod Benady 1993).
15 Field research diary Gibraltar, September 29, 1997.
16 Carlos, thus, describes exactly the sphere of action of the great godfather of smuggling in the Western Mediterranean, the aforementioned Juan March. To what extent Carlos worked within this network, I cannot say.
17 Field research diary Gibraltar, September 29, 1997.

could afford it. The poor died. The smuggler risks his life to make the important things accessible to the poor – of course to make money out of it. But still. The Spanish could get good quality tobacco in Gibraltar. It's like a service. In Tangier they sold watches at the price per kilo because they didn't have any in Spain. When I was a child, we took bread to Spain because Spanish bread was inedible. And at the border, customs officers sometimes took it from us.[18]

Carlos passionately advocated the cross-border ethics of smugglers. Smuggling was done with anything for which hardly any tax was payable on importation into Tangier, so that there were substantial profits on exportation (Ceballos López 2009: 174): Warnings such as those in the *Tangier Gazette* (1950) that smuggling – especially of tobacco products – damages the community's finances and would be punished with fines and prison sentences hardly seem to have stopped anyone from smuggling. Smuggling mainly concerned consumer goods such as "American cigarrillos americanos, liquors, silk stockings, expensive lighters, watches."

Tanjawi Zoubir Salihi (*1932) also smuggled for many years after World War II, namely with the ferry *Mons Calpe*. Mostly it was concerning goods from Gibraltar to Tangier: Radios, fabrics, all kinds of things. When it became too risky to disembark the goods in Tangier – that is, when the bribery of the customs officers failed – the goods were thrown into the water. They were then picked up by boats, which brought them ashore. Salihi himself transported goods and distributed them to merchants who transported them on to Casablanca or other cities in Morocco.[19]

Traditionally, smuggled goods from Gibraltar were offered for sale at the *Fondak Chijra* in Tangier (Guignet-Boulogne 2015: 59).

On February 18, 1956, a Hollywood-style chase of smugglers who were discovered in Tangier not far from Ghandori Beach and who fled by car across the city took place. Shots were also fired. The smuggled goods were worth over a million francs and consisted of American Parker pens and watches (Searle 2019: 56) to be taken to Gibraltar (La Dépeche Marocaine de Tangier 1956b).

Later, cross-border smuggling networks consolidated. Sir Joshua Hassan, former Prime Minister of Gibraltar, told me about smuggling in the mid-1990s:

---

18   Field research diary Gibraltar, September 29, 1997. I had the conversation with Carlos in his apartment in 1997. In preparation for my research on TanGib, I had fished this memory bag out of the chest again in the hope of being able to continue the conversation and the material. But it was not easy at all. After long research, I was able to locate one of his grandsons in 2019, and when I explained who I was and if it was possible to talk to his grandfather, the grandson said that Carlos would not remember me and was not interested. Initially offended, I came to the conclusion that there was no reason at all why he should have a conversation with someone he didn't remember. It was my interest, that of the ethnologist who was trying to defrost the memory bag. Why would that be of interest to Carlos?

19   Field research diary TanGib, February 20, 2020.

Gib fast launches taking hashish form Morocco to Spain. Moroccan ships leave Morocco with hashish, and in the Straits, passes it on to a launch which takes it to Málaga or to whatever they arranged with the carabinero, it's all arranged with them.[20]

Joe Moss, the Minister for Youth, confirmed: "These fast launches have enough horsepower to go from Gib to Morocco, from there to Spain and back to Gib."[21]

In the 1990s, journeys between Gibraltar, Morocco and Spain were coordinated by an infrared system installed on the top floor of one of the houses in the old town of Gibraltar, which belonged to a well-known smuggling family.[22]

The demand up to the coast in Spain is still there, the traffic has shifted: Gibraltar has closed down, so they are running it out of Ceuta, Tarifa, miles and miles of unprotected coastline where there are very lax registration laws and you can go in and out without any surveillance. You need a Spaniard to unload it in Spain, a Moroccan to supply it from Morocco, and a boat which could be a Spanish or a Gibraltarian boat. (Informant, *1967; Haller 2000a: 66)

In 1995, this system was politically scandalized and British authorities were forced to seize speedboats from Gibraltar (Haller 2000a: 241ff). Gibraltarians were particularly pleased to note that the then Spanish Foreign Minister, Abel Matutes, who had excelled in the scandal, himself came from a family of smugglers from Mallorca (Oliva 1985). It is also said that in the office of the main smuggling family, a photo of the head of the family with Matutes is hanging on the wall.

At about the same time – 1996 – the trials of 20 major drug lords in Morocco took place (Daoud 2017: 72), including Ahmed Bounekkoub, drug lord of Northern Morocco, affectionately known as H'midou or Derdib (Jackal),[23] during which

"other links between drug traffickers and government officials, including two advisors to former governors in the Tangier province, three civilian police colonels, the military police colonel in charge of coastal surveillance and three former chiefs of the Tangier urban judiciary and national security police service (Ketterer 2001: 32) became public."

The headquarters of Bounekkoub's smuggling was a hotel in Sidi Kankouch, which is directly connected to the sea by a channel. The estate is reminiscent of the command center of a villain from James Bond movies. However, Derdib was and still is widely regarded as a man of honor in Tangier because, unlike other smuggling

---

20   Interview with former Prime Minister Joshua Hassan, March 20, 1996.
21   Interview with Joe Moss, Minister for Education, Youth and Culture, April 12, 1996.
22   Field research diary Gibraltar, April 17, 1997.
23   In high Arabic, *dib* means both wolf and jackal, in Moroccan Arabic, however, it means jackal exclusively.

barons, he showed generosity towards the families of his employees and the corresponding communities. This kind of servant care, together with an unpretentious lifestyle and his origins in a poor fishing family gave him the reputation of a Robin Hood.

Illustration 61: 2013 Dedrib's headquarter, Sidi Khankouch

In Gibraltar, the smuggling crisis was framed as a local event, while in Tangier the Derdib case was also perceived as a local, or at best regional, event. I myself had interpreted this in the same way in my previous work. However, the simultaneous action against Gibraltarian smugglers and against Derdib is certainly no coincidence, although this statement has so far only been an assumption. I noticed this simultaneousness only while writing this book.

Here, the question arises as to how much we as researchers are guided by our own research results in the past, or rather, research over several decades transports the memory or documentation bags into the present whilst revisiting and, thus, creating a contemporaneousness that is hardly relevant for those involved at the time.

I found no sources about the simultaneity of the events in Gibraltar and around Derdib. Conversation partners also could or wanted to say little about it. In this respect, it would be the task of future political scientists or economists to investigate this question.

Today, smuggling still takes place between Morocco and Spain, Ceuta, on the African side of the Strait and the Costa del Sol. It is still tobacco, but there is also hashish, marijuana and harder drugs. The goods change, the networks remain.

The Civil Guard has confirmed that Moroccan networks are operating on the Spanish coast, particularly in Campo de Gibraltar and Almería, with logistical support from fishing boats, transporters and Spanish businessmen. Some employers working in the Strait of Gibraltar offer to transport immigrants across the Strait at a cost of between 100,000 Pesetas and 150,000 per service, according to the above-mentioned sources. (Barbero 1997)

It is not unusual that representatives of official bodies in Gibraltar, Morocco and Spain (The Gibraltar Chronicle 1997; GBC 2019b) are repeatedly involved in smuggling and sometimes profit from it (Peraldi 2007b). An informant says:

> Sometimes you have to transport 1000 kilos of hashish from Morocco and ask a boat owner if he would take over a load. The owner learns that the load is only 20 kilos. 50.000 GBP for a load, nobody would say no. Then the *big fish* would give the police a tip – because the police are often in cahoots and are corrupt. The poor smuggler is caught, the 20 kilos are gone, but while the police are busy with the operation, the remaining 980 kilos are transported unmolested.[24]

Illustration 62: 1990s, Tobacco smuggling, Gibraltar postcard

---

24 Field research diary Gibraltar, June 28, 1996.

And in Tangier, a smuggler confirms my question about the danger posed by the Moroccan coastguard and the Spanish civil guard: "They have all been bribed: Moroccans and Spaniards alike, that is not the problem."[25]

Tattoos can embody the relationships between Gibraltar and Morocco. A local tattoo artist says:

> Many of those who smuggled something illegally into La Línea and Gibraltar carried religious images of Christ and the Virgin Mary [...] symbols of protection when they are at sea. Many come to me and say: 'Oh, I have promised this or that, I have promised, 'if I am successful,' then I will have the face of Mary pricked, they think that the gods help them smuggle, for example: They are taken with so much weight (cargo), then something unexpected happens in court, they are acquitted and make a promise, like: 'When I am free, I will have the head of Jesus pricked.'[26]

It has even been claimed that drug trafficking is the only functioning industry in Tangier and the north of the country. After all, 40 per cent of the forests in the Rif region have been replaced by the cultivation of Kif (Daoud 2017: 69). And again and again, officials and police officers were involved in smuggling. A retired commissioner in Tangier told me:

> "In the past, I used to warn the smugglers in good time if action was to be taken against them. I've always wanted to help people. They were poor, they lived on it."[27]

Derdib, too, could probably only carry out its activities with a high degree of official protection (Ketterer 2001).

Drug money was frequently invested in the purchase of businesses, companies and established enterprises (Daoud 2017: 64ff). I was often told stories like the one of the most famous candy store in Tangier. The owners sold their property to a drug lord (who still owns it today). The drug lord, in turn, had no idea about confectionery production, he only needed the shop as a façade for money laundering. Therefore, the professional confectioners were dismissed.[28] A similar story is told about a textile factory which is now empty: The production of the garments had only served to make losses and, thus, to launder drug money.[29]

Everyone in Tangier knows that the building of *Café Giralda* on *Boulevard Pasteur* belongs – or used to belong – to Derdib. The money of the drug mafia is particularly well invested in the construction sector, and Peraldi (2007b) has conducted a

---

25   Field research diary Tangier, March 30, 2013.
26   Interview with Keith Tonna, July 16, 1996.
27   Field research diary Tangier, December 15, 2013.
28   Field research diary Tangier, April 27, 2013.
29   Field research diary TanGib, September 8, 2019.

masterful investigation of this branch of the economy. There is a connection between the drug economy and the decay of old, well-preserved buildings in Tangier: The old villas would be bought, demolished and then a large block would be built on the old, magnificent plot of land. Fortunately, Dar Zambaqía has not yet fallen victim to such barbarism, but many properties in the neighborhood have already met this fate. So, we come back to *Dar Zambaqía*.

That I moved into the property is a somewhat pompous statement: I rented a small studio there, which was located above the garage of the property: A big furnished room with kitchenette, internet access and satellite TV, a small bathroom with toilet. Windows to the garden and to the street.

In addition, the roof terrace, from which one could enjoy a view over *Mershan*, the *Dradeb* district on the right, *Villa Seruya* on the street, the floodlights of the old football stadium to the north and the Old Town on the left.

The rent of 4000 Dirham included the services of the cleaning lady, Ferdaouss, who took care of my apartment twice a week. I was allowed to use the garden of the house and the terrace of the main house, because my English landlord Charles left the house on the day I moved in: Charles underwent chemotherapy in London; he was to die of cancer in November 2013. Therefore, the property was largely empty except for me and one other tenant, Nuria. Nuria Fernandez-Vidal headed the office of the International Organization for Migration until spring 2014 as the officer responsible for the Tangier-Tetuán region.[30] For decades, the city has been a port of call for African migrants from the more southern parts of the continent and the starting point for their often cruel and deadly crossing in boats described as nutshells over to a Europe that seems tangible from Tangier and fires the imagination and desire of both locals and foreigners.

Nuria hosted friends in her apartment for over a month, and I also made friends with them: Mayte Carrasco, Spanish war reporter, filmmaker and writer, and her later husband Marcel Mettelsiefen, who was nominated for an *Academy Award* in the documentary category for his film *The Fate of the Children of Aleppo* in 2017.

Ferdaouss took care of the house and yard, feuded, cleaned and aired, washed my clothes and ironed. She sometimes brought food that she had cooked, but my friends advised me against eating it: All women practiced magic and sorcery, especially with food! In this way, they tried to bind a man to themselves and make him dependent. In particular, when strangers bring ready-cooked food into the house, one can be sure that the cook has other intentions than just to satisfy the hunger of the man being cooked for. I have to say that I never tasted the results of her cooking because I was uncomfortable with magic.

No, I have not found any magical items in my apartment that I could clearly identify as magic artifacts. This happened to the writer Jane Bowles, who was en-

---

30   https://www.iom.int/cms/about-iom.

chanted by her lover Khadija. In the course of my research, I was to discover that magical everyday practices were also commonplace in Tangier and that many lived in a world of magical realism (cf. Zillinger 2013: 67-99).

If you stepped into the garden through a green metal gate from the street, you entered an oasis of peace. In front was the main house, which for me was always just 'the villa,' with the terrace where garden furniture made taking tea a pleasure; the garden itself with its stone floor, trees and planters. To the right, the garage and above it, my studio, both shaded by a huge cherimoya tree, whose fruits were harvested in late summer. In *Dar Zambaqía*, I felt as I lived in the days of the International Zone of Tangier – a tolerant and free refuge beyond the moral and religious narrow-mindedness that largely characterizes everyday life in Tangier today. Sometimes, I thought of Barbary Lane 28 in Armistead Maupin's (1978) *Tales of the City*: An ideal space to live, dream, develop and work.

The brand-new, middle-class block *Mershan Gardens* where I lived before, about 400 meters from Dar Zambaqía, is quite different. This block in Rue d'Istanbul was built on the site of the old *Villa Rkaina*, right next to *Villa Delmar*. The entrance to a tunnel that connects *Mershan* with the port is there.[31]

A granddaughter of the owners of *Villa Delmar* is the Portuguese-American actress Daniela Ruah from the US TV series *Navy CIS: L.A*. A great-great-great-uncle of Ruah, Captain Artur Carlos de Barros Basto, a Portuguese *Dreyfus*, also lived in Tangier for some time. Like most of the Jews of Tangier and Lisbon, the Delmar originated in Tetuán. Relatives of the actress live in Gibraltar – the Marrache family, already mentioned several times, who are also related to the singer David Guetta and the music producer Bob Zaguri (who produced French actress Brigitte Bardot) through the family in Tangier.[32]

Joshua Marrache and his family have already appeared in this book several times. He is married to Corinne Senior from Marseille. Corinne is originally from Boudnib/Tafilalet in the Moroccan Sahara, but her family tree also includes Benchimols from Tangier.[33] Her great-grandfather Zaddiq Messaoud Senior was the cousin and closest friend of the greatest Jewish-Moroccan saint, Baba Sali (Rabbi Yisrael Abuhatzeira) from Tafilalet.

Corinne's family moved from Boudnib to Oran in Algeria; she herself was the last of her family to be born there in 1961; her mother had left the country in 1962

---

31 Field research diary TanGib, February 19, 2020.
32 Field research diary TanGib, March 4, 2020.
33 General Oufkir, the assassin against Hassan II in 1972, came from Boudnib, which is why Hassan II starved this very place. The young people from this place could not study and did not find work then, of course, not even the Jews.

and still keeps the bullet from the Algerian War of Independence which almost hit her when she stood on the balcony of her apartment with little Corinne.³⁴

Villa Rkaina and *Villa Delmar* are located opposite the small mosque Hajj Abdessalam El Fertakh, where the faithful have been holding Friday prayers since 1974. This was previously one of the youngest synagogues in Tangier, the *Esnoga Peretz*, which existed until 1968 and was donated by Doña Estrella Peretz Pinto. "De Peretz a Erez" (from *Mershan* to Israel) was then a dictum. The owner of the building who passed away in 2020, a Muslim who loved his city, has largely preserved the synagogal structure of the building.

Dar Zambaqia had a wall toward the street, about three meters high with broken glass on top and protected by the thick undergrowth of a tree. Up to now, shards of broken glass and branches would have deterred any intruder, according to my fellow tenant. I got a different impression when one night I saw children like cats climbing over the walls of the neighboring house, so fast and nimble, almost artistic and effortless, that my trust in the protection provided by our wall was deeply shaken. I must admit that I then switched on the beguiling night lighting of the garden not for romantic reasons but to simulate the presence of residents, especially when Nuria was traveling and I was alone in the square at night, as was often the case. Even when I left the studio in the evening, I would sometimes turn on the TV so that its flickering could be seen by potential riffraff from the street. "It's dangerous at night," Ferdaouss said, "Demons and ghosts come and drive you crazy."³⁵ The estate was also haunted – a former resident, Madame Bourveau from South Africa, had woken up one night and an old man was standing close to her bed. He disappeared into thin air. A murder had also taken place in my studio. Fortunately, I didn't know about it until spring 2020.³⁶

*Propriedad Magdalena, No. 3054*³⁷ – as the property was once called – originally had a floor area of 354 sq.m. and was named after the owner, British citizen Magdalena Sacarello, born in Gibraltar in 1899. Sacarello acquired the property in December 1947 from the larger Mazouari Tangier I, T. 219, whose owner was H.E. Si El Hadj Thami Ben Mohamed El Mezouaiu El Glaoui, the Pasha of Marrakech. He was said to own most of the land in Marrakech, as well as in Casablanca, Fez

---

34   Personal communication with Corinne Senior Marrache, March 29 and July 9, 2019.
35   One night she had been woken by an eerie knocking at the door, she was scared and became ill. Charles sent her to the doctor, who thought she was healthy. But Ferdaouss was frightened sick for two months.
36   Field research diary TanGib, February 19, 2020.
37   International Administration of the Tangier Area, Territorial Property Registration Service Year.

and even Tangier – and also that he owned large shares of the country's lead, cobalt and manganese mines. The Pasha was laid to rest on January 18, 1956.[38]

The purchase documents refer to "un terrain a bâtir" – a building plot. The purchase price was 106.200 pesetas. Sacarello had been married to Lorenzo Ferrary from Gibraltar since 1931. In the field research I had done in Gibraltar in the 1990s, I had got to know Gibraltarian Sacarellos and Ferraris. The purchase of the property took place in the immediate postwar period: Gibraltar's civilians had been evacuated during the war, many of them to Tangier. It was not foreseeable whether one could return to Gibraltar at all – a house in Tanger was the obvious choice for many. For a long time, the British authorities refused to allow civilians to return to Gibraltar. Many Gibraltarians had to wait until 1952 for a return to their homeland (Haller 2000a: 114).

Gibraltar and Tangier were very closely linked economically, but above all, through family networks, as the references to the Marrache family have already suggested. Many families active in Gibraltar had property on both sides of the Strait. British entrepreneur Ernest Waller, for example: He married the very young Ethel Maude Ryman in Tangier in 1898. She deceased in Gibraltar in 1921 but was buried in Tangier. They had a daughter, Ethel May Waller, who was born in Tangier, but lived with her husband Leonard Robinson (Robbie) in *Marina Court*/Gibraltar.[39] I lived in exactly this building during my research in 1985/86.

Waller founded the property company in 1894 and *Sociedad Waller & Co* (Laredo 1935: 125) joined it in 1921 with John Crichton-Stuart, 4th Lord Bute. Together they founded the *Compagnie Rentistica*[40] in 1928. Lord Bute was private financial advisor to British Kings George V and George VI, who owned the majority of Rentistica.[41]

Their main activity was the construction or acquisition of hotels: The Rentistica owned the *Rock Hotel* in Gibraltar and the *Minzah* in Tangier, as well as the *Mamounia* in Marrakech (where Alfred Hitchcock shot a central scene with Doris Day and James Stewart for his film *The Man Who Knew Too Much*), the *Reina Cristina* in Algeciras, the *Alhambra Palace* in Granada and the *Hotel Palace* in Madrid.[42]

---

38   The Gibraltar Chronicle, January 17, 1956. He died at the age of 84 and was the commander of a million Berber warriors. He was a friend of Winston Churchill and tried to oust Sultan Mohammed V (The Gibraltar Chronicle, January 17, 1956). His funeral was attended by his former opponents of the Istiqlal Party and the Democrats (The Gibraltar Chronicle, January 24, 1956).
39   Online Platform B, Ruthie García Mifsud (d.n.n).
40   Like other important groups, the *Rentistica* had its lobbyist in the Legislative Assembly of the Tangier Zone, the brother of the Marques of Bute.
41   Catherine, April 23, 2014: http://www.noblesseetroyautes.com/hotels-de-legende-the-rock-a-gibraltar/.
42   Catherine, April 23, 2014: http://www.noblesseetroyautes.com/hotels-de-legende-the-rock-a-gibraltar/; http://lavietouristique.com/index.php?option=com_k2&view=item&id=323:h%C3

Are you confused now? Wait and see, there's more ...

Manuel Peña and Esperanza Orellana built the *Teatro Cervantes* in 1913. Esperanza Orellana was the niece of Frasquito el Sevillano, who came to Tangier in 1850 and acquired a large and inhospitable area in the dunes, which is now bordered by *Rue de la Liberté*, *Rue de la Marine*, the *Playa*, *Monte Jilali* and the *Boulevard*. It is an area that today occupies a large part of the city center.

Esperanza's son Antonio Peña Orellana was a true Tangerino and diplomat of the Spanish Republic. He married Maria Luisa Gomez from Melilla. Her father, Agustin Gómez Morato from Valencia, in turn, was commander-in-chief of the Spanish troops in Spanish Morocco, a republican and superior of the later caudillo Francisco Franco. Antonio Peña Orellana's daughter Esperanza was born in exile in Mexico.

Esperanza's son, the writer Trino Cruz Seruya, now lives in Gibraltar. He became friends with Mohammed Choukri and another writer, Zoubir Ben Bouchta (Aujourd hui 2017). He is a school friend of the local government representative of Gibraltar in London and former editor of *TThe Gibraltar Chronicle*, Dominique Searle. Dominique's father Jon (1930-2011), my good friend, modeled the sculpture of James Joyce's Molly Bloom in the Alameda Gardens.

Jon was also a longtime editor of *The Gibraltar Chronicle* (1966-1987) and had consistently promoted cooperation between the *Journalists' Association of the Gibraltar Campo* and the *Journalists' Association of Northern Morocco*. The *Premio Jon Morgan Searle* was established to honor the cooperation between the two coasts. However, journalistic links between the two places had existed before, remembering the first printing houses that came from Gibraltar. American journalist David Woolman was also the *Moroccan Courier's* correspondent for Tangier and Gibraltar (Vaidon 1977: 275), regularly writing a column called *Zoco Chico* [Soq Dahkel] on Tangier and one on Gibraltar, entitled *Chips off the Old Rock* (Edwards 2005: 162). As Jimmy Joy, he wrote about gossip in Tangier in the *Tangier Gazette*, and in the same newspaper, now called the *Tangier Gazette and Times of Morocco*, there was a separate column News from Gibraltar in the late 1950s. On the corresponding page there were also advertisements for Gibraltarian shops and restaurants.

Esperanza was the closest friend of Désirée (Dizzy) Buckingham. I got to know her because together we rescued the overturned gravestone of the Georgian Princess Sonya Dragadze at the Anglican cemetery of St. Andrews.

The daughter of American engineer (and alleged spy) Winthrop Buckingham and Smyrna-born British socialite Ellen Ashe was friends with the Dragadzes. She still lives on the *Vieille Montagne* in the former accomodations where the Buckinghams needed to build a railway line from *La Vieille Montagne* to the port of Tangier.

%B4tels-de-tanger-au-xix-si%C3%A8cle--des-monuments-historiques-en-d%C3%A9perditio n.

Illustration 63: Conference of the Journalists of the Boughaz

The Buckinghams themselves built the *Hotel Farhar*, which became a meeting place for writers,[43] spies and glamorous guests.

Desirée is a friendly neighbor of Peter Hinwood, actor of *Rocky* from the *Rocky Horror Picture Show*, and lover of the late Christopher Gibbs (N.N. 2017b), whom I met in May 2013 at a garden party he hosted for the Anglican community. He is regarded as the inventor of the fashion of *Swinging London* in the 1960s, muse of Princess Margaret and Marianne Faithful, and introduced his friend Mick Jagger to the upper circles at the time.

Dizzy was portrayed in a short chapter by the anthropologist Jacques Vignet-Zunz (2016: 35ff). A student of anthropologist Ernest Gellner, Vignet-Zunz resear-

---

43   Jane and Paul Bowles stayed at the *Farhar* for a short time (Green 1992: 35).

Illustration 64: St. Andrews Cemetery

ched the Caribbean, Chad, Libya and Jbala, but he has also described his childhood at *Soq Barra*, the outer market of Tangier, in detail in a beautiful little publication (ibid.: 35ff). In his old age, Vignet-Zunz acquired a second foothold in Tangier, in a house of the Buckinghams in *Mujaheddin District*, in addition to his home in Casablanca.[44]

Back to Jon Searle in Gibraltar, whose widow Lina Danino I often met during my field research 2019/20 at *Café Jury's* on *Main Street*. She was the first physiotherapist in Gibraltar and the first local woman to hold the rank of officer, which was an extraordinary honor in those days, when natives were regarded as inferior.

In her long career, she treated film actor Errol Flynn, who sprained his finger while sailing, and several crew members of James Bond actor Timothy Dalton. Lina introduced me to her friends in 2019, including Lady Maxine Torrent del Prat. They meet regularly at *Jury's* and invited me to join them if I was in the area at that time of day.

Someone says that Pope Francis now has Mark Miles, a Gibraltarian, at his side, who accompanies him in countries where he has perfect Spanish and English.[45] A sworn community called the *Bloomsbury Circle* by Lina's son Dominique. I enjoy being together with Lina and her friends, the clever frozzies and funny exchanges. Everything is talked about, only Brexit is left out, as one of the circle has voted for a Brexit.

---

44 Field research diary TanGib, February 16, 2020.
45 Field research diary TanGib, August 19, 2019.

Several members of the circle are friends with an Australian journalist who lives in Tangier as well as in Gibraltar, where he is said to have moved into his main refuge. The journalist had already caught my attention with his deliberately colonial British appearance in 2013 in Tangier, where he could often be met at *Soq Dahkel*. He seemed to me at the time like a deliberately eccentric staging of zonal British life. Public photographs and the documentation of *Monthy Python* actor Michael Palin[46] show him in constant company of his rooster *birdie*.

The journalist's broker has placed a Gibraltarian couple in their *Villa* in the Kasbah. The couple preferably lives in Tangier. They once waited at the *Café de Paris* to be picked up by a "red dwarf"; a little man actually with a red fez came, just as the journalist had announced.

It led them to the journalist's apartment. This looks like an Oxford study room from the 1930s. He had an apartment full of *dwarfs*, which he also called "dwarfs," to serve the guests. After dinner they had to entertain the guests by performing all kinds of tricks. Then cock *birdie* made the rounds and marched through the apartment. A 90-year-old English lady without shoes but with a well-conducted headdress completed the evening party with the words, "now I need a big sip of gin." She lay down in an armchair and immediately snored like a sailor. The couple said they felt like they were in a Fellini film, and when they left the apartment, they wondered if this was really reality.[47]

Well? Is your head buzzing now? It should be, because this is where the stories of the worlds of Tangier, Gibraltar and beyond come together in most confusing ways. But that, dear reader, is the normal state of affairs, you know? Even today. *Normal* is that the connections between cultures and people are so diverse that they cannot be reduced to the dull black-and-white fever fantasies of Identitarians and lunatics. *Normal* is that we are interwoven, not everyone with everyone else and perhaps not as closely as in the examples presented here. But in diverse, interrelated ways.

Let's go back to *Mershan*. *Villa Seruya* was sold in 2017 and will probably soon be replaced by one of the new soulless blocks. The family still owns a tenement building behind the villa, the *Inmueble Seruya*, on *Avenue Hassan II*, formerly *Rue d'Alexandrie*. Luis Ayouch Tangir, a member of the Jewish community and Chief Commissioner, was a friend of the Seruyas and provided an apartment in the *Inmueble Seruya* for the property manager, also a former police officer, who is still alive in 2013.

Luis Tangir's mistress, his secretary Raquel Cohen, lived in Calle *Leon L'Africain* 1, a house which was exclusively occupied by Jewish families at the end of the Zone period. Raquel lived there with her brother Alberto Pimienta, who ran the music conservatory in the *Ras M'sallah* district. Sam Cohen, director of Bland (Golemo

---

46   https://www.palinstravels.co.uk/book-2008; Seealso N.N. (2017a).
47   Field research diary TanGib, September 1, 2019; See also N.N. (2017b).

2018), also lived there with his wife, as did the Soudrys, a poorer Jewish family. Albert Soudry was a boxer in his youth, later he was met at the *Cafe Tingis* on *Soq Dahkel*, where he worked as an "intermediary": "when someone had something to sell, he looked for somebody who could carry that out. They received a commission, and Soudry was gentle and trustworthy."[48] Albert Soudy's mother was a Christian from Córdoba. Her son died in a car accident and the mother fought for many years in court to get the insurance for the death of her son. An informant recalls that Señora Soudry always wore a headscarf like Grace Kelly and wore absolutely white make-up, with painted eyebrows.[49] The Soudrys had a daughter, Raquel, who called herself *Carlitos* because she felt like a man. She attended the school of the *Alliance Israélite* and was then sent by her mother to an apprenticeship as a tailor. Three inhabitants of the house *Leon l'Africain 1* (Golemo 2018), Alberto Pimienta, Sam Cohen and Raquel Soudry were, thus, homosexuals. Alberto Soudry had beaten up his sister at an early age because she dressed as a boy. She had been able to develop only after the death of her brother.[50] Raquel was well-known throughout the city; she was respected in the Zone time.[51] I had met *Carlitos* in 2013 in the Jewish retirement home, and it was one of the most shocking and unpleasant meetings, for which I am still deeply ashamed:

> The community leader, Abner Levy, said: "Raquel has always appeared dressed as a boy; she is a lesbian and has lived here in the Jewish retirement home for 20 years." Levy disparagingly said that she was not a good cherry to eat with. She was depressed and used to call herself *Carlitos*. "This woman has caused many problems. She lives on the upper floor and has developed a lesbian relationship with a simple woman from Tetuán who lives downstairs. Sometimes they would spend the night together. You have to put a stop to that, of course, because that's not acceptable," Levy says.

He went into her room, confronted her and headbanged her – just like Zinédine Zidane did in the World Cup final in Berlin in July 2006 – banging her forehead to show her what works and what doesn't (he physically demonstrates this) to me. And he beat her.

---

48   Online platform A, Maurice Castiel (d.n.n).
49   Personal communication, Paul Allemand, September 29, 2019.
50   Field research diary Tangier, December 20, 2013.
51   Personal communication Paul Allemand: "There is no real Tangerino that she does not know. Everyone knows her. She was accepted. She was like that, period. She was the archetype of the homosexual. [...] it was called, 'she's like Carlito,' or 'another Carlito.' She was the reference. The most famous lesbian because she didn't hide. Dressed like a man. She felt like a man." Field Research Diary Tangier, December 22, 2013; translation by the author.

"The woman was very dangerous; one day she had gone on a rampage and because the nurses could no longer control her," he – Levy – went into her room. Then she grabbed a knife and hurt his cheek. It was not a large wound, but it bled anyway. Then they were taken to 'the asylum' in Tangiers quartier *Beni Mekkada*. "Nobody wanted this Raquel, not even the Spanish consulate, although she is a Spanish citizen and receives a Spanish pension of 7000 Dh. Since she was Jewish, she was then admitted here" – according to Levy's version. He then made sure that she would only stay "upstairs" and "the other one" only downstairs.

After she had rioted, he himself had attached a metal lattice door to one of the empty rooms, behind which he then locked her in. "Such a thing is very rare here in the old people's home." He showed me this door, which was two or three rooms away from Raquel's present room. We went past there, he did not enter the room. He told me to just look at her, this "real guy," but not to talk to her, she was very dangerous. I felt terrible that this woman was presented like an animal. Levy had also behaved very paternalistically when visiting the other inmates – I found it disgusting. But while he was introducing the others to me personally, I stood in the doorway at *Carlitos* and he shouted: "Why don't you greet us, say hello, what's wrong with you today?" He was very harsh. The poor woman visibly wallowed uncomfortably in her armchair.[52]

I digress. As so often in this chapter. But the digressions are only supposed to be chitchat. They are meant to lead us back and forth between Tangier and Gibraltar on intricate paths and detours.

So back to Luis Tangir, the Commissioner. His son Joe made the acquaintance of my a friend of mine from Gibraltar, when he visited Tangier before his marriage in the 1970s and 80s.[53] Today, Joe lives in Israel.[54]

Like the Seruyas, another friend of mine, Estrella Abudarham has also a mixed Jewish-Christian family. Her father Abraham comes from a family in which Catholics were constantly married. Of the eleven siblings of her grandfather Mordejai, only two married Jewish. The children of such marriages often convert to Judaism. Mordejai's mother was a Benady from Corfou (formerly also an English colony).

Estrella's mother Sultana came from Oran in Algeria. Her brother David died in 1957 at the age of 23 in a bomb attack in Nedroma, Algeria. Sultana's father Haim Sebbag had lost his first wife early. He married a second time, but the new wife did not get along with her stepdaughter Sultana, beat her, so that Sultana left the house at the age of twelve. First to Casablanca and then to her cousin Aline Sonego,

---

52   Field research diary, December 19, 2013.
53   Personal communication, July 17, 2019.
54   Online platform A, Pedro Perales Cuesta (d.n.n).

who lived on the *Boulevard* in Tangier. Aline and Sultana are cousins of Mery Gabay-Bensimon, the aforementioned sister-in-law of Joshua Hassan.[55]

Estrella has been married since 1980 to Billy Abudarham, who runs the *Abudarham Synagogue* in Parliament Lane in Gibraltar. Both also ran a kosher grocery store, which they handed over to Hillel Edery at the turn of 2019/2020. This Gibraltarian Sephardi also comes from Tangier, where his grandfather Ambrosio Edery owned a butcher's shop and the restaurant *Al-Mabrouk*.

Avenue Hassan II on the edge of the *Mershan* plateau is dominated by two buildings: The *Villa Alster* and the aforementioned *Inmueble Seruya*, built in 1948.[56] The floor and walls of the courtyard are still decorated with large mosaics depicting orientalizing scenes from Don Quixote. Tiles with Spanish proverbs girded around the courtyard like a ribbon. An artist from Seville, a friend of old Mr. Seruya, designed the tiles.

The *Inmueble* consists of 44 apartments, 15 of which are vacant in 2014. Of the 44 tenants, only eight pay rent. Nobody would bother to collect the rent, says caretaker Jebbari.

Illustration 65: Inmueble Seruya

---

55 Estrella's grandfather Haim Sebbag was married to Estrella Benoliel, who is buried in Asilah. Field research diary TanGib, April 3, 2019.
56 It is unclear whether the patio of the building contained *Café L'Espagnole*, as some informants claimed. In any case, the heir to the estate, Trino Cruz Serruya, does not know about it (personal communication, September 30, 2019).

Whenever someone dies or moves out, the apartment is locked and not re-rented. That's why there are so many empty apartments. Those who pay rent and are long-established tenants pay 450 Dh per month [the rents have remained at the old level]; tenants who moved in later pay 1000 Dh, the most expensive rent is 2000. Up on the roof lives an old Englishman, who is the only non-Muslim today. Originally it was a Spanish Jewish house.[57]

The caretaker said that those tenants who don't pay rent would speculate that they might take over the apartment at some point. He said the legal titles were unclear. He himself also used to live in Gibraltar for half a year.

Neighboring *Villa Alster* got its name from the banker and gold speculator Jakob Alster and his wife Gerda, who had fled from Poland to Tangier during the war (Pons 1990: 105).

The administration of the *Inmueble Seruya* and *Villa Alster* was in the hands of Jewish family Benzecry, who had to change their name after independence because there were also Muslim Benzecrys. Mesod Benzecry, the guardian of the *Villa Alster*, named himself Sicsú el Fassi after his mother. He had a son, Youssef, who died in a traffic accident. A gaffer had stolen Youssef's ID because it was a foreign ID. Mesod searched in vain for this ID.[58]

Across the street lay *Hospital Benchimol*, the oldest hospital in the city. In 2010, it was demolished by order of the mayor in a night and fog operation to make way for a parking lot for the neighboring *Palais Moulay Hafid*.

The demolition of this building led to international entanglements, not least because the land was never officially sold to the government by the Jewish community that owned it. The Jewish community was as surprised by the demolition as the building guards who were arrested during the operation.

The palace itself was built for the Alawi Sultan Abd al-Hafid (1908-1912), who wanted to settle in Tangier after his resignation in 1912. He chose the property of the Belgian ambassador Abraham Sicsú. Sicsú's widow sold the villa, which was demolished for the construction of the Alawite palace. Since 1926, the palace has housed all Italian institutions. The Sicsú of Tangier are related to the philosopher Helene Cixous.

Ethnologist Elisa Chimenti, born in 1883 in Naples but raised in Tunis, came with her parents and siblings to Tangier, where she occasionally worked as a teacher. Elisa traveled the country with her father, who had been a doctor for Sultan Moulay Hassan, and served him – as she spoke Arabic very well – as an interpreter. Signore Chimenti died in 1907 from an unintentional overdose of a drug with which he treated himself. Elisa was briefly married to the Polish noble

---

57   Field research diary Tangier, December 15, 2013.
58   Field research diary Tangier, December 30, 2013.

Illustration 66: Hospital Benchimol destroyed

Illustration 67: Elisa Chimenti

Dombrowski, her sister Dinah to local doctor Dr. Gerard.[59] With her mother, she had founded the first Italian school in Morocco in 1914. In the late 1920s the school moved to *Palais Moulay Hafid*. The Chimentis lived opposite the palace in a villa

---

59   Personal Communication, Olga Benchekroun, December 29, 2019.

owned by the Laredo family. Elisa's sisters Dinah and Julia died in car accidents in the 1960s. In 1969 Elisa passed away; she was not only a respected and admired teacher, but also loved Arab culture and "her" Tangier, which she had described as an Andalusian city on African soil. Signora Chimenti collected, documented and published articles on the popular culture of *Tanjawis*, especially on the Jewish community.

At the beginning of the 20th century, she tells the Moroccan reality from the perspective of an attentive anthropologist – with participation, respect and love, so rare in her time. She is constantly exploring, discovering and revealing the roots and cultures of Morocco, starting from the myths of the civilizations that flourished around the Mediterranean, to take up the origins of Berber and Arabic culture, while respecting the tradition of oral histories from Black Africa and the Middle East. At a time when the borders of Africa were being drawn by the great powers at the Berlin Conference in 1884, Elisa Chimenti proved that culture is transversal, denouncing the nonsense of these border cuts (geometrical and geopolitical) that do not take populations into account. (Taburlini n.d.)

Back up in *Mershan, Dar Zambaqia*.

On September 7, 1948, another loan was taken out, with Tejuman Nenumal Aswani, a Hindu from Sindh, who lived in the Medina of Tangier. This time the mortgage was 75.000 pesetas (at 8 per cent interest). I also know the Aswani family from my research in Gibraltar. Since the middle of the 19th century, Sindhis have had a considerable trade network in the Mediterranean along the link between Great Britain and the jewel of the Empire, India. They are mainly members of the merchant caste of the Vishaya. During the Second World War, the Sindhis imported goods of all kinds to Tangier, bypassing the German submarine blockade. They not only earned money from trade, but also invested in real estate. Sindhis, for example, acquired the luxury *Hotel Cecil*, which no longer exists today, *Cine Vox* and *Café Fuentes* on *Soq Dahkel* (Woolman 1998: 107).

At a time when the influx of Indian women into the Crown Colony was forbidden so that they would not bear children there who could then have become British citizens, the women and children of Gibraltarian Sindhis lived for the most part in Tangier (Haller 2003).

In retrospect, it is impossible to reconstruct whether Sacarello had taken out the many mortgages to finance the construction of *Dar Zambaqia*, or whether he had already intended to buy it at a higher price.

In any case, on January 11, 1949, after only two years in Sacarello's hands, the property was sold to two buyers for a total price of 500.000 pesetas. Two-thirds went to American-French Princess Marthe-Marie de Chambrun, wife of Prince Alexandre Edmundo Ruspoli and daughter of French politician Pierre de Chambrun, whose sister Thérèse was married to French colonial hero Pierre Savorg-

Illustration 68: Jane Bowles and Marthe de Ruspoli

nan de Brazza. One-third went to Armenian-French lawyer Serge (Sarkis) Ter-Oganessoff, who came from Choucha in Nagorno-Karabakh. This temporary lover of the princess lived with his mother and sister in *Dar Zambaqia*. He died on January 31, 1963, one day after the household moved to the Jebel Kebir in Marthe's new house.[60]

Marthe de Chambrun was known in Tangier only as "Princesse Ruspoli," she played an important role in the best society of Tangier, descended from French General Lafayette, an uncle was married to the sister of the American President Teddy Roosevelt. Madame de Chambrun was educated at Oxford, spoke six languages fluently (Woolman 1989: 159; Ceballos López 2009: 296) and had been an enthusiastic amateur archaeologist, historian and Egyptologist (de Chambrun Ruspoli 1982). Marthe had the idea that the whole Mediterranean Sea as far as Egypt would have been settled from Atlantis and that the culture of the Mediterranean came from Atlantis. She had discovered the small Punic tombs in *Mershan*. She had always walked around with a walking stick, and once she discovered by chance that the

---

60 Personal communication, F05EE, December 5, 2019. Green (1992. 299) tells of the rumor that Ruspoli killed her lover Ter-Oganessof.

earth was loose there. She followed the matter up and, thus, discovered the Punic or Phoenician tombs.[61]

Her father, Pierre de Chambrun, was the only French senator to vote against France surrender in 1940. Marthe was arrested and imprisoned by the Nazis for supplying Allied soldiers in Paris with civilian clothes so they could escape undetected (Glass 2011).[62]

Madame de Chambrun and her husband, Prince Edmondo Ruspoli, were already living separately when she settled in Tangier in 1951. For several years Princess Ruspoli and Jane Bowles maintained a close friendship and at times a love affair (Finlayson 1992: 164, 168).

Jane Bowles and Madame de Chambrun were friends with the aforementioned Georgian Princess Sonya Dragadze and her Indian husband Narayan Kamalakar, through whom they met. Sonya had three children, the youngest being her daughter Tamara. Sonya was a concert pianist and played recitals with the celebrated Spanish dancer Mercedes Ruiz, who still lives in Tangier. After Sonyas death – she passed away in Marthes house – Narayan disappeared into a monastery in the Atlas Mountains. After its closure in 1965 (Green 1992: 340), he wandered as a mendicant monk with a donkey named Confucius towards Spain.

Tamara, Sonya's daughter, is another anthropologist with a relationship to Tangier – although she specializes professionally in the states of the Caucasus and only published a novel about Tangier in her youth – *Like Milk on the Fire* (Dragadze 1965). Already at the age of 12, Tamara was reported in the local press when she caught a burglar in her parents' house.[63] As Sonya's daughter, the redheaded beauty gained access to local celebrities, Marthe de Ruspoli, Jane Bowles and the Buckinghams. Thus, she temporarily took care of Marthe's correspondence, and later she kept the friends in Tangier connected to the clinic in Malaga where Jane Bowles was treated and died in 1973. Tamara's passion was and still is dancing, about which the *Tangier Gazette* already reports in 1959, when she danced in front of H.M. Mohammed V.[64] Today she lives in England, an anthropologist and author, and as a member of the Liberal Democrat Party she was a fervent representative of the Remainers in the Brexit campaign.

Ahmed Benchekroun stems from an important Moroccan family. He and his wife, Olga Alves Fonseca, were friends of the Kamalakars (Tamara's mother and stepfather), Jane Bowles and Marthe Ruspoli. Ahmed entered the service of Elisa

---

61   Field research diary TanGib, February 19, 2020.
62   Which had traumatic consequences for their children [...] one of the daughters successfully threw herself off the rocks not far from *Dar Zambaqía with* suicidal intent.
63   The Tangier Gazette, *Small Girl Catches Thief*, March 9, 1956: 5.
64   The Tangier Gazette, July 17, 1959.

*Illustration 69: 1961 Olga Benchecroun
and Tamara Dragadze*

Chimenti at the age of 23, and the couple founded and now manages the *Elisa Chimenti Foundation*. Olga had met Tamara when she herself was 17 years old. Ahmed will take me to his house, the magnificent *Villa Miramonte* in the *Brooks* district, in August 2019. The construction of this villa was finished in 1952 and belonged to Salomon Bergel.[65] *Brooks* was also the home of the Benaim family, who built the first villa in the district. But one after the other, it gets tricky again:

> Monsieur Bensadon emigrated from Tangier to Venezuela in the 19th century and then returned to his home town. His son David owned an import/export business in *Rue Leon l'Africain* and also worked for *Banco Pariente*. His daughter Alegria married Mimoun Benaim and, after their marriage in 1961 at the *Chocron Synagogue* in *Rue de Mexique*, the young couple moved to their father-in-law's villa in the *Brooks* district. Mr. Benaim had developed this area in the west of the Old Town together with his companions, Monsieur Cohen and Monsieur Azagury. Close friendships developed between the young couple and their peers in the neighborhood. One of the neighbors was Ruth, the daughter of Salomon Bergel, who now lives in

---

65   He "made a fortune by selling American Tobacco to American Troops in North Africa during the Second World War." Personal communication, Sidney Delmar, September 15, 2019.

Gibraltar. The Jewish-Gibraltarian *Restaurant Güitta*[66] – which for a time belonged to the American Mafia godfather Lucky Luciano – was also located right next to the father-in-law's villa. The Benaims produced shoes and owned several shops in Tangier, such as the traditional *Gigi* shop in the *Rue de Vigne*. When they moved to Gibraltar in 1970, the shop was sold to Rachid Tafersiti Zarouila, the city's leading home author, as mentioned above.

I met Alegría Benaim in 1996 in Gibraltar. In 2020 we have an in-depth interview. Her mother tongue is Spanish, at school she spoke French and, of course, she is fluent in the local Arabic dialect and the North African Jewish lingo, *Haketija*. She attended *Lycée Regnault* and became a clerk.

With her husband Mimoun Benaim she left the city relatively late – her parents had already moved to Israel in the 1960s. The couple settled down in Gibraltar in hope of a better economic environment than in Tangier, which at that time was slipping more and more into decay. However, it was not easy for them in the beginning because they hardly enjoyed any rights there. It took several years until the lawyer Sam M. Benady QC was able to win citizenship for them.

Alegría comes from the upper class and describes herself as privileged. She remembers the wonderful time she spent in Tangier. They had everything: English biscuits and chocolate, Swiss watches, the latest electrical appliances and cars, electricity, water, there was no need and everyone got along. Unlike in other Moroccan cities, there had hardly been any pogroms or attacks on Jews.[67]

Let's go back to *Villa Miramonte* in the neighborhood of the Benaims. Salomon Bergel sold his villa to an Algerian, who, in turn, sold it to Benchekroun, who is now (2020) trying to sell the villa for two million Euros.

Ahmed Benchekroun was Consul of Portugal, he is grandson of the Governor of Tangier during the time of the Spanish occupation in the 1940s, Caid Mohamed Temsamani. He sold his property in *Rue Shakespeare* to El Thani, the Emir of Qatar. On another plot of land on the mountain stands his *Villa Kepler*, where he lives with his wife Olga. Mr. Benchecroun was deslighted when I told him that Johann Kepplers mother ist related to my family. The villa is in the best neighborhood. The palace of the mother of King Mohamed VI is directly opposite. The Temsamani had sold the neighboring villa to the Belgian Robert van Kerckhove d'Hallebast, the last administrator of the International Zone of Tangier. The villa of Abdelkader Erzini is also located here: He was Honorary Consul of Sweden, his father was Honorary Consul of Morocco in Gibraltar.[68]

---

66   Online platform A, Pedro Perales Cuesta (d.n.n).
67   Field research diary TanGib March 1, 2020.
68   Field research diary TanGib February 19, 2020.

On the desks in Benchecroun's Miramonte and Kepler villas are photos with the future King Abdullah of Saudi Arabia, with Sultan El Thani of Qatar, with President Mario Soares of Portugal, with Elisa Chimenti and with Madame de Chambrun. "Marthe," as he also calls her, had been very active in the "Moroccan cause" at the UN in the course of independence and had translated many texts for the Moroccans.

On April 3, 1953, "Marthe" Ruspoli and Oganessoff took out a mortgage by mutual agreement with Caisse Neerlandaise de Credit, S.A., Tangeroise, in the amount of USD 4000, the interest for the current year and the fee for the policies.

On November 28, 1953, Princess Ruspoli sold one-sixth of her share to co-owner Ter-Oganessoff for the purchase price of 70.000 pesetas. On March 6, 1956, the two owners took out another mortgage – in the same amount as the 1953 loan from *Caisse Neerlandaise* – this time with *Société Hypothecaire de Tanger, S.A.Tangeroise*.

After Tangier was annexed to Morocco in 1956, a wave of nationalization set in that profoundly changed the international city in the years that followed. The street names were also changed. The Dar Zambaqía estate, for example, was no longer located in *Calle Ramón y Cajal* but in *Rue Imam Ibn Hanbal*.

The property was sold on November 30, 1962, to a Briton, Michael Parker, for 31.500 Dirham. He deceased in 1982 and left the property to a German, who, in turn, sold part of the property, 600 m2, to a Moroccan in 1991. The remaining property built on with the main house, consisting of ground floor, first floor and garage, now had the size of 3 hectare and 600m2. For a while, the German was tempted by a Belgian, who intended to buy the property to set up the Belgian honorary consulate there – the Belgian had applied for the position of Honorary Consul of his country. But in vain.[69] After the death of the German, my landlord bought the property. Some Gibraltarians still own property in Tangier today. As has been mentioned previously, the block of *Inmueble Seruya* in the Avenue Hassan II still belongs to a *transboughaz* family.

The current owner of the estate, writer Trino Cruz Seruya, descended from one of the mayors of La Línea on his father's side, his grandfather was impresario of the Teatro Cervantes de Tangier, also mentioned above. He married Paloma, daughter of Moses Seruya (*1880) from Gibraltar.

He himself had been expelled from his family (father from Gibraltar, mother from Oran) because he had married a Christian woman from Marbella. For a time, he sought his fortune in Iquitos, Ecuador, like so many Jews from TanGib (Malka n.d.). Moses returned to TanGib and finally acquired the villa from the Pasha de Marrakech El Glaoui.[70]

---

69 Field research diary TanGib, February 19, 2020.
70 As an anecdote: Elsewhere (Haller 2016: 144), I wrote that the current owner of *Dar Zambaqía* told me that his property belonged to El Glaoui the Pasha of Marrakech, who lived there with his wife and mistress. This story could not be true because *Dar Zambaqía* was not built until

Illustration 70: Plaque at Villa Seruya

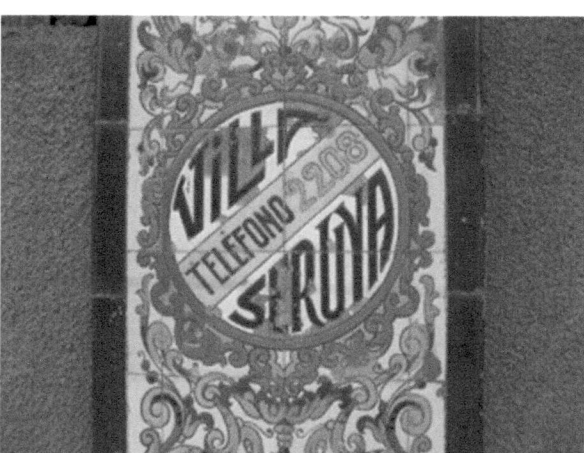

Villa Seruya is located opposite the *Dar Zambaqía*. Thus, a circle is closed, or rather, a dense fabric is completed. But there are still threads hanging here and there that make the whole thing seem unfinished. In the following chapters, we will see if the threads can be cut off or if it is possible to attach them. With threads of different colour, different density, different texture.

1948. Presumably, the property where the Pasha pursued his amorous preferences was *Villa Seruya*, which is located opposite *Dar Zambaqía*.

7. Reordering borders, dynamization and a new rapprochement

Territorial issues in the region are still diverse and the different national claims are linked to each other: Morocco regularly reacts when Spain claims Gibraltar for itself, for example, by demanding sovereignty over Ceuta and Melilla. Morocco, for example, occupied the small rocky island of Perejil off its coast one day after the announcement of a decision on the possible "Joint Sovereignty" of Great Britain and Spain over Gibraltar on July 11th, 2002. Perejil belongs to Ceuta according to Spanish interpretation. Spain and Morocco still argue about the sovereignty of the island, which is inhabited by two hundred goats of shepherdess Rachma Al Achiri. This led to the so-called Parsley War (or Perejil Island crisis) when Moroccan soldiers occupied the island on July 11th. Six days later, 1000 Spanish soldiers landed and expelled Moroccans. Since then, the issue has been controversial – even though Spain called on the Moroccan army in 2014 to expel 13 illegal migrants from the island (Sánchez/Olías 2014).

Illustration 71: Debatable Territory –Isla Perejil/Leila

Over the past 20 years, both parts of TanGib have undergone an unexpected spatial expansion, an urbanistic and infrastructural upgrading and an economic transformation – but in different ways.

While Tangier has eaten its way deep into the rural hinterland and even began to expand to the Atlantic shore, Gibraltar has transformed its hitherto little-used military bastions and defied the sea more and more to create residential, commercial and office space. In addition, the other side is slowly coming back into the focus in both cities.

7.1 Dynamization of TanGib

The apartment block *Marina Court*, where I lived during my research in the 1990s, was then the second tallest building on the marina, which was located behind the house. Boats were moored under my balcony and I could look across the Bay of Algeciras over to Spain. Today, *Marina Court* is the smallest building in the now so-called *Ocean Village*. Where the marina was located, a promenade with restaurants that protrude into the sea had been built and, on the right hand side, the new *Casino* that is modeled after a cruise liner. Luxurious skyscrapers with similar apartments draw the eye; *Marina Court* now seems dwarfish and out of time.

Illustration 72 : Land Reclamation in Gibraltar

Land reclamation has created new neighborhoods throughout Gibraltar. This is not only due to the fact that many foreign companies are required to be physically present with their staff. In Gibraltar, another lucrative branch was added to the financial industry, the *online gaming* or *gambling industry*. This created new local jobs, but also led to a large influx of Israeli, UK-British and Chinese workers. There are also preparations to offer local housing to Gibraltarians living in Spain until then, in case of political problems with Spain.

In Gibraltar, the 2019 election manifesto (YGTV 2019b) of the governing coalition of socialists and liberals (*GSLP-GLA*) is evidence of further planned land reclamations and the rededication of sites previously used by British Forces, such as the *Governor's Estate*, *The Mount*, the *Northern Defences* or the dockyards, of new and major plans.

In Tangier, various master plans (Haller 2016: 186ff) launched by King Mohamed VI in the new millennium were effective, for example, *Tangier-Métropole* (ibid.: 191ff). From the beginning of his reign in 1999, the then new king turned his attention to the north of the country, long neglected by his father, and in particular to the city of Tangier (ibid.: 176ff), which he chose as his favorite residence. Road and railway projects considerably dynamized urban space. The economic dynamization of Tangier is closely linked to such infrastructural projects. Not only have new areas been designated as a free trade zone, but the new port of *Tangier-Med* (ibid.: 181) and the production facilities at *Chrafate, Meloussa* (ibid.: 179ff) and *Mohamed VI Tangier Tech* have given the city an undreamt-of economic upswing, which, however, does not benefit large sections of the population (ibid.: 186f, 240ff). France, the Emirates, Qatar and China are investing heavily in the local economy. As in Gibraltar, there is no end in sight to the dynamism of Tangier. This was, of course, before the Corona Crisis.

7.2 Migration

Ever since I started working on the Strait of Gibraltar, migration from south to north has played an important role: What is happening in the Strait today is unfortunately not new historically but dates back to the 1990s. It is not the place to deal with the migration from Morocco to the EU, as this book focuses on the relations between Tangier and Gibraltar – and, in this respect, the migration disaster for the poor from the south plays hardly any role: Gibraltar is not a destination for migration. However, I would indirectly blame the focus of research on large migration movements towards the north for the fact that local relationships between Moroccan and Iberian cities are often out of focus: Social science research looks almost exclusively at migration and turns a blind eye to other, local phenomena and ties (Driessen 1992, 1995, 1996a, 1996b, 1999; Nyberg Sorensen 2000, 2006). These have been removed from the focus of research attention, which has given way to an economic view: What currently seems relevant is examined – and indeed relevant from the perspective of the national centers in which the respective academic cultures are integrated. TanGib is definitely not one of them.

The *Schengen Agreement* was signed in 1985. It provided for the lifting of controls at the internal borders of the Schengen states and their transfer to the external borders. Spain joined in 1991. Moroccans have not been able to enter Spain without a visa since then. Regarding Gibraltar, which is outside the Schengen area, Spain's reference to the agreement and the non-ratified *Convention on External Borders* served as an argument to justify a series of measures at the border: It was about controlling the illegal immigration of Moroccans into Spain via the Gibraltarian land border.

The Strait has increasingly become a problematic border for the legal movement of people. Until recently, Morocco itself was hardly present in the political and everyday discourse of Gibraltarians. Measures such as the cross-border EU program *Interreg II UK/Morocco Gibraltar*, which aimed to promote cooperation between the two territories, are largely unknown – even among local politicians. A first follow-up program, *Interreg III Gibraltar (UK)/Morocco*, ran from 2000-2006 and had a total budget of 850.000€.[1] No other succeeding programs have been launched.

The migration of Moroccans and other Africans via Moroccan Mediterranean ports to the EU is mostly directed towards the lonely coastal areas between Algeciras and Cadiz.[2] *Espaldas mojadas* – wet backs – they are called, immigrants who cross the 14 km wide Strait between North Africa and Spain in small boats to escape the hopelessness and poverty of their home countries. They came and still do come secretly and at night. Often the boats capsize and passengers drown. In the 1990s, the number of deaths on the wet border between Morocco and the EU rose, thanks to its militarization: Partly because Morocco feared losing its youth, partly because of pressure from the EU (Rickmeyer 2008: 19). In the case where they reached Europe successfully, they were mostly employed in agriculture or construction, or – like many Moroccan women who were promised jobs in the tourism industry – they ended up in the brothel of a rural town in southern Spain.

---

1 https://ec.europa.eu/regional_policy/de/atlas/programmes/2000-2006/european/interreg-iii-a-gibraltar-united-kingdom-and-morocco.

2 In 1996, 7741 illegal migrants were brought from Morocco to Andalusia; in the first two months of 1997, the *Guardia Civil* in Andalusia brought 768 illegal immigrants, 645 of whom were Moroccans. Siehe *Menores explotados en Almería*, in: El Pais, April 7, 1997; "Jams of more than two kilometres by the Spanish railway controls at the border crossing of Gibraltar," October 2, 1998; El Pais: "Gibraltar responds to controls at the fence by boarding a fishing boat," October 3, 1998.

Five dead, sixteen missing as search continues
A search last night continued for 15 Moroccans or Algerians and two Spaniards after the tiny boat in which they were part of a group of 30 being smuggled across the Strait of Gibraltar took on water and capsized. HMS York was Scene of Action Commander and led a group of Gibraltar rescue teams in a Spanish co-ordinated sea rescue after a French yacht Pichenbelle came across the sinking vessel, saw and rescued five men and brought them back to Gibraltar. Pichenbelle left at 7am from the Rock and found the men 500 yards off Tarifa's coast.[3]

Accidents of this kind have long been part of everyday life in the Strait of Gibraltar and neighboring regions. The secrecy and illegality of today's crossings are fatally similar to the circumstances under which Moroccan Jews fled in the 1950s and 60s.[4] So, news of illegal migration across the Straits of Gibraltar has accompanied me throughout my academic life. It is a human catastrophe, a political declaration of bankruptcy and a scientific impasse – everything has long been well documented and analyzed: At the time of my field research in Gibraltar (1995/96), through the reports of colleagues (e.g. Driessen 1996a, 1996b, 1999; Nyberg Sorensen 2000; Hannoum 2009; Rickmeyer 2009), in my research in Tangier (since 2013) and politically again since the increased monitoring of the routes via Lampedusa and the Aegean (since 2018).

While migration from North Africa is mainly to Spain, the well-guarded cliffs of Gibraltar itself are rarely approached and usually only the destination of the boats due to a navigational error. Refugees, such as two shipwrecked people who were picked up off Alborán in May 1997 by a Russian freighter and taken to Gibraltar, are immediately deported to Morocco.[5] Of the 34 illegal North African immigrants who landed in Gibraltar in the summer of 1996, 27 were deported to Morocco, the 7 remaining migrants "are being advised to contact relatives or others in Morocco who may be able to assist in the identification process."[6]

The UK, responsible for Gibraltar in immigration matters, performed its role as guardian of the EU's external border. This concerns all immigration to Gibraltar via the maritime border, such as the case of the five Abkhazian refugees who were stranded in Gibraltar after fleeing the civil war in Georgia. They were expelled at

---

3   The M@G – Gibraltar's Only Web-Zine, September 18, 1997. Also see *Las pateras de Caronte* – "Only six out of 30 immigrants managed to fight the old lady across the Strait that cost them their lives last Tuesday," in: EL PAIS, September 22, 1997.
4   The film *The March* by British director William Nicholson had already dealt in 1990 with the wave of immigration of the poor and hungry into rich Europe. From Morocco, the desperate refugees cross over to Spain and end up in the chic hotel complexes on the Costa del Sol. A European army faces them.
5   The Gibraltar Chronicle, May 21, 1997.
6   "Govt to act on illegal immigrants," in: The Gibraltar Chronicle, July 2, 1996.

the end of July 1996. A representative of the governor justified this with the domino effect that a positive decision could have on Algerians and Moroccans willing to migrate.[7] Since 2003, the EU has called for a tightening of the fight against illegal migration. In July 2006, Europe granted increased financial assistance to Moroccan authorities in the fight against migration. This included the repatriation of sub-Saharan migrants to their countries of origin, or simply their disposal in the desert (Rickmeyer 2008: 20f): The heat would do the trick!

7.3 Infrastructure: Transboughaz routes

The maritime border with Morocco became more impermeable not only because of tightened migration controls since 1991 but also because of the restriction of official transport links between Morocco and Gibraltar. Thus, at the beginning of the 1990s, for reasons of cost and independently of the process of European unification, the regular ferry service between Tangier and Gibraltar was discontinued. Afterwards, travelers from Gibraltar to Morocco had to either detour via the Spanish port of Algeciras or go by plane.

Moroccan workers in Gibraltar were perhaps the most relentlessly affected. For them, the restriction of ferry operations caused additional problems, as the costly level of air fares reduced the frequency of home visits and a detour via Spain was associated with time-consuming visa formalities. After Spanish authorities had made it more difficult for Moroccans to obtain transit visas from Gibraltar to Algeciras, ferry operations between Gibraltar and Tangier resumed in autumn 1996, albeit irregularly. The Gibraltarian based *Moroccan Workers Association* complained about the "unreliability, delays and confusion" surrounding the Gib-Tangier-Gib hydrofoil service. On several occasions the hydrofoil has gone to Algeciras in Spain instead of to Gibraltar. The irregularities of the ferry service were criticized by the *Moroccan Workers Association*, for example, "that there had been occasions when the hydrofoil had arrived in Gibraltar at 5am with workers who had to start work at 8 am."[8]

However, ferry and flight schedules between Gibraltar and Tangier have been repeatedly changed. On November 23, 1988, flights were suspended following a tragic accident in Tangier (Loftus 2013). In 1997, *GIB Airways* connected the colony with Tangier, Agadir, Casablanca and Marrakech with nine flights a week. In June

---

7   In August, the court ruled that the transfer in prison was against the law because the refugees could only be sent to prison by order of a Gibraltarian court. However, this did not happen (Reyes 1996).
8   The Gibraltar Chronicle, August 20, 2002: "MWA Complain about Hydrofoil."

1997, the private airline *Rock Air* started a 20-minute flight to Tangier four times a day.[9] Obviously, this connection was also soon discontinued.[10]

Illustration 73: Renewed Air Connections

After around 20 years, there is again a new flight connection between Tangier and Gibraltar: Twice a week with *Royal Air Maroc* since March 29, 2015.[11] In 2019, a helicopter service was set up to connect Gibraltar with Tangier and Tetuán,[12] and an irregular ferry service operates between the two north and south: At the time of my 2019/20 field research, a ferry by the company FRS operated, which runs every second Friday from Tangier to Gibraltar and every Sunday wends its way back.

7.4 Moroccan Gibraltarians

In 2013, Maroua Kharbouch became the first Gibraltarian with Moroccan roots to be elected Miss Gibraltar. Chief Minister Fabian Picardo explicitly pointed out in his speech on Gibraltar National Day 2019 that most Moroccans who came to Gibraltar 50 years ago as workers have now become British. They had helped to build modern Gibraltar and, together, all locals are now facing new challenges, such as Brexit. It's not that Gibraltar has always loved its Moroccans, as it is presented today (2020) in the self-presentation of the city as an open, multicultural place (López 2019: 38).

---

9   The Gibraltar Chronicle, April 21, 1997.
10 http://www.ukpoints.com/2015/03/29/worlds-shortest-intercontinental-flight-returns-gibraltar-tangier/.
11 https://www.gibraltarairport.gi/content/royal-air-marocs-inaugural-gibraltar-tangier-casablanca-flight-sunday
12 https://www.gibheli.com/gibraltar-helicopter-tour-africa/.

Rather, one wanted to get rid of Muslims just 20 years ago. In January 1998, for example, the local government announced that it would provide financial aid to encourage the voluntary return of 700 long-term unemployed Moroccans.[13]

However, there were also initiatives to defend the rights of Moroccan workers. The Independent Liberal Forum, for example, fought for the rights of Moroccan workers at an early stage. As early as 2002, they demanded that the 425.000 € that Gibraltar received from the EU to improve "economic cooperation between the Rock and Morocco"[14] should primarily benefit Moroccan workers. Still today, Moroccan workers

> have few legal rights. They are not allowed to apply for permanent residence until they have lived in Gibraltar for 25 years, and even then their applications are often ignored or mislead. This 25-year rule contravenes the EU recommendation that migrants should be eligible for residence after 10 years (Thatchell 2002).

The March for Justice protest in September 2000 presented the government with hundreds of applications for residence from Moroccans who have lived in Gibraltar for 25 years or more. Two years on, no response has been received by any of the applicants.

This lack of permanent residence status deprives migrant workers of many basic rights. They are entitled to only 13 weeks' unemployment benefit, and those who remain out of work for more than six months can be deported. The fear of deportation forces many to work for a pittance. Despite paying tax and national insurance, Moroccan workers are denied child benefit. No matter how long a male breadwinner has lived and worked on the Rock, his family is forbidden to join him. This forced separation of husbands from their wives and children is reminiscent of the migrant labour system under apartheid. As in the old South Africa, many immigrant workers live in squalid, dehumanising government-run hostels, behind a checkpoint barrier with a 24-hour guard. (ibid.)

The *Independent Liberal Forum* advocated "to increase human and social rights for all Gibraltar residents despite the apparent unpopularity of such an attitude in certain quarters on the Rock."[15]

The Gibraltar Independent quotes homeowner Charles Culatto on this subject:

> [Retired Moroccan workers] need to have an address here so they rent a room for £50 a month [...] Then they live in Morocco most of the time only coming here to pick up their pension and pay their rent. It's a complete waste of money for the Moroccan tenant and the landlord [...] But that would be easily resolved. There

---

13   The Gibraltar Chronicle, January 10, 1998.
14   The Gibraltar Chronicle, October 4, 2002, "ILF Welcome EU Funds for GIB-Morocco Links."
15   Ibid.

could be a government hostel with each Moroccan having their own P.O. Box. Then each of them would be able to stay there the length of time they need to be in Gibraltar. The main problem with the Moroccan community is that even though many have been living in Gibraltar for over 40 years, they were only given their British nationality five years ago. Until then they could not get on the housing list which means they are forced to live in these conditions until they go further up the list.[16]

Illustration 74: Gibraltar 1996

But many Gibraltarians see the precarious situation in which many guest workers lived as partly self-inflicted. Patrick Genovese tells about the purchase of a house:

> It was a cave, with a falling ceiling and rats and cockroaches. There was a Moroccan tenant who let a lot of his fellow countrymen live there illegally. But they had their own apartments in Gibraltar and Tangier, which they sublet. So they lived cheaply in this grotto and made money by renting out their actual apartments.[17]

I receive a similar assessment one day later:

---

16 The Gibraltar Independent 2019, "Who is at fault for decrepit state of Gibraltar private rented housing?," April 25, 2019. http://gibraltarindependent.com/who-is-at-fault-for-decrepit-state-of-gibraltar-private-rented-housing/.
17 Field research diary TanGib, November 1, 2019.

Moroccans had demanded in the 1980s that they be given dignified housing. My interlocutor Charles Newbury said that Gibraltarians themselves were still living in cramped conditions at that time and had to worry about somehow getting out of housing misery. If the Moroccans were living in bad situations, it was because they had made this decision. Because most Moroccans just transferred their money to Morocco or Tangier, where they built their own apartments. 'From a human point of view, this is all understandable,' says my interview partner, 'but you can't complain to the community afterwards about the choice you made.'[18]

A Moroccan couple lived in the old town in modest circumstances. Both saved all their lives for a house in Tangier. The wife would rather have a small apartment for the elderly in Tangier, where one could then enjoy the savings. In the end, her husband prevailed and the house was built: A large house with a converted ground floor for a shop, several floors for the children and a large plot of land. Now the husband has passed away and the widow does not know whether she can use the house in Tangier herself. It is too big. It is also not clear whether the children will move in with their families. So the survivor stands with a house that she never wanted.[19]

A colleague from Tangier[20] had previously confirmed to me

Many Moroccans working in Gibraltar were not the typical migrant workers but had opened shops in Tangier and elsewhere selling goods from Gibraltar. Alternatively, they may have brought goods from Gibraltar with them which could be bought cheaply there and then sold them through some shop in Tangier. They were often tobacco shops. I remember when I was a child, I could see perfume or cosmetics in tobacco shops without them being sold there regularly. They came from Gibraltar.

But once again, Charles Newbury:

"one cannot demand politically that one is compensated in Gibraltar for investing the money elsewhere. That is the price. Also the locals cannot afford two apartments."[21]

After the story Patrick Genovese had told me earlier, the position of my interlocutor is another facet in the assessment of *Tanjawis* living in Gibraltar. Namely, that Moroccans prefer to live in miserable circumstances, but in doing so, they built their apartments in Tangier or in Morocco and then sublet them. However, my

---

18   Field research diary TanGib, November 2, 2019.
19   Field research diary TanGib, February 29, 2020.
20   Field research diary TanGib, October 25, 2019.
21   Field research diary TanGib, November 2, 2019.

Illustration 75: Moroccan Gibraltarian on National Day 1996

interlocutors distinguish the first generation of Moroccan workers from today's Gibraltarians of Moroccan descent:

> The latter are Gibraltarians, you can see that from the children, for example, on the ferry to Morocco. There are the Spanish, there are Moroccans from Morocco and there are Moroccans from Gibraltar. And their children would be just as Gibraltarian in mentality as all other inhabitants of the rock.[22]

7.5 Cultural heritage

The common history of the region seems to have been hardly present in either place until recently. There are only tentative signs of attempts to promote the awareness of cultural similarities on both sides, for example, by founding a monthly magazine, *Lifestyle*, which was launched in the summer of 1996. *Lifestyle* was to be published trilingually (in English, Spanish and French) after a start-up period and aimed at an intellectual and culturally interested readership via a distribution network in

---

22 Field research diary TanGib, November 2, 2019.

Gibraltar, Spain and Morocco. Its focus was not only on cultural commonality but also on the economic consideration of rediscovering the region as a common market for local economies. The magazine was soon discontinued.

My good friend Jon Searle founded the aforementioned journalists' association in the 1980s because he believed that Gibraltar could provide a neutral ground for the exchange between Spanish and Moroccan journalists who, until then, had had no contact with each other.

Illustration 76: 1996, Building the Mosque (Gibraltar)

One event that was to tie in with the regional and historical commonality of Gibraltar and the Islamic world was the construction of a mosque on the southern tip of the peninsula, which had already been planned in the 1970s and was completed in the 1990s. However, the project, financed by the Saudi *King Fahd Foundation*, was originally not geared to the religious needs of the only Muslims that by then lived in Gibraltar, the Moroccan workers. One of their spokespersons explained to me in 1996 that during the planning phase, the Saudi builders had refused to allow "these dirty people" to enter the mosque at all. The construction of the mosque was, therefore, initially a primarily symbolic project. A period of 1286 years after the conquest of Gibraltar by Tariq ibn Ziyad (711) and 505 years after the expulsion of the Moors from the Iberian Peninsula, the mosque was built and solemnly opened on August 8, 1997, in the presence of high Saudi dignitaries.[23] For the Saudi

---

23 The area of the mosque is 5002 m^2 and its construction cost over 30 million Saudi riyal. The building can hold 2000 believers. The minaret is 16 meters high. The building houses a library,

Minister of Justice, Al Sheik, the construction of the mosque confirms the role of Saudi Arabia as a guardian of Islam and servant of all Muslims.[24]

How do key players in the cultural sector deal with cultural heritage issues? At the beginning of this book, I referred to *Knightsfield Holdings Ltd.* who had produced the video on the history of Gibraltar. The Finlayson family are responsible for this production: Tommy, Gibraltar's longtime archivist, Clive, the Director of *The Gibraltar Museum* (now: *The National Museum*) and his spouse Geraldine, Director of the Civic Center *John Mackintosh Hall*.

On March 31st, 1989, the Bossano government dissolved the *Museum Committee*, and the obligations of care and conservation of the monuments were transferred to the *Gibraltar Heritage Trust*. Some members of the disbanded *Museum Committee* took over board positions in the *Heritage Trust*. The position of curator was filled by the biologist Clive Finlayson as part of the restructuring. An advisory sub-committee was established [...]. So, although *de jure* under the aegis of the *Heritage Trust*, the Museum was now *de facto* under the influence of the government through the sub-committee. The sub-committee awarded the operation of the Museum to a private company, *Knightsfield Holdings Ltd.* whose board member was the new curator, Clive Finlayson. (Haller 2000a: 223)

The business was recently handed over to their son Stewart. The Finlaysons were instrumental in founding the University of Gibraltar, and Clive Finlayson was rewarded by the Minister of Culture, John Cortés, on September 23, 2019, with the title of Beacon Professor.

Finlaysons dominate and control Gibraltar's historiography, access to archive material and the contouring of the dominant national narrative of Gibraltarian identity through their concentrated activities.

I have already analyzed this narrative elsewhere (Haller 2001b). Publications, conferences and the Museum itself are the crucial pieces of local identity production. There is no need to critically examine these activities in their entirety again. They do, however, lend themselves to a small-scale study of how heritage and history can be woven together, consolidated and politically instrumentalized – in a sense, a didactic play on the ethnicization of a society and the genesis of a nation. This

---

a conference room, a school with six classes (where religious studies and Arabic language are taught) and the Imam's living quarters.

24   The Saudi Intelligence Service's website expresses the symbolic meaning of the mosque as follows: The minaret looks like "a distinguished landmark for anyone who passes through the entrance of the Gibraltar peninsula or anyone who lands at its airport in the view of the mosque location near an area which is a converging point for the Mediterranean Sea and the Atlantic Ocean." URL: www.alqimam.com.sa/saudi_info/news/9-aug.html (Last modified on August 9, 1997).

became evident as the institution's name changed from *The Gibraltar Museum* to *The Gibraltar National Museum*.

The naturalization of the nation (including the recourse to prehistory) plays a central role: In the narrative on the history of Gibraltar presented in the *Museum*, it is the Rock itself – *Calpe* – which tells the "story of its children." And from a Neolithic jawbone found in Gorham's Cave, a reconstructed bust of a woman was immediately given the Latin name *Calpeia*.[25]

Young and new nations all over the world need a foundational narrative, and everywhere specialists knit together such a narrative in a halfway plausible way. This is even more necessary in the context of decolonization: Populations must first salvage and document the set pieces of their civil past. Critical accompaniment of such processes is an important and necessary task for social scientists. It is noticeable, for example, that certain set pieces that had a decisive influence on the history of the colony are loudly absent in the relevant publications.

I have already written about the concealment of Jewish contributions elsewhere (Haller 2000a).[26] The relationship to Tangier in the national narrative presented in the Museum and in publications can be evaluated critically with new expertise. Gibraltar is formulated as a self-sufficient entity that has its roots in Great Britain and the Romanic part of the Mediterranean – but the Moroccan coast nearby and the life-supporting influence of the ties with Morocco are not discussed anywhere. Neither Tangier nor Tetuán nor Morocco as a whole play a role in the *Gibraltar Museum* or the publications of academic laymen, such as the Finlaysons (and other local historians, whose concern is to focus more on the *inside* of society than the ties to the outside). A children's book on the history of Gibraltar (Skipworth/Lloyd 2017), for example, does not mention any Jewish, Hindu or Moroccan impact on the community. All this may well make sense politically if one wanted to present Gibraltar as a non-Spanish and Christian entity (without Jews, Muslims and Hindus). However, this does not meet scientific requirements. For decisive set pieces of the diverse, contradictory and partly conflict-laden history of civilians are kept silent. To quote Gibraltarian archaeologist Kevin Lane (2019):

> "It is interesting to note that we seem to have found the original Gibraltarian in the Palaeolithic." For Lane, "our newfound sense of us, such that the success of our Neanderthal heritage" is not an indication of an obligation to a past that must be preserved, but "a status symbol of our nascent nation and identity politics by other means (ibid.)."

---

25   The fact that the DNA of the bone remains had a 90 per cent origin from *Anatolia* does not harm the national history of *Mother Gibraltar*.

26   Lane (2019) argues that other legacies of the past are not taken into account either, such as the local architecture and class society that separated Gibraltarians from the British rulers.

One cannot put it more accurately. Thus, Finlayson's narrative certainly has an effect on Gibraltar's self-image. The concealment or neglect of ties to Morocco fits very well into a national project oriented towards *native* autonomy in the sense of the book *Making of a People* (1994). The author, Joseph Garcia, was a young historian when the book was published, but today he is Deputy Prime Minister.

It may be that the narrative will change over time, for example, when it seems opportune to emphasize the ties to North Africa. There is evidence that Garcia supports the establishment of new ties with Morocco, which we will encounter in the next chapter.

7.6 Other links between Tangier and Gibraltar

In addition to migration, routes, the labor market and cultural identity, other links have developed between Gibraltar and Tangier, which can only be touched upon briefly at this point.

The supply of food, raw materials and other materials, for example, through the *Gibmaroc Group*, is certainly most important. Its Managing Director George R. Desoisa, explains:

> Gibraltar and the Gibraltarians being the survivors and true entrepreneurs that we are, we turned things around and I would say that 48 hours after the referendum there was a different emphasis, there was a different thrust, and Gibraltarians were already looking to run it around in our favor and how could we approach the challenge. (Euronews 2018)

Illustration 77: Food Supply

Cooperation has also developed in the field of the military. Since 2000, the British Army and Commander British Forces – the local defense forces of Gibraltar

(*The Royal Gibraltar Regiment*) – have been conducting joint military manoeuvres with Moroccan armed forces every year under the name Exercise Jebel Sahara[27]. In 2015, for example, a one-month infantry manoeuvre took place in the inorth of Marrakech with 500 British and Moroccan soldiers.[28]

Finally, there is also a binding force between the two cities in terms of civil society involvement. In 1985, the *Cheshire Homes Support Group* from Gibraltar set up a facility in Tangier to care for disabled children and adults, providing them with accommodation and food. The facility is located in *Dar El Hana* (House of Affection), which was made available by the Portuguese government in 1962. In Gibraltar, Brother Murphy of the Irish Brothers was particularly active in raising funds and support, and the Lions Club and various schools were particularly active.[29]

---

27   See, for example, "Royal Gibraltar Regiment returns from Morocco deployment," *The Gibraltar Chronicle* November 14, 2019. https://www.chronicle.gi/royal-gibraltar-regiment-returns-from-morocco-deployment/.

28   Panorama, November 20, 2015. http://gibraltarpanorama.gi/15209/149935/a/exercise-jebel-sahara-a-shining-example-of-defence-cooperation-with-morocco.

29   Panorama, January 22, 2015. "Local support group wants to take charity work in Tangier to new level." http://www.panorama.gi/localnews/headlines.php?action=view_article&article=12822.

8. Brexit: An ethnography of agony with hopeful glances to the other side of the Strait

Today is October 31st, 2019. Today would be Brexit if Britain had kept to it. I cross the border between Gibraltar and La Línea to find traces of Brexit. But apart from a call by the union to demtrate against the Brexit on October 9, I find nothing. They are small leaflets stuck to masts and I take one with me.

In the local bookshop I ask about local Brexit, because in the shop window there is a book about it. It is just a novel without any relationship to the region.[1]

> Lina Searle invites me to meet her friends. As mentioned in the last chapter, the *Bloomsbury Circle* meets almost every morning in a local café. They talk about travel, political views, art and local gossip, but: Brexit is excluded. 'Almost everyone in Gibraltar has voted to stay in the EU,' says Lina. But not everyone from the circle of friends. 'Life's too short,' she adds, 'to be divided over such things.' Everyone agrees: You can't influence Brexit from Gibraltar anyway.[2]

As has already been mentioned, I have spent many years researching the border of Gibraltar with Spain and Morocco. For a long time, it seemed as if the situation had frozen: Spain and Gibraltar within an EU (but Gibraltar outside the *Schengen Agreement*), and Gibraltar and Spain vis-à-vis a Morocco located outside of the EU. Now, however, with the referendum on the withdrawal of Great Britain from the EU, the situation had changed: Until the actual withdrawal date of January 31, 2020, it remained uncertain whether and when the UK (and, thus, Gibraltar) would leave the EU, and what this would mean for relationships between Spain, Gibraltar and Morocco. There has been uncertainty about it since the 2016 referendum on Brexit:

1 Whether Brexit would take place at all, and if so
2 when this would occur and
3 under what conditions?

---

1 Field research diary TanGib, October 31, 2019.
2 Field research diary TanGib, November 3, 2019.

Illustration 78 : Anti Brexit manifestation, La Línea

In any case, my research in 2019 is characterized by these uncertainties: Basically, I am researching an event that might or might not happen. In this respect, most of my research was not about Brexit but about the preparations for a possible Brexit.

A look back: On June 23rd, 2016, the referendum on UK membership within the EU took place. A narrow majority of 51.9 per cent voted for a Brexit. Gibraltar, the only British overseas territory belonging to the EU, also voted: 95.9 per cent voted in favor of remaining inside the EU. However, as the territory's membership of the EU is dependent on Great Britain, Gibraltar has to submit to the vote of the mother country and will follow it. An online article (Barahona 2019) describes the reaction of young Gibraltarians who had not experienced the closure themselves: "With the Brexit result, all the stories of the parents came up again [...] back when the border was completely closed between 1969 and 1985." Older people go into shock:

A friend tells me that Brexit was a shock. The day after the Referendum took place, they went to Seville, where the son took part in a basketball gymnastics tournament. She and her husband did not talk about Brexit during the whole trip. The first person to raise the subject was the receptionist at the hotel in Seville, who said with a glance at her Gibraltarian passports: 'What have they done to you!' My fri-

8. Brexit: An ethnography of agony with hopeful glances to the other side of the Strait 217

Illustration 79 : Brexit Results in Gibraltar

end said that Gibraltarians were in shock. They avoided talking about it. She herself describes how she had felt like a cockroach on its back for nine months with depression. In April 2017, after Clause 24, which refers to Spain's say in the fate of Gibraltar,[3] she felt as if a bucket of cold water had watered her head, which tore her out of her depression and since then, she has been a woman who says: 'We will continue to live like this and make the best out of it.' She calls herself a convinced European, but totally disillusioned.[4]

During my field trips in 2019 and 2020, the mood of Gibraltarians regarding Brexit was full of cynical revulsion and helpless refusal to deal with it again after three years of uncertainty.

As for Brexit, Martha Coreggio says that people do not like to talk about it because they have no control over it at all. That is why there is no graffiti or stickers or other visible signs here.[5]

Heidi Viñas Coreggio twists her eyes: She has given up thinking about Brexit. She doesn't want to hear anything about it, she doesn't want to see anything. She looks

---

3 "After the United Kingdom leaves the Union, no agreement between the EU and the United Kingdom may apply to the territory of Gibraltar without the agreement between the Kingdom of Spain and the United Kingdom." (GBC 2017)
4 Field research diary TanGib, April 3, 2019.
5 Field research diary TanGib, March 31, .2019.

up and rejects her hands. This is certainly not an artificial gesture. I have actually only experienced Gibraltarians who have surrendered to fate, who don't want to hear anything about it.[6]

This is not the place to trace in detail what has happened around Brexit since 2016. What is important here is the way in which Gibraltar and its inhabitants have dealt with a possible Brexit since the referendum. Because a Brexit would affect all aspects of life in Gibraltar which touch on different aspects and range from physical reactions, legal measures and infrastructural planning to questions of security of supply and the establishment of new economic relations.

Gibraltar authorities have adapted as well as possible:

> Philipp Chester fears the worst for Gibraltar. He thinks that with papers without the European flag on them, you would not be able to get to Spain. He says that you can only change 1000 identity cards, for example, because you don't have any more of them in stock. So it would take forever for everyone to get their identity card without the European flag on it. So a complete disaster. He does not believe that the border will be closed, but that difficulties at the border will be enacted.[7]

Brexit is a traumatic issue for both Gibraltar and the Spanish hinterland; But it divides families and circles of friends less than in the mother country because support for remaining in the EU was almost unanimous. Various dates for Brexit have been set. The situation was, therefore, one of long-dormant agony. Gibraltarians were tired of the subject during my research periods. It would be best not to talk about it. It's no use anyway and only makes you crazy to get tangled up in the loops of what-if. In the spring of 2020, it still seemed to be in the repression phase. According to a survey by *The Gibraltar Chronicle* in March 2020, only 2.9 per cent of those questioned said that Brexit had affected their "mental health" (Reyes 2020a: 1, 2).

The Gibraltarian Government, on the other hand, had to face up to the possible dangers; it prepared itself early on for all possible scenarios, twists and turns of a possible No-Deal-Brexit. This now benefits Gibraltar in the Corona crisis. Chief Minister Picardo points out on March 22, 2020, that in preparation for Brexit, everything was stored for a possible border closure in order to survive months of isolation.

Chief Minister Picardo speaks of the "political hell of Brexit" to be faced in the local early parliamentary elections three weeks before one of the announced Brexit dates, October 31, 2019. The local government of *GSLP* and *Liberal Party of Gibraltar*

---

6   Field research diary TanGib, March 31, 2019.
7   Field research diary TanGib, Agust 15, 2019.

"know Brexit inside out" and has developed specific political plans to master Brexit. An office had been set up in *Main Street* to provide information about these plans.[8]

8.1 Political status

'Those files there, they all have to do with Brexit. When I started as Brexit Minister, I had two files. Now there are more than 60. It's insanely complex. At first, all I had to do was deal with the exit agreement and make sure that Gibraltar was not left out. But over time, three new strands have been added. First, we have to prepare for the worst-case scenario – an unregulated Brexit. Secondly, we need to be prepared in case the British Parliament finally accepts the negotiated agreement. And thirdly, we must ensure that after Brexit we have the same relationship with the EU as Britain. This concerns around 40 different issues,' said Joseph Garcia, Deputy Prime Minister of Gibraltar. (Frantzen 2019)

Early elections in Gibraltar had been scheduled for October 17, 2019. In view of the unclear and threatening situation to which Gibraltar was exposed by Brexit, Chief Minister Fabian Picardo wanted to obtain a new vote for a policy by the population.[9] The election was also scheduled so that it could be held before possible new elections in the UK. Although the ruling coalition lost a lot of votes, it was still able to achieve an absolute majority of 52.5 per cent. Due to a complicated electoral law, it retained its majority of 10 to 7 seats in the local parliament.

The election manifesto of the governing parties also speaks of "further commercial ties between Gibraltar and Morocco." The opening of an office of the *Gibraltar and Morocco Business Association (GMBA)* in Morocco is explicitly welcomed and supported. The descendants of the Moroccan guest workers of the 1960s and 70s living in Gibraltar are now acknowledged as enrichment and part of the national identity (López 2019: 38). In addition to Mandarin, Arabic would also to be offered as a school subject (ibid.: 94). A daily flight to Casablanca or Tangier as (ibid.: 119) well as forms of cultural exchange with Morocco are to be established (ibid.: 134).

In dealing with the Brexit trauma, it helps Gibraltarians to have made out two enemies: Spain and the EU. Because, of course, as on other occasions before, Spain would be trying to take every opportunity to play poker on the status of Gibraltar, whose independence has never been recognized by Madrid (Haller 2000a).

---

8   Field research diary TanGib, 05.03.2020.
9   "We have the expertise, we have the team and we have the plan to deliver a safe Brexit to the people of Gibraltar. We ask for them to vote on our record, to vote for us on the basis of what we are going to do but also on the potential implications Brexit may have on Gibraltar," added Dr Joseph Garcia, leader of the Liberals. (Lopez 2019)

According to November 2018, Spain

> could blow the exit deal. The reason: Gibraltar. [...] Spain wants to negotiate directly with Great Britain about the future of the strip of land in the south of the Iberian Peninsula. This must be laid down both in the Brexit Agreement itself and in the accompanying political declaration on the future relationship between Britain and the EU. If this does not happen, 'we cannot support the agreement,' said Foreign Minister Borrell. (Becker 2018b; translated by the author)

"Reactions in London were outraged, prominent Conservatives even hinted at waging war on Gibraltar if necessary (Becker 2018a; translated by the author)." The UK government told Spain to resolve its problems with Gibraltar in harmony with the other EU states (Reyes 2018a). Spain is interested in finding a lever to bring about the secession of Gibraltar from the negotiating package with the UK, because Gibraltar has a constitutional right to a say in its political future. Consequently, Chief Minister Picardo referred to precisely this right to a say, which Spain wanted to deny. Mr Picardo explained that the future of Gibraltar is linked to the United Kingdom, since the mother countries

> 'unwavering commitment' that it will negotiate future trade and other arrangements with the EU that work for all of the British family of nations, including Gibraltar. Even though Gibraltarians had voted overwhelmingly to remain, Gibraltar would exit the EU alongside the UK because Britain guaranteed the Rock's 'security, prosperity and the rule of law'. (Reyes 2018b)

In view of the decades of constant attempts to make Gibraltar part of Spain, it is no wonder that local hatred is directed against Spain.[10] Now, however, the resentment of Gibraltarians is also directed against the EU. The European Parliament and the 27 member states had agreed in April 2019 to a resolution on visa regulations in which Gibraltar was called a *colony* (Sánchez 2019). However, Gibraltar has been fighting against the designation as a colony since the 1960s. What may appear to be a pettiness to readers unfamiliar with the circumstances of Gibraltar's sensitivities, strikes a sore point in Gibraltar itself: Colony status would mean that the United Nations would have to "solve" the Gibraltar problem and that Gibraltarians would not be allowed to decide on their own affiliation. The vote of the EU Parliament and the other member states is, therefore, interpreted as a betrayal of the ideals of the right of self-determination. During my research, this was repeatedly conveyed to me in this way by a wide variety of actors – especially by those who had fought particularly fiercely for remaining within the EU.

---

10   See Haller (2000a: 88ff) on "borderland hysteria."

8.2 Foreign policy implications

What have been the consequences of Brexit so far for Gibraltar's foreign policy? Certainly until Corona, the feared consequences of Brexit on the border with Spain have not yet been noticed at the end of the field research.[11]

Nevertheless, Brexit is already showing foreign policy reactions. In Morocco, the question of sovereignty of Ceuta and Melilla is back again on the agenda. In the event of greater Spanish intervention in Gibraltar, such as a joint administration by Spain and the UK, Morocco will also put forward the idea of joint administration of the two Spanish exclaves by Morocco and Spain. There would also be problems regarding Western Sahara because Spain's position is contradictory: For the future of Western Sahara, Madrid is demanding the Sahaouris' right to self-determination, while ignoring the self-determined referenda in Gibraltar for remaining part of Britain (Masiky 2018). The closure, for example, of Morocco's land border with the Spanish exclave of Ceuta in spring 2020 is widely interpreted as a reaction to the fascist regional government of the Spanish city and to the economic problems of the surrounding area (Handaji 2020). Gibraltarians, on the other hand, are convinced that Morocco will once again – as in the case of the Parsley Island crisis – bring its own regional power to bear in the event that Spain increases the pressure on Gibraltar.

In January 2020, Chief Minister Picardo launched an unusual initiative to address the issue of Gibraltar in the structure between the UK and the EU: Gibraltar is considering joining the Schengen area in order to ensure smooth border traffic even after Brexit.

'Does it make sense for the EU that 2.5 square miles at the southernmost tip of the Iberian Peninsula should not be accessible to EU citizens? I don't think so,' said Gibraltar's head of government Fabian Picardo on Friday […] Alluding to Liechtenstein, Picardo said that other European micro-states were also taking advantage of the Schengen Agreement without being fully integrated into the Schengen Information System. Gibraltar's accession would be 'a positive step.' (ntv 2020)

Spanish Prime Minister Pedro Sánchez responded that it was appropriate to overcome the age-old question of sovereignty and to explore new ways of cooperation. The British government, on the other hand, reacted negatively – it was still the UK that was negotiating with the EU on its relations with Gibraltar (BBC 2020).

---

11   Field research diary TanGib, February 27, 2020.

8.3 Economy

Placa, the food market on *Soq Barra* in Tangier. There I discover references to goods from Gibraltar. My friend Noreddine Chraibi had told me that there was a stand selling goods from Gibraltar. But he did not know if it still exists today. 'You have to go up the stairs at the olive sellers.' I find the stand with British goods from Gibraltar. I can see that from the names of the supermarket chain *Morrison's* on the food. I take pictures of oatmeal, rice and honey with *Morrison's* label on them. Then I walk down the stairs to the meat and vegetable market where I also discover traces of *Morrison's* – shopping bags – on the stalls. I also find a stand advertising the Union Jack, the Moroccan flag and the Rock of Gibraltar, and a photograph of the Saccone & Speed staff. Obviously, there are still economic links between Gibraltar and Tangier.[12]

Illustration 80: Placa, Tangier 2019

Mr. Jamal, whose last name I don't know, runs this business. He has lived and worked in Gibraltar for 47 years. However, he came to the colony before the border was closed in 1969. Jamal has worked for several employers on the Rock. Like most Moroccans of his time, he stayed in the mass accommodations at Casemate Square, those narrow and oppressive rooms with many bunk beds.

Today, Mr. Jamal lives in his own house in a middle-class part of Tangier, in Buena Vista. He has no family left on the other side, but he has many friends. The goods in his shop are mainly drugstore products, cosmetics and light medicines. *Tanjawis* would still prefer to get them from Gibraltar.

---

12   Field research diary TanGib, October 23, 2019.

He shows me an old shopping bag from *Safeway's*, the predecessor operator of the current *Morrison's*. The advertising sign of the stand is also already several years old. So he has run the business for at least 15 years. He only travels there rarely and to buy his goods, the crossing is expensive.[13] As the ferry to Gibraltar leaves every second Friday and returns on Sunday, he stays overnight in a cheap hostel.

A few days later Mr. Jamal sees me in *Main Street* of Gibraltar and greet me. I almost didn't recognize him. He is carrying two of the staple – empty – jumbo shopping bags and pulls an equally empty rolling bag behind him. He is on the way to purchase his wares.[14]

Mr. Jamal isn't the only one who brings goods from Gibraltar to Tangier. Several Moroccans transport bags with goods to Tangier. They either do this, like Mr. Jamal, for their own business, or they transport them for customers. One of them delivers goods to the household market in Tangiers *Casabarata* district every week. Customers pay between 20 and 30 € for the transport of one of the jumbo bags. Translate to Morocco with a small van loaded with full bags will quickly make a good profit. Some of the people who transport are connected in both Spain and Morocco, which makes border crossing smooth, noiseless and safe.[15]

> A network of smugglers that transported 47 Moroccans via Gibraltar to Spain and thus to the EU was dismantled in January 2020. Gibraltar had been monitoring the suspicious organisation since the end of 2018; it issued false short-stay visas to Moroccans, with which a total of around 130 migrants entered Gibraltar and were then transported across the land border to Spain. It is suspected that Moroccans were charged between 7000 and 8000 € each. The organisation claimed 'a logistical network of drivers, taxi-drivers and other collaborators in Spain who were allegedly paid up to 200 euros per migrant.' Obviously police forces in Spain and Gibraltar jointly observed the work of that illegal network, just as the network in turn observed the working methods of the police: 'The group is said to have used complex and sophisticated counter-surveillance measures and adapted rapidly whenever one of its members was picked up (Gulraj/Reyes 2020).' This points to cross-border networks of an official (police) and unofficial (smuggler/smuggler) nature.

These ventures have nothing to do with Brexit causally. Certainly, in times of post-Brexit, Gibraltar can build on already established relations with Tangier and North Morocco.

---

13   Field research diary TanGib, February 25, 2020.
14   Field research diary TanGib, March 1, 2020.
15   Field research diary TanGib, March 1-3, 2020.

What are Gibraltar's economic problems in the wake of the 2016 referendum? Since then, the official authorities in Gibraltar have been preparing as pragmatically as possible for a possible No-Deal Brexit (GBC 2019c).

'I think we've managed to protect ourselves as best we can. 90% of our trade is with Britain, not the EU. The most crucial thing was to ensure that we had access to the UK market after Brexit. That was important to our service providers, especially the car insurers: 20 percent of British car policies are sold by providers in Gibraltar. Of course, Brexit creates uncertainty. But we have protected our economy extremely well. They have to understand that when they are small, they have two advantages: they can change direction more quickly and diversify more easily,' says Deputy Chief Minister Joseph Garcia. (Deutschlandfunk 2019)

This sounds like a whistling in the woods. At Saccone & Speed, Gibraltar's largest food importer, I am told that Brexit has led the small territory into agony.

At first, the company had prepared for the end of March 2019 and filled up all of its storage facilities with food. When Brexit did not arrive in April, everything had to be sold quickly. In November 2019 now the same story. It is assumed that the new date in January or February 2020 will be the same again. The uncertainty was driving everyone crazy. It is an agony that drags on. Saccone & Speed would now also have to consider military tunnels that lie inside the rock. For storage. The problem is that these tunnels have not been used for a long time and some of them have to be secured first. Of course, this would not be possible overnight. In this respect, Brexit is a logistical challenge.[16]

The problem of storage of goods is widely discussed. Here, the many tunnels within the rock prove to be a stroke of luck.

"Debbie Harrington Rossi said they've been stockpiling drugs until next year."[17] Sidney Delmar told me back in April that they had already stored food and supplies until June 2019. He's referring to a television discussion on the *Viewpoint Programme* on the local TV, *GBC*.

The Manager of Marks & Spencer said that they had enough stock, both clothes and food, until June. [...] A week later [...] the leader of the GSD, Philip, was asking Fabian [Picardo]. Fabian said that from the moment Brexit was mentioned, the Government of Gibraltar was preparing itself for 'any' eventuality, be it a hard or a soft Brexit. They have been planning for the past two years. Fabian was able to say that if there was a hard Brexit and even if the frontier was closed. That products would be brought in, either from Morocco, Portugal or the United Kingdom and

---

16   Field research diary TanGib, November 1, 2019.
17   Field research diary TanGib, August 15, 2019.

that the prices on the shelves would stay as they are. One thing you must remember, Gibraltar's situation makes it unique, in the sense that only 32.000 people live in a tiny place with a budget of over eighty million pounds. The third wealthiest 'per capita' place in the world. The money that is generated will be used for the needs of the people. This why we hardly felt the 2008 recession.[18]

The economic consequences of the 2016 referendum include not only precautionary measures and the mitigation of possible economic risks but also the search for new economic opportunities to safeguard Gibraltar's existence. Gibraltar's status as a financial center derives much of its importance from the fact that it is a territory with special tax rights within the EU. This would probably be jeopardized by a Brexit.

Gibraltar was already affected by economic setbacks in the run-up to Brexit. Especially in the *gambling* sector. In 2010, 2000 people (12 per cent of the workforce) were employed at *Bet365*, *Stan James*, *William Hill*, *888Casino*, *BetVictor* and others in Gibraltar (Castles 2010). Denise Coates, the woman with the highest income in the world, moved her company *Bet365* to Gibraltar in 2015 (Picco 2020). A company pays 1 per cent of its income in tax, but no more than £ 500.000. However, *Gambling Companies* are slowly leaving Gibraltar in whole or in part as a result of Brexit. Bet365, for example, is reducing 80 % of its Gibraltar-based empoyees and turning to Malta instead(Stradbrook2019). This affects 400 of its 500 local employees.

Many of those employed in the gambling industry live in Spain, as housing prices in Spain are much cheaper than in Gibraltar. Andrew Lyman, Executive Director of the Gibraltar Government's Gambling Division, points out that the possibility of a *No-Deal Brexit* already deeply unsettles employees.

> There is now more focus and some angst around 'no-deal' planning and what that means at an individual level. Most operators have already planned on a worst-case scenario basis. We are hoping for the withdrawal of Article 50 or for a managed exit. The industry can deal with IT structures and EU licensing issues, but the border remains a concern. (Joyes 2019)

Although it is possible to work for gambling companies in Gibraltar from their (Spanish) home, the situation is deeply unsettling.

Gibraltar is, thus, increasingly looking to new business relationships or those that already exist and are considered to be unproblematic. Portugal, for example, is considered a possible partner alongside Morocco in order to maintain the local economy. The largest construction company *Casais* that is building many of the new

---

18 Personal communication Sidney Delmar, September 24, 2019.

blocks in Gibraltar is already Portuguese: According to the company's own information,[19] *Casais Gibraltar* consists of approximately 450 employees, 60 of them locals. Moreover, several Gibraltarian hotels have already been bought by Portuguese.[20]

Particular hopes are placed on the *British-Moroccan Free Trade Agreement* of autumn 2019. It is considered to be particularly helpful for the local economy. However, the British Ambassador in Rabat warns Morocco against too close ties with Gibraltar:

> 'If we talk about Gibraltar and try to forge links between Gibraltar and Morocco, you Moroccans will have problems with the Spaniards,' [the ambassador, Thomas Reilly] said at one point during the interview on Radio Luxe.[21]

As expected, the Government of Gibraltar reacts by rejecting this statement. But things are in flux. In April 2020, a local weekly paper, *Panorama*,[22] refers to the increased economic cooperation between Gibraltar and Morocco, which is embedded in Britains strategy for the exploitation of oil reserves between Morocco and the Canary Islands.

8.4. Gibraltar and Morocco Business Association (GMBA) and Strait of Gibraltar Association (SGA)

> '[…] we can obviously start doing more trade through Morocco, they have one of the biggest ports in the Mediterranean, so they have a lot of trade that comes through Mediterranean and out to the rest of the world, and they come past Gibraltar, so it comes through and some of them use the Moroccan port, they've got a free port there. I would think that if we actually did start looking to Morocco; then we would actually be able to trade more easily with the rest of the world, it would just be a question of getting things as they are parked there and then bringing them over to Gibraltar,' sagt Christopher Bourne, Direktor des Gibraltar Business Centre. (Sputniknews 2019)

---

19   https://www.casais.pt/en/2-institutional/6-casais-in-the-world/6-gibraltar/
20   Field research diary TanGib, March 29, 2019.
21   The Gibraltar Chronicle Online, 2019, https://www.chronicle.gi/govt-complains-to-uk-over-un acceptable-comments-by-uk-ambassador-to-morocco/.
22   "The whole issue has surfaced with Morocco having approved new laws about the delimitation of territorial waters, with an exclusive economic Zone of 200 miles and up to 350 for its continental shelf, which has raised concern over territorial waters overlapping with the Canary Islands. It opens up the exploration of valuable petrol and natural gas resources in the area, over which British energy companies have already shown interest." (Garcia 2020).

One way out of the current orientation towards the EU is to attract Moroccan tourists. In December 2016, Minister of Economy Albert Isola, Minister of Tourism Gilbert Licudi, and Nicky Guerrero from the *Gibraltar Tourist Board* visited the cities of Marrakech, Casablanca and Tangier to promote Gibraltar as an economic opportunity to Morocco (The Maghreb Times 2016).

On March 23rd, 2019, the GMBA (The Gibraltar Chronicle, March 23rd, 2019) was founded, because it is expected that the supply of Gibraltar would have to be secured again via Morocco and that workers would also have to be recruited from Morocco if Spain were to close the land border again after a Brexit.

Illustration 81: GMBA

On August 8th, 2019, the Online Journal *noticiasgibraltar* published that the president of the SGA, Clive Reed, other members of the Association, and Deputy Chief Minister Joseph García want to develop new foreign markets in the context of Brexit. It is explicitly stated several times that this is a private sector initiative (noticiasgibraltar 2019).

On August 9th, 2019, English-language newspaper *Sur* (Bartlett 2019) reported that the *GMBA* would open an office in Tangier to boost economic and cultural exchange. The newspaper points out twice that this activity is not related to Brexit but to the Gibraltarian government's general search for new economic ties. *Sur* refers to a press release which assumes that Spain would not close the border like in Franco's time. Both sides – Gibraltar and Spain – would only lose if the border were to be closed, because Gibraltar imports goods and raw materials from Spain for about 1.5 trillion euros a year, and 15.329 Spanish residents work in Gibraltar, 9705 of whom are Gibraltarians.

The continued reference to the private sector nature of the *GMBA* is based on the fact that Gibraltar is not allowed to take any foreign policy initiatives – foreign policy is still the responsibility of the UK. But the leader of *GMBA*, Steven Marin, is a long-standing member of the ruling party *GSLP* and a friend of Deputy Chief Minister Garcia. The *GMBA* is modeled on the relations between Japan and Taiwan, as these two countries do not recognize each other either, but relationships in business and culture are at the forefront on the private and regional level. The office in Tangier would be established in the city center, probably on the *Boulevard* or nearby. A Gibraltarian flag will be raised there, which is particularly important to Steven Marin. Brahim Krikaz, Marin's husband and also a driving force of the *GMBA*, emphasizes that the interest of the two cities in each other is actually not very great. The first task of the office would be to create an awareness of mutual possibilities. There is no reason why Gibraltarian companies, for example, should not produce in the *Economic Free Zone* in Tangier. Brexit is providing the necessary impetus.[23] It can be assumed that the employment of an Arabic teacher at *Gibraltar College* is connected with these efforts (Gomez 2019).

The opening of the *GMBA* office in Tangier, scheduled for October 2019, had to be postponed due to the early elections in Gibraltar. As late as mid-November, it was still not clear which of the two locations – the *Ibn Battouta Mall* or a building opposite the *Grande Poste* – would eventually house the office. However, the *GMBA* is already active in Tangier at this time. It participated in the *MEDays Forum*, which took place in mid-November 2019 in Tangier. Workshops were held on Brexit and its impact on Africa.

The *SGA* appointed Henry and Priscilla Sacramento as its patrons on November 19, 2019. "Every club in Britain has a patron or several patrons who would have a socially well-connected stand. Honour means that you don't get paid for it," Henry says with a wink.[24]

On November 23rd, 2019, the *GMBA* announces that the office will be located in *Avenue Youssef Ben Tachfine*. On December 2nd, 2019, the office is scheduled to move in and will open in January 2020.[25]

Although the office is operational at the time of my visit in February 2020, no official opening had taken place. The entrance door to the building is decorated with signs of both organizations (*GMBA, SGA*), and the Gibraltarian flag is attached to a side window, which unfortunately is somewhat difficult to see from the street.

The reception room has two desks and a shelf with brochures. Several rooms, including a meeting room for about 40 guests, complete the office's inventory.

During the first weeks of the office's existence, the visitors are mainly Gibraltarian tourists who want to find out about the activities of the association. Others are Moroccans who have an interest in Gibraltar and different projects, intentions or ideas. In this phase, according to the office manager, it is crucial to first explore

---

23   Field research diary TanGib, August 19, 2019.
24   Field research diary TanGib, February 25, 2020.
25   Online platform G (d.n.n).

the potential and be open to everything. *Tanjawis* generally know very little about Gibraltar; some consider it an island. In Gibraltar, the interest in Tangier is much greater. Therefore, it is important to first hold events in Tangier to arouse interest in the other side.[26]

As Gibraltar is a face-to-face society, the effectiveness of social initiatives is generally assessed less ideologically and more in terms of the specific actors involved.

The head of the office worked in Tunis until recently and is originally from Casablanca. She has had nothing to do with Gibraltar since then and has never been there. She was probably hired because she speaks perfect English, having lived in the U.S. for about 17 years. Not only does she have no connections to Gibraltar, she is also completely unfamiliar with Tangier. She has neither family nor friendly ties there.[27]

In addition to the specific actors, the office has existed for just a few months when my field research was completed in March 2020.[28] After such a short time, one can hardly expect that structures would have already been established that are viable and permanent.[29]

In Gibraltar itself, the *GMBA* promotes local initiatives – even small ones – that strengthen ties with Morocco, for example, the distribution of argan products in Gibraltar by *June & Simo*, who presented their initiative on November 4th, 2019.

8.5. Social and Cultural links

Individual Gibraltarians are also active at other levels in establishing or maintaining links with Northern Morocco, in particular Tangier.

Three charitable initiatives are particularly noteworthy here.

Charles Trico, whom I met in the 1990s in Gibraltar in his Bar *Hole in't Wall*, regularly visits the neighboring city to support Ayuda a casa de acogida Tangier. Together with a friend, he has organized orphan aid in a poor district of the city. The initiators of the orphan foundation describe their commitment as purely private, which has nothing to do with the *GMBA* or the *SGA*.[30]

While his friend has no family ties with Northern Africa, Charles descends from important Northern African Rabbis.

---

26 Field research diary TanGib, February 27, 2020.
27 Ibid.
28 Field research diary TanGib, February 18, 2020.
29 Field research diary TanGib, February 22, 2020.
30 Field research diary TanGib, February 18, 2020.

The first visit to the official orphanage in Tangier showed them that the children are very well placed there, said Charles. However, there were also initiatives in districts that were less well equipped. Charles met a woman, for example, who took care of children in a poor district. She sent him videos of the initiative, which were terrible, a few children in the poorest conditions. The woman had made an effort to care for them but with few resources. Charles collected food, money and toys in Gibraltar. But most of the things they had bought in Tangier. In the meantime, the woman has moved into a better place with a garden. Since then, the conditions have been quite pleasant, but the rent has increased from 700 Dirham to 1000 Dirham. Local supporters in Tangiers could not cope with that. So the supporters in Gibraltar try to do what they can, but they can still only help a little, Charles says.[31] Charles' brothers and sisters-in-law also support the project. In October 2019, I accidentally discover a table in the women's charity *Darna* where Charles' sister-in-law is offering small handicrafts for sale[32] – the proceeds go to the orphanage.

Illustration 82: Private Charity at Darna

The second charity initiative, the aforementioned *Cheshire Homes Support*, is older but still provides support for disabled and homeless young people. Members of the initiative regularly bring food, tools and equipment of all kinds to Tangier. In November 2019, 100 sleeping bags, dog toys and dog food were collected to help the homeless in Tangier: "Together we are making Tangier a better place for all."[33]

Thirdly, there is the Maroc Atlas and Gibraltar 4x4 Club.

---

31 Ibid.
32 Field research diary TanGib, October 25, 2019.
33 Online platform G (d.n.n).

MarocAtlas Gibraltar 4x4 Club is Gibraltar's first and only official 4x4 club. The group was originally formed in 1994 as a solidarity group taking supplies to children in the remotest parts of Morocco. In 2011, we formalised the group and expanded to form a Club and a nonprofit organisation, organising the yearly raids to Morocco as well as monthly and bi-monthly trips to off road circuits, routes and family trips in Spain & doing charities events locally. Being officially a nonprofit org, our Solidarity Raids to Morocco are always done through volunteer work where everyone pays for their own costs during the trip with no extra costs. The club is promoting motor sports back to Gibraltar by participating with other European countries in competing rally's.[34]

In addition to these organized initiatives, culturally active individuals also live in both cities. An Australian journalist is one of them.

I run into him on *Main Street* in Gibraltar. He recognized me and greeted me in a friendly way. My companion then says that the journalist is now living in Gibraltar. I told him that here they believe that he lives in Gibraltar, but in Tangier they are convinced that he lives in Tangier. He probably lives in both places.[35]

Dar Henpris in the Kasbah, named after the couple Henry and Priscilla Sacramento mentioned already, who were appointed by the *SGA* as their patrons, has become a meeting point for Gibraltarians in Tangier and a meeting place for *Tanjawis* and Gibraltarians. Former police commissioner Henry and his wife Priscilla love Moroccan culture and the Strait they frequently cross. One can see the Rock of Gibraltar from their roof terrace in good weather. Priscilla is a writer of novels about the region.

I present local writer Mohamed Larbi Mechtat to her in November 2019. Priscilla had commissioned a friendship cake, which was eaten after dinner: Tangier-Gibraltar was written on it. Larbi Mechtat was currently writing the seventh of his novels, all of which are set in the Medina of Tangier. The two writers do not speak each other's language of publication – Larbi Mechtat no English and Sacramento no Arabic – so Spanish and French are used. They agree to organize joint cultural events, such as readings, in both cities.

Similar cultural events are already taking place in Gibraltar, such as a *Tangier & Gibraltar Art Exhibition* in December 2019 in *John Mackintosh Hall*, supported by the Gibraltarian Ministry of Culture and others. Minister John Cortes opens the exhibition:

---

34   https://www.facebook.com/groups/mag4x4committee/about/
35   Field research diary TanGib, October 30, 2019.

The exchange will marry both communities and integrate through culture the understanding of one another. I am very confident this exchange will be of great benefit to both artistic communities and will be the gateway for future cultural exchanges with other small nations and neighboring towns. (YGTV 2019a)

Communication between the two cities via digital media also creates a binding force. Several online platforms focus on Tangier or Gibraltar, and I myself founded the Facebook Group *TanGib* in 2019 in order to help my research project. Furthermore, in October 2019, I posted a video on YouTube about *Tangier in Gibraltar, Gibraltar in Tangier*.[36]

Other rather informal or private activities, such as a Moroccan Night of the local waterfront are organized. There are also sporting links between the two cities, especially boat rallies.

Several informants have pointed out to me that several Gibraltarians (mainly women and some men) of an already set age (40+) now have *Tanjawi* boyfriends. Some of these couples have married in the meantime. One can imagine that the rumors about "unsatisfied women" and "Moroccans looking for a place to stay" are sprouting from their mouths.

There's one who got ripped off by her Moroccan boyfriend. She was warned by another Moroccan: You can see that the man is a crook. In any case, she financed an apartment for him in Tangier and showered him with expensive gifts. Once she wanted to visit him in the apartment she was paying for. He wouldn't let her in. After he got his residence permit, he married someone else. Gay Gibraltarians have also had such experiences. An elderly gentleman let himself be ripped off by a Moroccan for 15 years.[37]

'It happened to my niece,' says another informant. 'She married a Moroccan and when he got his residence permit, he dropped her. That happens to quite a few people here. Especially the hard-to-get ones: The fat one, the ugly one, the crooked one.'[38]

Today there are hardly any marriages between the Jewish community of Gibraltar and Moroccan Jews. A rare exception arose in Corona times when I was invited to attend a Gibraltar-Moroccan wedding via Zoom. On August 16th, 2020, the son of a family friend married his girlfriend from Casablanca. When a speech was announced at the reception and the guests were asked to be quiet, the groom's Gibraltarian mother knocked on a glass and shouted: "Silence please," while her daughter-in-law began the typical Moroccan praise *"ulululu."*

---

36   https://www.youtube.com/watch?v=obZ8vTuK9tU&fbclid=IwAR3cDWo7Zxs-SyLZS4TB_4geHP9gDN4eosONE2ialp8VTmNaONyAZNOhPFJs.
37   Field research diary TanGib, February 29, 2020.
38   Field research diary TanGib, March 3, 2020.

8.6. Conclusion

Today is January 30th, 2020. At 00.00 tomorrow evening, Britain will leave the EU after 47 years. I will not be in Gibraltar, but I will visit the Rock and Tangier in 5 weeks, *inchallah*. On the web pages of *The Gibraltar Chronicle* one presents oneself, as so often, as a mere chronicler of the events. One does not get to know anything about the atmosphere in the city. On the online platforms I researched, the subject of Brexit is also largely nonexistent: No cheering, no moaning, no grumbling, not even gallows humor. The pages focus almost exclusively on personal concerns regarding health, family celebrations, school performances or professional life in Gibraltar itself. Socially and politically relevant topics are missing. Only the liberation of the Auschwitz concentration camp 75 years ago is remembered. If I interpret this absence correctly in the context of the mood since the Referendum, there is something like the breathless silence before the knot really bursts. In order to really believe it, it has to happen.

The three-year process since the Referendum initially led to widespread shock in Gibraltar. The overwhelming majority of residents had voted for Britain to remain in the EU, so the local outcome hardly caused any upheaval within families, circles of friends or neighborhoods. This state of shock gave way to agony, as in the three years of Brexit, any sign in British politics that could prevent Brexit was too often disappointed. It was preferable to stop talking about the issue and to ignore it. In public spaces, neither graffiti nor posters or bumper stickers expressed any opinion on the subject. For Brexit was not only contrary to the political or economic interests of Gibraltarians, it once again made them aware of their own powerlessness: There was absolutely no possibility of influencing the politics of the mother country. So, two options opened up: Either they surrendered to their fate or they tried to take it into their own hands and develop their own initiatives. Among the latter, one can note the orientation towards the neighboring country Morocco and the initiative by Chief Minister Picardo to join the Schengen area. Both initiatives are astonishingly courageous and testify to a new self-confidence, as Gibraltar still has no authority to shape its foreign relations which remain in the hands of the UK.

The initiatives can also be read as signs of the defiant and pragmatic activism that followed the shock and agony. Self-confidence and a look ahead were evident in most of the talks in March 2020 in which Brexit was touched upon. There are existing resources for this: The commitment of individual actors, charitable initiatives, informal economic relationships, illegal networks, cultural activities and love relationships.

One day before the final Brexit on January 1st.2021, a solution was found for Gibraltar: the territory will join the Schengen area, just as Picardo had requested. For the residents of Gibraltar, this means - unlike other British people - full freedom of movement in the countries of the Schengen area. The job and employment opportunities of the residents of the *Campo* in Gibraltar are secured.

On January 9th, 2021, it was reported that Boris Johnson's government was considering the project of a tunnel from Morocco to Gibraltar (Urteaga 2021). In the process of going to print, it is not possible to determine the seriousness of the source. In any case, building a tunnel into Gibraltar, which is now part of the Schengen area, would secure and strengthen Great Britain's influence on the EU's North Africa policy. One day later, Spanish daily El País announced that Great Britain and Spain had agreed to remove the border fence between La Línia and Gibraltar (Martín/Gonzáles 2021).

This gives rise to a new attitude: My previous experience in Gibraltar was more of a fateful devotion to the role of a puppet depending on Britain and Spain. But now there was a third reference point – the EU. After all, Gibraltarians had been citizens of Europe for 47 years. Even if the EU is currently perceived as a toothless and unwilling partner who is not affected by Gibraltar's fate, Gibraltarians have, nevertheless, built up networks within the EU.

8.7. Addendum: Corona

It can happen that fast. Brexit just established or strengthened bonds between Gibraltar and Morocco, I could finish my last field research phase, leave Gibraltar on March 6th, 2020, and start the flight home from Málaga. And now this: The measures against the coronavirus are affecting relations between states and, of course, between Gibraltar, Spain and Morocco.

The Government of Gibraltar calls on all Gibraltarians living in the Spanish hinterland to adapt to and respect the Spanish measures against the spread of the virus. Border crossings into Spain should be limited to the minimum necessary. Spaniards working in the hotel and catering industry in Gibraltar will not be allowed to cross the border because, firstly, the curfew in Spain affects many of the frontier workers and Spaniards working in Gibraltar and, secondly, relevant companies in Gibraltar will be closed for 21 days for the time being (Reyes 2020b).

Some Gibraltarians stranded in Morocco may board a ferry to Gibraltar via Ceuta in Spain. This is because the shipping connection from Morocco to Gibraltar and to Spain has also been discontinued (The Gibraltar Chronicle 2020a).

On March 15th, 2020, the British Embassy in Rabat called on all British citizens to leave Morocco, and flights from Tangier to Gibraltar were also to be suspended. The *GMBA* leaders Marin and Krikaz went to Ibn Battouta airport to assist insecure travelers. These had already been advised in advance to get to the airport as early as possible. The *GMBA* office was closed the next day.

Illustration 83: Covid19 – Directing British nationals back to Gibraltar. GBME leaders at Ibn Battouta airport

On March 15th, 2020 Morocco cancels all flights to 25 other countries (The Gibraltar Chronicle 2020b). A few days later, Chief Minister Picardo explains that the preparations for Brexit, especially the extensive storage of food, medicine and other supplies, will make it possible to guarantee the supply of the population for a longer period of time during the Corona crisis.

Priscilla and Henry Sacramento remain in Tangier during the crisis. Originally, they wanted to return to Gibraltar at the beginning of Ramadan at the end of April 2020, but this was not possible until July. From the roof of their house they can at least see Gibraltar (Peralta 2020).

On May 8th, 2020, 23 Gibraltar-resident British nationals were repatriated from Morocco. These were in the North African country on March 12th, the day the Moroccan borders were closed. The action was carried out through the cooperation of the U.K., Moroccan and Gibraltarian governments. The *Gibraltar Chronicle* reported that there were still 38 British citizens remaining in Morocco. On arrival in Gibraltar, passengers were checked for elevated temperatures. All were advised to self-isolate for 14 days (The Gibraltar Chronicle 2020c).

9. Conclusion

9.1. What is the next step with TanGib?

Of course, nobody knows what will happen with TanGib. One could express it religiously: Only the Lord himself knows; or: It is written what will happen, *inchallah*. It can also be formulated in a social scientific way: The future is contingent. Prognoses are not my business – neither as a human being nor as a scientist. Nevertheless, it may be possible to gather evidence that can help us to approach the question of how things might go on with TanGib. The starting point is the original assertion that TanGib exists at all. Let us look at the elements that led me to consider TanGib as one city: Informal and formal structural relationships in different fields.

TanGib has never existed as an administratively anchored city. But there were times when both cities were so closely connected with each other and the surrounding regions that one can speak of a cultural area.

On the informal level, family ties still exist across the Strait, be it Gibraltarian property in Tangier (and also *Tanjawi* property in Gibraltar), be it smuggling networks (which surround TanGib but go beyond it) (Ingelmo 2018), be it Moroccans living in Gibraltar or Gibraltarians living in Tangier. Informal cross-border networks such as those between Gibraltar and Tangier, between Tangier and Andalusia or between Gibraltar and the Spanish *Campo de Gibraltar* continue to play an important role.[1] In addition, on the level of habitus, sensory perceptions and narratives, there is still a basic understanding of and sometimes identification with the other side: *Boughazidad*. It consists of the internalization of the other, the highlighting of commonalities and the negation of otherness.

We find structural similarities on the level of natural conditions: Wind, light, currents and waves. Social and cultural similarities between the two cities are currently shaped more from Gibraltar than from Tangier: Today the Rock is economically more dependent on Tangier than Tangier on Gibraltar. Thus, *transboughaz*

---

1   Until 2013, for example, the local bus business in La Línea was operated by the CMT (*Compañía de transporte de Marruecos*). Online platform A, Julián Nunes Rocha (d.n.n).

initiatives in the fields of journalism and economy, as well as charity, have been taken by Gibraltarian actors.

Regarding military cooperation between Gibraltar and Northern Morocco, I cannot say which side is more active or more interested.

On the level of cultural memory, however, a more national or nationalistic view is cultivated on both sides. In Tangier, local politics, local journalism and civic engagement show little historical awareness of their own city. Ruralization, land speculation, rural exodus and orientation towards the national Moroccan discourse are exemplary of the the decisive keywords here. How should one develop an awareness of the city on the other side which one could not easily visit?

In Gibraltar, the national narrative is based on the assertion of a uniqueness that unambiguously demarcates the territory and its inhabitants from Spain and the Spanish. This 'native' narrative, as I like to call it, sacrifices both historical precision and cross-border networks. I suspect that the silence about the networks that have existed is based on two aspects: Firstly, informal cross-border networks are easily denounceable as illicit and illegal (such as smuggling); secondly, the silence is a collateral damage of the demarcation against Spain: The relations with Tangier were rarely merely bilateral (i.e. between Tangier and Gibraltar), but mostly included Spain or the Spanish, as could be shown by many family networks. This, however, is the crux in the national Gibraltarian narrative: Its focus on prehistory relieves the community from turning to historically closer periods in which there were undeniable mixes with Morocco and Spain.

Looking away from local and regional conditions presents an even more complete picture. For Tangier and Gibraltar, it is no longer just a matter of connecting, because the city of TanGib is dependent on the regional and global context: Spain and Gibraltar are on one side of the fortress walls of Europe, and Tangier and Morocco are on the other. This need not be mentioned further. National animosities still smolder: Morocco (e.g. occupation of Perejil in 2002, closure of the border with Ceuta in 2020) is remembered as a power factor to be reckoned with if the balance of power in the Strait is to be changed. Nevertheless, Spain and Morocco are, in many respects, closely linked politically and economically. This may also prevent the GMBA office in Tangier from consolidating and developing in the future. The local government's support for the office is so cautious "because they know that Spain can always ask the Moroccan government to close the Gibraltar office in Tangier."[2]

But it is not the only political framework that needs to be taken into account when considering the relations between Tangier and Gibraltar. The resistance to the Moroccan monarchy is still smoldering in the Rif mountains and around Alhucemas. Moreover, there is rumbling in nearby Algeria, even though long-time

---

2 Sidney Delmar, Field research diary TanGib, February 23, 2020.

president Bouteflika gave up his fifth presidential candidacy on March 11, 2019, after intense protests. In Andalusia, the fascist party Vox won important votes in the regional elections (2018) for the first time since the death of General Franco, especially in the border municipalities of San Roque (12.53 per cent), La Línea (14.77 per cent) and Algeciras (19.49 per cent). In neighboring Ceuta, Vox even became the strongest party in the national elections in November 2019, which prompts the SGA to formulate "Vox wins this means more than ever Gibraltar and Morocco needs each other.[3]

Gibraltar itself had to reposition itself several times in the period of the announced Brexit, and importantly, the basic conditions have been constantly changing since 2016. Nothing was certain.

As a result of Brexit, Great Britain is again becoming increasingly active in the Strait. Britons are particularly present in two zones that are designated for major tourism projects in northern Morocco, Marina Smir near Tetuán and Marchica near Melilla. The forecasts for a line for renewable energies are also ambitious. An electric cable is to be laid to Gibraltar to benefit from Morocco's development in the field of renewable energies. In return, Gibraltar plans to share its financial sector experience with the Alawite Kingdom. Military cooperation between Gibraltar and Morocco is also to be expanded. All of this is perceived with concern in Spain. In addition, cooperation in agriculture is to be expanded, which would particularly hit the farmers in the Spanish province of Huelva hard: "Here we pay salaries and social security, a worker costs more than 60 euros, in Morocco 12 euros. How should we compete with it? "Says the farmer Antonio Luis Martín' Curi 'from the province of Huelva. In addition, the UK sees Morocco as a stepping stone to West African markets. In the first trade dialogue between Morocco and Great Britain in June 2020, Morocco offered itself to Britain as a gateway to Africa, and the former British Minister Conor Burns already announced "the triangulation of Morocco, Africa and Great Britain"(Moreno 2020c).

The major powers are still present: Gibraltar can still be used by the U.K. and the U.S. as an ideal aircraft carrier in the Mediterranean and the Middle East. A Moroccan initiative in July 2020 could be suitable for changing the conditions at the entrance to the Mediterranean once again: So far, the U.S. has two military bases, the air force base in Morón near Seville and the naval port of Rota on the coast of Cádiz, from which operations in the Mediterranean and the Middle East can be carried out. According the Spanish Online Journal *El Español*, Morocco is now offering the Americans the opportunity to close them and exchange them for several bases in the vicinity of Tangier: In particular, a territory has been reserved for the (American) military next to the overseas port of Ksar el Shgir, as well as facilities at Guercif, Taourirt and Monte Arruit (Moreno 2020b). As this is a recent information

---

3   Online Platform H (d.n.n).

Just before this book goes into print, I couldn't check if the source is trustworthy or fake news, as some say. A development like that would upset the existing balance of power in the region and weaken the Spanish position in the area. Against the background of the simultaneous withdrawal of troops from Germany, this would mean, from the point of view of the European security architecture, a weakening of NATO as a whole and a deliberate snubbing of Germany and Spain by the US. From a Spanish reading, however, Moroccan policy is also aimed at weakening the Spanish exclave of Ceuta in the immediate vicinity of Ksar el Sghir and is linked to the Moroccan offer to the Jewish communities of Ceuta and Melilla not only to invest more in Northern Morocco but also to resettle there (Moreno 2020a). The offer also applies to the Sephardim of Gibraltar (Yaabouk 2020). All these communities are historically, economically and family-wise closely connected with Northern Morocco and especially with Tangier. If they were to relocate to Morocco on a larger scale, this would mean a double weakening of Spain and the exclaves to which Morocco has always laid claim. For Tangier, the presence of American soldiers with their families and the arrival of the Sephardic Ceuta and Melilla could return to a cosmopolitan era. Perhaps the restorations that have been carried out in Tangier over the past two years on long-neglected buildings from the Zone's time are already symbolic signs of a reflection on a new cosmopolitanism that accompanies geostrategic efforts?

At the same time, however, many EU companies – Renault, Dacia, Zara – are also represented with production facilities in the Tangier area. In addition, there is a new player: The construction of the Chinese production city of Tangier Tech[4] on an area of 467 ha for companies of the most varied kinds indicates that China also intends to occupy the region as a field of activity.

Tangier, the actual economic center of the region, has so far only been able to keep the promise of an economically prosperous and peaceful future for a small minority of its inhabitants. Most ordinary citizens are not benefiting from growth, the rates of unemployment, illiteracy and poverty are high, and the lack of prospects for the young generation is frightening. Not for the first time since the 1990s, the Strait is currently once again the preferred illegal migration route from Africa to Europe. Many *Tanjawis* and other Moroccans still or already want to leave for Europe because they see no future prospects in their home country. And quite a few poorer Spaniards move to Morocco because they can live better from their support there. How Corona will affect the two cities is not foreseeable.

---

4 The companies come from the automotive and aerospace industries, "renewable energies, leather and textile industry, mechanical engineering, electrical and electronic industry, plastics industry, agri-food industry, chemical and semi-chemical industry and building materials industry" (Maghreb Post Online 2019).

Hopelessness in Morocco is widespread, and no one knows whether it will not be revealed in a second Arab spring or a catastrophic winter. All in all, unfavorable starting conditions for the successful future of TanGib. But, wasn't it always like this here?

Again, these are turbulent times for the region. Gibraltar's interest in Tangier and TanGib is growing in any case thanks to Brexit. Tangier's interest in Gibraltar, on the other hand, first has to be reawakened, ventilated and revitalized. Informal, habitual and, to some extent, structural resources are already in place.

9.2. Conclusions regarding the theoretical approaches

If one refers back to Graebner's metaphor, then the region probably no longer represents a cultural area today, since it is no longer a frequently condensed network of relationships. TanGib was once – until about 1956 – a *Single Border Society* – and perhaps it will be again: At present, it is not. The ethnographic view of the present alone tempts us to deny the cultural area: Tangier is much more closely connected to the other regions of Morocco, to the diaspora in Europe and, via the port of Tangier-Med, to the commercial metropolises of the globe than to Gibraltar, 14 kilometers away. However, the future is contingent. There are first signs that TanGib is slowly being ventilated again at the moment. With a view to the present, it can be said that TanGib and the surrounding areas no longer represent a cultural area today – but they do exhibit features of a cultural area that can and will be reactivated again.

With the image of breathing, the old concept of cultural circles can also be updated: Contrary to what Graebner and Frobenius assumed, these are not stable or permanent circles of exchange but rather processual entities; they may narrow or expand at times. They may connect to other regions or encapsulate themselves, so they have no fixed form. This depends on the general geopolitical situation, trade flows, migration routes and other factors.

If this is so, why do I still insist so much on the concept of the cultural area? Because the image of locality linked to the vastness, as celebrated at the height of globalization, is just as false as the image of narrowness, which is primarily related to the national. We still find, or have already found, many times denser interdependencies in cultural and social reality which – if they are maintained over a long period of time – are able to create privileged commonalities that do not exist with other regions.

Economic and military institutions maintain relations between the two cities or regions. Social conditions that can underpin these relations still exist but have a different value for Gibraltar than for Tangier. The networks through which I have traversed in Chapter 6 are more relevant to Gibraltar today than to Tangier as a whole – more Gibraltarians have ties or property in Tangier than vice versa, due to different demographic and political processes. Even if Tangier had not experienced massive population growth in the last 50 years, its ties with Gibraltar would still have been weakened: By the Moroccanization of the companies that expelled Europeans, by the emigration of Jews and the departure of many Muslim *Tanjawis*. Religious, ethical and family networks that were crucially responsible for TanGib's close ties have disintegrated, and there are no significant Jewish or Christian diasporas. But the Moroccan diaspora in Gibraltar has the potential to stabilize and expand *transboughaz* social ties – I am not talking about conscious identification. This would require sensitive ethnological research in the future.

In addition to the recently emerging institutions (GMBA, SGA), which emphasize such commonalities, cultural and psychological identifications represent crucial resources for anchoring these institutional commonalities in people's consciousness. For TanGib, I have coined the term *Boughazidad* for this. This means that one knows the other side only too well, because one has internalized it over centuries in one way or another. This knowledge does not always have to be explicit: This is where the nationality manufacturers in Gibraltar are currently failing, as is the education system in TanGib. It can also be implicit, and it can manifest itself in the automatic knowledge of looks, sounds, gestures, movements, family stories, smells and colors, sea currents and winds. An analysis of the rhythms, in the sense of Lefebvre and Regulier, was quite appropriate here, for it turns precisely to implicit conditions. One can judge the people of the other side because one has internalized them. When informants from Tangier tell me that Gibraltarians and Andalusians are "like us," while the English, Soussi and Castilian are different; and when I am told in Gibraltar that they know what makes the *Tanjawis* tick, then these are proofs of a *Boughazidad* that cannot be dismissed. But, of course, this is also subject to constant change: Many people who have moved in from the south of Morocco are simply not familiar with Mediterranean commonalities and Gibraltarians are more concerned with ties to Great Britain than with those to their close neighborhood. In this respect, it can be concluded that my understanding of the cultural sphere and of *Boughazidad* represents two sides of the same coin: The more explicit/institutional and the more implicit/cultural and habitualized side of a breathing, pliable category.

Transregionality like *Boughazidad* therefore can offer better means of understanding and an alternative way of thinking about - mainly - ethnic and religious identity. First, because it foregrounds social and cultural practice rather than confession. This could be shown on thorough empirical grounds. And second, because ethnicity has been constantly thought as linked to descendence – whether biologically taken for granted, symbolically claimed, invented, imagined or believed. Neither *Tanjawis* nor Gibraltarians can honestly claim descendence as a common ground for identification. Rather, it is social space wherein identitfication unfolds through practice: by internalizing and deeply knowing about the other.

Illustration 84 : Chez Kébé, Tangier

I have introduced the term 'memory bags' to refer to information from earlier conversations with informants that comes to light in later conversations themselves. I recall the example of Michael Gómez and Patrick Grénard. I met Gómez in Gibraltar in the 90s, Grénard in Tangier in the 2010s. By chance, I learned that they knew each other, since they were in the same school class. For me this was a real treat because I thought I had found an example of *Boughazidad*. But I had to be careful not to overstress the example. *Boughazidad* means the internalization of the other side and, thus, the creation of a common ground. But what does "common ground" mean here? Gómez and Grénard recognized each other in the photo, they had kept a common ground in their memory bags, but it didn't mean anything in the everyday life of either of them 40 years after their time together at school. It was the ethnologist who first recognized the common student body, then named it to them and, in a third step, tried to revitalize the relationship. Neither one nor the other had any honest interest in this. They had little to do with each other in the past, so why would they now stage something that had neither existed in the past nor would they want today? The only one who was interested in such a production was me. This unpleasant realization of the eager researcher about his own contribution in creating the conditions to which he turns, requires an insistent humility towards his own material, so that one does not cut it up as if it were only following his own need in his own argumentation. Yes, Marshall Sahlins is right: The worlds of our informants do not revolve around our worlds (Sahlins 2013: XIII).

It is more a matter of curbing one's own academic exuberance after reduction and making rather cautious statements: *Boughazidad*, therefore, refers to the underpinning of the common ground between Southern Spain, Gibraltar and Morocco, on the basis of which structural, institutional and action-oriented commonalities can develop but not the structures, institutions and actions themselves.

In many regions of the Mediterranean, cosmopolitan elements, present or past, are a resource for being transformed into political ideologies. Cosmopolitanism in Gibraltar and Istria (Prekodravac 2013; Zorko/Fontana 2014) tends to be local and regional, while Pharaonism (Kaufman 2001) in Egypt, Kahanoff's Levantinism (Ohana 2016) and Lebanese Phoenicianism (Rejwan 2009) were national.

This work on TanGib has not really contributed to a new understanding of cosmopolitanism. I have already distinguished between a scientific and philosophical understanding, on the one hand, and a cultural understanding, on the other, in earlier works: A philosophical draft such as Kant's is just not the same as Tafersiti Zarouila's work in Tangier or that of the Finlaysons in Gibraltar. I would be a bad ethnologist if I were to consider the latter to be less important than the thoughts of the Königsberg philosopher. But neither Kant's designs nor those of the hobby historians in Tangier and Gibraltar can be equated with lived cultural and social relationships. Tafersiti Zarouila is undoubtedly concerned with preserving the memory of a past time that was his own childhood and saving it for the future through a variety of publications; Finlaysons, in a post-colonial sense, weave a Gibraltarian national narrative for a new community.

Tangier and Gibraltar provided their development across nations and religions. Regarding the identification with Tangier, Gibraltar and TanGib, it can be said – analogous to the development of a Levantine identification in Smyrna:

> [T]he process of dispossession of the 'national' traits of the word in the period, reaching the cosmopolitan status registered in the following centur[y], was made possible by its manipulation as a 'container' of identities that could work as a facilitator in the merchants' world and in the building of social inter-relationships. (Tagliaferri 2016: 90)

When one looks at the contemporary cultural and social practices of cosmopolitan coexistence in Tangier and Gibraltar, one finds that cosmopolitanism in Tangier refers to the zone's past and tends to underestimate contemporary forms, such as the presence of sub-Saharan, other immigrants and Chinese investors, which are not perceived as valuable. This can be seen not least in the rejection of *Arobis* by *Tanjawis de Verdad*. However, they are now in a minority position and, therefore, cultivate a rather defensive cosmopolitanism. Perhaps the possible establishment of American military bases and the influx of Jews from Ceuta and Melilla may indicate the basis for a new cosmopolitanization of Tangier. Cosmopolitan in Gibraltar, on the other hand, in the sense of interfaith and -ethnic ties, is not just a hollow phrase but a social reality cultivated and lived on many levels. In short, as an ethnologist, I do not understand cosmopolitanism in the sense of Kant or political scientists such as Nussbaum (1996, 2020) and others but as a lived reality. And here it is important to distinguish political ideologies from cosmopolitan structures and from everyday reality

Whether the memory of cosmopolitanism will one day serve as a resource for a political ideology, for example, to assert Tangier's regional independence within Morocco, is rather unlikely from today's point of view.

9.3 Final remark

Ethnologists have shown that the ethnological perspective makes it possible to argue about rehearsed scientific categories and approaches on the basis of each cultural group and to question them: This is the task of the subject in the Boasian sense. However, its unique location between Europe and Africa, the Atlantic and the Mediterranean, the Western and the Islamic world, makes the Strait of Gibraltar probably a particularly privileged place for this endeavor. Not only Western concepts, such as nation, state, borders, religion and culture, are put to the test here but also the Islamic categories of purity, *baraka*, submission and spirituality. Everything, routes, paths and people cross here. In a double sense. This focus on the crossroads allows us to look at the human, which is opposed to a world of separation, isolation, fanaticism and identity struggle: By this, I mean practical social and cultural negotiation.

We will see if and how *Boughazidad* will develop in the future. Sensual bonds still play an important role, myths are still present and some architectural similarities and several networks of relationships from earlier times have survived. It is possible that all these resources will reappear in the echo of Brexit, reactivated. A first hint is given by the local novels, which place *transboughaz* family stories at their center. Perhaps the resources will also be used politically again – probably in Gibraltar at first, after all, relations with Tangier have always been particularly important when Spain threatened the status of Gibraltar. This may become all the more necessary as the gaming industry, which has made a significant contribution to Gibraltar's economy in recent years, is already turning its attention to other locations that will give them access to the European single market (Reyes 2019). In any case, Morocco and Tangier are once again seen as partners to cushion the hardships of EU withdrawal. The establishment of the GMBA is an expression of this interest. In Tangier itself, Gibraltar is only a second o third class economic opportunity, among other things – the economic area in the North of Morocco has developed too far around Tangier and has been integrated into the worldwide network for Gibraltar to be of decisive importance at the present.

It is possible that the relationship between the two cities will be considerably enhanced after Brexit. Morocco may be granted a privileged special status, allowing local and regional networks to strengthen and develop. It is possible that Tangier less than Morocco as a whole will play an important role for the civilian population of Gibraltar and will gain in importance. On the other hand, Morocco is currently experiencing a political and economic revaluation, as a privileged partner of both the EU and UK. We will see which partnerships become significant, but there are certainly enough starting points to expect increasingly transnational links on a *transboughaz* basis. The Strait can wait.

References

Bibliography

Abbas, Akbar (2000): "Cosmopolitan De-scriptions: Shanghai and Hong Kong", in: Public Culture 12/3, pp. 769-786.

Abu-Shams, Leila/ Gonzales-Vazquez, Araceli (2014): "Juxtaposing Time: An Anthropology of Multiple Temporalities in Morocco", in: Revue des mondes musulmanes et de la Méditerranée 136, pp. 33-45.

Adams, Susan/Bosch, Elena/Balaresque, Patricia L./Ballereau, Stéphane J./Lee, Andrew C./Arroyo, Eduardo et al. (2008): "The Genetic Legacy of Religious Diversity and Intolerance: Paternal Lineages of Christians, Jews, and Muslims in the Iberian Peninsula", in: American Journal of Human Genetics 83, pp. 725-736.

Agrell, Olof/Lempriere, Will (1798): Neue Reise nach Marokos welche im Lande selbst gesammelte interesante, historisch-statistische Nachrichten bis in das Jahr 1797 enthält, Translated from Swedish, Nürnberg: Adam Gottlieb Schneder und Weigel.

Aidi, Hisham (2017): „Juan Goytisolo – Tangier, Havana and the Treasonous Intellectual", in: Middle East Report 282, pp. 19-31.

Aixelà-Cabré, Yolanda (2017): "El activismo nacionalista marroquí (1927-1936). Efectos del protectorado español en la historia del Marruecos colonial", in: Illes i Imperis 19, pp. 145-168.

Aleko, Lilius (1956): Turbulent Tangier. London, Elek Books.

Ali Bey (Badía y Leblich, Domingo) (1814): Voyages d'Ali Bey el Abbassi (pseud.) en Afrique et en Asie pendant les années, 1803, 1804, 1805 … Paris: S. Didot.

Andersen, Hans Christian (1863a): Spanien. H.C. Andersens Samlede Skrifter Ottende Bind, Anden Udgave, Kjøbenhavn C.A. Reitzels Forlag 1878, Bianco Lunos Bogtrykkeri. (https://www.hcandersen-homepage.dk/?page_id=64717, last visited: 11.11.2020).

Andersen, Hans Christian (1863b): Spanien. H.C. Andersens Samlede Skrifter Ottende Bind, Anden Udgave, Kjøbenhavn C.A. Reitzels Forlag 1878, Bianco Lunos Bogtrykkeri. (https://www.hcandersen-homepage.dk/?page_id=28761, last visited: 11.11.2020).

Anderson, Benedict (1983): Imagined-Communities – Reflections on the Origin and Spread of Nationalism, London: Verso.

Ange, Olivia/Berliner, David (eds.) (2015): Anthropology and Nostalgia, New York: Berghahn Books, p. 235.

Antweiler, Christoph (2004): "Urbanität und Ethnologie. Aktuelle Theorietrends und Methodik ethnologischer Stadtforschung", in: Zeitschrift für Ethnologie 129/2, pp. 285-307.

Antweiler, Christoph (2018): "Urbanization and urban environments", in: The International Encyclopedia of Anthropology. Oxford, UK: John Wiley & Sons, Ltd., pp. 1-10

Aramoni, Aniceto (1972): "Machismo", in: Psychology Today 5/8, pp. 69-72.

Assayag, Isaac J. (2000): Tanger - Regards sur le passé. Ce qu'il fut. Tanger, o. A.

Bahloul, Joelle (1994): "The Sephardic Jew as Mediterranean: A View from Kinship and Gender", in: Journal of Mediterranean Studies 4/2, pp. 197-207.

Bahrami, Beebe (1998): "A Door to Paradise: Converts, the New Age, Islam, and the Past in Granada, Spain," in: City & Society 10/1, pp. 121-132.

Banfield, Edward C. (1958): The Moral Basis of a Backward Society. Glencoe, Illinois: The Free Press.

Barbero, Luis (1997): "Las redes de contrabando de hachís de Marruecos toman el control del 'mercado' de la inmigración", in: El País April 7.

Barcía Trelles, Camilo (1968): "Pasado, Presente y Futuro de un Problema Colonial: Gibraltar." Revista de Política Internacional 96, pp. 127-154.

Baroja, Pio (1989). "Tánger", in: Abdellah Djbilou (ed.), Tánger, puerta de África. Antología de textos literarios hispánicos 1860-1960. Madrid: Editorial CantArabia, pp. 39-45.

Barth, Fredrik (1969): "Introduction." In: Fredrik Barth (ed.), Ethnic Groups and Boundaries, Oslo: Norwegian University Press, pp. 9-38.

Benady, Mesod (1974-1978) "The settlement of the Jews in Gibraltar, 1704-1783", in: Jewish Historical Society of England Transactions, Vol. 26, pp. 87-110.

Benady, Mesod (1979-1980): "Who is a Gibraltarian? The Roots of Gibraltarian Society and Culture", in: Calpe News, March 1, 1979 – January 25, 1980, 24 Issues.

Benady, Mesod (1989): "The Jewish Community of Gibraltar", in: Richard Barnett/Walter Schwab (eds.), The Western Sephardim, Grendon, Northhants: Gibraltar Books Ltd., pp. 144-179.

Benady, Mesod (1992): "The Role of Jews in the British Colonies of the Western Mediterranean", in: Transactions of the Jewish Historical Society of England. Paper presented to the Society on November 19, pp. 45-63.

Benady, Mesod (1993): "Las comunidades del norte de Marueccos", in: Henry Méchoulan (ed.), Los judíos de España. Historia de una diáspora. 1492-1992, Madrid: Trotta, pp. 507-514.

Benady, Mesod (1996) The Streets of Gibraltar - A short history, Grendon, Northhants: Gibraltar Books Ltd.
Benady, Sam (1994): Civil Hospital and Epidemics in Gibraltar, Grendon, Northhants: Gibraltar Books Ltd.
Benady, Sam M. (1993): Memoirs of a Gibraltarian (1905-1993), Grendon, Northhants: Gibraltar Books Ltd.
Benady, Sam/Chiappe, Mary (2011): The Pearls of Tangier: Bresciano in Morocco, Gibraltar: Rock Scorpion Books.
Bendelac, Abraham/Miège, Jean Louis (1995): Chronique de Tanger, 1820-1830: Journal de Bendelac, Marokko: La Porte.
Bornemann, Fritz (1967): "Chronologie, Kulturkreis und Urkultur in der kulturhistorischen Forschung", in: C. A. Schmitz (ed.), Historische Völkerkunde, Frankfurt am Main: Akademische Verlagsanstalt, pp. 79-121.
Borutta, Manuel (2014): "Frankreichs Süden: Der Midi und Algerien, 1830–1962", in: Francia 41, pp. 201-225.
Borutta, Manuel/Lemmes, Fabian (2013): "Die Wiederkehr des Mittelmeerraumes: Stand und Perspektiven der neuhistorischen Mediterranistik", in: Neue Politische Literatur 58, pp. 389-419.
Bosch, E./Calafell, F./Pérez-Lezaun, A./Clarimón, J./Comas, D./Mateu, E. et al. (2000): "Genetic structure of North-West Africa revealed by STR analysis", in: European Journal of Human Genetics 8/5, pp. 360-366.
Bourdieu, Pierre (1991) "Identity and Representation. Elements for a Critical Reflection on the Idea of Region", in: Pierre Bourdieu, Language and Symbolic Power. Cambridge: Polity Press 1991.
Bourdieu, Pierre (2010): Algerische Skizzen, Frankfurt am Main: Suhrkamp.
Boutayeb, Rachid (2017): "Nachbarschaft für Anfänger", in: Kuckuck – Notizen zur Alltagskultur 1/17, pp. 12-17.
Brandes, Stanley (1981): "Like Wounded Stags – Male Sexual Ideology in an Andalusian Town", in: Sherry Ortner/Harriet Whitehead (eds.), Sexual Meanings – The Cultural Construction of Gender and Sexuality, Cambridge, pp. 216-239.
Burke III, Edmund (2014): The Ethnographic State, France and the Invention of Moroccan Islam, Oakland: University of California Press.
Canessa, Andrew (ed.) (2019): Bordering on Britishness, Palgrave Studies in European Political Sociology, Cham: Springer Nature Switzerland AG.
Cañizares y Moyano, Eduardo (1998): "Description of Tangier", in: Crónicas del norte, Spanish Travellers in Morocco. Anthology, Tetouan: Tetuan Asmir Association, pp. 39-44.
Ceballos López, Leopoldo (2009): Historia de Tanger – Memoria de la ciudad internacional, Córdoba: Editorial Almuzara.
Ceballos López, Leopoldo (2015): Tánger, Tánger, una saga tangerine, Barcelona: edhasa.

Ceballos López, Leopoldo (2019): Tánger, Tánger, una saga tangerina, 2nd edition, Letra de Autor.

Cecilia, Myra (2009): "RosalindaPowellFox,DaughteroftheRajandSpain", in: EyeOnSpain July 16. https://www.eyeonspain.com/blogs/myracecilia/1798/rosalinda-powell-fox-daughter-of-the-raj-and-spain.aspx

Chimenti, Elisa (1935): Eves Marocaines, Tanger: Les Editions Internationales.

Chimenti, Elisa (1964): Le Sortilège et autres contes sépharditв, Tanger: Les Editions Marocaines et Internationales.

Chimenti, Elisa (2003): Cuentos del Marruecos Español, Madrid: Clan Editorial.

Chipulina, Neville (2013): "1861 – Sir William Codrington – The Jewish Refugees." (https://gibraltar-intro.blogspot.com/2013/08/1861-sir-william-codringtоn-lady.html).

Chirop, John/Martínez, Francisco Javier (eds.) (2018): Mediterrannean Quarantines, 1750-1914. Manchester: Manchester University Press.

Choukri, Mohamed (1973): For Bread Alone, University of Virginia: P. Owen.

Coccia, Emanuele (2018): Die Wurzeln der Welt, München: Carl Hanser Verlag.

Cohen, Anthony S./Fukui, Katsuyoshi (1993): Humanizing the City? Social Contexts of Urban Life at the Turn of the Millennium, Edinburgh: Edinburgh University Press.

Coon, Carleton (1933): The Riffian. Boston: Little, Brown and Company.

Coon, Carleton (1980): A North Africa Story: Story of an Anthropologist as OSS Agent. Ort: Gambit Publications

Coon, Carleton Stevens (1939): The Races of Europe. New York: The Macmilan Company. (https://archive.org/details/racesofeurope031695mbp/page/n4, last visited: 11.11.2020).

Corbin, John R./Corbin, M. S. (1987): Urbane Thought, Gower Pub Co.

Cordero Torres, José María (1966): "La población de Gibraltar." In: Revista de Política Internacional 85, pp. 7-31.

Corrales Castilla, José Manuel (2003): "Molly Bloom en Gibraltar", in: Almoraima – Revista de Estudios Campogibraltareños 30, pp. 83-91.

Cousin, Abert (1902): "Tanger." Paris: A. Chalame. (http://www.culture-islam.fr/contrees/maghreb/victo-cousin-tanger-1902, last visited: 11.11.2020).

Daoud, Zakya (2017): Le Détroit de Gibraltar, Frontière entre les Mondes – De Tanger aus clandestins, Casablanca: La Croisée des Chemins.

de Amicis, Edmondo (1897): Morocco – Its People and Places. Philadelphia: Henry T. Coates & Co.

de Chambrun Ruspoli, Marthe (1982): Le Retour du Phénix. Paris: Les belles lettres, Vol. 1.

de Reparaz, Gonzalo (1922): Aventuras de un geografo errante. Madrid: Sintes.

de Tejada, Vicente Diez (1906): Cosas de los Moros – Impresiones de la vida en Tanger, Barcelona: F. Granada Editores.

del Castillo Navarro, Luis Alberto (2003): "Luna Benamor. Una Historia de amor impossible", in: Almoraima – Revista de Estudios Campogibraltareños, 30, pp. 95-111.

del Manzano Pratts, Miguel A. (2019): Así vivíamos en La Línea de la Concepción a Mediados del Siglo XX. La Línea.

Díaz, Beatriz (2018): Con cuatro tablas y cuatro chapas – vivir en Barracas. Bilbao: Autoedición.

Donnan, Hastings/ Wilson, Thomas M. (eds.) (1999): Border - Frontiers of Identity, Nation and State. Oxford/New York: Berg.

Dragadze, Tamara (1965): Like Milk on the Fire. London: Chatto & Windus.

Driesen, Henk (1992): On the Spanish-Moroccan Frontier. New York/Oxford: Berg.

Driessen, Henk (1983): "Male Sociability and Rituals of Masculinity in Rural Andalusia", in: Anthropological Quarterly 56/4, pp. 125-133.

Driessen, Henk (1995): "Transitional Tangier – Some Notes on Passage and Representation", in: kea Stadtdschungel pp. 149-163.

Driessen, Henk (1996a): "At the Edge of Europe: Crossing and Marking the Mediterranean Divide", in: Liam O'Dowd/William M. Wilson/Thomas M. Wilson (eds.), Borders, Nations and States: Frontiers of Sovereignty in the New Europe, Avebury, pp. 179-198.

Driessen, Henk (1996b): "What Am I Doing Here? The Anthropologist, the Mole, and Border Ethnography", in: Waltraud Kokot/Dorle Dracklé (eds.), Ethnologie Europas, Berlin: Dietrich Reimer Verlag, pp. 287-299.

Driessen, Henk (1999): "Smuggling as a Border Way of Life: A Mediterranean Case," in: Tobias Wendl/Michael Rösler (eds.). Frontiers and Borderlands, Frankfurt am Main: Peter Lang, pp. 117-127.

Du Taillis, Jean (1905): Le Maroc pittoresque. Paris: E. Flammarion.

Duran, Khald (1992): "Andalusia's Nostalgia for Progress and Harmonious Heresy", in: Middle East Report 178, pp. 20-23.

Edwards, Brian T. (2005): Morocco Bound: Disorienting America's Maghreb, from Casablanca to the Marrakech Express. Durham/ London: Duke University Press.

El Ouriaghi, Musatafá (2013): Yannatu al-ard, Rabat: Manchurat AlÊbara.

Elbaz, Vanessa Paloma (2015): Muslim Descendants of Jews in Morocco: Identity and Practice. Journal of Spanish, Portuguese and Italian Crypto-Jews. (https://doi.org/10.17863/CAM.40057, last visited: 11.11.2020).

España, Alberto (1954): La Pequeña historia de Tánger. Recuerdos, impresiones y anécdotas de una gran ciudad. Tanger: Distribuciones Ibérica.

Fabian, Johannes (2007): Memory against Culture, Durham/London: Duke University Press.

Fabian, Johannes (2009): "Why Does Anthropology Need Time", in: T. Sunier (ed.), Anthropologie in en zee van verhalen, Amsterdam: Aksant, pp. 185-199.

Feld, Steven (1984): "Sound Structure as Social Structure", in: Ethnomusicology 28/3, pp. 383-409.
Finlayson, Iain (1992): Tangier – City of the Dream. London: Flamingo/HarperCollins Publ.
Finlayson, Thomas J. (1991): The Fortress Came First, Grendon, Northants: Gibraltar Books Ltd.
Finlayson, Thomas J. (1996): Stories from the Rock, Gibraltar: Aquila Services Ltd.
Finlayson, Thomas J. (2018): The Boundaries of Gibraltar, Gibraltar: Charles Trico Printers.
Fort, G. (1859): Coos-coo-soo – Letters from Tangier in Africa, Philadelphia: J.S. M'Calla Printer.
Fowler, David (2009): National Service, Elvis and Me, Lulu.com
Frattini, Eric (2004): The Entity: Five Centuries of Secret Vatican Espionage. New York: St. Martin's Press.
Frembgen, Jürgen Wasim (2014): „Ergriffenheit und Ekstase an den Schreinen der Sufi-Heiligen. Ein Plädoyer für Toleranz und Pluralität", in: C. Schmid-Hahn (ed.): Islam verstehen – Herausforderung für Europa. Innsbruck: StudienVerlag, pp. 87-93.
Fuhrmann, Malte (2007): "Meeresanrainer-Weltenbürger? Zum Verhältnis von hafenstädtischer Gesellschaft und Kosmopolitismus", in: Comparativ, Zeitschrift für Globalgeschichte und vergleichende Gesellschaftsforschung 17/2, pp. 12-27.
Gaggero, James (2011): "Mons Calpe 1954 – 1986", in: Gibraltar Heritage Journal 18, pp. 28-36.
Galliano, Paco (2003): The Smallest Bank in the World: The History of Galliano's Bank 1855-1987, Gibraltar: Gibraltar Books Ltd.
García, Joseph J. (1994): Gibraltar – The making of a People: The Modern Political History of Gibraltar and Its People, Gibraltar: Medsun.
Garcia, Richard J. M. (2014): Wholesome Wines & Kindred Spirits: Saccone & Speed, 1839-2014, Gibraltar: Saccone & Speed.
Ghouirgate Abdellatif (1996): "Tanger dans un récit de voyage marocain du XIXème siècle", in: Horizons Maghrébins – Le droit à la mémoire, N°31-32, Tanger au miroir d'elle-même, pp. 154-160.
Gilmore, David (1986): "Mother-Son Intimacy and the Dual View of Women in Andalusia: Analysis through Oral Poetry", in: Ethnos 14/3, pp. 227-251.
Gilmore, David (1987): Aggression and Community. Yale Univ Press.
Gilmore, David/Gilmore, Margret (1978): "Sobre los machos y los matriarcados: el mito machista en Andalucía", in: Ethnica 14, pp. 147-160.
Gilson Miller, Susan (1991): "The People of Tangier and the French Bombardment of 1844", in: Middle Eastern Studies 27/4, pp. 583-596.

Gilson Miller, Susan (2001): "Watering the Garden of Tangier: Colonial Contestations in a Moroccan City", in: Susan Slyomomovics (ed.), The Walled Arab City in Literature, Architecture and History: The Living Medina in the Maghrib, London: Frank Cass, pp. 25-50.

Gilson Miller, Susan (2010): "The Beni Ider Quarter of Tangier in 1900: Hybridity as a Social Practice", in: Susan Gilson Miller/Mauro Bertagnin (eds.), The Architecture and Memory of the Minority Quarter of the Muslim Mediterranean City, Aga Khan Program on Islamic Architecture, the Graduate School of Design, Harvard University. Cambridge, MA: Harvard University Press, pp. 138-172.

Giraldo, Octavio (1972): "El machismo como fenómeno psicocultural", in: Revista Latinoamericana de Psicología 4/3, pp. 295-309.

Glass, Charles (2011): Americans in Paris: Life and Death Under Nazi Occupation, Penguin Books.

Goffman, Erving (1963): Stigma. Notes on the Management of Spoiled Identity, Englewood-Cliffs, NJ: Prentice-Hall.

González Vázquez, Araceli (2015): "La institución del culto a la santa-mártir judía Lalla Solika de Fez y su revitalización contempornánea. Reflexiones desde la Historia, la Antropología y la Literatura", in: Quaderns-e de l'Institut Català d'Antropologia 20/2, Barcelona: ICA, pp. 126-143.

Graebner, Fritz (1911): Methode der Ethnologie. Heidelberg: C. Winter.

Green, Michelle (1992): The Dream at the End of the World, London: Bloomsbury.

Guessous, Widad J. (1977): Volkskundliche Arabische Texte aus Marokko – Aus der Sammlung des Konsuls Karl Emil Schabinger von Schowingen (1877-1987), Frankfurt am Main et al.: Verlag Peter Lang.

Guignet-Boulogne, Philippe (2015): Socco – une promenade dans la vielle Ville de Tanger, Tanger: Slaiki Akhawayne.

Guillen, P./Miège, J.L. (1965): "Les débuts de la politique allemande au Maroc (1870-1877)", in: Revue Historique 234/2, pp. 323-352.

Gulraj, Priya/Reyes, Brian (2020): "Cross-border operation targets people-trafficking network using Gibraltar as gateway to Europe", in: The Gibraltar Chronicle Online, 12.01.2020.

Hall, Stuart (2005): "Whose Heritage? Un-settling 'the Heritage', Re-Imagining the Post-Nation", in: J. Littler/R. Naidoo (eds.), The Politics of Heritage: The Legacies of 'Race', London: Routledge.

Haller, Dieter (1992): Machismo und Homosexualität – zur Geschlechtsrollenkonzeption des Mannes in Andalusien. Dissertation, Heidelberg University. Published on microfiche, March 1992.

Haller, Dieter (1996/97): Feldforschungstagebuch Gibraltar.

Haller, Dieter (2000a): Gelebte Grenze Gibraltar – Transnationalismus, Lokalität und Identität in kulturanthropologischer Perspektive, Wiesbaden: Deutscher Universitätsverlag – Soziologie.

Haller, Dieter (2000b): "Romancing Patios: Die Aneignung der Stadt im Rahmen der ethnischen und nationalen Neubestimmung in Gibraltar", in: Waltraud Kokot/Thomas Hengartner/Kathrin Wildner (Eds.), Kulturwissenschaftliche Sichtweisen auf die Stadt, Berlin: Dietrich Reimer, pp. 225-251.

Haller, Dieter (2000c): "The Smuggler and the Beauty Queen: The Border and Sovereignty as Sources of Body Style in Gibraltar." In: Ethnologia Europaea 30/2, pp. 57-73.

Haller, Dieter (2001a): "Transcending Locality – The Diaspora Network of Sephardic Jews in the Western Mediterranean", in: Anthropological Journal on European Cultures 9/1, pp. 3-31.

Haller, Dieter (2001b): "Das Lob der Mischung, Reinheit als Gefahr: Nationalismus und Ethnizität in Gibraltar", in: Zeitschrift für Ethnologie 126/1, pp. 27-61.

Haller, Dieter (2003): "Place and Ethnicity in Two Merchant Diasporas: A Comparison of the Sindhis and the Jews of Gibraltar", in: Global Networks 3/1, pp. 75-96.

Haller, Dieter (2007): Lone Star Texas – Ethnographische Notizen aus einem unbekannten Land, Bielefeld: transcript.

Haller, Dieter (2013/14): Feldforschungstagebuch Tanger.

Haller, Dieter (2015): "Cosmopolitanism as Heritage – Remembering the Liberties of Tangier", in: Dieter Haller/Achim Lichtenberger/Meike Meerpohl (eds.), Essays on Heritage, Tourism and Society in the MENA Region – Proceedings of the International Heritage Conference 2013 at Tangier, Morocco, Paderborn: Verlag Ferdinand Schönigh, Reihe Mittelmeerstudien, pp. 123-143.

Haller, Dieter (2016): Tanger – der Hafen, die Geister, die Lust, Bielefeld: transcript.

Haller, Dieter (2018): "Geister im Raum: Cultural Areas in Zeiten der der ontologischen Wende", in: Steffen Wippel/Andrea Fischer-Tahir (eds.), Jenseits etablierter Meta-Geographien. Der Nahe Osten und Nordafrika in transregionaler Perspektive, Baden-Baden: Nomos, pp. 71-90.

Haller, Dieter (2019): Feldforschungstagebuch TanGib.

Haller, Dieter (2020): Wie Maghribisch sind die Sozialwissenschaften? – Von Köpfen und Ideen: Internationalisierung einmal anders, revised version of lecture „Wie Maghribisch sind die Sozialwissenschaften? – Von Köpfen und Ideen: Internationalisierung einmal anders" held in SoWi Kolloquium, RUB, 17.04.2019. (https://www.sowi.rub.de/mam/content/sozanth/haller_mghr_20.pdf, last visited: 11.11.2020).

Haller, Dieter/Romer, Brunhilde (eds.) (1992): Sevilla – ein Stadtbuch, Kassel: Verlag Jenior & Pressler.

Hannoum, Abdelmajjid (2009): "The Harraga of Tangiers", in: Encounters 1/, pp. 231-245.

Hart, David (1957): "An Ethnographic Survey of the Rifian Tribe of Aith Wariyaghir", in: Middle East Journal 11/2, pp. 153-162.

Harvey, David (2000): "Cosmopolitanism and the Banality of Geographical Evils", in: Public Culture 12/2, pp. 529–564.

Heeter Smith, Rachel (2016): A Disgrace to Her Colours: The Mediterranean population Problem & Tactics of Governmentality in Eighteenth-Century Gibraltar, Dissertation submitted in partial fulfillment of the requirements for the degree of Doctor of Philosophy in History in the Graduate College of the University of Illinois at Urbana-Champaign.

Herbert, David (1990): Engaging Eccentrics – Recollections, London: Peter Owen.

Hermans, Hubert J.M. (2001): "The Dialogical Self: Toward a Theory of Personal and Cultural Positioning", in: Culture & Psychology 7/3, pp. 243–281.

Herzfeld, Michael (1987): Anthropology through the Looking Glass: Critical Ethnography in the Margins of Europe, Cambridge/New York: Cambridge University Press.

Hillali, Francine, (1988): Le Centre de Tanger: bi ou multipolarité? Dissertation. Tours, Université François Rabelais.

Honorio, Carol (2015): Antonio Cavilla british photographer in Morocco 1885 - 1908. Opensource. (https://www.academia.edu/40636499/Antonio_Cavilla_british_photographer_in_Morocco_1885_1908).

Howes, H.W. (1991): The Gibraltarian – The Origin and Development of the Population of Gibraltar from 1704, 3rd ed, Gibraltar: Medsun.

Ilbert, Robert (1997): Alexandria 1860-1960: The Brief Life of a Cosmopolitan Community, Alexandria: Harpocrates Publishers.

Ingham, John (1964): "The Bullfighter", in: American Imago 12, pp. 95-102.

Jackson, Sir William G.F. (1987): The Rock of the Gibraltarians – A History of Gibraltar. Farleigh Dickinson U.P., Assoc. Univ. Press.

Jackson, Sir William G.F./Cantos, Francis (1995): From Fortress to Democracy – The Political Biography of Sir Joshua Hassan, Grendon, Northants: Gibraltar Books.

Jankélévitch, Vladimir (1983): L'irréversible et la nostalgie, Paris: Flammarion.

Jebrouni, Randa (2019): La letra y la ciudad. Tánger en las literaturas española y marroquí actuales, Edición: Rocío Rojas-Marcos Albert.

Joffé, E. G. H. (1985): "The Moroccan Nationalist Movement: Istiqlal, the Sultan, and the Country", in: The Journal of African History 26/4, World War II and Africa, pp. 289-307.

Kaufman, Asher (2001): Phoenicianism: The Formation of an Identity in Lebanon in 1920. Middle Eastern Studies.

Keesing, Roger (1981): "Theories of Culture", in: Ronald W. Casson (ed.), Language, Culture, and Cognition, Macmillan Publishing Co., Inc., pp. 42-66.

Ketterer, James (2001): "Networks of Discontent in Northern Morocco – Drugs, Opposition and Urban Unrest", in: Middle East Report 218 – Morocco in Transition 31, pp. 30-33, 45.

King, Charles (2020): Schule der Rebellen. Wie ein Kreis verwegener Anthropologen Race, Sex und Gender erfand, München: Carl Hanser Verlag.

Kleingeld, Pauline/Brown, Eric (2002): "Cosmopolitanism", in: Stanford Encyclopedia of Philosophy. (https://plato.stanford.edu/entries/cosmopolitanism/, last visited: 11.11.2020).

Kockel, Ullrich (2007): "Reflexive Traditions and Heritage Production", in: Ullrich Kockel/Máiréad Nic Craith (eds.), Cultural Heritage as Reflexive Tradition, Houndsmill: Palgrave Macmillan, pp. 19-34.

Kramer, Fritz (1987): Der rote Fes. Über Besessenheit und Kunst in Afrika, Frankfurt am Main: Athenäum.

L'Eurafricain (1955): La singulière Zone de Tanger, Paris: Ed Eurafricains.

Lagerborg, R. (1951): Edvard Westermarck och verken från hans verkstad, Helsingfors: Holger Schildts förlag.

Lakhmari, Sami (2016): "Putsch sur l'université", in: Zamane February, pp. 6-13.

Lamelas, Diego (1992): The Sale of Gibraltar in 1474, Grendon, Northants: Gibraltar Books.

Landau, Rom (1952): Portrait of Tangier, London: Robert Hale Ltd.

Lane, Kevin (2016): "Entre mitos y moros: un nuevo acercamiento a la historia de Gibraltar desde la arqueología (711-1462)", in: Almoraima. Revista de Estudios Campogibraltareños 45, pp. 203-227.

Lane, Kevin (2019): "Buildings of the past, foundations of our future", in: The Gibraltar Chronicle 8 April, p. 5.

Laredo, Isaac (1936): Historia de un Viejo Tangerino, Madrid: Bermejo.

Laskier, Michael M. (1990): "Developments in the Jewish Communities of Morocco 1956-76", in: Middle Eastern Studies 26/4, pp. 465-505.

Lefebvre, Henri/Régulier, Catherine (2004): "Attempt at the Rhythmanalysis of Mediterranean Cities", in: Henri Lefebvre (ed.), Rhythmanalysis – Space, Time and Everyday Life, translated Stuart Elden/Gerald Moore, London: Continuum, pp. 85-109. (Originally published as 'Essai de rythmanalyse des villes méditerranéennes', Peuples Méditerranéens, 37, 1986, reprinted in Éléments de rythmanalyse: Introduction à la connaissance des rythmes, Paris: Éditions Syllepse, 1992, S. 97–109).

Lenz, Oskar (1884): Timbuktu; Reise durch Marokko, die Sahara und den Sudan, ausgeführt im Auftrage der Afrikanischen Gesellschaft in Deutschland in den Jahren 1879 und 1880, Leipzig: F. A. Brockhaus.

Limbrick, Peter (2020): Arab Modernism as World Cinema. The Films of Moumen Smihi, Oakland: University of California Press.

Löfgren, Orvar (1999): "Crossing Borders: The Nationalization of Anxiety", in: Ethnologia Scandinavica 29, pp. 5-27.

Lombard, Anthony (1997): "The Roman Catholic Abudarham Family", in: The Gibraltar Heritage Journal 4, pp. 75-91.

López García, Bernabé (2012): "Los Españoles de Tánger", in: AWRAQ. Revista de análisis y pensamiento sobre el mundo árabe e islámico contemporáneo, 5-6, pp. 1-45.

López García, Bernabé (2018): "Una jornada particular: el 30 de marzo de 1952 en Tánger", in: Laura Feliu/Josep Lluís Mateo Dieste y Ferran Izquierdo Brichs (eds.), Un siglo de movilización social en Marruecos, edicions bellaterra, pp. 239-259.

Malo, Pierre (1953): Le vrai visage de Tanger, Tanger: Éditions Internationales.

Manzi, Ítalo (2005): "Entrevista a Emilio Sanz de Soto", in: Cuadernos hispanoamericanos 661-661, pp. 235ff.

Marco, Carlos (1913) "La Comisión de Higiene y de Limpieza de Tánger: su historia, sus poderes, sus reglamentos, sus concesiones y otros datos de interés local." Madrid: J. M. Bollo.

Martínez Antonio, Francisco Javier (2010-2011): "El doctor Severo Cenarro y los proyectos médico-sanitarios de la España africana (1884-1898)", in: Cuadernos del Archivo Central de Ceuta 19, pp. 255-296.

Martínez García, Ramón (1989): "Una excursión en diez y seis Jornadas", in: Abdellah Djbilou (ed.), Tánger, puerta de África. Antología de textos literarios hispánicos 1860-1960. Madrid: Editorial CantArabia, pp. 25-33.

Martínez Ruiz, José Ignacio (2005): "De Tánger a Gibraltar: El Estrecho en la praxis comercial e imperial británica (1661-1776)", in: Hispania LXV/3/221, pp. 1043-1062.

Martínez, Iñaki (2016): La ciudad de la mentira, Barcelona: Ed. Planeta.

Martinez, Rafael Ma (1953): "Romance a Tanger", Cosmópolis, 30.10.1953.

Maupin, Armistead (1978ff): Tales of the City, Reinbek bei Hamburg: Rowohlt.

Meier, Mischa (2019): Europa, Asien und Afrika vom 3. bis zum 8. Jahrhundert n.Chr. – Geschichte der Völkerwanderung, München: C.H. Beck Verlag.

Meyer, Eliah (2014): The factual list of nazis protected by Spain. (https://archive.or g/details/THEFACTUALLISTOFNAZISPROTECTEDBYSPAIN/page/n1/mode/2 up, last visited: 11.11.2020).

Michaux-Bellaire, Edouard (1921): Tanger et sa Zone, Paris: Ernest Leroux.

Miège, Jean Louis (1991): La propriété immobilière a Tanger d' après un plan du XIXè siècle, Maroc-Europe – Tanger: entre deux mondes, Rabat: El Maarif El Jadida, pp. 85-90.

Miège, Jean Louis (1996a): Le Maroc et l'Europe 1822-1906, Tomo II, Rabat: El Maarif El Jadida.

Miège, Jean Louis (1996b): Le Maroc et l'Europe 1822-1906, Tomo IV Vers la Crise, Rabat: El Maarif El Jadida.

Miège, Jean Louis/Bousquet, Georges/Denarnaud, Jacques (eds.) (1992): Tanger: porte entre deux mondes, Courbevoie: ACR Ed. Internationale.

Mitchell Serels, M. (1996): Los Judios der Tanger en los Siglos XIX y XX, Caracas: Ed. De la Asociación Israelita de Venezuela y del Centro de Estudios Sefardíes de Caracas.

Moreno, Aviad (2012): "De-Westernizing Morocco: Pre-migration Colonial History and the Ethnic-oriented Self-representation of Tangier's Natives in Israel", in: Quest. Issues in Contemporary Jewish History. Journal of Fondazione CDEC, 4 November (https://www.quest-cdecjournal.it/focus.php?id=313, last visited: 11.11.2020).

Mousjid, Bilal (2018a): "Une enfance Tangeroise," in: Le Mag 2-8 March, pp. 44-45.

Mousjid, Bilal (2018b): "Comment Hassan II a tué la philosophie", in: Telquel 820/13-19 July, pp. 32-41.

Müller, Klaus E. (1987): Das magische Universum der Identität: Elementarformen sozialen Verhaltens, Frankfurt am Main/New York: Campus.

N.N. (2000): Half the Nation, Gibraltar: The Gibraltar Business Network.

Nasri, Chourouq (2006): "Tangier: a Place Reinvented, Made and Unmade by Anouar Majid in Si Yussef", in: Larbi Touaf/Soumia Boutkhil (eds.), Representing Minorities: Studies in Literature and Criticism, Cambridge: Cambridge Scholars Press, pp. 1-14.

Neumann, Wolfgang (1981): Der Mensch und sein Doppelgänger, Wiesbaden: Franz Steiner Verlag GmbH.

Nic Craith, Máiréad (2007): "Cultural Heritages: Process, Power, Commodification", in: Ullrich Kockel/Máiréad Nic Craith (eds.), Cultural Heritage as Reflexive Tradition, Houndsmill: Palgrave Macmillan, pp. 1-19.

Nussbaum, Martha C. (1996): "Patriotism and Cosmopolitanism", in: Martha C. Nussbaum, For Love of Country: Debating the Limits of Patriotism, Boston: Beacon Press, pp. 2-20.

Nussbaum, Martha C. (2020): Kosmopolitismus – Revision eines Ideals, Darmstadt: WBG Theiss.

Nyberg Sorensen, Ninna (2000): "Crossing the Spanish-Moroccan Border with Migrants, New Islamists, and Riff-Raff", in: Ethnologia Europaea, Special Issue on borders pp. 87-101.

Nyberg Sorensen, Ninna (ed.) (2006): Mediterranean Transit Migration, Danish Institute for International Studies.

O'Donnell, Patrick (2014): Operatives, Spies, and Saboteurs: The Unknown Story of the Men and Women of World War II's OSS, Simon and Schuster.

Oda Ángel, Francisco (2003): "La sociología de las Fronteras. Una visión desde la Literatura", in: Almoraima 30, pp. 15-21.

Ohana, David (2016): "Jacqueline Kahanoff – Between Levantinism and Mediterraneanism", in: Mihran Dabag/Dieter Haller/Nikolas Jaspert/Achim Lichtenberger (eds.), New Horizons, Münster: F. Schönigh Verlag, pp. 361-385.

Örs, I. (2002): "Coffeehouses, Cosmopolitanism, and Pluralizing Modernities in Istanbul", in: Journal of Mediterranean Studies 12, pp. 119-145.
Ortíz, Fernando (1940): "El fenómeno social de la transculturación y su importancia en Cuba", in: Revista Bimestre Cubana, 46, pp. 273–278.
Ortner, Sherry (1984): "Theory of Anthropology Since the Sixties", in: Society for Comparative Studies of Society and History pp. 126-166.
Pack, Sasha (2015): "Turismo, urbanismo y colonialismo en Tánger, 1880-1939", in: Cuadernos de Historia Contemporánea, Vol. 37, 45-65.
Pasolini, Pier Paolo (1955): Ragazzi di vita, Berlin: Wagenbach.
Pastor de Maria Campos, Camila (2019): "Esa puta llamada Tanger, That Whore Called Tangier: Tropes and Practices of Tangerine Prostitution in Hispanophone Memoir and Fiction", in: The Journal of North African Studies 24/1, pp. 62-85.
Pennell, C. R. (1994): "Accommodation between European and Islamic Law in the Western Mediterranean in the Early Nineteenth Century", in: British Journal of Middle Eastern Studies 21/2, pp. 159-189.
Peraldi, Michel (2007a): "Aventuriers du nouveau capitalisme marchand. Essai d'anthropologie de l'éthique mercantile." (https://www.cairn.info/voyages-du-developpement--9782845869400-page-73.htm, last visited: 11.11.2020).
Peraldi, Michel (2007b): "Economies criminelles et mondes d'affaire à Tanger", in: Cultures & Conflits 68, pp. 111-125.
Peristany, J. G. (ed.) (1976): Mediterranean Family Structures, Cambridge: Cambridge University Press.
Petermann, Werner (2004): Die Geschichte der Ethnologie, Wuppertal: Edition Trickster im Peter Hammer.
Pickering, Michael/Keightley, Emily (2006): "The Modalities of Nostalgia", in: Current Sociology 54, pp. 919-941.
Pitt-Rivers, Julian (1961): The People of the Sierra, University of Chicago Press.
Pons, Dominique (1990): Les riches heures de Tanger. Paris, Le Table Ronde.
Posac Mon, Carlos (1990): "Las relaciones comerciales entre Tánger y Tarifa en el período 1766-1768", in: Almoraima 4, pp. 61-73.
Prekodravac, Milena (2013): "Bericht". in: Jahresbericht des Zentrums für Mittelmeerstudien AKADEMISCHES JAHR 2012/13, p. 72.
Press, Irwin (1979): The City as a Context: Urbanism and Behavioral Constraints in Seville, University of Illinois Press.
Qadery, Mustafa (2016): "L'Allemagne et le Maroc pendant la Grande Guerre", in: Dieter Haller/Steffen Wippel/Helmut Reifeld (eds.), FocussurTanger–Làoùl'A friqueetl'Europeserencontrent, Rabat: Konrad Adenauer Stiftung, Bureau du Maroc, pp. 23-37.
Rachik, Hassan, (2012): Le proche et le lointain. Un siècle d'anthropologie au Maroc, Marseille & Aix-en-Provence: Editions Parenthèses & MMSH.

Ramirez Copeiro de Villar, Jesus (1996): Espías y neutrales: Huelva en la II Guerra Mundial, Huelva.

Reifeld, Helmut (2016): "Préface: Tanger – modèle ou exception?", in: Dieter Haller/Steffen Wippel/Helmut Reifeld (eds.), FocussurTanger–Làoùl'Afriquee tl'Europeserencontrent, Rabat: Konrad Adenauer Stiftung, Bureau du Maroc, pp. 7-9. (https://www.kas.de/laenderberichte/detail/-/content/tanger-im-fokus, last visited: 11.11.2020).

Rejwan, Nissim (2009): Arabs in the Mirror: Images and Self-images from Pre-Islamic to Modern Times, Austin: University of Texas Press.

Rickmeyer, Stefan (2009): Nach Europa via Tanger, Tübingen: Tübinger Verein für Volkskunde.

Rico, Gumersindo (1967): La Población de Gibraltar (sus origenes, naturaleza y sentido), Madrid: Editorial Nacional.

Robertson, Roland (1992): Globalization. Social Theory and Global Culture. London: Sage Publications.

Römhild, Regina/Westrich, Michael (2013): "Kosmopolitismus an der Grenze – Der Mittelmeerraum als Laboratorium für transversalen Gemeinsinn", in: Zeitschrift für Kulturwissenschaften 1/2013, pp. 85-08.

Romero, Eugenio María (1837): Martirio de la joven Hachuel, ó, la heroina hebrea, Gibraltar: Imprenta Militar.

Rousseau, Dominic (2019): Rachel Muyal – La Mémoire d'une Tangéroise, Casablanca: La Croisée des Chemins.

Rubin, Jonah (2016): Review of Olivia Ange and David Berliner (eds.): Anthropology and Nostalgia. New York: Berghahn Books, 2015, in: *Anthropos* 111, pp. 660-661.

Sacramento, Priscilla (2016): Invisible Threads, AuthorHouseUK.

Sahlins, Marshall (2013): "Foreword", in: Philippe Descola/Marshall Sahlins/Janet Lloyd (eds.), Beyond Nature and Culture, Chicago: University of Chicago Press, pp. XI-XIV.

Sancho Bisquerra, Enrique (2019): Esperanza en Tánger, Selbstverlag (Books on demand). (https://www.esperanzaentanger.es/?fbclid=IwAR23fz9eKAqRTVz6lOm9RZJlMxDaCIjdPclZZR9rxqoMe7Rl62LKswEmp1c).

Santamaría, Antonio (1985): "El machismo sus identificaciones", in: Revista de Psicoanálisis 5, pp. 1127-1144.

Sasse, Dirk (2006): Franzosen, Briten und Deutsche im Rifkrieg 1921-1926. München: Oldenbourg.

Savory, Isabel (1903): In the Tail of the Peacock, London: Hutchinson & Co. (https://archive.org/details/intailpeacock00savogoog, last visited: 11.11.2020).

Sawyer-Lauçanno, Christopher (1989): An Invisible Spectator – A Biography of Paul Bowles, New York: Weidenfeld & Bicolon.

Schabinger Frhr. von Schowingen (1967) Weltgeschichtliche Mosaiksplitter. Erlebnisse und Erinnerungen eines kaiserlichen Dragomans, Baden-Baden: K. F. Schabinger Frhr. von Schowingen.

Schroeter, Daniel (1994): "Orientalism and the Jews of the Mediterranean", in: Journal of Mediterranean Society 4/2, pp. 183-196.

Schroeter, Daniel J. (2002): The Sultan's Jew: Morocco and the Sephardi World, Stanford: Stanford University Press.

Searle, Lina (2019): 1936-1982 – Gibraltar: Physiotherpy in its early Years, Gibraltar.

Sebat, Georges (2016): "Histoire des noms et prénoms des Israélites du Maroc" Juif du Maroc, 22.08.2016. (http://juifdumaroc.over-blog.com/histoire-des-noms-et-prenoms-des-israelites-du-maroc.html, last visited: 11.11.2020).

Serfaty, A.B.M. (1958): The Jews of Gibraltar under British Rule, Gibraltar: Gibraltar Garrison Library.

Simenel, Romain (2014): L'origine est aux frontières, Paris: Éditions de la Maison des sciences de l'homme.

Simmel, Georg (1908): Soziologie. Untersuchungen über die Formen der Vergesellschaftung, Berlin: Duncker & Humblot Verlag, pp. 483-493.

Simmons, Mark (2018): Ian Fleming and Operation Golden Eye: Keeping Spain out of World War II, Casemate Publishers. (https://books.google.de/books?id=nsnXDwAAQBAJ&pg=PT121&lpg=PT121&dq=ian+fleming+tangier&source=bl&ots=5t75tMICvY&sig=ACfU3U0-OcqntBR4-eksjkoWzIDn6E0McA&hl=de&sa=X&ved=2ahUKEwjA_YTlue3oAhUNDuwKHdqKD5oQ6AEwAXoECAsQLg#v=onepage&q=ian%20fleming%20tangier&f=false, last visited: 11.11.2020).

Skipworth, Patrick/Lloyd Christopher (2017): The Story of Gibraltar, Tonbridge: What on Earth Publishing Ltd.

Spain. Ministry of Foreign Affairs (1965): Documentos sobre Gibraltar (The Spanish Red Book), Madrid: Sucesores de Rivadeneyra.

Stanton, Gareth (1991): "Guests in the Dock – Moroccan Workers on Trial in the Colony of Gibraltar", in: Critique of Anthropology 11/4, pp. 361-379.

Stanton, Gareth (1994): "The Play of Identity: Gibraltar and Its Migrants", in: Victoria Goddard/Josep R. Llobera/Cris Shore (eds.), The Anthropology of Europe, Oxford/Providence: Berg Publ.

Stanton, Gareth (2009): "The Oriental City – A North African Itinerary", in: Third Text Africa 1/2, pp. 3-38.

Stockey, Gareth (2019): "Us and Them: British and Gibraltarian Colonialism in the Campo de Gibraltar c. 1900–1954", in: Andrew Canessa (ed.), Bordering on Britishness, Palgrave Studies in European Political Sociology, pp. 91-120.

Stoddard, Charles Augustus (1892): Spanish Cities; with Glimpses of Gibraltar and Tangier, New York: C. Scribner's sons.

Streck, Bernhard (2010): "Bedarfsarbeit, Faulheit und Fleiss ausserhalb der Leistungsgesellschaft", in: Alke Dohrmann/Nicole Poissonnier (eds.), Schweifgebiete: Festschrift für Ulrich Braukämper, Münster: Lit-Verlag, pp. 1-18.

Suolinna, Kirsti (1995): "Abdessalam El-Baqqali as a Key Person and Friend of Edward Westermarck", The third Nordic conference on Middle Eastern Studies: Ethnic encounter and culture change, Joensuu, Finland, 19-22 June 1995.

Sydney Morning Herald (1944): "German Consul to Leave Tangier", 05.02.1944.

Tafersiti Zarouila, Rachid, (2012): Tanger – Réalités d'un Mythe. Le mythe resiste, Tanger: Edition Zarouila.

Tagliaferri, Filomena Viviana (2016): "In the Process of Being Levantines. The 'Levantinization' of the Catholic Community of Izmir (1683–1724)", in: Turkish Historical Review 7, pp. 86-112.

Téllez Rubio, Juan José (2003): "Más allá de los viajeros romanticos. Referencias al Estrecho de Gibraltar en algunos escritores anglosajones des siglo XX", in: Almoraima 30, pp. 125-141.

Trevisan Semi, Emanuela/Sekkat Hatimi, Hanane (2011): Mémoire et Répresentations des Juifs au Maroc – Les voisins absents de Meknès, Ed. Publisud.

Trimborn, Hermann (1958): "Von den Aufgaben und Verfahren der Völkerkunde", in: Leonhard Adam/Hermann Trimborn (eds.), Lehrbuch der Völkerkunde, Stuttgart: Ferdinand Enke, pp. 1-26.

Twain, Mark (1920): The Writings of Mark Twain (author's national edition), Toronto: Robarts – University of Toronto.

Umbría Quiñones, Diego Andrés (2019): Los Contrabandistas de tabaco por el Campo de Gibraltar y la Serranía de Ronda (1945-1965) – A caballo, a pie y con perros, La Línea.

Vaidon, Lawdom (1977): Tangier. A Different Way, Metuchen: Scarecrow Press.

Vásquez Molina, Ángel (1962): Se enciende y se apaga la luz, Barcelona: Planeta DeAgostini.

Vásquez Molina, Ángel (1976): La vida perra de Juanita Narboni, Barcelona: Planeta.

Vásquez Molina, Ángel (2009): La vida perra de Juanita Narboni. 5th Ed. de Virginia Trueba. Madrid: Catedra, Letras Hispánicas.

Ventzlaff, Helga (2018): "Zur Verwendung von Vögeln in der Volksmedizin Marokkos" (Reprint 1979), in: Curare 40/1+2, pp. 71-91.

Vernay, Alain (1968): Les paradis fiscaux, Paris: Editions de Séuil.

Vignet-Zunz, Jacques (2016): Une enfance au Socco, Tanger: Khbar Bladna.

Wallace, Edgar (1922): Angel of Terror, New York, A.L. Burt Company.

Weidner, Stefan (2018): "Gesegnet seien die Fremden", in: The Turn (Zero) – Daseinsgrenzen, pp. 25-37.

Westermarck, Edward (1909): Ursprung und Entwicklung der Moralbegriffe, Vol. II, Leipzig: W. Klinkhardt.

Westermarck, Edward (1920): The belief in Spirits in Morocco, Abo: Abo Akademi Press.
Westermarck, Edward (1933): Pagan Survivals in Mohamedan Civilisation, Amsterdam: Philo Press.
Westermarck, Edward (1968): Ritual and Belief in Morocco, New Hyde Park: University Books.
Wippel, Stefan (2000): "Die 'feste' Verbindung mit Europa", in: Asien Afrika Lateinamerika 28, pp. 631-676.
Wolf, Eric (1988): "Inventing Society." In: American Ethnologist, Vol. 15, No. 4, pp. 752-761.
Woolman, David (1998): Stars in the Firmament – Tangier Characters 1660-1960, Pueblo: Passegiata Press.
Zambrano, María/Ortega y Gasset, José (1984): Andalucía sueño y realidad, Granada: Biblioteca de la Cultura Andaluza.
Zillinger, Martin (2013): Die Trance, das Blut, die Kamera. Trance-Medien und Neue Medien im marokkanischen Sufismus, Bielefeld: Transcript.
Zorko, Marta/Fontana, Matija (2014): "A Geopolitical Background of "Istrianism": An Analysis of Istrian Regional Identification", in: suvremene TEME 7/1, pp. 78-95.

Dailies and Weeklies - Journals

Aourid, Hassan (2019): "Mission civilatrice ou Apartheid?", in: Zamane 102, pp. 34-37.
Barahona, Pepe (2019): "Abgeschottet: Warum junge Menschen in Gibraltar den Brexit verfluchen", in: Vice August 6. (https://www.vice.com/de/article/qv7yvb/warum-junge-menschen-in-gibraltar-den-brexit-verfluchen, last visited: 11.11.2020).
Bartlett, Debbie (2019): "As Brexit looms, Gibraltar Welcomes the Idea of a Tangier Trade Office", in: Sur August 9. (http://www.surinenglish.com/gibraltar/201908/09/brexit-looms-gibraltar-welcomes-20190809110344-v.html?ns_campaign=surinenglish&ns_mchannel=web&ns_source=noticias-relacionadas&ns_linkname=pos-1&ns_fee=0&fbclid=IwAR0WOEVCbpVD2NTQgtxiRn8aRDwvS7ppPgwL_ijxl1foEC3IfgjiIcblpKQ, last visited: 11.11.2020).
Becker, Markus (2018a): "Der Brexit und die Gibraltar-Frage- Zoff um diesen Zipfel", in: Spiegel Online November 15.
Becker, Markus (2018b): "Widerstand aus Madrid – Spanien droht mit Brexit-Blockade – wegen Gibraltar", in: Spiegel Online November 19.
Benjelloun Abdelmajid (1996): "Le mouvement nationaliste marocain à Tanger", in: Horizons Maghrébins – Le droit à la mémoire, N°31-32. Tanger au miroir d'elle-même, pp. 24-29.

Cartwright, Richard (2009): "Past Imperfect", in: Gibraltar Magazine March 2009, pp. 80-81.
Caudex, Yann A. (1973): "Die Wirtschaft wird 'marokkanisiert'", in: Das Ostpreussenblatt August 18, 33, p. 20.
Chimenti, Elisa (1950): "Women's Magic", in: The Tangier Gazette January 27.
Doering, Martina, (2007): "Vierzehn Kilometer bis Europa", in: Berliner Zeitung, 21.05.2007.
Golemo, Kelsey (2018): "The Life and Times of Sam Cohen", in: Moorish Tides, 14.03.2018. (https://www.moorishtides.com/profiles/the-life-and-times-of-sam-cohen/, last visited: 11.11.2020).
Gómez Rubio, Juan José (1997): "Contraband, Money Laundering and Tax Avoidance", in: The Times 03.03.1997.
Gomez, Carmen (2019): "Minority groups in Gibraltar?", in: Panorama Online, 16.10.2019. (http://www.gibraltarpanorama.gi/167046, last visited: 11.11.2020).
Handaji, Madelaine (2020): "Closure of Borders Exposes Ceuta, Melilla Dependence on Morocco", in: Moroccoworld Online, 15.02.2020. (https://www.moroccoworldnews.com/2020/02/293762/closure-of-borders-exposes-ceuta-melilla-dependence-on-morocco/, last visited: 11.11.2020).
Ingelmo, Pedro (2018): "Qué es el narcotráfico en el Estrecho – Cártel", in: Diario de Cádiz, 20.05.2018. (https://www.diariodecadiz.es/noticias-provincia-cadiz/Cartel_0_1246975814.html, last visited: 11.11.2020).
Insight Magazine, December 2001.
Insight Magazine, July 2003.
Insight Magazine, November 2003.
Insight Magazine, October 2001.
Insight Magazine, September 2001.
Kabbaj, Marouane (2018): "De plus en plus d'échanges entre le Maroc et Israël", in: Maroc Hebdo Online, 11.08.2018. (https://www.maroc-hebdo.press.ma/de-plus-plus-dechanges-entre-maroc-israel, last visited: 11.11.2020).
La Dépeche Marocaine de Tanger (1956): Douze inculpes dans une grave affaire de Contrebande, 13.07.1956.
La Dépeche Marocaine de Tanger (1956a): Déclarations sensationnelles de M. Balafrej – Le regime liberal de Tanger sera garanti par une convention internationale, 04.09.1956.
La Dépeche Marocaine de Tanger (1956b): Euphorie Générale et les tre justifiée a Tanger apres la declaration de M. Ahmed Balafrej, 05.09.1956.
La Dépeche Marocaine de Tanger (1956c): Tanger sera dotée d'un statut special en matière bancaire, financière et économique, 08.09.1956.
La Dépeche Marocaine de Tanger (1956d): Statut special economico et d´financier pour Tanger, 08.09.1956.

La Dépeche Marocaine de Tanger (1956e): La fermeture des débits de boissons en médina et des maisons de tolérance, 14.09.1956.

La Dépeche Marocaine de Tanger (1956f): Les cafés du Petit Socco demeuront, 14.09.1956.

Maghreb Post Online (2019): "Marokko – Tanger Tech – Projekt kommt wieder in Bewegung", 24.04.2019. (https://www.maghreb-post.de/wirtschaft/marokko-t anger-tech-projekt-kommt-wieder-bewegung/, last visited: 11.11.2020).

Martín, Maria/Miguel Gonzáles (2021): "El texto del acuerdo entre España y el Reino Unido prevé demoler la verja deGibraltar", in: Moroccoworldnews Online, 10.09.2021. (https://elpais.com/espana/2021-01-10/el-texto-del-acuerdo-entre-espana-y-reino-unido-preve-demoler-la-verja-de-gibraltar.html/, last visited: 16.01.2021).

Masiky, Hassan (2018): "Brexit: Gibraltar Offers a Diplomatic Opening for Morocco to Reclaim Ceuta, Melilla", in: Moroccoworldnews Online, 26.02.2018. (https://www.moroccoworldnews.com/2018/12/260298/brexit-gibraltar-diplomatic-m orocco-reclaim-ceuta-melilla/, last visited: 11.11.2020).

Milikin, H. F. (1966): "Keine Spur blieb zurück - In Tanger verschwand eine Bank", in: ZEIT Online, 28.10.1966. (https://www.zeit.de/1966/44/keine-spur-blieb-zu rueck/komplettansicht, last visited: 11.11.2020).

Moreno, Sonia (2020a): "Marruecos invita a los judíos a irse de Ceuta y Melilla para invertir al otro lado de la frontera", in: El Español Online, 18.06.2020. (https://www.elespanol.com/espana/politica/20200618/marr uecos-invita-judios-ceuta-melilla-invertir-frontera/498451541_0.html, last visited: 11.11.2020).

Moreno, Sonia (2020b): "Marruecos ofrece a EEUU una base para cerrar Rota: Mohamed VI da facilidades a los americanos", in: El Español Online, 06.06.2020. (https://www.elespanol.com/espana/20200705/marruecos-eeuu-rota-moha med-vi-facilidades-americanos/502700238_0.html?utm_campaign=socialbu tton&utm_source=whatsapp&utm_medium=social&fbclid=IwAR1WlbHePM DPKRdAjsbBqr-nm2OC4ls5-rDbutpx_wC_LS4hieLDDiTcpq8, last visited: 11. 11.2020).

Naba, René (2018): "Maroc-Israël: Hassan II, la grande imposture", in: Afrique-Asie Online, 25.12.2018. (http://www.afrique-asie.fr/maroc-israel-hassan-ii-la -grande-imposture-1/, last visited: 11.11.2020).

Norton, Tommy (2020): "Secret documents shed light on British attempts to fuel tension between Spain and Morocco over Gibraltar", in: The Gibraltar Chronicle, 24.06.2020. (https://www.chronicle.gi/secret-documents-shed-light-on-britis h-attempts-to-fuel-tension-between-spain-and-morocco-over-gibraltar/, last visited: 11.11.2020).

noticiasgibraltar (2019): "Gibraltar estudia abrir una oficina comercial en Tánger", in: Noticiasgibraltar, 08.08.2019. (https://noticiasgibraltar.es/gibraltar/noticia

s/gibraltar-estudia-abrir-una-oficina-comercial-tanger?fbclid=IwAR3_EYRiIV 3GwyFB7uWdz5rgMnb7od3dwMloHHWUuPhyTyx7Jx5ZdGzNfg8, last visited: 11.11.2020).

Oliva, Paco (1985): "Border opening no immediate effect on Campo unemployment", in: The Gibraltar Chronicle 12.3.1985.

Panorama (2015): "Local support group wants to take charity work in Tangier to new level", in: Panorama-Online, 22.01.2015.

Peralta, Gabriella (2020): "Gibraltarians in isolation abroad – 40 days in lockdown and counting for local couple in Morocco", in: The Gibraltar Chronicle, 24.04.2020.

Reyes, Brian (1996): "Refugees detention unlawful", in: Panorama, 19-26 August, p. 21.

Reyes, Brian (2018a): "Gibraltar, UK and Spain reach agreement on Brexit", in: The Gibraltar Chronicle, 21.11.2018.

Reyes, Brian (2018b): "Last-minutedealdefusesGibBrexitrow,butopinionsdifferonw hatitmeans", in: The Gibraltar Chronicle, 24.11.2018.

Reyes, Brian (2019): "bet365toscaledownGibraltaroperationandrelocatetoMalta,citi ngBrexit", in: The Gibraltar Chronicle Online, 23.05.2019.

Reyes, Brian (2020a): "Poll suggests Gibraltarias shrug off Brexit and global warming fears", in: The Gibraltar Chronicle Online, 02.03.2020.

Reyes, Brian (2020b): "New Spanish measures not expected to impact on cross-border movement essential to Gib", in: The Gibraltar Chronicle Online, 29.03.2020.

Sánchez, Álvaro (2019): "EU Parliament pushes out British negotiator over Gibraltar 'colony' dispute", in: El Pais Online (English Version), 02.04.2019. (https ://elpais.com/elpais/2019/04/02/inenglish/1554189331_930101.html, last visited: 11.11.2020).

Sánchez, Gabriela/Olías, Laura (2014): "Las fuerzas marroquíes entran en Perejil y devuelven a los 13 inmigrantes llega dos a la isla Española", in: El Diario ONLINE, 03.06.2014. (https://www.eldiario.es/desalambre/Cerca-inmigrantes-lle gan-Isla-Perejil_0_266673396.html, last visited: 11.11.2020).

Schmid, Ulrich (2018): "Der jüdische Exodus in Nordafrika", in: NZZ Online 25.03.2018. (https://www.nzz.ch/international/die-koscheren-marokkaner-ld. 136683,lastvisited:11.11.20200).

Shkolnik, Daniel (2017): "Inside the Moroccan Cafe Where the Rolling Stones Got Stoned", in: Vice, 17.04.2017. (https://www.vice.com/en_us/article/vvae78 /inside-the-moroccan-cafe-where-the-rolling-stones-got-stoned, last visited: 11.11.2020).

Stein, Hannes (2014): "Willst du nur was mit Dschihadisten zu tun haben?", in: WELT Online, 29.12.2014. (https://www.welt.de/kultur/literarischewelt/article 135806359/Willst-du-nur-was-mit-Dschihadisten-zu-tun-haben.html, last visited: 11.11.2020).

Thatchell, Peter (2002): "Gibraltar's case is tarnished by its abysmal human rights record", in: The Guardian: The Rock shows it is a hard place, 07.11. 2002.
The Diplomat (2016): "Dominique Searle, Gibraltar's new representative in London after the Brexit", 04.07.2016. (https://thediplomatinspain.com/en/2016/07/dominique-searle-gibraltars-new-representative-in-london-after-the-brexit/, last visited: 11.11.2020).
The Gibraltar Chronicle (1997): "La Línea Customs head arrested in 'Operacion", 19.04.1997.
The Gibraltar Chronicle (2019): "New Gibraltar Morocco Business Association launches", 19.03.2019.
The Gibraltar Chronicle (2020a): "Morocco Suspends Passenger Ferry to Gibraltar", in: The Gibraltar Chronicle Online, 13.03.2020.
The Gibraltar Chronicle (2020b): "Morocco halts flights with 25 more countries, including Gibraltar", in: The Gibraltar Chronicle Online, 08.05.2020.
The Gibraltar Chronicle (2020c): "Three governments coordinate rescue mission across the Strait, bringing Gibraltarians home", In: The Gibraltar Chronicle Online, 15.03.2020.
The Maghreb Times (2016): "Gibraltar puts focus on Morocco", 05.12.2016. (https://themaghrebtimes.com/gibraltar-puts-focus-on-morocco/, last visited: 11.11.2020).
The Tangier Gazette (1950): "Contraband Tobacco", 27.01.1950.
The Tangier Gazette (1960): "It was reported…", 22.01.1960.
Time Magazine (1933): "Spain: March to Gibraltar," Monday, November 13, 1933
Time Magazine (1952): "Tangier: Nylon Sid & the Jolly Roger," Monday, December 29.
Times of Israel Staff (2018): "Les discrètes mais fructueuses relations israélo-marocaines", in: The Times of Israel Online, 13.11.2018. (https://fr.timesofisrael.com/les-discretes-mais-fructueuses-relations-israelo-marocaines/, last visited: 11.11.2020).
Zamane Online (2019): "Insolite: une fatwa pour Hercule et Ibn Battouta", 07.05.2019. (https://zamane.ma/fr/insolite-une-fatwa-pour-hercule-et-ibn-battouta/, last visited: 11.11.2020)
ZEIT ONLINE (1972): "Putschversuch in Marokko", 26.08.1972. (https://www.zeit.de/1972/34/putschversuch-in-marokko, last visited: 11.11.2020).
ZEIT ONLINE (2018): "Gibraltars Regierungschef kritisiert Spaniens Veto-Drohung", 23. November.
ZEIT ONLINE (2020): "Gibraltar strebt Beitritt zum Schengen-Raum an", 18.01.2020. (https://www.zeit.de/politik/ausland/2020-01/brexit-gibraltar-schengen-raum-europaische-union, last visited: 11.11.2020).

Filmography

EL CHERGUI (1975) (MAR, R: Moumen Smihi)

TV and Audio Sources

Bayerischer Rundfunk (2012): Magiera, Birgit "18. Dezember 1923 – Tanger wird 'Internationale Zone'", BR, 18.12.2012. (https://www.audiolibrix.de/de/Podcast/Episode/291096/tanger-wird-internationale-zone, last visited: 11.11.2020).

Bayerischer Rundfunk (2018): Grasberger, Lukas "Die Straße von Gibraltar – Nadelöhr der Weltgeschichte", Bayerischer Rundfunk, RadioWissen. 13.08.2018. (https://www.br.de/radio/bayern2/programmkalender/sendung-2069730.html, last visited: 11.11.2020).

BBC (2018): The bribe that prevented Hitler from taking Gibraltar from the British and controlling the Mediterranean. October 7, 2018. (https://www.bbc.com/mundo/noticias-45754336, last visited: 11.11.2020).

BBC (2020): "Brexit: UK to Decide on Gibraltar-EU Travel Deal. In: BBC Online January 20. (https://www.bbc.com/news/world-europe-51173850, last visited: 11.11.2020).

Deutschlandfunk (2019): Frantzen, Michael: "Gibraltar und der Brexit - Forever british, Never spanisch, gerne europäisch." Deutschlandfunk 18.07.2019 (https://www.deutschlandfunkkultur.de/gibraltar-und-der-brexit-forever-britisch-never-spanisch.979.de.html?dram:article_id=454055, last visited: 11.11.2020).

Euronews (2018): Lazaro, Ana "Brexit & Gibraltar: The Rock and a hard place" in: Euronews Online 17.10.2018. (https://www.euronews.com/2018/10/17/brexit-gibraltar-the-rock-and-a-hard-place, last visited: 11.11.2020).

GBC (2017): "EU Council confirms Gibraltar clause remains in Brexit negotiating guidelines – Picardo insists treatment unfair." GBC Online, 30.04.2017, (https://www.gbc.gi/news/eu-council-confirms-gibraltar-clause-remains-brexit-negotiating-guidelines-picardo-insists-treatment-unfair-35097, last visited: 11.11.2020).

GBC (2019a): "Gibraltar Morocco Business Association welcomes 'well overdue' plaque honouring Moroccan workers." GBC Online, 03.05.2019, (https://www.gbc.gi/news/gibraltar-morocco-business-association-welcomes-well-overdue-plaque-honouring-moroccan-workers, last visited: 11.11.2020).

GBC (2019b): "Policia Nacional officer based in La Linea expelled from the force for collaborating with smugglers", GBC Online, 31.07.2019, (https://www.gbc.gi/news/policia-nacional-officer-based-la-linea-expelled-force-collaborating-smugglers, last visited: 11.11.2020).

GBC (2019c): "DCM casts further light on No-Deal Brexit preparations", GBC Online, 02.09.2019. (https://www.gbc.gi/news/dcm-casts-further-light-no-deal-brexit-preparations, last visited: 11.11.2020).

ntv (2020): "Nach dem Brexit – Gibraltar erwägt Schengen-Beitritt", ntv-Online, 19.01.2020. (https://www.n-tv.de/politik/Gibraltar-erwaegt-Schengen-Beitritt-article21518306.html, last visited: 11.11.2020).
Radiosefarad (n.d.): El Tánger de Carlos Colón. (http://www.radiosefarad.com/el-tanger-de-carlos-colon/?fbclid=IwAR2GWI2loy5jbeeoHmxt3AvWKnNNOpTH MYfA51j7bbrswWy3rkOGmmRSmWk, last visited: 11.11.2020).
rtve (2018): "Se entrega el líder de Los Castañas, huido de la Policía y que reapareció en un videoclip de reggaeton", rtve Online, 17.10.2018. (http://www.rtve.es/noticias/20181017/se-entrega-lider-castanas-uno-principales-clanes-narcos-del-campo-gibraltar/1820640.shtml, last visited: 11.11.2020).
YGTV (2019a): "Gibraltar And Tangier Cultural Exchange", 26.11.2019. (https://www.yourgibraltartv.com/society/20377-gibraltar-and-tangier-cultural-exchange?fbclid=IwAR021fljcETPnv5mWdb4vrcCe_ocK3-_GFVxNBwkL2NoIWwSpzdB kAg4bP8, last visited: 11.11.2020)
YGTV (2019b): Lopez, Ariana "GSLP Liberals 'Aspire To The Best Gibraltar' as They Launch Their Manifesto." YGTV Team, 03.10.2019. (https://www.yourgibraltartv.com/politics/20030-gslp-liberals-aspire-to-the-best-gibraltar-as-they-launch-their-manifesto?fbclid=IwAR3-UdQhwvCP8iIumSUi5GDZTkhPIfGEx-oNE9 RDNE8PnmNGWYAM6tG4IGM, last visited: 11.11.2020).

Nonscientific Websources

André (2003): Les reines de Tanger. Dafina.net, November 16. (https://dafina.net/forums/read.php?52,79463,page=1, last visited: 11.11.2020).
Aujourd'hui (2010): "Zoubeir Benbouchta: Lalla Jmila évoque des faits historiques de Tanger", November 4. (https://aujourdhui.ma/regions/zoubeir-benbouchta-lalla-jmila-evoque-des-faits-historiques-de-tanger-73805, last visited: 11.11.2020).
Babas, Latifa/Benargane, Yassine (2018): "Diplomates marocains #12: Jacob Benider, l'ambassadeur juif originaire de Gibraltar." Yabiladi Online August 3. (https://www.yabiladi.com/articles/details/67741/diplomates-marocains-jacob-benider-l-ambassadeur.html?fbclid=IwAR2BfP5nhQouvFGQZdAtIGBd59z WjlCo7Nzq3W4aWwohFhT6-ukqhxmsP-c, last visited: 11.11.2020).
Benady, Sam (2020): "JamesJoyceandVicenteBlascoIbañez." Blog (http://keysofcity.blogspot.com/2020/04/james-joyce-and-vicente-blasco-ibanez.html, last visited: 11.11.2020).
Brufal de Melgarejo, Michael (2008): "Mariola Russo", Gibraltar Rock Jottings July 21.
Chipulina, Neville (2014a): "1860 – James Richardson – Smuggling Cattle" (https://gibraltar-intro.blogspot.com/2014/04/1860-james-richardson-smuggling-cattle.html, last visited: 11.11.2020).

Chipulina, Neville (2014b): "1750 – The Jews of Gibraltar – The Establishment" (https://gibraltar-intro.blogspot.com/2014/05/1750-jews-of-gibraltar-establishment-by.html, last visited: 11.11.2020).
Chipulina, Neville (2016): "1910 – A. Benzaquen – Postcards from Tangier" (https://gibraltar-intro.blogspot.com/2016/04/1910-a.html, last visited: 11.11.2020).
Chipulina, Neville (2017): "1721 – Abraham Benider – The Butcher of Gibraltar" (https://gibraltar-intro.blogspot.com/2017/05/1721-abraham-benider-butcher-of.html, last visited: 11.11.2020).
Cosquieri, Francis (2015): "Other Stories from the Evacuation: Spending the Second World War in Tangiers" Entretien 12.03.2015 (http://www.findglocal.com/GB/Colchester/176579716037568/Bordering-on-Britishness, last visited: 11.11.2020).
Garcia, Joe (2020): "Britain and Morocco to strengthen relations", Panorama Online, 14.04.2020 (http://www.gibraltarpanorama.gi/170128, last visited: 11.11.2020).
Holman Reynolds, Libby (n.d.): "Jane Bowles, Libby Holman Reynolds and Barbara Hutton" (http://www.paulbowles.org/photosjanebowles.html, last visited: 11.11.2020).
Joyes, Nathan (2019): "Closing Gibraltar's border: does anyone win?", in: Gamblinginsider, 02.09.2019. (https://www.gamblinginsider.com/news/7781/closing-gibraltars-border-does-anyone-win, last visited: 11.11.2020).
Lisenbee, Kenneth (n.d.): "Chronology of the Life of Paul Bowles (Part II, 1947-2000)" (http://www.paulbowles.org/chronologytwo.html, last visited: 11.11.2020).
Loftus, Gerald (2013): "When Tangier & Gibraltar Were 'Tan-Gib'", Tangier American Legation, 13.08.2013. (https://legation.ipower.com/blog/?p=113, last visited: 11.11.2020).
Malka, Jeff (n.d.): "Indiana Jones meets Tangier Moshe" (https://www.jewishgen.org/Sephardic/amazon.HTM, last visited: 11.11.2020).
Mas Garriga, Jordi (2013): "Mershan." (http://tingisaecid.com/v2/file/monograph/14_qtSiO2ffYjNYAFBDpam6KeaWGCLrBsoTW88vkb6HZfI5ZeAlOf_12-Marchan/12-Marchan.pdf, last visited: 05.08.2015).
Mribti, Youssef (2015): Beitrag in Facebook/Siempretanger, 27.02.2015, (https://www.facebook.com/groups/122089227881843/permalink/774672752623484/, last visited: 11.11.2020).
N.N. (2012): "UnrecuerdodeTangeryunolvidodeEspaña." (http://blogdetanger.blogspot.com/2012/09/?m=1, last visited: 11.11.2020).
N.N. (2017a): "Tangier with Micheal Palin" (https://www.youtube.com/watch?v=GeciyS5Y4mw, last visited: 11.11.2020).
N.N. (2017b): "The Aesthetes: Expats in Tangier" (https://www.youtube.com/watch?v=hpfPsW-TTe4, last visited: 11.11.2020).

Picco, Ernesto (2020): "Gibraltar: un viaje a la resaca del imperio británico bajo la sombra del Brexit" (https://www.fronterad.com/gibraltar-un-viaje-a-la-resaca-del-imperio-britanico-bajo-la-sombra-del-brexit/, last visited: 11.11.2020).

Sanahuja Albiñana, Vicente Luís (2011): "Mons Calpe" (https://vidamaritima.com/2011/03/mons-calpe/, last visited: 17.09.2014).

Soto, Fernando (2014): "El doctor pirata", 18.09.2014. (https://ocultismocadiz3000.blogspot.com/2014/09/el-doctor-pirata.html, last visited: 11.11.2020).

Sputniknews (2019): "Gibraltar Could Bolster Trade With Morocco to Offset Brexit Damage – Local Businessman", in: Sputniknews Online, 17.10.2019. (https://sputniknews.com/analysis/201910171077075622-gibraltar-could-bolster-trade-with-morocco-to-offset-brexit-damage--local-businessman/?fbclid=IwAR1C2YfBxtBGczzelIB5zzwa95hkWY5AhPCT08O9NxQftSVQGobzifoNqKI, last visited: 11.11.2020).

Stradbrook, Steven (2019): "Bet365cutting80%ofGibraltarstaffaheadofMaltamove", Calvinayre, 29.08.2019. (https://calvinayre.com/2019/08/29/business/bet365-cutting-400-gibraltar-staff/, last visited: 11.11.2020).

Taburlini, Maria Pia (n.d.): "Elisa Chimenti (Naples 1883 – Tanger 1969)." (https://www.elisachimenti.org/biographie_fr.html, last visited: 11.11.2020).

Toledano, Ralph (2010): "Fin du Patrimoine Juif Tangérois ?" (http://www.darna.com/phorum/read.php?13,171291,171342, last visited: 15.05.2015).

Urteaga, Diego (2021): "Reino Unido estudia construir un túnel que una Gibraltar y Tánger," atalayar Online, 09.01.2021. (https://atalayar.com/content/reino-unido-estudia-construir-un-túnel-que-una-gibraltar-y-tánger, last visited: 16.01.2021).

Vásquez Molina, Ángel (2012): "Antonio Vazquez Molina" (http://www.cronicadetanger.com/antonio-vazquez-molina/, 21.05.2012, last visited: 14.03.2016).

Wikipedia (n.d.a.): "Coon, Carleton Stevens." (https://de.wikipedia.org/wiki/Carleton_S._Coon, last visited: 11.11.2020).

Wikipedia (n.d.b.) "Pillars of Hercules." (https://en.wikipedia.org/wiki/Pillars_of_Hercules, last visited: 11.11.2020).

Wikipedia (n.d.c.) "Marga d'Andurain." (https://de.wikipedia.org/wiki/Marga_d%E2%80%99Andurain, last visited: 11.11.2020).

Yaabouk, Mohammed (2020): "Les Juifs de Ceuta, Melilla et Gibraltar, futur investisseurs à Fnideq et Nador ?", in: Yabiladi Online, 16.06.2020. (https://www.yabiladi.com/articles/details/95127/juifs-ceuta-melilla-gibraltar-futurs.html, last visited: 11.11.2020).

List of Illustrations

1 View of the Straits from Gibraltar, 02.04.2019. Source: author's photography.
2 (a-c) The Anthropologists of Tangier. Different sources.
3 El Boughaz. Source: https://fineartamerica.com/featured/strait-of-gibraltar-topographic-map-natural-color-top-view-frank-ramspott.html?product=throw-pillow (last visit: 05.11.2020).
4 Limestone Gibraltar. Source: The Gibraltar Story – Jurassic Rock, produced by Knightsfield Ltd. in 1994.
5 View from Dar Baroud, Tangier, across the Strait. Source: author's photography, 30.05.2013.
6 Closed border between Gibraltar and La Línea. Source: https://www.gbc.gi/news/gibraltar-and-la-linea-commemorate-50-years-frontier-closure (last visit: 05.11.2020).
7 Proyects of fixed railway connections. Source: Lombardi, Giovanni 2010 Der Tunnel unter der Meerenge von Gibraltar. Swiss Tunnel Congress Luzern, Juni 2010. Minusio. https://www.lombardi.ch/en-gb/SiteAssets/Publications/1334/Pubb-0514-E-Ein%20alter%20Traum%20-%20Der%20Tunnel%20ounter%20der%20Meerenge%20von%20Gibraltar.pdf (last visit: 05.11.2020).
8 Travels of Oscar Lenz source: https://pictures.abebooks.com/LUCIE/155838663 85.jpg (last visit: 05.11.2020).
9 Ferry between Tarifa and Tangier 2013. Source: author's photography, 13.02.2013.
10 Cafe Makina, 2018: Source: author's photography.
11 Patio Schott (Gibraltar), 1996. Source: author's photography.
12 Patio Laredo (Tangier), 2019 Source: by courtesy of Said Akhnak.
13 Cafe Gibraltar, Tangier: Source https://www.facebook.com/photo?fbid=638535096277806&set=gm.778534512237308 (last visit: 05.11.2020).
14 View from Reclaimed Land onto the Rock of Gibraltar. Source: author's photography, 31.03.2019.
15 1Hoopoe as medicine, Tangier. Source: author's photography, 22.03.2017.
16 Hoopoe, Alameda Gardens, Gibraltar. Source: author's photography.
17 Cosmopolis Source: author's photography.
18 Malabata. Source: author's photography.
19 Sindhis Source: Bharat Ratna, March 1993.
20 Jewish-Tangerino colony in Iquitos. Source: Chahid, Soufiane 2020 L'incroyable histoire des juifs marocains en Amazonie. Telquel 14 JUIN 2020, https://telquel.ma/2020/06/14/lincroyable-histoire-des-juifs-marocains-en-amazonie_164940 3 (last visit: 05.11.2020).
21 Jon Morgan Searle. Source: author's photography, 26.10.2010.
22 A gibraltarian-tangerino familytree. Source: author's sketch.

23 Simita Benatar. Source: del Castillo Navarro, Luis Alberto 2003 Luna Benamor, und Historia de Amor Imposible. In: Almoraima 30, Pg. 110.
24 Trance and Possession, Zaouia Hamdouchia. Source. author's photography, 14.09.2018.
25 A Takeaway in Gibraltar. Source. author's photography, 21.08.2019.
26 Cabaret Prisma, Sevilla. Source. author's photography, 1985.
27 Mediterranean Contraband Triangle. Sources. Málaga, Great Britain 1954. Movie by Richard Sale; https://artsandculture.google.com/entity/juan-march-ordinas/m0b41cl (last visit: 05.11.2020).
28 Tangier Ville. Source: author's photography, 30.05.2013.
29 Borders at the Strait of Gibraltar. Source: https://www.facebook.com/GibMaroc/photos/a.128861367771638/536970630294041/?type=3&theater (last visit: 05.11.2020).
30 Culture Area. Source: https://modis.gsfc.nasa.gov/gallery/individual.php?db_date=2017-08-21 (last visit: 05.11.2020).
31 Gibraltarian Currency. Source: https://www.worldbanknotescoins.com/2015/05/gibraltar-5-pounds-banknote-1995-queen-elizabeth.html(last visit: 05.11.2020).
32 Portuguese Tangier. Source: https://www.avuncularamerican.net/2014/06/the-skeletons-of-portuguese-tangier.html (last visit: 05.11.2020).
33 Commercial City. Source: Bartlett, W.H. 1851 Gleanings on the Overland Route.
34 Source: AlfredDehodencq ca 1869 Execution of a Moroccan Jewess (Sol Hachuel).
35 Jewish Refugees in Gibraltar, 1859. Source: https://gibraltar-intro.blogspot.com/2015/04/1859-jewish-refugees-purchase-of.html (last visit: 05.11.2020).
36 Source: Sloma, Diane 1994 Character and Styl of the early Gibraltar Chronicles. In: Gibraltar Heritage Journal, Vol. 2, pg. 31.
37 Rue du Télégraphe Anglais. Source: https://tangier-vip.skyrock.com/2397563223-Tanger-rue-du-telegraphe-anglais.html (last visit: 05.11.2020).
38 Steamship Hercules. Source: https://gibraltar-intro.blogspot.com/2015/02/1810-bland-line-reputable-tavern-owner.html (last visit: 05.11.2020).
39 Moroccan Poultry Merchant in Gibraltar, 1930. Source: https://www.facebook.com/photo.php?fbid=10218326704933652&set=gm.2707354382685501&type=3&theater&ifg=1 (last visit: 05.11.2020).
40 Pig Sticking in Forêt Diplomatique 1930: Source. https://www.facebook.com/photo/?fbid=2864180863635262&set=gm.2872908069466598 (last visit: 05.11.2020).
41 Royal Calpe Hunt. Source: https://gibraltar-intro.blogspot.com/2011/10/chapter-22.html (last visit: 05.11.2020).
42 Pension Gibraltar, Tangier. Source: author's photography, 11.05.2012.

43 1904 - Kidnapping Ion Perdicaris, Tangier. Source: https://www.pinterest.nz/ pin/350366046008893949/?amp_client_id=CLIENT_ID(_)&mweb_unauth_id={ {default.session}}&simplified=true (last visit: 05.11.2020).
44 The International Zone of Tangier. Source: https://de.wikipedia.org/wiki/Inter nationale_Zone_von_Tanger (last visit: 05.11.2020).
45 The Gumpert family, Kap Spartel lighthousel. Source: http://germangumpert.t ripod.com/caboespartel/espartela.jpg (last visit: 05.11.2020).
46 Notice about d'Andurains possible assessination. Source: https://docplayer.es/ 51656036-La-condesa-marga-d-andurain-protagonizo-una-vida-propia-de-la-mejor-novela-de-aventuras-nacida-en-el-seno-de-una-familia-de-la-burgues ia.html (last visit: 05.11.2020).
47 EGOZ after drawning (Gibraltar). Source: https://gibraltar-intro.blogspot.com /2016/03/1961-sinking-of-pisces-jack-garofalo.html (last visit: 05.11.2020).
48 Source: Moumen Smihis movie "El Chergui" 1975.
49 Christian woman dressed as jewish bride. Source: by courtesy of Manolo Bautista Nieto.
50 1955 Riots in Souq Barra, Tangier. Source: https://www.facebook.com/photo .php?fbid=610261039032995&set=gm.538963842861044&type=3&theater&ifg=1 (last visit: 05.11.2020).
51 1956 Announcement of a Special Status for Tangier. Source: La Dépèche Marocaine, Sept. 4th 1956.
52 Tangier Excentrics and Celebrities. Source: https://www.vogue.it/en/people-ar e-talking-about/vogue-arts/2011/04/portraits-of-tangier (last visit: 05.11.2020).
53 Tangier-Gibraltar Connections. Announcement. Sources: https://www.facebo ok.com/photo.php?fbid=10202578636926622&set=gm.537211676369594&type=3 &theater&ifg=1 (last visit: 05.11.2020).
54 Announcement Saccone Speed. Source: https://gibraltar-intro.blogspot.com/2 015/12/blog-post.html (last visit: 05.11.2020).
55 Gibraltar Commemorates Moroccan Workers. Source: https://www.gbc.gi/new s/unite-commemorates-moroccan-worker-contribution (last visit: 05.11.2020).
56 Transboughaz Tourism. Source: author's photography.
57 1965 Rabbi Yamin Cohen. Source: https://dbs.anumuseum.org.il/skn/en/c6/e 134968/Photos/Rabbi_Yamin_Cohen_Blessing_a_Baby_Girl_at_a_Fadas_ (last visit: 05.11.2020).
58 Dar Zambaquia in Mershan district
59 Edward Westermarck with co-workers and servants in the 1920s, Åbo Akademi University Library. Source: https://docplayer.net/65708870-Approaching-religi on-part-ii-edited-by-tore-ahlback.html (last visit: 05.11.2020).
60 The Reichmann Family. Source: https://www.yumpu.com/en/document/rea d/6343831/the-reichmann-family-history-pdf-businessweek (last visit: 05.11. 2020).

61 2013 Dedrib's headquarter, Sidi Khankouch. Source: author's photography, 2013.
62 1990s Tobacco smuggling. Source: Gibraltar postcard.
63 Congreso de Periodistas del Estrecho. https://asociacionprensajerez.com/category/apcg/ (last visit: 05.11.2020).
64 St. Andrews Cemetery. Source: author's photography, 2013.
65 Inmueble Seruya Source: author's photography, 22.11.2013.
66 Benchimol Hospital destroyed. Source: http://www.darnna.com/phorum/read.php?13,171291,page=3 (last visit: 05.11.2020).
67 Elisa Chimenti. Source: https://www.elisachimenti.org/ (last visit: 05.11.2020).
68 Jane Bowles and Marthe de Ruspoli. Source: http://www.paulbowles.org/photosjanebowles.html.
69 Olga Benchecroun und Tamara Dragadze, Hotel Cecil 1961. Source: by courtesy of Olga Benchecroun and Tamara Dragadze.
70 Plaque at Villa Seruya. Source: author's photography
71 Debatable Territory – Isla Perejil/Leila. Source: https://elpais.com/diario/2002/07/21/espana/1027202406_850215.html (last visit: 05.11.2020).
72 Land Reclamation in Gibraltar. Source: https://oceanvillage.gi/ (last visit: 05.11.2020).
73 Renewed Air Connections Source: https://picclick.co.uk/Gibraltar-Airways-Gibraltar-Tangier-Twice-Daily-Airline-Luggage-392725821972.html (last visit: 05.11.2020).
74 1996 Moroccan Bazar. Source: author's photography.
75 Moroccan Gibraltarian on National Day. Source: author's photography, 10.09.1996.
76 Moschee, 1996. Source: author's photography.
77 2020 Food Supply. Source: author's photography.
78 2020 Anti Brexit manifestation, La Línea. Source: author's photography.
79 Brexit Results in Gibraltar. Source: https://elpais.com/politica/2016/06/24/actualidad/1466766657_153654.html (last visit: 05.11.2020).
80 Jamal, 2019. Source: author's photography.
81 GMBE. Source: https://www.gmbe.me/ (last visit: 05.11.2020).
82 2019 Private Charity at Darna. Source: author's photography.
83 Covid19 – Directing British nationals back to Gibraltar. GBME leaders at Ibn Battouta airport. Source: by courtesy of Steven Marin, 23.10.2020.
84 Chez Kébé. Source: https://www.facebook.com/ChezKebe/photos/a.169450433237911/414404238742528/ (last visit: 05.11.2020).

Cultural Studies

Gabriele Klein
Pina Bausch's Dance Theater
Company, Artistic Practices and Reception

May 2020, 440 p., pb., col. ill.
29,99 € (DE), 978-3-8376-5055-6
E-Book:
PDF: 29,99 € (DE), ISBN 978-3-8394-5055-0

Elisa Ganivet
Border Wall Aesthetics
Artworks in Border Spaces

2019, 250 p., hardcover, ill.
79,99 € (DE), 978-3-8376-4777-8
E-Book:
PDF: 79,99 € (DE), ISBN 978-3-8394-4777-2

Krista Lynes, Tyler Morgenstern, Ian Alan Paul (eds.)
Moving Images
Mediating Migration as Crisis

May 2020, 320 p., pb., col. ill.
40,00 € (DE), 978-3-8376-4827-0
E-Book: available as free open access publication
PDF: ISBN 978-3-8394-4827-4

All print, e-book and open access versions of the titles in our list
are available in our online shop www.transcript-publishing.com

Cultural Studies

Andreas Sudmann (Ed.)
The Democratization of Artificial Intelligence
Net Politics in the Era of Learning Algorithms

2019, 334 p., pb., col. ill.
49,99 € (DE), 978-3-8376-4719-8
E-Book: available as free open access publication
PDF: ISBN 978-3-8394-4719-2

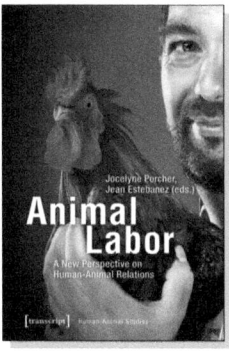

Jocelyne Porcher, Jean Estebanez (eds.)
Animal Labor
A New Perspective on Human-Animal Relations

2019, 182 p., hardcover
99,99 € (DE), 978-3-8376-4364-0
E-Book:
PDF: 99,99 € (DE), ISBN 978-3-8394-4364-4

Ramón Reichert, Mathias Fuchs,
Pablo Abend, Annika Richterich, Karin Wenz (eds.)
Digital Culture & Society (DCS)
Vol. 4, Issue 1/2018 – Rethinking AI: Neural Networks,
Biometrics and the New Artificial Intelligence

2018, 244 p., pb., ill.
29,99 € (DE), 978-3-8376-4266-7
E-Book:
PDF: 29,99 € (DE), ISBN 978-3-8394-4266-1

All print, e-book and open access versions of the titles in our list
are available in our online shop www.transcript-publishing.com